CANADIAN LOCAL GOVERNMENT

CANADIAN LOCAL GOVERNMENT

AN URBAN PERSPECTIVE

ANDREW SANCTON

OXFORD
UNIVERSITY PRESS

OXFORD
UNIVERSITY PRESS

8 Sampson Mews, Suite 204, Don Mills, Ontario M3C 0H5
www.oupcanada.com

Oxford University Press is a department of the University of Oxford.
It furthers the University's objective of excellence in research, scholarship,
and education by publishing worldwide in

Oxford   New York

Auckland   Cape Town   Dar es Salaam   Hong Kong   Karachi
Kuala Lumpur   Madrid   Melbourne   Mexico City   Nairobi
New Delhi   Shanghai   Taipei   Toronto

With offices in

Argentina   Austria   Brazil   Chile   Czech Republic   France   Greece
Guatemala   Hungary   Italy   Japan   Poland   Portugal   Singapore
South Korea   Switzerland   Thailand   Turkey   Ukraine   Vietnam

Oxford is a trade mark of Oxford University Press
in the UK and in certain other countries

Published in Canada
by Oxford University Press

Library and Archives Canada Cataloguing in Publication

Sancton, Andrew, 1948–
Canadian local government : an urban
perspective / Andrew Sancton.

Includes bibliographical references and index.
ISBN 978–0–19–542756–1

1. Municipal government—Canada. I. Title.

JS1710.S36 2011   320.8'50971   C2011-900507-7

Cover image: Thomas Northcut/Getty

Oxford University Press is committed to our environment. This book is printed on Forest
Stewardship Council certified paper, harvested from a responsibly managed forest.

Mixed Sources
Product group from well-managed
forests and other controlled sources
www.fsc.org Cert no. SW-COC-000952
© 1996 Forest Stewardship Council

Printed and bound in Canada.

1 2 3 4 — 14 13 12 11

CONTENTS

PREFACE AND
ACKNOWLEDGEMENTS

I have been teaching courses in Canadian local government at the University of Western Ontario for more than 30 years. Like all instructors I have never found a perfect textbook. Until recently, however, I have resisted the temptation to try to write my own—there have always been too many other projects and priorities and too many aspects of the subject about which I did not feel ready to write. By 2007, however, such excuses seemed feeble, especially when I came up against the persuasive reasoning of David Stover and Kate Skene from Oxford University Press Canada.

I am under no illusions that other instructors and their students will find my attempt at a text to be perfect. Their priorities will doubtless be different from mine. All readers, however, have a right to know the kinds of influences that have shaped my own particular approach. Since the mid-1980s I have taught courses at Western designed for managers in Canadian municipalities, first in our Diploma in Public Administration program that was developed by the late Professor Allan O'Brien, and then in the Master of Public Administration program. Allan, a former mayor of Halifax and past president of the Federation of Canadian Municipalities, convinced me that, as a then-young academic with no experience working in municipal government, I had something to offer our manager-students.

In retrospect, I think he was right. More importantly for this book, my experience in these classes has profoundly affected how I approach my subject. It is a cliché to claim that instructors always learn from their students, but for me it has been obviously true. I lecture about the broad principles of local government organization and politics and am happily interrupted by managerial stories about how they relate to 'the real world'. I came to have a profound respect for the kinds of problems senior Canadian municipal managers must grapple with daily, a respect I hope is reflected in this book. The practical result of all this for my current readers is that, more so than in other texts, they will find this book rooted in practical problems and issues. But just as municipal managers need to be able to think abstractly as well as practically, this book does contain some abstract sections grounded in various theoretical approaches to the study of political science and public administration. Such sections are always meant to illuminate practical issues rather than to minimize them.

Given that non-managers will constitute the vast majority of my readership, how does my own personal history with such managers affect my approach in this book? Above all, it means that readers will learn about Canadian local government from the perspective of someone who takes it very seriously as a vital component of Canada's overall system of government. For me, local government is important for what it is and what it does, not simply as part of some broader theoretical argument about, for example, the nature of cities in capitalist economies or how market competition promotes efficiencies in local service provision. If both practising municipal managers and students of political science and public administration feel that this book engages them, then in my eyes it will have been successful.

One of the great attractions of life as a professor is being able to pursue one's own academic interests. Western has always been a most hospitable place for local government research, especially in recent years after my colleague and friend, Robert Young, obtained a very large grant from the Social Sciences and Humanities Research Council of Canada (SSHRC) involving the study of Canadian municipalities. The book that he and I co-edited for this project, *Foundations of Governance: Municipal Government in Canada's Provinces* (Toronto: University of Toronto Press, 2009), has provided much important raw material for this text. From 1990 to 1995, I benefited from my own SSHRC standard research grant, a project that delivered less in published form than was originally promised. Some of the material from this project is published here for the first time, especially in Chapter 10. My debts to the SSHRC in general and Bob Young in particular are gratefully acknowledged. A sabbatical leave from Western in the first half of 2010 made possible the final push to get this project done.

Except for David Siegel at Brock University and for two reviewers who remain anonymous, other colleagues have generally been spared prior exposure to what I have written here. David has been especially helpful: in his formal review; in making subsequent suggestions for improvement; and in sharing with me his experience as a very successful textbook co-author. Colleagues who have not seen the manuscript will be familiar with my approach to some of the topics I cover, especially those relating to the governance of city-regions and to municipal amalgamations. Hopefully, they will appreciate the different context required by a text and the fact that I have tackled some related subjects (see especially Chapter 5) about which I previously knew little. Some students in my 2009–10 classes read preliminary drafts of a few of the early chapters. I take their general reluctance to offer much in the way of criticism as tacit approval in some cases, and in most as reluctance to cause trouble for themselves or their professor. In any event, I do appreciate the comments I received.

After having completed this manuscript I now more fully understand the challenges faced by all those who have previously attempted texts on this subject. I think especially, however, of Professor Donald J.H. Higgins of St Mary's University, whose pioneering texts, *Urban Canada: Its Government and Politics* (1977) and *Local and Urban Politics in Canada* (1986), paved the way for the rest of us among his generation of political scientists. Don's tragic death in 1989 took from us a scholar who had a great deal more to contribute.

Once I started writing, I received helpful and prompt guidance from my developmental editor at OUP Canada, Rebecca Ryoji. Informed and skilful copy-editing was provided by Dr Richard Tallman and Laurna Tallman. My thanks go to all who have been involved in this project. I, of course, remain solely responsible for all errors and omissions. I hope those who discover them will let me know.

Above all, textbooks are for students. This book is dedicated to all of mine: past, present, and future.

Andrew Sancton
asancton@uwo.ca
London, Ontario
October 2010

INTRODUCTION

Most Canadians live in cities or their suburbs. Even a statement as simple as this raises many questions about how the words 'cities' and 'suburbs' are defined, questions that are crucial to the subject matter of this book and that will be addressed at various points, especially in Chapter 5. Because Canada is primarily an urban nation, many Canadians confront significant urban problems every day: traffic congestion, expensive or ineffective public transit, homelessness, the ugliness of commercial sprawl. Many more use urban services that are usually taken for granted here, but which are highly problematic in some of the world's most populous cities: the supply of clean drinking water, the safe removal of liquid and solid waste, policing of public spaces so as to provide security for all who wish to move around. Local governments are intimately linked to urban problems and services, and that is one good reason why we should know about them.

As we shall see throughout this book, however, local governments often do not have exclusive jurisdiction over urban problems and issues; the most intractable problems usually involve other levels of government as well, sometimes in dominant decision-making roles. Analyses of the politics of urban problems often refer to 'multi-level governance', a process whereby various levels and varieties of government act collaboratively to address issues that transcend the jurisdictional responsibilities of each of them. This book focuses neither on urban problems nor on multi-level governance. It focuses instead on local governments as political institutions. Its objective is to attempt to answer all the big questions political scientists ask about any political institutions: How are they defined? Why do we have them? What do they do? How do they relate to other political institutions? How is power attained and distributed within them? How do decisions get made and implemented? Where does their money come from and how does it get spent? Answering these questions will require us to consider many important urban problems but, at its heart, this book is about local government, not about urban issues and problems. It takes local governments seriously in that it assumes that we need to know as much about how our local governments work as we know about other levels of government. No one can pretend that studying the politics and government of Canadian local government has as much initial appeal as studying international terrorism, American presidential elections, or the dominance of the prime minister in Canadian government. But most readers—if they are not already—will be working and/or raising families in Canadian cities, relying on local public services, and paying property taxes. Knowing about Canadian local government facilitates urban living.

Although some of the material in the book is clearly relevant to local government in rural areas, those with special interests in rural local government will be disappointed. If this book gave as much attention to rural as urban, its subtitle would not be 'an urban perspective'. A more important disclaimer is that in the Canadian context 'local government' does not include any form of Aboriginal self-government. Although some of the administrative challenges of local and Aboriginal governance are no doubt similar, their political origins are so different that comparisons within a political and governmental context—which is the context of this book—are quite irrelevant. Aboriginal self-governance relates in some way to the concept of 'nation'; local government does not. In Chapter 5, we shall touch briefly on the subject of Aboriginal Canadians who live in cities, but this is about as close as we shall get to Canada's First Nations.

This book is designed as a textbook for political science courses in Canadian local government at both the undergraduate and graduate levels. It should also serve as a reference book on the subject for any interested citizen. It assumes no prior knowledge of local government, and only a rudimentary knowledge of the basic principles of Canadian government. There are no elaborate theoretical frameworks, and every effort has been made to limit the use of academic jargon, except where it is absolutely necessary to understand particular contributions to our knowledge of urban governance. Long-time scholars in the field might be surprised by the fact that their names generally appear only in the notes, but not in the main narrative. As much as is possible, this is a book about Canadian local government, not a book about how various scholars have contributed to our current knowledge of Canadian local government. Nor is it a book about the urban geography of Canadian cities or about the urban sociology of Canadian cities.[1]

The four chapters that comprise Part I of the book are concerned with the legal and political framework of Canadian local government. More so than other levels of government, local governments are generally the result of some deliberate design, either by provincial governments or by groups of local citizens who at some point in the past have taken action, in accordance with provincial laws, to provide themselves with some degree of self-government. Because of this element of self-conscious design, we need pay some attention in these first chapters to the principles that are relevant for the institutional design of systems of local government.

Part II is concerned with how structures of local government are adapted to urbanization. Chapter 5 deals with different definitions and characteristics of Canadian urbanization. In one way or another, the remaining three chapters in this part deal with changing boundaries of local governments. The fact that boundaries of local governments—unlike those of national or provincial governments—are always open for discussion and change is a key distinguishing characteristic of local government. To ignore boundaries when studying local government is to ignore the essence of the subject.

Part III of the book is about power, politics, and management within major Canadian municipalities. This is the part of the book that will seem most familiar to readers familiar with books about the politics of particular provinces and countries. Here we explore the roles and behaviours of local voters, councillors, mayors, developers, citizens' groups, and managers. Part IV is about money, a subject of great importance to all governments but one of special importance at the local level where much money is needed, where local governmental access to various tax resources is relatively limited, and where there is much debate about the desirability of change. In this section we explore the property tax in some detail, a subject of essential knowledge for anyone claiming to know anything about local government in Canada. The final chapter, by way of conclusion, addresses issues that relate to the future of Canadian local government.

Understanding the nature of political institutions almost invariably requires an understanding of their historical evolution. There is much history in this book, but it does not all appear near the beginning.

Relevant historical background is covered wherever it appears neces-sary. Canadian local government has its origins in Britain's deep his-torical past. If we have no understanding of these origins, there is much about local government in Canada that is difficult to understand. We examine these origins in Chapter 1, whose object is to define what local government is.

PART I
The Legal and Political Framework

1 What Is Local Government?

'Local government' is a slippery term, used in different ways in different places in different circumstances. For the purposes of this book, the term includes both municipalities and all other governmental entities with territories smaller than provinces that have their own governing bodies with some capacity for autonomous decision-making. At this stage, such a definition raises as many questions as it answers. The main purpose of this chapter is to explain what the definition means.

Nowhere in Canada can we find any kind of constitutional or legal definition of local government. This situation is different from that of many European liberal democracies in which local governments are legally established and protected by the national constitution and in which local governments therefore comprise an important part of the of the state apparatus. In the United States, each state government has its own constitution and most of these documents establish and define local governments in one way or another. Canada and other countries from the old British Commonwealth are distinct in not providing any form of constitutional recognition for local governments. The only way to understand what they are is to explore their historical origins. Such an exploration forms the first part of this chapter.

Municipal Corporations in the English Tradition

Municipal corporations—also known as municipalities—are the most important components of Canadian local government. Canadian municipalities are the direct descendants of English municipal corporations. To understand the legal context of Canadian municipal government, we need to know about English municipal corporations, and to know about

English municipal corporations we need to understand their relationship to the monarch. In Britain, the monarch is the government. Everything that the British government does is done in the name of the monarch. The prime minister is the monarch's prime adviser. Everyone who works for the government serves the Crown, hence the term 'civil servant'. The reality, of course, is that the monarch decides virtually nothing herself, but symbolically she is everywhere.

The first English municipal corporations derived from royal charters. For example, the charter of the City of London can be traced back to 1075. By the mid-fourteenth century a distinct corporate body had emerged, consisting of a mayor, aldermen, and councillors, the forerunner of the City of London Corporation that exists today and governs the square-mile territory at the heart of London known as 'the City'.[1] Later municipal corporations were established by parliamentary statute rather than by royal charters. A municipal corporation is legally entitled to do whatever its charter or statute says it can do.

Municipal corporations act on behalf of themselves and their residents, not on behalf of the Crown. For many centuries in Britain there was great tension between the Crown and many municipal corporations. Some of the provisions in the Magna Carta of 1215 are directed at protecting municipal corporations against arbitrary royal action. Until the nineteenth century, municipal corporations carried on their business with little or no supervision from the monarch and his government, and certainly without any form of public control through democratic elections. Their 'business' varied from place to place, but it usually involved regulating public markets and nuisances, investing in what we would now call public infrastructure, and raising funds through various charges and taxes. In fact, distinctions between municipal corporations and other corporations were hazy at best. Municipal corporations engaged in commercial trading, and some trading corporations with royal charters (the Hudson's Bay Company in Canada) were granted legal authority by the monarch to govern vast territories of land that had been claimed for Britain by colonial explorers.

The approval in Britain of the Municipal Corporations Act in 1835 started a long process whereby Britain's municipal corporations became part of a regularized, democratic system of local government that extended throughout the entire country. This process began at about the same time as Canada's first municipal corporations were established. Saint John, New Brunswick, Canada's first municipal corporation, had been created by royal charter in 1785 but municipal incorporations elsewhere in what is now Canada did not begin until the 1830s and 1840s. In 1849, the legislature of the pre-Confederation Province of Canada approved a Municipal Act (commonly known as the Baldwin Act, after its sponsor Robert Baldwin) for Canada West that provided the basis for Ontario's municipal system for more than a century.[2] By this time, municipal corporations in Britain, the United States, and Canada were increasingly being recognized as a form of government rather than as an unusual variant of a private business corporation,[3] although campaigns by business interests to remove such corporations from all forms of 'municipal trading' (i.e., commercial businesses) were commonplace until well into the twentieth century.

After 1867, legislatures in all the Canadian provinces eventually approved laws that established townships, counties, or districts as the basic units of rural municipal government. Residents in urban settlements, if they followed certain procedures laid out in the various provincial laws, could then initiate a process whereby their settlements, depending on population size, became incorporated as villages, towns, or cities. Although all municipalities ultimately owe their existence to provincial law, it is important to realize that incorporated villages, towns, and cities often owe their existence to initiatives taken by local citizens many years previously. Frequently, systems of municipal government seem so complex that it is impossible to imagine that a rational policy-maker in a provincial capital could ever have devised them. In reality, the complexity derives largely from the past actions of thousands of individuals in their local different communities rather than from a single omnipotent centre.

We have already seen that early English municipal corporations were quite separate from 'the government' as represented by the monarch. But are today's municipalities part of 'the government'? The answer is not as simple as it seems. For traditionalists, municipalities can never be on the same level as a government whose very existence is inseparable from the Crown. For strict federalists in the United States and Canada, it is clear that the federal constitution establishes two—and only two—levels of government, with governments at each of the two levels deriving their existence directly from the respective constitutions of each country. But, for all practical purposes, most citizens recognize that they pay taxes to, and are regulated by, three distinct levels of government: federal, provincial (state in the United States), and municipal.

Occasionally, however, it is still sometimes suggested that municipalities are not really governments at all. For example, in 1999, a senior adjudicator for Ontario's Chief Information and Privacy Officer ruled that the city of Toronto was not a government under the terms of Ontario's Freedom of Information and Protection of Privacy Act. He refused to accept the city's contention that certain information it provided to a provincial ministry need not be made public because it would 'reveal information received in confidence from another government',[4] which is grounds for exemption under the Act. The adjudicator went on:

> if a municipality was considered a government for the purposes of section 15 of the *Act*, a letter from a local library board could be placed on the same footing, and qualify for the same exemption as a document received from the government of another nation. This would greatly expand the number of records that could be withheld from the public indefinitely.[5]

A much more common and authoritative position was expressed by the Supreme Court of Canada in 1997 when it was asked to decide whether the Canadian Charter of Rights and Freedoms applied to certain employment practices of the city of Longueuil in Quebec.

> The ambit of s. 32 of the Canadian *Charter* is wide enough to include all entities that are essentially governmental in nature and is not restricted merely to those that are formally part of the structure of the federal or provincial governments. As well, under s. 32, particular entities will be subject to *Charter* scrutiny in respect of certain governmental activities they perform, even if the entities themselves cannot accurately be described as 'governmental' *per se*. Since municipalities cannot but be described as 'governmental entities', they are subject to the Canadian *Charter*. First, municipal councils are democratically elected by members of the general public and are accountable to their constituents in a manner analogous to that in which Parliament and the provincial legislatures are accountable to the electorates they represent. Second, municipalities possess a general taxing power that, for the purposes of determining whether they can rightfully be described as 'government', is indistinguishable from the taxing powers of the Parliament or the provinces. Third, and importantly, municipalities are empowered to make laws, to administer them and to enforce them within a defined territorial jurisdiction. Finally, and most significantly, municipalities derive their existence and law-making authority from the provinces. As the Canadian *Charter* clearly applies to the provincial legislatures and governments, it must also apply to entities upon which they confer governmental powers within their authority. Otherwise, provinces could simply avoid the application of the *Charter* by devolving powers on municipal bodies. Further, since a municipality is governmental in nature, all its activities are subject to *Charter* review. The Canadian *Charter* is therefore applicable to the residence requirement at issue in

this case. The particular modality a municipality chooses to adopt in advancing its policies cannot shield its activities from *Charter* scrutiny. All the municipality's powers are derived from statute and all are of a governmental character. An act performed by an entity that is governmental in nature is thus necessarily 'governmental' and cannot properly be viewed as 'private.'[6]

This passage is a clear a statement as to why, for legal purposes at least, municipalities meet all the requirements for being 'governmental entities', although they are notably never referred to as 'governments'. It is also very clear from the passage that the governmental authority of municipalities derives solely from provincial legislation and from nowhere else.

Different Kinds of Canadian Municipalities

If municipalities are clearly governmental entities, how do we determine which governmental entities are municipalities and which are not? The official name of Chatham–Kent in Ontario is the Municipality of Chatham–Kent, so that is a good clue that it is indeed a municipality. So are all incorporated places that are cities, towns, and villages. Things get more complicated when we think about rural areas or 'governmental entities' whose territories seem quite large.

The first point to realize is that much of Canada's territory is not included in any municipality. Such areas could be Indian reserves or territory belonging to autonomous First Nations. But most of it is simply 'unincorporated', meaning that there is no municipal government with jurisdiction in that area. The relatively few people who live in unincorporated areas are troublesome to provincial governments because they require some minimal government services (local roads, for example) that elsewhere are paid for and provided by municipalities. These same people often resist incorporation, or inclusion in the territory of a neighbouring municipality, because they rightly expect that they would end up paying higher taxes, even if they also would receive a higher level of local services.

The second point is that most populated agricultural areas are covered by rural municipalities. They go by such labels as township, rural district, or county. But the issue of terminology is not quite so simple. In northern Ontario, for example, many 'geographical townships' are not incorporated and hence have no municipal government of their own (although some geographical townships are included within the territory of a municipality that has another name, such as Timmins or Greater Sudbury). In Ontario, Nova Scotia, and Alberta, some rural municipalities are known as counties.

But in Ontario most counties are examples of what are known as upper-tier municipalities. They provide some municipal services for the whole territory of the county, but this same territory also contains lower-tier municipalities (usually towns, villages, and townships) that provide more local municipal services. In Quebec, the analogous institution is a 'municipal regional county' (MRC). Ontario also has six 'regional municipalities' that are generally more urban than counties. People who live within the jurisdiction of an upper-tier municipality are said to live within two-tier systems of municipal government.

In British Columbia, 'regional districts' act as upper-tier municipal governments in all places where there are also lower-tier municipalities. For otherwise unincorporated areas, they act as the single-tier of municipal government. In provinces other than Ontario, Quebec, and British Columbia, the entire municipal system is single-tier because there is no part of the province covered by two distinct tiers (or levels) of municipal government. We shall analyze the historical evolution and relative merits of these different forms of municipal structure in Chapter 7.

New Brunswick is another somewhat special case because 37 per cent of the province's population live within the territory of 'local service districts',[7] but these people are considered to live in unincorporated areas because these entities are not subject to the province's Municipalities Act.

Finally, Quebec has two 'supra-regional governments' that cover the entire urbanized areas around Montreal and Quebec City, respectively. Some people living on the outer fringes of this area are actually subject to three levels of municipal government: local municipality, MRC, and supra-regional (known in Quebec as the 'metropolitan community'). Table 1.1 shows the total number of municipalities for each province, including the number of upper-tier and supra-regional municipalities, where applicable.

Special–Purpose Bodies

We saw earlier that when the Ontario information adjudicator was trying to determine whether or not he should consider municipalities to be governments, he was concerned that 'a letter from a local library board could be placed on the same footing . . . as a document from the government of another nation.' Why did he refer to library boards when he was supposed to be concerned with municipalities? The answer is

Table 1.1 Municipal Governments in Canada, 2008

Province/Territory	Total Municipalities	Upper–Tier Municipalities	Supra–Regional Municipalities
Alberta	353		
British Columbia	155	27	
Manitoba	203		
New Brunswick	103		
Newfoundland and Labrador	280		
Nova Scotia	55		
Northwest Territories	33		
Nunavut	25		
Ontario	415	30	
Prince Edward Island	75		
Quebec	1,141	86	2
Saskatchewan	801		
Yukon	8		
Total	3,647	143	2

Source: Commonwealth Local Government Forum, *Canada Profile*. At: <www.clgf.org.uk/user–files/1/File/2008_Country_Files/CANADA.pdf> (23 June 2010).

that library boards in Ontario are both connected to municipalities and separate from them. Such boards and commissions are usually referred to as special-purpose bodies.

Special-purpose bodies are very similar to municipalities except that they are established to carry out a single governmental function, as distinct from municipalities, which have multiple functions. Those who govern special-purpose bodies are either democratically elected or are appointed by people who are democratically elected. They have the authority to levy a tax themselves, to claim tax revenues from another body, or to charge user fees for essential services or utilities. They also have the authority to make laws (i.e., binding rules) and to enforce them within their respective assigned territories. Although municipalities and most special-purpose bodies derive their authority from provincial law, some local special-purpose bodies (e.g., port and airport authorities) are under federal jurisdiction. We shall explore this further in Chapter 4.

Determining which local institutions qualify as special-purpose bodies, and therefore as 'governmental entities', is not easy. Fortunately, for our purposes, we do not have to make clear distinctions. We need only recognize that some special-purpose bodies are almost as powerful as municipalities and others are so weak that they are hardly like governments at all. Elected school boards with the authority to levy their own taxes are the strongest special-purpose bodies in Canada. Library boards in Ontario are among the weakest.

Figure 1.1 Components of Local Government in Canada

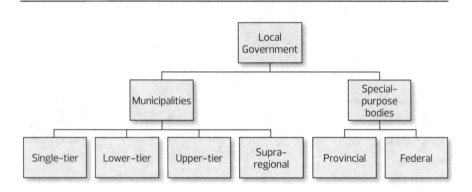

Understanding the definition of special-purpose bodies can be aided by pointing out some examples of institutions that clearly are not special-purpose bodies. Committees of municipal councillors that report to the entire municipal council are not special-purpose bodies, because they can make no final decisions themselves. The same applies to local advisory committees of citizens that may be appointed by any level of government. Business corporations that are partly or wholly owned by municipal governments are not special-purpose bodies because they have no more authority than any other business corporation to appropriate taxpayers' money or to make any kind of binding rule or law. Local non-profit institutions such as hospitals and universities receive large sums of public money, mostly from provincial governments, but simply receiving public money does not make them special-purpose bodies.

Statistics Canada defines 'local governments' as including municipalities and their associated 'autonomous boards, commissions and funds . . . [and] school boards'.[8] In short, local governments in Canada include municipalities and local special-purpose bodies. Such a definition is commonly accepted[9] but is far from crystal clear, as we shall explore in more detail in Chapter 4.

Financial Significance of Local Government

In 1913 local governments accounted for 36 per cent of government spending in Canada, while provinces were responsible for only 17 per cent. By 1948 the percentages were 14 and 18, respectively.[10] Since then, the proportion of provincial spending to the total has risen to the same level as the federal, while the proportion of total spending that is local remains much the same. Spending by local governments in Canada is significant and important, but it is wrong to claim that it is becoming more important relative to other levels of government.

Another way of seeking out what is very similar information is to look at local government's share of total revenue that each level of government raises from its own sources. By looking at 'own-source' revenue for each level of government, we eliminate the effect of transfer payments from one level of government to the other. Figure 1.2 shows the total revenue raised by each level of government without counting transfers received from other levels.

Figure 1.2 Own–Source Revenues for Federal, Provincial, and Local Governments

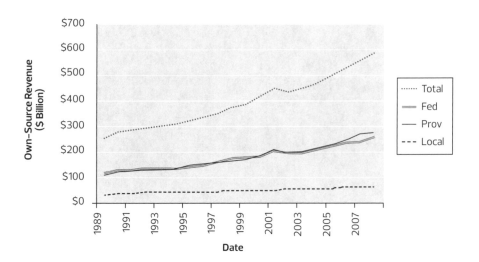

Source: Statistics Canada, CANSIM Table 3850024.

Conclusion

In this chapter we have defined what local government is and looked at its financial significance in relation to other levels of government in Canada. But this information is only important in the real world if we know what it is that local governments actually do and what they spend their money on. This is what we turn to in the next chapter.

RESOURCES

See Andrew Sancton and Robert Young, eds, *Foundations of Governance: Municipal Government in Canada's Provinces* (Toronto: University of Toronto Press, 2009), which contains essays on the municipal systems of each of the 10 provinces.

STUDY QUESTIONS

1. Why is it not strictly accurate to say that people who work for municipalities are civil servants?
2. What is the difference between a single-tier municipality and an upper-tier municipality?
3. Do you currently reside in a two-tier municipal system or a single-tier system?

2 Why Local Government?

In theory, we do not need to have local government at all, because all of what they do could be carried out directly by provincial governments. This chapter tries to explain why provincial legislatures—and the legislatures of most other democratic jurisdictions in the world—have established systems of local government within their borders. It then moves on to discuss what Canadian local governments actually do. Not surprisingly, the functions of local government are generally related to some of the theoretical reasons why local governments have been created in the first place.

Imagining Provinces without Local Government

For most aspects of Canadian local government, provinces are central governments; they are the ones in control. For the purposes of this discussion, we shall refer only to provinces and local governments to keep things as simple as possible. For now, we need not worry about Canada being a federation, with two levels of government above the local.

It is not difficult to imagine provinces without local governments. This is especially so in Prince Edward Island, which has a total population only slightly in excess of 135,000. In many ways, the provincial government of PEI is little more than a local government itself, so it is not surprising that the provincial government makes many apparently local decisions.[1] For other provinces, especially the larger ones, imagining a complete absence of local government is much more difficult. In such a state of affairs, the province would make all the decisions about all the matters within its constitutional sphere of jurisdiction. It would decide how garbage gets collected, where buildings can be built, which teachers will teach in which schools, and how water supply systems will be built and financed. It would not necessarily have to make laws relating to each of these issues in each place, but it would have to establish its own procedures for deciding each of these issues, and many more.

There are at least three major questions a provincial government would have to address in the absence of any kind of local government:

1. Are all places going to be treated the same way?
2. If not, for which functions of government will there be local flexibility?
3. Will the bureaucracy remain in the capital city or will it be 'deconcentrated' to outlying areas?

Each question will be treated in turn.

The question regarding equal treatment for all places is not about services being identical everywhere. Clearly, no one would contemplate having as many police officers patrolling a rural road as a busy downtown street. Levels of service can always be adjusted in accordance with some kind of rational formula to determine need (number of cars on the road, number of people living nearby, record of recent crimes in the area, etc.). But it would not be easy to develop appropriate formulas for every government service that would produce satisfactory results everywhere in a large province. It would be even harder to administer it fairly and efficiently. A small army of bureaucrats would be needed simply to collect all the required data.

Let us assume, however, that it is theoretically possible to work out the appropriate formulas and to administer them. Will these allow for flexibility? What can we do if citizens in one area want to be treated differently from those in another? For some matters—provision of health insurance, for example—the provincial government would be unlikely to allow variation. But what if people in one area of a province want more police (or recreational facilities, or public gardens) than the formulas provide for? Or what if they want less so that they can reduce their levels of taxation? To accommodate such preferences, the central government would have to develop mechanisms for determining these preferences, for implementing them, and for taxing different groups of people at different rates so that each group pays for its own level of preferred services. Making these kinds of adjustments in taxes and service levels to allow for local preferences, while not impossible, would add a dramatic additional burden to the work of the provincial government.

As for centralizing or 'deconcentrating' the machinery of government—i.e., the bureaucracy—obviously the government could not manage all the different local activities from its headquarters in the capital city.

Not only would there need to be large numbers of government employees in major urban centres to actually provide the services, but their managers would have to be nearby to ensure that central policies and procedures were properly followed. To the extent that central officials are located outside the capital, we say that the government is 'deconcentrated'.

If this all sounds like some kind of bureaucratic and administrative nightmare, it is meant to. Many people think that having multiple layers of government—and multiple governments at every layer except for the whole country—is itself a nightmare. One of the major objectives of this chapter, and of this book as a whole, is to show that healthy systems of local government, while far from perfect, are much more preferable than the kind of centralized system described above. The argument here is not that local governments always work well and will always do what they are supposed to do.[2] Rather, if a system of government for any territory larger than a single small city includes a well-functioning system of local government, then it will work better than a centralized system containing no local government. The next section analyzes why this is so.

Efficiency

The most important reason why central governments establish systems of local government is to promote efficiency. Two senses of 'efficiency' are relevant here. The first has to do with economies and diseconomies of scale, a concept from economics that refers to how unit costs change for different products depending on the number of units produced. For example, if electricity were required to serve a few isolated households, no one would decide to serve them by building a nuclear power plant; the cost would be too great for the small amount of electricity needed. Because there are economies of scale in nuclear generation of electricity, such a method could well be cheaper for each household if the whole system were designed to serve millions of people.

Sometimes it is assumed that there are economies of scale for every product. But common sense suggests that this cannot possibly be true. If there were economies of scale in commercial lawn mowing, we would expect to see entities such as a Canadian Lawn Mowing Company or, in this age of globalization, International Lawn Services Incorporated. The reason such companies do not exist is simple: there are no economies of scale in lawn mowing. A giant company cannot compete with a person who owns a single lawn mower and is able to move it around from customer to customer within a small area (and even that person cannot compete with an underemployed teenager who has free access to his parents' lawn mower when it is not being used to cut the family lawn).

The same factors are at work in government services. If citizens want their own highly sophisticated system for common defence against perceived external threats, they are going to be better off if they are part of a very large group who can pool their resources to buy all the latest high-tech equipment. But if the same citizens all desire that their residential neighbourhoods are served by well-maintained and attractive urban parks, they are not likely to be well served by a national 'Ministry of Neighbourhood Parks'. To prevent the diseconomies of scale that would emerge from having layers of bureaucrats supervising a national system of neighbourhood parks, it is simply more efficient to have hundreds of quite separate organizations providing such parks. In the real world, such organizations are part of local government.[3]

But there is also a different type of efficiency—allocative efficiency—that can be promoted by local government. Allocative efficiency in government involves ensuring that the bundle of services and taxes provided by government matches as closely as possible what it is that people actually want. Local governments are well suited for promoting allocative efficiency. They provide a mechanism that enables citizens in different territories to adjust the level of government services to match what they want. Such a mechanism is, of course, far from perfect. Within the same small territory served by the same local government, young families might prefer that their tax money be spent to provide lifeguards for local wading pools while their older neighbours might want more large-print books in the public library. One way or another, the local political process works out compromises between these conflicting interests. The point is that different outcomes are likely in different places and, if the system is relatively open and democratic, such different outcomes reflect a crude measure of allocative efficiency.[4]

There is, however, a potential dark side to allocative efficiency. What if all the richer older people end up living close to each other and the poorer younger families live somewhere else? What if they are separated from each other by the boundaries that create different local governments for each group? If public education were provided exclusively by local governments, the old rich people could decide to have no schools at all, and the poor young families could not afford to provide them for their own children. It is precisely to prevent such a state of affairs that public education in Western countries is now so closely supervised and controlled by central governments (provinces in Canada).

If citizens in the richer area use their local government to pay for a luxurious recreational and cultural centre that the poorer area clearly cannot afford, the issues are trickier. Some people will argue that it is unfair and therefore unacceptable for rich people to have better public facilities in their areas than poor people can have in theirs, especially if the two areas are relatively close to each other and the use of the luxurious facility is in some way restricted to residents of the area that paid for them. If this argument is extended to claim that rich people should not be allowed to keep their riches, then at least it is consistent. But if the position is that it is acceptable for rich people to use their riches to build swimming pools in their respective backyards, but unacceptable for them collectively to decide to pay high taxes to their local government so as to provide themselves with one superlative swimming facility, then it is hard to see the logic. Can we reasonably accept that different people will have different levels of individual financial resources but that all local governments must have similar resources and provide similar levels of services? What about the differences in resources between the governments of Alberta and New Brunswick? More tellingly, what about the differences between the governments of Canada and Bangladesh?

Raising these questions shows that allocative efficiency is potentially a controversial concept. Sensible people can have legitimate disagreements about the extent of differences in service levels that societies should tolerate among their different local governments. But, at a minimum, there is surely agreement that groups of citizens in different places, regardless of their financial resources, are likely to have different preferences for some government services and that it is wasteful to ignore such differences by providing a common level of services and taxes everywhere. Local governments enable differentiation in levels of service for different groups of citizens in different areas.

Two other potential arguments about how local governments promote efficiency need to be considered. The first has to do with the benefits of competition. By definition, if there are no local governments within a given jurisdiction, then the one central (e.g., provincial) government in that jurisdiction is a monopoly in the sense that it is the only provider of government services. Monopolies are notorious for being inefficient and for passing on their excessive costs to their captive consumers. Establishing a system of local government involves establishing governments whose levels of services and taxes can at least be compared with each other. Citizens therefore have some idea about the relative efficiency of their own local governments and can at least vote accordingly. Indeed, a large body of literature considers the extent to which people and businesses actually move from one jurisdiction to another in search of the local government that best matches their preferences. This literature was originally sparked by an academic article by the American economist

Charles Tiebout, who famously argued that governments can be made to be as efficient as private firms by ensuring that there are enough of them to compete with each other to attract taxpaying residents and businesses. Under Tiebout's assumptions, residents and businesses 'vote with their feet' when they are dissatisfied with the actions of local governments, and the threat of losing taxpayers forces them to be as efficient as possible. We need not accept fully the 'public-choice' framework that flows from Tiebout's analysis to accept that competition among different local governments to do a better job can sometimes be beneficial.[5]

So far the arguments about efficiency have related to local governments in general, both municipal governments and special-purpose bodies. But the last argument relates only to municipal governments, which, as seen in Chapter 1, are by definition responsible for a number of different governmental functions. The existence of municipalities enables them to benefit from 'economies of scope', which involve efficiencies deriving from the fact that an organization is doing more than one thing at a time. For example, a municipality can benefit from the fact that it can use its own parks and community centres to run recreational programs. Or under-occupied road maintenance workers can be used to fix sewers. If the central government were responsible for these functions (or if they were each provided by a different special-purpose body), then local co-ordination across different functional areas would likely be more difficult. Economies of scope for functions within the jurisdiction of the same municipality are not guaranteed. Most people can recall seeing municipal workers digging up a municipal roadway one day to fix a sewer only to have it dug up again a few weeks later to fix something else.

In fact, local governments in general do not have a popular reputation for great efficiency. Images of outside workers standing around waiting for equipment to arrive or of inside workers pushing paper from one office to another are probably predominant in many people's minds when they (infrequently) think about local government. Many such images are simply unfair and inaccurate. But that is not what concerns us here. What is relevant is that local government enhances the potential capacity of government in general to be more efficient. Perhaps the only institutions that would be less efficient than local governments in providing local public services would be agencies of central governments.

Participation

There are many exaggerated arguments about how the existence of local governments facilitates citizen participation in local decision-making. Such arguments often conjure up images of deliberative assemblies in ancient Athens, town meetings in New England, or the claim by the English political philosopher John Stuart Mill that local governments are 'the chief instrument for the public education of the citizens'.[6] What these images all have in common is an assumption that citizens have a keen interest in local issues, a recognition that they are to be settled by the actions of local governments, an understanding of how such institutions work, and a belief that their own actions will make a difference in the local decision-making process. In fact, however, much evidence suggests that each of these assumptions is wrong.

Paul E. Peterson, an American political scientist, urges us to recognize some of the harsh facts about local government, especially in North America, many of which we will return to in later chapters of this book. Turnout at elections is low, in part because party involvement is limited, making it difficult for all but the best-informed electors to know whom to vote for. Issues at the local level often seem technical and legalistic, especially in comparison with the broad policy issues with which national legislatures usually occupy themselves. Media attention to local politics is cursory at best, making it more likely that citizens actually know more about what is going on in their national capitals than in their city halls.[7] In these circumstances, how can anyone possibly claim that local government is even partially justified by its ability to enhance citizen participation?

The claim must be based on particular circumstances and issues rather than on generalized claims about the day-to-day activities of local government. Many citizens—even ones who have owned their own houses in the same neighbourhood for a long time—can go for years without having much participatory involvement in local government. They expect the normal municipal services, complain about taxes, and might even vote if they feel they know the candidates. But when someone proposes to make a significant change in their immediate built environment that is perceived to be negative, they often quickly become involved, fully expecting that 'their' councillor will support their position. This is where local political activity can be intimate and highly participatory. Councillors generally do respond to groups of enraged local citizens; they encourage them to show up at committee and council meetings; and the citizens actually watch their complaint get dealt with. Thousands of people in Canada become involved in local politics each year in precisely this way and many subsequently run for election. Some of these people then get elected to decision-making positions themselves and some of these subsequently enter provincial or federal politics. These are some of the ways that local government promotes meaningful citizen participation in politics.

This is not to pretend that all participation in local politics is prompted by ordinary citizens trying to defend or improve their neighbourhoods. Some people get involved because their livelihood involves local real estate and they know that local governments are very important to the local market. Others become involved in local politics because they are really interested in eventually making a political career at another level and they know that local politics is a good 'training ground' and a place to get one's name known. In short, local government decision-making is often, if not usually, intimately connected to complex calculations about short- and long-term political advantage rather than to simply enabling ordinary citizens to have their say on issues that are of concern to them.

These considerations about the participatory and political aspects of local government should cause us to examine how they affect the capacity of local governments to be efficient. In the previous section of this chapter, local governments were portrayed as though they were neutral mechanisms for transforming citizen preferences into public policies and public services. An extreme example of this perspective is represented by the 'public-choice' approach, where local governments are perceived as acting so much like private firms that their decisions are expected to be determined more by market forces than by preferences expressed through such political mechanisms as elections. But even if we dispense with the fiction that local governments are exclusively engaged in some kind of market competition with each other, we still cannot conclude that is possible for them to somehow be non-political. The fact that the makeup of their governing boards (councils) is determined through a relatively open electoral process, and that people who get elected usually want to be re-elected, means that participation matters. This is good. Yet, as we shall see in more detail in later chapters, not all citizens are equal when it comes to participation, so not all citizen preferences are accurately and fairly represented in the local decision-making process. This is a fact that not only reflects badly on the capacity of local governments to promote participation but it also undermines their capacity to be allocatively efficient.

Having acknowledged all this, we are once gain left to contemplate what our political life would be like in the absence of local government. Would there be alternative opportunities for citizens to become politically engaged? What participatory avenues would be open to citizens who wanted to affect a central-government decision that affected only their own immediate area? Could such avenues be effective if the political or bureaucratic futures of those in the central government were in no way determined by what people in the area actually wanted? Indeed, if there were no local government, our collective political lives might well seem even more limited and powerless than they already are.

Pluralism

A pluralistic political system is one in which there are many sources of power. The opposite of a pluralist system is a totalitarian one, in which the state controls everything and no other sources of power are tolerated. Totalitarian states do not have local governments that are in any sense independent of the central state. In the aftermath of Nazi Germany, and to a lesser extent in the aftermath of the Soviet Union and its Eastern European empire, much attention focused on establishing local governments so that they could act as bulwarks against the re-emergence of totalitarianism. Although it is doubtful that the existence of local governments can prevent dictatorship at the centre, it is certainly true that local governments provide a source of political power that can serve as counterpoint to the central authority.

In liberal democracies political power emanates from many sources, which is why they are sometimes called pluralist democracies. Big businesses, trade unions, social movements (such as environmentalism), and interest groups (of which there are thousands, such as associations of pharmacists) are all sources of political power, either because they control financial resources and jobs (big business) or because they have the capacity to influence votes at election time. Unlike the other sources of pluralist political power mentioned above, local governments—especially municipal governments—can claim a special legitimacy based on the fact that their governing bodies are subject to election by universal franchise within their designated territories. This territorial base, combined with their special claim to democratic legitimacy, means that municipal governments can plausibly claim to represent people within these territories.

This doesn't mean they will necessarily get what they want from the central government, but it does mean they are a distinct voice in the pluralist universe. Although federal and provincial legislators represent distinct territories, the boundaries of their constituencies (which are designed to be roughly equal in population within any given province) mean that they often represent areas that are larger or smaller than those of the territorial communities that have the most meaning to people. Municipal boundaries can be more congruent with such communities (although we shall see in later chapters that this is not always the case) and so mayors, for example, have a potentially greater capacity to speak on behalf of territorial communities. If there were no local governments, there would be no mayors.

Functions of Canadian Local Governments

In practical terms, local governments exist to do what cannot be done so well by either central governments or by the private market. In the discussion earlier in this chapter about economies and diseconomies of scale in government services, we saw that some government services can be provided more efficiently if they are provided by organizations that are smaller than the central government. Such functions of government are natural candidates to be placed under the direct jurisdiction of local government. But, as we shall see, some functions of government are carried out locally in the absence of such a compelling economic imperative. Such services tend to be closely supervised, and sometimes subsidized, by central governments.

If we were to look at local governments around the world,[8] we would find a huge variety in their functional responsibilities. Indeed, if we allow for central intervention and supervision, it is almost impossible to think of a government function that could not be provided locally. If we do not make such an allowance, it is almost impossible to think of government functions that will be exclusively local, because almost all local services are subject to some form of central guidance. In any event, in the discussion that follows, we shall not be attempting universally applicable descriptions of the functions of local government but shall instead be focussing on what local governments in Canada do. Even this is difficult, however, because there is considerable variation among the provinces.

Ontario is the special case.[9] Unlike other provinces, its municipalities are responsible, under close provincial supervision and with massive provincial subsidies, for delivering income and employment assistance for able-bodied people who have run out of money. The program is called OntarioWorks, but is more universally recognized as 'welfare'. Again, unlike municipalities in other parts of the country, those in Ontario provide subsidized child care to low-income parents and subsidized housing to people unable to afford market housing. They do so with extensive provincial supervision and subsidies, but the latter are never enough as far as the municipalities are concerned.

Within all Canadian provinces, municipalities—both urban and rural—have at least some legal authority to act in relation to each of the following functions:[10] fire protection; animal control; roads (but only in the cities of Charlottetown and Summerside in PEI); traffic control; solid waste collection and disposal (but not in PEI); land-use planning and regulation; building regulation; economic development; tourism promotion; public libraries; parks and recreation; cultural facilities; licensing of businesses; emergency planning and preparedness; rural fences and drainage; regulation and/or provision of cemeteries; airports (though not major airports formerly operated directly by the federal government); and weed control and regulation of cosmetic pesticides (although recent provincial legislation in Ontario removes cosmetic pesticides from municipal jurisdiction).

The following are additional functions that are generally carried out by *urban* municipalities: public transit; regulation of taxis; water purification and distribution; sewage collection and treatment; downtown revitalization; and regulation of noise.

Except in Newfoundland and Labrador, where it is a responsibility of the Royal Newfoundland Constabulary, urban municipalities are generally responsible for policing, although there are various kinds of special-purpose bodies in different provinces (as will be outlined in Chapter 5) to insulate police from the direct control of municipal councils. Some urban municipalities obtain their policing through contracts with the Royal Canadian Mounted Police (RCMP) or with provincial police forces (Ontario and Quebec). The RCMP or provincial police forces generally provide policing in rural areas. Arrangements vary from province to province concerning the extent to which rural municipalities contribute to the cost. In Ontario, rural municipalities have paid the full cost since 1998.

As we have seen, Ontario is the only province in which municipalities have the statutory responsibility to provide social services and contribute to their funding. In Alberta, municipal governments contribute to the funding of certain preventative social service programs and lodges for low-income senior citizens. Arrangements for municipal seniors' residences in Ontario are similar, except that they are operated directly by cities and upper-tier municipalities rather than by separate non-profit corporations. In British Columbia, larger urban municipalities (especially the city of Vancouver) are engaged in social planning functions mainly aimed at attracting funding from other levels of government, co-ordinating the work of non-profit agencies, and providing modest municipal subsidies to various kinds of social service organizations, including community centres and non-profit child-care centres. In other provinces, there is even less municipal involvement in social services, ranging from none at all to minor expenditures for non-recreational programs in community centres and for the staffing of social planning groups.

Quebec and Ontario are the only provinces in which cities have any financial responsibility for social housing. The city of Vancouver manages subsidized housing for seniors and people with disabilities but has no financial responsibility for these units. Even the management costs are paid by other levels of government. Regional districts in British Columbia manage rental units for low-income people but make no financial contribution.

Municipalities in Ontario are responsible for providing land-ambulance services. The city of Winnipeg has a contractual arrangement with the regional health authority to provide ambulance services within its territory, but this appears not to be a municipal responsibility elsewhere in the province.

The regulation of air quality is a municipal (regional district) responsibility in British Columbia. Public health is explicitly a municipal responsibility only in Ontario, where it is often carried out through regional or county public health units. In Manitoba, municipalities have responsibility for the inspection of food service establishments and for insect control.

Public utilities (other than water supply) are difficult to categorize. For example, electrical distribution in Ontario's urban areas is the responsibility of business corporations, most of which are still owned by municipalities. Some small municipalities own local telephone companies and others own their own natural gas distribution systems.

In many developed countries, municipal governments have direct responsibility for public education. In Canada public education is the responsibility of local school boards, although their authority varies significantly from province to province. Only in Saskatchewan and Quebec do school boards still have the authority to levy their own taxes to help finance local schools.

We can conclude from all this that the core functions of Canadian local governments—especially municipalities—involve planning, regulating, protecting, and providing infrastructure services for our built environment. In the urban areas in which most of us live, such a responsibility is crucial to the quality of life, and this is why municipalities are so important. Notwithstanding the suitability of municipalities for controlling the built environment, no one can sensibly claim that each individual municipality should be able to do as its residents please. Most of us are now painfully aware, for example, that residential development that requires inhabitants to drive cars to live their everyday lives is damaging not just to the health of the individual residents but also to the environment that we all must share. That is why central governments are increasingly legislating the general principles under which municipalities regulate local development, and this in turn is why intergovernmental relations, in Canada and elsewhere, are becoming increasingly complex, leaving us much to contemplate in subsequent chapters.

Conclusion

The built environment is under local jurisdiction in Canada and most other countries because it is physically located in a particular place. For efficiency reasons discussed above, it makes sense that one central government is not directly responsible for all aspects of the built environment in hundreds of different settlements, large and small. By establishing local governments to manage the built environment—and to perform certain other services designated by central governments—we can concurrently provide valuable opportunities for political participation and engagement as well as enhance pluralism by creating alternative sources of political power rooted in elected territorial governments rather than in big businesses, trade unions, social movements, and interest groups.

RESOURCES

Lionel Feldman, ed., *Politics and Government of Urban Canada: Selected Readings*, 4th edn. (Toronto: Methuen, 1981), Part I, 1–86, contains classic and conflicting articles on the relationship between local government and democracy by Georges Langrod, Keith Panter-Brick, Leo Moulin, L.J. Sharpe, Robert A. Dahl, and Warren Magnusson.

STUDY QUESTIONS

1. What are 'economies of scale' and why are they important in debates about local government?
2. What does it mean to 'vote with your feet'? Should local governments pay attention to this phenomenon? Why or why not?
3. Do you believe that local governments in most provinces could be replaced by 'deconcentrated' provincial governments? Explain your reasoning.

3 Central Governments and Local Governments

L ocal governments are part of Canada's multi-level system of government. We saw in Chapter 1 that local governments are sometimes
divided into two levels. But in this chapter we are concerned with the
governments that cover larger territories than local governments, the
ones that we have called central governments. Canada is a federation in
which two levels of government, the federal and provincial, are established by the Constitution. In different ways, both of these levels of government have profound impacts on what local governments can do and
cannot do. This chapter is about those impacts and how municipalities
organize themselves to respond to them.

Constitutional Role of Federal and Provincial Governments

Canada's written Constitution consists of the Constitution Act, 1867
(originally titled the British North America Act) and the Constitution
Act, 1982 and their amendments.[1] In these documents, there are no
references to the terms 'local government' or 'municipality'. However,
the term 'municipal' is mentioned twice, both times in section 92 of
the Constitution Act, 1867, which is concerned with 'exclusive powers
of provincial legislatures'. Subsection 8 lists 'Municipal Institutions in
the Province' as one of the exclusive provincial powers and subsection 9
lists 'Shop, Saloon, Tavern, Auctioneer, and other Licences in order to
the raising of a Revenue for Provincial, Local, or Municipal Purposes'.
Subsection 16 adds to provincial jurisdiction 'Generally all Matters of
a merely local or private Nature in the Province'. This is the sum total
of what the Canadian Constitution says about provincial authority over

municipalities. It has been enough for judges, commentators, and politicians over the years constantly to claim that Canadian municipalities are 'creatures of the provinces'. Such a characterization is accurate as far as it goes, because municipalities under the Constitution rely on the provinces for their legal existence. A corollary to this statement is that any federal law purporting to alter the legal status of a municipality would be unconstitutional. But, as we shall see throughout this chapter, there are lots of actions that the federal government can take, and does take, that directly affect what municipalities actually do.

For one thing, when the federal government is acting for purposes within its own spheres of jurisdiction, it is not bound by municipal regulations that might apply to other property-owners or employers in the municipality. This is important, because the federal government is the country's largest property-owner and employer. In many Canadian municipalities—especially ones that contain, or are near to, major military bases, national parks, or other major federal facilities—the federal government's presence is crucial to the local economy. Federal policies concerning such matters as immigration, ports and airports, depreciation of buildings for income tax purposes, and the funding of research can also be crucial to local economies. So it is absolutely wrong to claim that, just because the federal government has no constitutional responsibility for Canadian municipalities, it is irrelevant to them. As we shall see, in recent years municipalities have been especially active in seeking new funds from the federal government, an objective that is perfectly constitutional because the federal government faces few restrictions on its ability to spend. In any event, most federal funds destined for municipalities are channelled through their respective provincial governments.

In order to think more carefully about the meaning of the Constitution with respect to Canadian local government, it is interesting to contemplate whether or not the federal government could establish elected local special-purpose bodies within its field of jurisdiction. For example, as the result of an amendment to the Constitution approved in 1940, unemployment insurance is clearly within federal jurisdiction. What if the federal Parliament approved a law dividing Canada into multiple territories for this purpose and establishing local elected bodies in each territory to decide on local details of implementation? Such authorities would be local governments under federal jurisdiction. It is hard to see how such a law could be subject to a constitutional challenge. As we shall see in the next chapter, federally established authorities to operate ports and airports are essentially local special-purpose bodies, although the members of their governing bodies are not elected.

The National Capital Commission (NCC), comprising 15 members all appointed by the federal government, can be seen as a local special-purpose body under federal jurisdiction. In its earlier institutional manifestations it played a major role in drawing up and implementing a regional plan for the entire capital area, the most notable feature of which is a greenbelt around the original city of Ottawa. The NCC also is also responsible for significant green spaces and recreational areas on the Quebec side of the river. An important constitutional ruling of the Supreme Court of Canada in 1966 held that 'the federal government had the power to plan for the National Capital Region, and to expropriate land for its purposes, including land for the Greenbelt.'[2] Such a power related exclusively to the fact that the area in question was the federal capital. Similar federal powers do not exist in other Canadian cities.

'Municipal institutions' are not in any way protected by the Canadian Constitution. They are simply placed under provincial jurisdiction. It is wrong, however, to claim that there is no protection for *any* form of local government in the Constitution. This is because the Constitution contains important provisions relating to the ability of certain kinds of local minorities to control their own public schools. Section 93 of the Constitution Act, 1867 places education under provincial jurisdiction but prevents provincial legislatures from removing rights possessed by designated religious minorities (Roman Catholic and Protestant) in certain provinces (now Ontario, Saskatchewan, and Alberta) at the time that they entered Confederation. This means that in the affected provinces, Roman Catholics have the right to elect their own school boards. By extension, it seems that public school supporters in those provinces have the same constitutional right. Since the passage of the Constitution Act, 1982, various decisions of the Supreme Court of Canada have held that the rights of French and English linguistic minorities in each province to minority-language education include rights to manage and control such education. But such rulings on language rights have done little to protect the local nature of educational governance because in six provinces a single French-language school board covers the entire province.[3]

Provincial Statutes Relating to Local Government

Unlike American states, Canadian provinces do not have their own written constitutions. Provincial legislatures are free to enact any kind of law they want, as long as it does not violate the Charter of Rights and Freedoms, impinge on federal jurisdiction or on the protected rights of religious minorities concerning education, or affect the office of

Lieutenant-Governor (the Queen's representative appointed by the federal government). This means that there is no form of constitutional protection for municipalities in Canada, a situation contrasting with that in many American states where state constitutions provide for various kinds of municipal protection, often known generically as 'home rule'.[4]

In Canada, every province has at least one general law, or statute, that establishes the basic rules for municipal government. In some provinces there are different laws for urban and rural municipalities. Many of Canada's largest cities, including Toronto, Montreal, Vancouver, and Winnipeg, are generally exempt from such general laws because they have their own special provincial laws applying only to them, often called 'charters'. The existence of such charters must not be confused with the kind of 'home rule' that exists in many American states. A city charter in Canada is nothing more than an ordinary provincial statute. It provides no extra constitutional protection for the municipality to which it applies. Its provisions can be changed by the provincial legislature at any time without any form of approval from the municipality. The only sense in which a city charter is especially important is if it grants more authority than that which is found in general provincial legislation applying to municipalities.

These general laws that apply to other municipalities are usually known as 'municipal acts', but it does not really matter what they are called. What matters is what is contained within them. In the last decade or so provincial legislatures have tended to try to simplify such laws by granting municipal governments various forms of general jurisdiction over a relatively wide range of subjects related to local affairs. Past practice involved detailed lists of exactly what it was that municipalities were allowed to make rules about. The apparent requirement for such lists derived from the fact that Canadian courts generally adopted what American jurists refer to as 'Dillon's rule', 'as set down by Iowa Supreme Court Judge John F. Dillon in the 1860s, who equated municipalities with business corporations, both of them limited to the powers expressly granted through their incorporation'.[5] 'Express authority' (or power) refers to matters explicitly listed in provincial legislation as being under municipal jurisdiction. The advantage of having express authority was that, if a subject appeared on the list, it was extremely difficult for anyone to claim in a court of law that a municipality was acting illegally by attempting to regulate it. The problem, however, was that, every time a new local issue emerged, municipalities would have to ask the provincial legislature to amend the law to grant them the required jurisdiction. Now that in most provinces the assignment of municipal jurisdiction is more general, we can expect municipalities to test their jurisdictional limits and for affected individuals and companies to challenge such apparent jurisdiction in the courts. The important principle here is that municipalities can do nothing without some kind of authorization by a provincial law. If a municipality is regulating taxi fares, it is doing so either because it has express authority to do so or because it is acting under a more general provincial grant of authority such as 'all matters related to public vehicular transportation'.

In recent years there has also been a provincial trend to grant 'natural person powers' to municipalities. A 'natural person' is an adult human being. With natural person powers, municipalities can generally do what persons can legally do, such as enter into contracts and borrow money. Municipalities already had most of these powers anyway and no provincial law envisions municipalities doing *all* the things a person can do (e.g., get married, adopt children), so the granting of natural person powers has hardly caused a revolution in municipal law. Nevertheless, Richard Tindal and Susan Nobes Tindal are right to point out that the additional natural person powers granted to municipalities provide them with a wider range of tools to carry out their assigned functions.[6]

It would be a huge mistake to assume that the only places to look for such laws governing municipalities are in the general municipal statutes or in the special ones (charters) that apply in some of the large cities. For one thing, provincial governments often sponsor laws that apply only to particular municipalities or groups of municipalities. These laws are just as valid as more general ones, so any lawyer or researcher needs to know the contents of all of them. More importantly, a great many other provincial laws relate to a wide variety of subjects that grant authority to municipalities. For example, if one wanted to know what municipalities in a particular province could do with respect to controlling traffic, it might well be more fruitful to search in laws regarding roads and transportation than in the relevant Municipal Act. Some of these laws establish local special-purpose bodies and outline how such bodies will relate to municipal government. Laws having to do with municipal police forces and with land-use planning are especially relevant here.

So far we have not referred to private statutes. These are often of considerable importance in understanding how provincial law applies to particular municipalities. Private statutes are enacted by provincial legislatures only on the application of an individual, a municipality, or a corporation; they relate only to the particular interests of the applicant. Municipalities frequently request private statutes so that they can solve some particular local problem for which there is no other legal remedy. These statutes are usually sponsored by the local member representing the area in which the statute is meant to apply; they are never sponsored by a cabinet minister.

In dealing with private statutes, the legislature follows special procedures to make sure that any affected person or corporation gets a chance to make known how their interests are affected. All statutes that are not private statutes are known as public statutes. For most public-policy questions, researchers need only know about public statutes, but when we are studying the legal authority of particular municipalities in particular circumstances, we often need to know about the relevant private statutes as well.

Provincial Ministries and Ministers

Each province has a cabinet minister designated to look after the municipal system within the province. The most common title is 'Minister of Municipal Affairs', but others are used as well. For example, in British Columbia it is the Minister of Community Development. These ministers are all responsible for ensuring that legislation is in place and implemented so that municipalities can do their jobs effectively, efficiently, and democratically. In some provinces the legislation gives the minister considerable authority to control what municipalities do; in others there is much less in the way of central supervision. Similarly, there is considerable variation in the number of provincial public servants who assist the minister in carrying out these functions. These and other matters of common concern are discussed at annual meetings of Provincial and Territorial Ministers Responsible for Local Government that are organized by the Canadian Intergovernmental Conference Secretariat.[7]

It is important to note that, even though municipalities are legally 'creatures of the provinces', no provincial minister is in a hierarchical relationship with respect to municipalities; except in the most unusual circumstances specified by law, no minister can order a mayor or municipal council what to do. Provincial law establishes municipalities as institutions that are separate from the provincial government. Provincial ministers responsible for municipal affairs frequently find themselves defending the desirability of municipal autonomy against attacks from ministerial colleagues who might wish to impose highly detailed rules about what municipalities can do concerning their own spheres of concern, such as roads. This is an important function, because almost all provincial ministers must deal with municipalities in one way or another. In general, ministries of municipal affairs are the only provincial ministries with a direct interest in enhancing the participatory and local democratic features of municipal activities. Other ministries tend to see municipalities only as convenient mechanisms for the local delivery of some of the provincial services for which they are responsible.

Some of these other ministries have responsibility for the smooth operation of local special-purpose bodies that operate within their spheres of jurisdiction. The best examples are the provincial ministries responsible for education; their relationship to school boards is analogous to that of ministries of municipal affairs to municipalities. Similarly, provincial ministries responsible for policing are generally responsible for whatever local special-purpose bodies are established to govern local police services. A frequent dynamic within provincial governments is that, whenever there is uncertainty about who should have power over what at the local level, ministers of municipal affairs defend the interests of municipalities while the other ministers defend their respective special-purpose bodies. We shall return to this issue in the next chapter.

Administrative Tribunals

Many provincial statutes, especially those concerned with land-use planning, either require that certain municipal decisions be approved at the provincial level before they come into effect or they provide opportunities for aggrieved local citizens to appeal such decisions to the provincial government. One mechanism for deciding on these approvals or appeals is to require action from the relevant minister. For matters of important policy in which the provincial government has a clear interest, it makes sense for the issue to require a ministerial decision. But no minister wants to be burdened with having to decide the exact meaning of a particular policy in every possible circumstance or to referee relatively routine disputes between citizens and their local governments. Fortunately, there is an alternative. Such matters can be referred to a provincial administrative tribunal.

Most provinces have some kind of administrative tribunal or tribunals relating to municipal affairs and/or land-use planning. The authority of each varies dramatically from province to province. The extremes are British Columbia and Ontario. In British Columbia there is no provincial appeal tribunal for local land-use planning, and general complaints about abuse of process or funds by municipalities go to a single provincial official, the Inspector of Municipalities. In Ontario, there is an extremely powerful tribunal, the Ontario Municipal Board, which we shall soon examine in a bit more detail.

In British Columbia, municipalities must gain approval of the Agricultural Land Commission[8] if they wish to authorize development within the province's reserve of agricultural land. Apart from that, regional districts and municipalities in BC have remarkable autonomy to make their own final decisions about the use of land. Provincial legislation does require that, prior to any changes in land-use regulation, municipal councils must consult with affected parties and hold at least one formal public hearing on the matter. Such changes directly affect the value of people's property, and the general common-law principle is that everyone potentially affected by the changes has a right to be heard and to be part of a fair process of decision-making. This principle also applies, of course, in the other common-law provinces (all except Quebec), which is why municipal decisions that directly affect particular individual interests can usually be appealed to the courts. But appeals to courts can only be based on the *process* by which the municipal decision-making process was carried out. Appeals to administrative tribunals are usually about the *substance* of the municipal decision, which is why they exist separately from the courts. Two of the most obvious differences between municipal councils, on the one hand, and the federal and provincial legislatures, on the other, are that municipalities are corporations exercising delegated authority from provinces and that they routinely make decisions directly affecting the property rights of particular individuals. These characteristics mean that municipal decisions are much more susceptible to various forms of appeal, thereby causing municipal decision-makers constantly to wonder if their actions on a particular matter will eventually end up in a court of law or an administrative tribunal.

Because of its great power and status within Canada's largest province, the Ontario Municipal Board (OMB) deserves special attention. It was created in 1906 as the Ontario Railway and Municipal Board, charged primarily with hearing applications for, and regulating, intra-provincial railways and street railways within municipalities.[9] It became the OMB in 1932 after its railway functions had atrophied and its supervisory roles concerning municipal finances and land-use planning had greatly increased.[10] The OMB has about 35 members, all appointed by the provincial cabinet for renewable three-year terms. Most are lawyers, land-use planners, or former municipal councillors. Almost all their hearings—conducted by panels comprising one to three members—now relate to land-use planning. Virtually all municipal planning decisions or non-decisions, ranging from a new official plan for the entire municipality to a minor variance in zoning affecting a single property-owner, can be appealed to the OMB. What the municipal council actually did or did not do is of little consequence to the OMB. It wants to hear the *reasons* for the municipal action and the *reasons* why the appellants think it acted wrongly. This usually involves costly expert opinions on both sides that are gathered and cross-examined by the lawyers for the various parties involved in the dispute. If declared 'provincial policies' appear to be relevant, then the OMB is supposed to take these into account as well.

The key point is that the OMB effectively substitutes its own judgement for that of the relevant municipal council. Because all the actors in any municipal decision-making process about the use of land in Ontario know that an appeal to the OMB is always possible for almost any conceivable reason, municipal decision-making is often seen as simply a step in the process rather than its culmination.[11] There has been much rhetoric in Ontario recently about the empowerment of municipalities in general and the city of Toronto in particular. But as long as the OMB maintains its power, Ontario municipalities will be among the weakest in North America when it comes to their ability to control their own land use. Meanwhile, all the lawyers and consultants involved in OMB hearings are powerful opponents of change. So are developers—and sometimes even citizen groups—who tend to believe that OMB decision-making is more predictable and consistent than that of elected municipal councils.

Administrative tribunals exist for local government functions other than land-use planning. For example, most provinces have some form of tribunal that regulates municipal police services, hears appeals from police officers about disciplinary issues, and investigates province-wide policing issues (investigating citizen complaints against particular officers is usually carried out by yet another body). In Ontario, the Ontario Civilian Commission on Police Services is also charged with refereeing disputes between municipal councils and local police services boards (which are special-purpose bodies) about the financing of local police services.

Money

Local governments, such as police services boards and municipalities, need money. Ultimately, the province decides how they can get it. Provincial legislatures approve laws that specifically authorize certain forms of local taxation, the levying of user charges, and formulas for the transfer of money from the provincial treasury to local governments. We shall examine these transfers further in Chapter 14; for now, however, we need to note that they can be for general purposes (unconditional) or for specific purposes (conditional). Specific-purpose grants are allocated on the condition that they are used to help finance an objective that the provincial government deems to be desirable, such as support for low-income housing.

Generally, provincial legislatures do not place restrictions on how organizations and individuals might voluntarily bestow funds on local governments, but Quebec legislation requires that federal funding of Quebec municipalities must receive prior provincial approval.[12] In Manitoba, British Columbia, and Saskatchewan, provincial governments have been explicit partners in tri-level 'urban development agreements' involving the federal government and the cities of Winnipeg, Vancouver, Regina, and Saskatoon. In these agreements all three levels of government participate financially in attempting to remedy targeted urban problems. The agreements have received considerable academic attention,[13] but the Vancouver one is probably the best known because it has provided for 'Insite', the supervised injection site for drug addicts located in the Downtown Eastside. The agreements expired in 2010 and renewal by the Harper government seems unlikely. Prime Minister Stephen Harper, contrary to Prime Minister Paul Martin (2004–6), has frequently expressed the view that the federal government should not be signing formal intergovernmental agreements with municipalities, not to mention that, ideologically, his government is generally opposed to such 'liberal' projects.

Provincial policies about local government funding are hugely important. In theory, a province could allow its local governments to have the same taxing authority as the province itself, so there could be local personal and corporate income taxes and sales taxes, just as there are now in some American states. In the past, there have been isolated examples of municipal income and sales taxes in Canada; Montreal's authority to levy a municipal sales tax was removed in 1964.[14] In fact, the main local tax has always been a tax on real (i.e., land and buildings) property. Issues relating to property tax often dominate local politics because revenues from it are crucial to the quality of local services and property tax levels are often forefront in the minds of any owners of property—residential, commercial, or industrial. We shall return to the property tax in Chapter 14.

Whether or not municipalities should have access to other taxes has been a controversial issue in recent years. Municipal officials have often argued for new taxation authority, but what they seem most interested in is getting a guaranteed share of various federal and provincial taxes, especially sales taxes, including the federal goods and services tax (GST). Effective in 2007, Toronto was granted the authority to tax land transfers, the renewal of motor vehicle registrations, public entertainment (such as movies), tobacco products, and alcohol served in bars and restaurants. So far, after huge political battles within its council, Toronto has levied a land transfer tax of 2 per cent and an annual $60 municipal tax on vehicle registrations. The other possibilities have not yet been implemented. The fear is that these other possible taxes would have the effect of driving customers of commercial operations elsewhere. This might not be a problem in downtown Toronto, but who would want to own a bar or movie theatre near the city's outer border if there were bars and movie theatres a few blocks away in a neighbouring municipality whose patrons were not required to pay the tax?

Municipalities have generally been more successful in obtaining *shares* of particular federal and provincial taxes. Their most important victory came in the 2005 federal budget when the Liberal government promised to send five cents a litre of its federal gas tax to Canadian municipalities for the next five years. The Conservative government has since extended this commitment until 2013–14. The money is allocated to each province in accordance with its share of the Canadian population. Allocation to the municipalities is determined by a federal agreement with each province.[15] In British Columbia and Ontario, the provincial association of municipalities is a party to the agreement and in Ontario the city of Toronto has its own agreement. The federal conditions for sharing the funds are relatively lax, resulting in the claim by municipalities that this is the way all federal funds should be disbursed locally. Nevertheless, even federal tax-sharing on gas is in fact a form of federal grant, subject to some real conditions: municipalities can only use the funds for 'environmentally sustainable capital infrastructure'. If the federal and municipal governments were literally sharing revenue from a common tax, the municipalities could make their own decisions about their portion of the rate in accordance with whatever intergovernmental agreement they were able to negotiate. They could then spend the proceeds as they wished, just as the federal government does.

Municipal Organizations

Much of the campaigning for additional municipal financial resources was conducted by associations of municipalities: the Federation of Canadian Municipalities (FCM) based in Ottawa and similar groups in each province. The existence of these associations points to an obvious tension in the status of municipalities within the Canadian political universe. On the one hand, they are clearly elected governments, having to deal daily with interest groups clamouring for lower taxes, a cleaner environment, better roads, and more housing for people who cannot afford market prices. On the other hand, from the perspective of the federal and provincial governments, municipalities make their case as though they themselves were just another interest group. There are too many municipalities for each one to make its own case and, in any event, they share a great many common interests. But, once they join together in an association, they lose much of what makes them distinct. Precisely this problem helps explain why neither the city of Toronto nor the city of Montreal is a member of its respective provincial association of municipalities. Both are so much larger than other municipalities in their provinces that their leaders consider they can do a better job of representing their interests to their provincial governments themselves. But both cities remain as members of the FCM.

The FCM has existed since 1901. Its membership comprises almost 1,800 municipalities, under half the Canadian total of 3,800. But most of the non-members are the very smallest. Many are indirectly represented by the 18 provincial and territorial associations of municipalities that are also FCM members. (Some provinces have both francophone and anglophone associations, and some have separate associations representing big cities and smaller and rural municipalities.) The FCM operates exclusively at the federal level, lobbying constantly to direct federal funds towards municipalities.[16] In recent years it has been especially successful in relation to infrastructure (including the sharing of the federal gas tax) and in obtaining $550 million from the federal government for the Green Municipal Fund, which the FCM administers as loans and grants to Canadian municipalities to enhance community sustainability.[17] The FCM also managed in 2004 to convince the federal government to give municipalities a 100 per cent rebate on amounts that they pay for the GST.

The FCM has obviously been favourable to a strong federal presence in relation to matters of importance to Canadian municipalities. In the 1970s it was a firm supporter of the short-lived federal Ministry of State for Urban Affairs. In 2004 Prime Minister Martin appointed a Secretary of State for Cities and Communities, but the cabinet position did not survive when Prime Minister Harper took office in 2006. In both of these cases the federal plan was not to try to take over provincial jurisdiction in relation to municipalities but rather to co-ordinate more effectively the many federal activities with direct consequences for municipalities.[18] But this is a sensitive matter, especially in Quebec, so it is unlikely that yet another federal institution for cities will emerge anytime soon. Meanwhile, the FCM carries on its lobbying activities in whichever federal agencies seem relevant to the policy concerns of Canadian municipalities.

In the same way that provincial governments are much more important for the day-to-day activities of municipalities than the federal government is, provincial associations of municipalities are generally more important than the FCM. They are key players in any provincial policy-making that affects municipalities and their annual conferences generally command the presence of a wide array of provincial cabinet ministers. Their main problem is the difficulty of building political unity among municipalities, except on the vaguest of principles. While all municipalities in a particular province might agree that their provincial government should transfer more funds to them, they soon disagree among themselves about the criteria for disbursement or the local programs for which it should be targeted. For example, large urban municipalities might want funds for public transit while rural municipalities might be preoccupied with the need to improve the drainage of agricultural land. It is often extremely difficult to reach inter-municipal agreement, which is another reason why Toronto and Montreal have left their respective provincial associations. Much of the day-to-day work of provincial associations of municipalities involves participating in various forms of consultative committees established by provincial ministries, many of which can be of considerable significance for provincial policy-making. The associations' role, of course, is to ensure that the municipal voice is heard while important decisions affecting them are being made. Often they do a highly effective job. But municipal politicians in big cities usually feel they should be consulted directly on any matter of concern to them, which is another reason why they sometimes feel they can get along without the associations.

Table 3.1 Provincial Associations of Municipalities in Canada

Alberta Association of Municipal Districts and Counties

Alberta Urban Municipalities Association

Union of British Columbia Municipalities

Association des municipalités bilingues du Manitoba inc.

Association of Manitoba Municipalities

Municipalities Newfoundland and Labrador

Association francophone des municipalités du Nouveau–Brunswick

Cities of New Brunswick Association

Union of Municipalities of New Brunswick

Union of Nova Scotia Municipalities

Association française des municipalités de l'Ontario

Association of Municipalities of Ontario

Fédération Québécoise des Municipalités

Union des Municipalités du Québec

Federation of Prince Edward Island Municipalities

Saskatchewan Association of Rural Municipalities

Saskatchewan Urban Municipalities Association

Source: <www.fcm.ca/english/view.asp?x=498>.

Municipal interests are so different that, as can be seen in Table 3.1, six provinces have more than one association. In three cases (Manitoba, Ontario, and New Brunswick), there are separate associations for municipalities that operate at least partly in French. But far more significant for our purposes is the fact that in three other provinces (Alberta, Saskatchewan, and Quebec) there are separate organizations for urban and rural municipalities, meaning that municipalities in these provinces do not generally even attempt to arrive at common positions with respect to provincial policies. Whether this makes much difference in the overall scheme of things is unclear. For example, the Association of Municipalities of Ontario (AMO), representing both urban and rural municipalities in Ontario, is subdivided into six caucuses and nine groups and organizations, each of which elects varying numbers of representatives to a board of directors comprising more than 40 members.[19]

It is important to remember that, because both the FCM and the provincial associations represent the municipalities as corporate entities, they in fact represent the wishes of the people comprising the municipal councils. In short, they are controlled by elected municipal politicians. A panoply of other organizations represents *employees* of municipalities, everything from the Canadian Association of Municipal Administrators (CAMA) (comprising about 400 city managers, chief administrative officers, and other senior municipal appointed officials) to provincial associations of building inspectors, tax collectors, and municipal clerks. Such organizations are primarily concerned with providing services to their members, including opportunities for professional development, but they sometimes express policy to provincial governments as well, positions that are not always identical to those of their political masters. In summary, the network of municipal organizations in Canada is extremely complex and it is often difficult to identify common objectives as municipalities interact with the federal and provincial governments.

Conclusion

Despite the frequent assertion that municipalities are mere 'creatures of the provinces', in practice they form an integral part of Canada's system of multi-level governance, even taking account of the Harper government's disapproval of formal tri-level agreements. In recent years, acting mainly through the FCM, municipalities have had a significant impact on federal politics and policies. They have certainly been successful in raising awareness across Canada about the need for all governments to invest more in physical infrastructure, much of which is built and maintained by municipalities.

For all kinds of reasons, municipal involvement with the provinces is much deeper than with the federal government. Indeed, provincial–municipal interactions are crucial to everyday activities of almost all Canadian residents. Analyses of these interactions will recur in various forms throughout the rest of this book. One of the many complicated features of the provincial–municipal relationship is the existence of local special-purpose bodies, to which we turn for more detailed study in the next chapter.

RESOURCES

The website of the Federation of Canadian Municipalities—<www.fcm.ca/English/view.asp?x=1>—is the most useful website in relation to the subject matter of this chapter. A thorough exploration of all of its parts, including the links to some of the FCM members and provincial organizations, provides a detailed portrait of multi-level governance in Canada. Another helpful website is operated by the largest academic research project ever to investigate tri-level intergovernmental relations in Canada: Public Policy in Municipalities and based at the University of Western Ontario. See: <www.ppm-ppm.ca/index.htm>. One of the books resulting from the project of particular relevance to this chapter is Robert Young and Christian Leuprecht, eds, *Municipal–Federal–Provincial Relations in Canada* (Montreal and Kingston: McGill-Queen's University Press, 2006).

For a sophisticated discussion by a political theorist of alternative approaches to the constitutional status of Canadian municipalities, see the following articles by Warren Magnusson: 'Are Municipalities Creatures of the Provinces?', *Journal of Canadian Studies* 39, 2 (2005): 5–31; 'Urbanism, Cities, and Local Self-Government', *Canadian Public Administration* 48, 1 (2005): 96–123; 'Protecting the Right of Local Self-Government', *Canadian Journal of Political Science* 38, 4 (2005): 897–922.

STUDY QUESTIONS

1. What is the constitutional status of Canadian municipal governments? Why is it not possible for them to have 'home rule' under current constitutional arrangements?
2. What is a 'private legislation' and why is it sometimes important for local governments?
3. What are administrative tribunals and why are they important for municipalities in most provinces?
4. Why is it often difficult for provincial associations of municipalities to arrive at common positions?

4 Special-Purpose Bodies

We saw in Chapter 1 that local special-purpose bodies are local governments that have responsibilities only for a specific function, such as public education or policing. In Chapter 3 we noted that in some provinces a particular form of special-purpose body, Roman Catholic school boards, have a degree of constitutional protection. Although less visible than municipal governments, special-purpose bodies deserve our attention because they make important decisions for communities and spend significant amounts of money. They are also important because their relations with municipalities can sometimes be quite difficult, and frequent proposals are made, from the municipal side at least, for their power to be curbed. Municipalities generally want to control local services and expenditures within their territories and special-purpose bodies are often a direct threat to their ability to do so. Any student of Canadian local government needs to know why special-purpose bodies were created and why they persist. As we survey different types of special-purpose bodies in this chapter, we shall attempt to address these issues. Unfortunately, so much variation exists among special-purpose bodies that it can be difficult sometimes to keep them all straight. But complexity is endemic to local governments. Its institutions have generally been designed to help solve real problems in the real world rather than to look neat on an organization chart. It is more important to gain a feel for the reasons behind this complexity than it is to know exactly how each different body is organized. Nevertheless, this chapter explores special-purpose bodies in some detail because the rest of the book will be primarily concerned with municipalities and future chapters will deal with special-purpose bodies only in passing.

School Boards

The first schools in Canada were originally operated by the Roman Catholic Church in New France. Protestant churches became involved after British conquest and settlement, especially in the early nineteenth century. Early legislation in the British North American colonies provided mechanisms for parents to organize and collectively finance public schools in their own immediate areas. Such legislation generally predated the establishment of municipalities. By the early 1840s, municipalities were more common and were generally made responsible for raising funds for schools from the general tax levies they charged on local property.[1] Meanwhile, locally elected school boards emerged out of the skeletal organizations of parents that had created the first public schools earlier in the century. In the Province of Canada (now Ontario and Quebec), the 1840s were marked by considerable uncertainty about whether school boards or municipalities were locally responsible for public schools. For a brief period, the Toronto municipal council was responsible for appointing school board members as well as paying for the schools themselves. In 1848 it closed the public schools during a dispute with the board about costs. The conflict was resolved in 1850 when the law was amended to provide again for the election of school board members and to establish their right to levy their own tax on property.[2] The fundamentals of this arrangement remained in place in Ontario until 1998.

Both before and after Confederation in 1867, legislatures in British North America reinforced the role of elected school boards as the local bodies in charge of public schools. In doing so, they were generally following American models, although there have always been many more examples in the United States of places where mayors and municipal councils retained some form of control over school boards and local schools.[3] Locally elected school boards were created in England and Wales in 1870, in large measure to emulate American success in providing basic education to large numbers of children. But they were abolished in 1902,[4] when local education became a direct responsibility of municipalities (or 'local authorities' as municipalities are generally known in Britain). The existence of relatively powerful local school boards is very much a North American phenomenon. Their importance did not derive from Britain or Europe.

Denominational Rights

A special feature of school boards in Canada has been the creation of rights for some Christian denominational minorities in some provinces to establish their own school boards. Such rights were first legislated in the Province of Canada in 1841 when Catholic and Protestant minorities were allowed to establish their own 'dissentient' school boards in each township and parish. The general rights of these religious minorities in Ontario and Quebec were perpetuated and protected by section 93 of the British North America Act (now the Constitution Act, 1867) at the time of Confederation. They were extended to Manitoba, Alberta, and Saskatchewan when these provinces were admitted to Canada, but were controversially removed in Manitoba in 1890.[5] The case of Newfoundland (now Newfoundland and Labrador) is especially interesting. When it joined Canada in 1949, school boards for Roman Catholics, Anglicans, Methodists, Congregationalists, the Salvation Army, Seventh Day Adventists, and two varieties of Presbyterians were all constitutionally protected. Pentecostals were added in 1954.[6] Under the terms of the Constitution Act, 1982, these constitutional guarantees can be amended only with the approval of the relevant provincial legislature and the Parliament of Canada. After considerable political turmoil, the guarantees to religious groups enabling them to have their own school boards have been abolished in both Quebec and Newfoundland, in 1997 and 1998 respectively.

Linguistic Rights

Political agreement in Quebec was facilitated by the Supreme Court of Canada's interpretation of constitutional guarantees for linguistic minorities contained in the Canadian Charter of Rights and Freedoms (sections 1–34 of the Constitution Act, 1982). English-speaking Quebecers, who had been holding on to Protestant boards so as to control their own local educational systems, became convinced that the constitutional protections for English-language school boards were just as secure as the religious guarantees had been. The end result of the Supreme Court's decisions on minority-language educational rights, as we saw in Chapter 3, was the establishment in all provinces of at least one minority-language school board. In 1996, the New Brunswick provincial legislature enacted the Progressive Conservative government's plan to replace all the province's school boards with one English-language provincial board and one French-language one. Local influence over schools was to be provided by elected parent committees for each school. However, in 2000, a Liberal government sponsored legislation that re-established school boards.

Current Status of School Boards

Although local, elected school boards currently exist in all 10 Canadian provinces, their authority to levy their own taxes has been greatly eroded over the past few decades. There are now only two provinces, Saskatchewan and Quebec, in which school boards have independent

Table 4.1 Types of School Boards in Canadian Provinces

	English Public	French Public	English Catholic	French Catholic
Newfoundland and Labrador	3	1		
Prince Edward Island	2	1		
Nova Scotia	7	1		
New Brunswick	9	5		
Quebec	9	60		
Ontario	31	4	29	8
Manitoba	35	1		
Saskatchewan	18	1	10	
Alberta	42	4	18	1
British Columbia	60	1		

Note: Table does not include three school boards for indigenous peoples in Quebec

Source: Websites of provincial ministries of education.

authority to levy taxes on property. Nevertheless, subject to varying degrees of control by provincial ministries of education, they still make many important decisions about local schools, decisions that can be crucial to the viability of particular communities and neighbourhoods. School trustees are generally elected at the same time as members of municipal councils, so voting turnout generally depends on municipal turnout. In Quebec, however, where school boards have their own election dates, turnouts have been abysmally low: 8.4 per cent in 2003 and 7.9 per cent in 2007.[7]

Police Boards

As with public schools, policing in a rudimentary form existed in Canadian cities and towns before municipalities did. Originally, 'constables' were appointed in Britain and in Canada by local justices of the peace, who also performed many of the local regulatory functions that were later passed on to municipalities. Constables were simply local citizens who took their turn in watching for fires, patrolling at night, issuing summonses, and making arrests. But their connection with justices of the peace marked the beginning of a kind of special status for police that has survived long since they became part of professional police forces in the late nineteenth century. In Charlottetown, Prince Edward Island, the city police force remained under the direct control of a local judge until as late as 1941. More commonly elsewhere, municipal councils themselves initially inherited some of the judicial authority of justices of the peace. The original law incorporating the city of Toronto established the elected council as the 'Mayor's Court of the City of Toronto' whose jurisdiction extended over 'crimes and misdemeanours arising within the City'.[8] Because of these early judicial functions, mayors are sometimes anachronistically referred to as 'chief magistrates'.

Although municipal councils have long since lost their judicial functions, police officers when performing their duties in Britain and Canada (but not in the United States) are still considered to possess a degree of legal independence from their political masters that is not extended to other government employees. The exact nature of such independence will be discussed later. In any event, just as the council of the city of Toronto once had complete control over public education, it also had complete control over policing from 1834 until 1858, at which time a new law for Upper Canada required that each city (but not other types of municipalities) establish a Board of Commissioners of Police, comprising the mayor and up to two local magistrates or two citizens appointed by the council.[9]

Ontario remains as the province in which police boards are the most powerful. No municipal council has direct control over a police service, although municipal appointees always comprise the majority of the members. Budgets for police services are drawn up by the police services board; if the municipal council does not approve it, the board can appeal to the Ontario Civilian Commission on Police Services, which will make the final determination. The situation is similar in British Columbia, except that there are only 11 municipal police boards, one for each of the municipal police services. Most BC municipalities are policed by contract with the RCMP. Under these circumstances, municipal police boards are not required. Where they are required, the boards are chaired by the mayor; one other member (not a councillor) is appointed by the municipal council; and up to five members are appointed by the provincial government.[10] If disagreement arises between a municipal council and a board about the budget, the final decision is taken by the provincial director of police services, an official in the Ministry of the Attorney General.

Local police boards are also mandatory for municipal police services in Alberta, Saskatchewan, and Nova Scotia, but final responsibility for the police budget rests with the municipal council. In New Brunswick, police boards are optional. In Newfoundland and Labrador municipal policing is carried out by a provincial force, the Royal Newfoundland

Constabulary. In Quebec, Prince Edward Island, and Manitoba there are no municipal police boards, but Manitoba is in the process of reviewing its legislation about local police governance.

Quebec deserves special attention because, like Ontario, it contains large cities but, unlike Ontario, municipal councils directly control the police. The chief of the Montreal police service, the second-largest municipal police service in Canada, reports to the municipal council in the same way as any other department head. Under Montreal's legislative charter, the council must establish a public security commission made of councillors and one provincial appointee, but its functions are purely advisory.

With respect to the governance of municipal police in Canada, at least two important questions must be asked: (1) Is there any sense in which the police are constitutionally independent of the municipal corporation that they serve? (2) To the extent that they are, do they need a special-purpose body to protect such independence?

Independence of Police Officers

Are municipal police constitutionally independent of their respective municipal corporations? This important legal question has received considerable attention from judges and scholars in the Anglo-American democracies. The question is essentially the same whether it involves the RCMP in relation to the federal government, provincial police forces in relation to provincial governments, or municipal police forces and municipalities: To what extent do constitutional conventions allow civilians to direct the activities of police officers? This has been an issue of considerable political controversy in Canada in recent years, the most notable recent example being how Ontario politicians and civil servants related to the Ontario Provincial Police (OPP) in 1995 during the occupation of Ipperwash Provincial Park by the Chippewas of the Kettle and Stoney Point First Nation. The fact that the OPP shot and killed Dudley George, one of the occupiers, led to the creation in 2003 of a judicial inquiry, presided over by Mr Justice Sidney Linden. Mr Justice Linden devoted an entire chapter of his report[11] to 'Police/Government Relations'. Linden's treatment of this subject was backed up by extensive legal research.[12]

Linden cites a famous British judicial decision in 1968, which has had a huge influence in advancing the cause of police independence. In the decision, Lord Denning wrote that no police authority can tell a chief constable what to do. 'The responsibility for law enforcement lies on him. He is answerable to the law and to the law alone.'[13] In 1999 the Supreme Court of Canada stated that 'A police officer investigating a crime is not acting as a government functionary or as an agent of anybody. He or she occupies a public office initially defined by the common law and subsequently set out in various statutes.' The Court noted that this principle 'underpins the rule of law' and 'is one of the fundamental and organizing principles of the Constitution.'[14]

But Mr Justice Linden was quick to point out that both federal and provincial statutes in Canada *do* give ministers of the Crown authority to direct many police activities and that the Supreme Court has never questioned the constitutional validity of these statutes. What ministers clearly *cannot* do is direct police activities with respect to particular criminal investigations. The Ontario Police Services Act states that municipal police service boards 'shall not direct the chief of police with respect to specific operational decisions or with respect to the day-to-day operation of the police'.[15] This provision reinforces the prohibition against civilian involvement in criminal investigations, but it also widens the sphere of police independence to include 'specific operational decisions'. It is important to note, however, that in Canada there is no *constitutional* protection for police independence in *all* operational decisions. Such protection only applies with respect to criminal investigations.

In theory, Parliament or a provincial legislature could approve a law overriding constitutional conventions about police independence in criminal investigations and authorizing civilian government officials to direct such investigations. Any such law would no doubt be challenged on the grounds that it violates the Charter of Rights and Freedoms. But the key point here is that the police are not alone among municipal employees in being immune from certain kinds of administrative or political direction. For example, provincial laws prevent any employers, including municipalities, from directing professionals such as physicians, lawyers, and accountants in the carrying out of their professional responsibilities. If we consider the police as professional investigators of criminal activities, their position is really no different.

The Necessity of Police Boards?

To what extent do municipal police services need special-purpose bodies to protect their constitutional independence? In light of the previous discussion, the answer should be obvious. Because municipal police have the same constitutional status as the RCMP and provincial police services and because these police services (and many municipal police services in Canada) are not governed by special-purpose bodies, there is no obvious reason why there should be any local special-purpose bodies for police. Whether they exist or not is simply a matter of provincial policy and law. In Ontario, where police service boards are especially strong, there have been many proposals over the years that they be abolished, or at least made optional, with the decision about their existence to be taken by the municipal council.[16] Police organizations have successfully defended their special-purpose bodies, in part by appealing to the unique constitutional status of the police. But, as we have seen, the principle of non-interference in criminal investigations does not require that police be governed by special-purpose bodies. With no obvious necessity for local police special-purpose bodies, there can be no obvious conclusions about how they should be structured or how they should relate to municipal councils. Generally speaking, police organizations want them to be almost totally independent of municipal councils, while the councils want to be able to control expenditures without taking on direct responsibility. Even in cities where police special-purpose bodies are weak or non-existent, most individual councillors are reluctant to criticize police practices in public for fear of being tarred as anti-police.

Excessive emphasis on the notion of police independence and the continued existence of strong local police special-purpose bodies combine to severely limit political debate in Canadian municipalities about police priorities and policies.[17] In the case of the Ipperwash occupation, the issue was not whether the relevant provincial minister could issue general instructions to the OPP (Mr Justice Linden concluded that he could), but whether the government's position was communicated to the OPP clearly and through the correct channels. It is obvious, in regard to municipal police services, that mayors, individual councillors, and even individual members of police service boards cannot attempt to instruct any police officer about what to do about anything. Acting collectively and officially, however, municipal councils or police boards (depending on which group has the statutory authority) can and should openly instruct chiefs of police about matters of policy. Mr Justice Linden was not afraid to take on the difficult task of outlining the distinction between a policy decision and an operational decision. He claims, for example, that a decision about whether to use force or to negotiate with protestors is a policy decision 'even when the policy was first made in the context of a specific dispute', but that such a policy decision 'should be generally applicable to similar disputes.'[18] It is rare indeed for a municipal council or a police services board to have an open debate about such an issue.

The Vancouver Park Board

The provincial legislation that establishes and governs the city of Vancouver (the Vancouver Charter) requires that there be a park board whose members are directly elected for three-year terms at the same time as the Vancouver city council. The board currently has seven members, but this number can be changed by the city council.[19] The board has its origins in the city's acquisition of Stanley Park from the federal government in 1887. Stanley Park was initially managed by a park committee established by council, but this became a directly elected board in 1890. The board subsequently became responsible for other parks and for recreation programs. Although it raises some funds from user fees, it relies on grants from the city council for more than half its annual budget of about $80 million.[20]

The continued existence of the board no doubt reflects the great attachment that citizens of Vancouver have for their parks, especially Stanley Park. Nevertheless, financial control of the city's parks and recreation programs rests firmly with the city council, because it determines annually the amount of money that is transferred to the park board.[21]

Library Boards

Large cities in Canada operate public libraries. Except in Quebec, these libraries are governed by special-purpose bodies made up of municipal councillors, citizens appointed by municipal councils and/or school boards, and sometimes provincial representatives. Nowhere are the boards directly elected. The boards are reliant on municipal councils for funds, but generally have considerable freedom to make policy on non-financial matters, especially relating to decisions about collections policies. In fact, this is one of the main reasons for having the boards, to ensure that decisions about what books to order are not decided by councillors who might have little or no interest in libraries or who might not be sufficiently committed to principles relating to the free flow of a wide variety of religious, social, and political information. Another reason is that the boards are seen as better able than councils to harness the enthusiasm and commitment of library users. In smaller communities, and especially in smaller provinces, public libraries are often run directly by the province or by provincial–municipal partnerships. In these latter cases, library boards facilitate representation from the various municipalities that are involved in a region-wide multi-municipal system.

Local Transit Systems and Utilities

Many local special-purpose bodies exist because they provide a service that in large measure is financed by user fees. In short, they are operating a form of business, even if that business is significantly subsidized from the public purse. A common belief in Canada and elsewhere is that services generating significant independent revenues should have a degree of freedom from the direct control of municipal councils so that they have the flexibility to respond quickly to use their revenue where it is needed most to meet their business objectives. In fact, however, there is not much logic behind different institutional arrangements for different revenue-producing local services. For example, public transit services are usually run by special-purpose bodies even though they receive significant public subsidies, while water supply systems are usually directly run by municipalities even though they have become increasingly self-financing in recent years as water meters have become almost universal in most towns and cities.

Most local public services for which there can be user fees were originally provided by private companies. British North America's first water mains were built in Montreal by Joseph Frobisher's Company of Proprietors of the Montreal Water Works. Toronto started to receive a communal water supply in 1843, when the Toronto Gas, Light and Water Company began pumping from Lake Ontario.[22] Companies operating street railways appeared in both cities in the 1860s[23] and electricity companies in the 1880s.[24] In each of these cases the municipal council had to grant the company a franchise, meaning that the company was granted the exclusive right to install infrastructure for its service on municipal land within a defined territory. Franchises of this nature are generally granted when the service in question can be provided, in practical terms, by only one supplier within a given territory. Because there cannot be competing systems of underground water pipes, or of rails and wires on public streets, we say that the service is a natural monopoly. The alternative to granting a franchise is for the government to run the service itself. In the case of municipal governments, they often do so through special-purpose bodies.

Utilities and Private Companies

Before examining such special-purpose bodies in more detail, it is interesting to think about various natural monopolies that are still usually in the hands of private companies. In Canadian cities, the most common ones are natural gas distribution systems, traditional telephone lines or fibre optic cable, coaxial cable (used by cable TV companies), and district heating and cooling systems (found in the downtown cores of some major cities). Companies that benefit from having natural monopolies require heavy regulation to prevent them from taking unfair advantage of their monopolistic position. Such regulation occurs through the terms of their franchise agreements or through regulatory institutions established for this purpose. Natural gas distribution systems are generally regulated in Canada by provincial governments; various telecommunication cable systems are regulated federally by the Canadian Radio-television and Telecommunications Commission (CRTC); and district heating and cooling systems are overseen by municipal governments. But even the natural gas and telecommunications companies are subject to municipal regulation concerning the physical placement of their pipes and wires.

Federal and provincial regulation of these natural monopolies has changed dramatically in recent decades. For both natural gas and telecommunications, regulators have generally forced the owners of distribution systems to open up their systems to other service providers to create new forms of market competition. For natural gas, however, there is always only one physical system for distribution. For telecommunications, new technology has allowed for competition even in distribution systems, especially in relation to telephones and broadband Internet provision. These systems are subject to strong competition from wireless providers. Hundreds of television channels are distributed by competing providers of coaxial cable and satellite service. As far as wires are concerned, however, there is no more than one network of fibre optic cable and one network of coaxial cable in any given Canadian territory.

Although most Canadian city-dwellers are familiar with such private companies as Heritage Gas (Nova Scotia), Bell Canada (telephones in Ontario and Quebec), and Shaw Communications (cable TV in western Canada, and satellite TV in other parts of the country), many might not be aware that various municipal governments in different parts of the country have provided some of these services themselves for quite a long period of time. For example, Thunder Bay in Ontario owns its own telephone company and Kitchener, Ontario, has a natural gas distribution system, which is run directly by Kitchener Utilities, a division of the municipal government that is also responsible for the water supply system. Especially interesting for students of Canadian municipal government is the fact that two of Canada's major utility corporations, EPCOR and Telus, had their origins as line departments of the city of Edmonton, providing electricity, natural gas, and telecommunications services within the city limits. Since being privatized by the city, many of their operations have spread throughout Canada (e.g., wireless telephone service from Telus) and to many parts of the world.

In most parts of Canada electricity is distributed to consumers through wires owned by provincial Crown corporations (Hydro-Québec, BC Hydro, etc.). Until 1998, electricity distribution networks in most cities and towns in Ontario were operated by municipal special-purpose bodies generally known as public utilities commissions (which often ran the water supply system as well) or by hydro commissions that bought their electricity from Ontario Hydro. Since then, however, Ontario municipalities have been required to transfer their electricity operations to corporations established under the Ontario Business Corporations Act. This means that, in legal terms, they have similar corporate structures to those of private businesses in the province, except that in most cases the sole shareholder remains the municipal corporation. In some ways, a municipally appointed board of directors of a municipally owned corporation established to distribute electricity is very similar to a local special-purpose body, even though in legal terms it is just like a private corporate board of directors. Under the 1998 provincial legislation that established these arrangements, municipalities are free to sell their electricity distribution systems, but almost all remain municipally owned in one form or another.

Transit in Toronto and Montreal

Special-purpose bodies for user-fee services are particularly important in public transit, especially in Canada's two largest provinces, Ontario and Quebec. The largest municipal transit system in Canada is operated by the Toronto Transit Commission (TTC), the current members of which are nine Toronto city councillors appointed for two-year terms by the Toronto city council. The TTC has direct responsibility for constructing, maintaining, and operating Toronto's subway, streetcar, and bus system, but it is far from being totally independent because it relies on city council for funds to make up the difference between its total costs and its revenues, almost all of which derive from user fees (fares). In 2007, the city contributed $365 million of the TTC's total operating expenses of $1.2 billion.[25] It is therefore a crucially important part of the city's annual budget. Nevertheless, the TTC does not appear in the city's official chart of its 'administrative structure'[26] and its General Manager of Transportation Services has no administrative responsibility for the TTC. The councillor serving as chair of the TTC often speaks publicly on behalf of the Commission, but its formal independence certainly does not prevent the city's mayor, who is usually not a member, from being the best-known political advocate for the TTC both within the city and outside.

Arrangements for transit in Montreal are similar. The Société de transport de Montréal (STM) is governed by a board of directors comprising nine members, seven of whom are elected municipal officials.[27] Two members are transit users' representatives. It is quite clear, however, that the special-purpose bodies for transit in Montreal and Toronto are dominated by city councillors. Apart from the administrative convenience of separating a huge transit operation from an even larger municipal corporation, it is difficult to see why these special-purpose bodies exist. In many respects they are simply products of the historical development of each transit system. But this history is itself important for understanding some of the issues involved in the existence of special-purpose bodies for transit.

The Toronto and Montreal transit systems were taken over from private companies by the municipalities in 1920 and 1951 respectively. In each case the advocates of municipalization promised to continue to run the system like a business while simultaneously improving service. The Toronto Transportation Commission originally comprised three prominent local businessmen appointed by the council. As early as 1925, Commission members clashed with city council as they tried to maintain financial self-sufficiency while certain councillors pushed for policies that served their own particular political interests.[28] But the TTC was managed so successfully as a business (aided eventually by wartime prosperity combined with the absence of new automobiles) that it accumulated a reserve fund of $25 million that was used to finance most of the initial construction of the Toronto subway.[29]

When the TTC was renamed the Toronto Transit Commission in 1953, the sales of automobiles were exploding. It became increasingly difficult for the TTC to be self-financing. By the time construction for the Bloor Street subway started in 1955, the TTC was able itself to finance only 45 per cent of the cost.[30] As the years went on, the TTC required more extensive capital subsidies, and then operating subsidies, although it remained in better financial shape than virtually all other North American transit systems. Not surprisingly, as municipal politicians became increasingly responsible for financing public transit, they were less likely to want to have the system governed by outsiders, which explains why all nine members of the TTC are now city councillors and why key budgetary decisions are taken by the council as a whole. As far as transit decision-making is concerned, this situation is not much different from places such as Calgary and Winnipeg where the transit systems are just another department of city government reporting to city council in the same way as other city departments.

Inter-Municipal Special-Purpose Bodies

Inter-municipal special-purpose bodies are established so that two or more municipalities can partner with each other to provide a particular service. A special-purpose body, comprising representatives from the participating municipalities, acts as the governing body of the partnership. These kinds of special-purpose bodies can be required by provincial policy or they can result from voluntary inter-municipal agreements. We shall briefly examine examples of both, starting with conservation authorities in Ontario.

Conservation Authorities in Ontario

Most of the territory of the populated portions of Ontario is covered by 36 special-purpose bodies known as conservation authorities.[31] Their existence derives from provincial legislation approved in 1946 that was designed to facilitate inter-municipal co-operation for the purposes of flood protection. Perhaps their most notable feature is that their boundaries are constructed so as generally to follow boundaries of watersheds rather than of municipalities. This means that some municipalities belong to more than one conservation authority. Boards of directors of conservation authorities comprise municipal councillors from each participating municipality chosen by the municipal council as a whole. Municipal voting strength on each board generally correlates with its financial contribution, which in turn relates to each municipality's share of the assessed value of property within the authority's territory.

Although the original conservation authorities were designed to result from local initiative, municipalities are now required to participate, largely because the authorities form a crucial part of Ontario's land-use planning and water-source protection policy. In this regard, their actions are tightly regulated by provincial policy, but this does not mean there is no room for local variation, especially in revenue-producing activities such as the provision of campgrounds on authority land. In other provinces the functions carried out by conservation authorities in Ontario are generally carried out by the province itself.

TransLink in British Columbia

An important example of a provincially mandated inter-municipal special-purpose body is the South Coast British Columbia Transportation Authority, commonly known as TransLink. It is charged with overseeing roads and public transit in the Vancouver metropolitan region. The history of institutional arrangements for the provision of roads and public transit in British Columbia in general and Vancouver in particular is quite complex.[32] The latest changes for the Vancouver region were made in 2007. The new legislation provided for a nine-person board of directors chosen by the Mayors' Council on Regional Transportation, comprising the mayors of 21 municipalities and the chief of a First Nation served by the system. Each mayor or chief casts one vote for every 20,000 people residing within his or her municipality. In appointing the board, however, they can only choose from among a list of 15 potential nominees (none of whom can be elected officials) established by a 'screening panel' comprising one appointee named by each of the following: the provincial government; the Mayors' Council, the Institute of Chartered Accountants of British Columbia; the Vancouver Board of Trade; and the Greater Vancouver Gateway Council (a business group concerned primarily with import-export issues). The Mayors' Council also must approve transportation plans, levels of municipal funding, and borrowing limits for the authority. Finally, it appoints a Regional Transportation Commissioner who has certain independent regulatory functions, including the authority to rule on fare increases for public transit that are requested by the board. TransLink is the most complex and powerful regional transportation authority in Canada. It plans for future development for both public transit and roads; allocates funds for major improvements in the road system; and, either directly or indirectly, is responsible for the operation of public transit in the entire area. In addition to drawing on property tax revenues from member municipalities, it also has direct access to funds from taxes on parking lots and gasoline. For many residents of the Vancouver area, it is probably the branch of local government that has the most immediate impact on their daily lives.

Inter–Municipal Water Authorities

As one would expect, inter-municipal special-purpose bodies that result from particular agreements among particular municipalities take a wide variety of forms. Many are established to operate particular municipal facilities built by more than one municipality. Rinks, fairgrounds, and other athletic facilities are perhaps the most common examples. But some crucial municipal services are also run by inter-municipal special-purpose bodies. For example, London, Ontario, receives its water from two treatment plants, one on Lake Huron and the other on Lake Erie. Each system is governed by an inter-municipal special-purpose body, because municipalities situated along each of the pipelines connecting the plants to London can opt into the system so as to use treated lake water rather than water from wells. Representatives from London's city council dominate each governing body, but all municipalities served by the system are represented as well. Interestingly, each of the joint boards of management, as they are called, has contracted out the management of their treatment plants and the pipelines to a private company, American Water Services Canada Corporation.

One of Canada's most durable inter-municipal special-purpose bodies is the Buffalo Pound Water Administration Board, which has supplied treated water since 1951 to both Regina and Moose Jaw, which are 60 kilometres apart. The board's water treatment facility is at Buffalo Pound Lake, located a little to the north of both cities but closer to Moose Jaw.[33] The board is made up of three members: two senior administrators (one from engineering and one from financial services) from Regina and one (an engineer) from Moose Jaw. Because the population of Regina (180,000) is more than five times that of Moose Jaw (32,000), the latter has the majority of members on the board. In reality, though, both sides must agree on significant changes, regardless of the makeup of the board. Because the board members are municipal staff, they are careful not to stray far from the political direction of their respective councils. Although the board is technically a separate legal entity and is therefore the employer of the plant's workers, collective agreements tend to follow settlements in Regina, which are in turn similar to those in most urban municipalities in the province. Most of the board's human resources functions are carried out by Regina's human resources department. Water rates are set by the board. Both councils seem to accept the notion that the setting of the rates is a technical issue appropriately determined by staff. In any event, the senior staff who are members of the board have never acted in such a way as to provoke political controversies about rate levels. Financial services for the board are provided by Regina.

This long-standing inter-municipal body has provoked little or no controversy or disagreement over the years. Why has it been so successful? Perhaps because the municipalities are far apart and consequently there are no inter-municipal irritants relating to other subjects that can impinge on a good working relationship concerning water. Perhaps it is because the board membership comprises senior staff rather than elected politicians who might want to use the board for other political purposes. Why has staff control of the board not itself caused difficulty in terms of accountability? Although formal mechanisms are not in place, staff members seem extremely sensitive to the need to consult with their respective councils on any issue that goes beyond the technical concerns of the water treatment plant itself. Why do administrative costs of running a completely separate board appear not to be an issue? The answer here surely relates to the informal arrangements whereby many of the non-engineering functions are in fact carried out by the city of Regina. The Buffalo Pound Water Administration Board stands as an apparently permanent voluntary inter-municipal institution. It shows that municipalities can get along with each other for a productive purpose over a long period of time.

Intergovernmental Special–Purpose Bodies

To the extent that police services boards (discussed above) contain representatives of both provincial and municipal governments, they are intergovernmental special-purpose bodies. But there are also other intergovernmental special-purpose bodies whose services are not directly financed by municipalities. As we saw above in regard to local transit systems and utilities, there are often few practical differences between institutions formally established as special-purpose bodies and others established as government-controlled corporations. Major ports and airports in Canada are operated by corporations established by the federal

Table 4.2 Canadian Port Authorities

Belledune Port Authority (near Bathurst, NB)
Halifax Port Authority
Hamilton Port Authority
Montreal Port Authority
Nanaimo Port Authority
Port Alberni Port Authority
Prince Rupert Port Authority
Quebec Port Authority
Saguenay Port Authority
Saint John Port Authority
Sept-Îles Port Authority
St John's Port Authority
Thunder Bay Port Authority
Toronto Port Authority
Trois-Rivières Port Authority
Vancouver Fraser Port Authority
Windsor Port Authority

Note: The Port of Churchill, Manitoba, is operated by the Churchill Gateway Development Corporation, a non-share public–private partnership created in 2003. For details, see: <www.portofchurchill.ca/cgdc/about/#>.

Source: <www.tc.gc.ca/eng/programs/ports-cpalinks-1109.htm>.

government, and their boards include representatives appointed by all three levels of government. The reason for federal leadership is that ports and airports are under federal jurisdiction. During the 1990s, significant changes were made to legislation governing Canada's major ports and airports. In general, less important ones were turned over by the federal government to a wide variety of private and public bodies, including municipalities. The establishment of local boards for major ports and airports was primarily an attempt to promote entrepreneurialism and better adaptation to local circumstances.

Federal Port Authorities

The Canada Marine Act became law in 1998. Under its provisions, 17 local port authorities have been established (Table 4.2).

The Act provides that both provincial and municipal governments listed in the regulations establishing each authority are entitled to name a minority of the members of the boards of directors, although they cannot be elected politicians. The work of these authorities is extremely important for the economic development of the communities in which the ports are located. In the cases of Vancouver, Halifax, Montreal, and Thunder Bay, it is of considerable importance to the entire Canadian economy.

The Toronto Port Authority does not have much of a port to run, but its activities have been politically contentious because, despite the fervent opposition of David Miller, the former mayor of Toronto (2003–10), it has successfully expanded the operations of its small airport on Toronto Island. The friction between the city and the Toronto Port Authority has been one of the most dramatic examples in recent years of an open conflict between a special-purpose body and an associated municipal government.[34]

Federal Airport Authorities

Canada's National Airports Policy was articulated during the 1990s as part of an effort to systematize the federal government's approach to the country's wide variety of airports, ranging from Pearson in Toronto to isolated landing strips in the Far North. For our purposes, the most important part of the policy is the designation of 26 airports as part of the National Airports System. These 26 airports (Table 4.3) serve a provincial capital and/or serve 200,000 passengers annually. Each is governed by an airport authority with its own board of directors, some of whose members are nominated by the governments of the provinces and municipalities they serve.

These airport authorities are supposed to be self-financing, even after paying annual rents to the federal government for the land on which the airports are situated. Consumer and business groups complain that this

Table 4.3 Canadian Airport Authorities

Aéroports de Montréal

Aéroport de Québec Inc.

Charlottetown Airport Authority Inc.

Edmonton Regional Airports Authority

Gander International Airport Authority Inc.

Greater Fredericton Airport Authority Inc.

Greater London International Airport Authority

Greater Moncton International Airport Authority Inc.

Greater Toronto Airports Authority

Halifax International Airport Authority

Ottawa Macdonald–Cartier International Airport Authority

Prince George Airport Authority Inc.

Regina Airport Authority

Saint John Airport Inc.

Saskatoon Airport Authority

St John's International Airport Authority

The Calgary Airport Authority

Thunder Bay International Airports Authority Inc.

Vancouver International Airport Authority

Victoria Airport Authority

Winnipeg Airports Authority Inc.

Source: <www.tc.gc.ca/eng/programs/airports-mapcaa-64.htm>.

policy has greatly contributed to the high cost of flying in Canada and has thereby hindered economic development in some communities. Many of these authorities manage more than one airport. For example, the Edmonton Airports Authority manages four, including the Edmonton city airport that for a long period of time offered short-haul scheduled flights after Edmonton International airport was built. The airport authority in Montreal converted that city's second airport, Mirabel, into a cargo-only facility and centralized all passenger flights at Trudeau airport in Dorval.

As we have seen, the Toronto Island airport is *not* operated by the Greater Toronto Airports Authority (GTAA). The GTAA has been involved in ongoing studies about developing a second Toronto airport on federally owned land in Pickering, east of Toronto, but any action on such a project is a long way off. Most of the territory of Pearson airport, west of Toronto, is actually part of the city of Mississauga. There has been considerable conflict between the GTAA and Hazel McCallion, Mississauga's long-serving mayor. The issues involved municipal nominees to the GTAA board of directors, airport noise and its impact on present and future residential development, and the extent to which the GTAA has to comply with various municipal rules and regulations. In general, McCallion achieved little success in her various battles with the GTAA, a state of affairs to which she was otherwise unaccustomed.[35]

In the case of the airport authorities, the board itself actually makes new appointments to the board, even in the cases of the provincial and municipal nominees. For Mayor McCallion, this was a major irritant, especially when the GTAA turned down two of Mississauga's original nominees.[36] Regardless of who formally makes the appointment, members of any board are legally required to act in what they consider to be the interests of the board itself, not in the interests of the body that nominated them. This is a major reason why, simply because municipalities often name members to various special-purpose bodies, the municipalities do not necessarily have direct influence over their actions.

Agence métropolitaine de transport in Montreal

The intergovernmental authorities for ports and airports have involved all three levels of government. An example of such a body that only involves the provincial and municipal levels is the Agence métropolitaine de transport (ATM) in Montreal, which is charged with planning for public transit for the whole metropolitan region. Established in 1995, it also operates the commuter rail system, whose operating deficits are funded by the provincial government and by area municipalities. The Quebec government appoints four of the seven board members, including the chair, while the other three are municipal elected officials, one each from the cities of Montreal and Laval and another representing the other municipalities in the region.[37] The ATM is not nearly as strong an authority as TransLink in Vancouver because it has no jurisdiction over road development and because, except for commuter rail, it has no operational control over public transit.

Local Special–Purpose Bodies with No Municipal Involvement

All of the local special-purpose bodies examined so far have involved municipal governments in one way or another. Even school boards, which in most provinces have been remarkably independent of municipal government, have relied on municipalities for the administration of elections and/or the collection of property taxes. In recent years, however, some provincial governments have established boards and agencies to make particular public policy decisions for particular defined territories. To the extent that these boards and agencies have a degree of independence from provincial governments and otherwise meet the definition of local government outlined in Chapter 1, they can be considered local special-purpose bodies. The first such body to be discussed, Metrolinx in Toronto, is similar in purpose to TransLink in Vancouver and the ATM in Montreal.

Metrolinx in Toronto and Hamilton

The Greater Toronto Transportation Authority was created in 2006 but its name was changed to Metrolinx in 2009. Its territory covers the cities of Toronto and Hamilton and the regional municipalities of Durham, York, Peel, and Halton. Its main functions are to plan the future public transit system for the area and to operate GO Transit, the existing commuter rail and regional bus system. In the past, municipalities have helped subsidize GO Transit and have been represented on the Metrolinx board and its predecessors. In accordance with amendments to the Metrolinx Act in 2009, the provincial government now appoints all 15 members of the Metrolinx board, none of whom are elected officials. As we shall see in Chapter 5, this is part of a clear effort by the Ontario government to take greater control of major urban issues facing the larger Toronto region rather than to leave such issues in the hands of local elected officials. Metrolinx already makes important decisions about fares and services for GO Transit and, through its planning functions for future transportation investment, has the potential to be increasingly important in the future.

Regional Health Authorities

The greatest growth in non-municipal local and regional special-purpose bodies has been in health care. Regional health authorities exist in one form or another in all provinces except Alberta and Prince Edward Island.[38] Excluding authorities that are province-wide in scope, Table 4.4 shows the number and name of these authorities in the remaining eight provinces.

In all cases, members of the boards of the authorities are named by the provincial government and receive virtually all of their funds from that source. Their mandates vary from province to province, but one of their main common objectives is to enable regional community leaders rather than provincial bureaucrats to develop mechanisms for local

Table 4.4 Sub-provincial Health Authorities

British Columbia: 18 health authorities

Saskatchewan: 13 regional health authorities

Manitoba: 11 regional health authorities

Ontario: 14 local health integration networks (LHINs)

Quebec: 18 Agences de la santé et des services sociaux

New Brunswick: 2 regional health authorities

Nova Scotia: 9 district health authorities

Newfoundland and Labrador: 4 regional health authorities

Sources: Websites of provincial ministries of health.

health institutions, especially hospitals, in order to use resources more rationally. Another common function is the provision of public health programs, such as vaccinations and services for pregnant women. In Ontario, however, public health programs are delivered and partially financed either by municipalities or by special-purpose bodies (boards of health, district health units) that are directly linked to municipalities.

Regional health authorities have the potential to become extremely important, but their track record since they were first introduced in some provinces in the 1970s and 1980s has not been especially impressive. Some local hospital leaders have been reluctant to take orders from regional authorities and have sometimes successfully used their influence at the provincial level when regional decisions have gone against them. The problem with the regional boards is that they lack democratic legitimacy. Few of us could name a member of our own regional health authority. There have been attempts to elect members of regional health boards in Quebec and Saskatchewan, but turnouts were so abysmally low that such practices have neither been continued nor adopted elsewhere.

A major report for the Quebec government in 1999[39] recommended that upper-tier regional municipalities take over some responsibility for health and social services. The recommendation met almost unanimous opposition from all affected parties and was never implemented. It is therefore highly unlikely that local and regional decision-making for health and social services will become more closely linked to municipal government in the foreseeable future. Elections at the local level in Canada will likely have little to do with health; board members of regional health authorities will almost certainly not think of themselves as being involved in local politics. Similarly, Canadian students of health policy and of local government will likely pay little attention to each other.

Conclusion

This chapter has shown that there is a huge variation in the nature of Canadian local special-purpose bodies. Some might think that the net has been cast too wide. If we restrict our definition to ones clearly linked to municipal government, then some scholars claim that school boards do not qualify.[40] For some, library boards might be too weak to qualify as local governments. Non-profit or Crown corporations established by other levels of government are obviously suspect, even if they do operate major local public facilities such as ports and airports and even if their boards do contain municipal nominees. Regional health authorities are perhaps beyond the pale, but if we exclude them, then what justification would we have for including Metrolinx, an institution that, in form and finance, looks remarkably like Ontario's LHINs? One of the differences is that the territory covered by Metrolinx is much larger than any of the Toronto-area LHINs, so that LHINs are more 'local' than Metrolinx. But it would be absurd to exclude Metrolinx from a textbook concerned with the local governance of Canadian cities just because elected municipal politicians have been recently been removed from its governing body. Similarly, it would be absurd to exclude Metrolinx and include TransLink just because of differences in financing and in mechanisms for making appointments to their respective boards.

The difficulty of defining and categorizing local special-purpose bodies is one of the features of local government that makes its study complex and complicated. As we shall see, one of the reasons for promoting municipal amalgamations is that they sometimes eliminate the need for inter-municipal special-purpose bodies. Within particular municipalities, there are often frequent calls to eliminate particular special-purpose bodies such as police services boards or transit commissions. Without any local special-purpose bodies, local government in Canada would definitely be simpler and easier to understand, but it would likely not be better equipped to improve the quality of our urban life. Municipal councils can do a great deal, but they are not necessarily well suited to govern our schools, and perhaps not even our police services. There are strong reasons why various utilities that can raise their own revenues from consumers might be better off being run as separate business-like operations. And there are certainly reasons why inter-municipal special-purpose bodies should not always be replaced by amalgamated municipalities. Amalgamating the cities of Regina and Moose Jaw because they share the same water treatment plant, for example, does not seem like enlightened public policy. So, even if we could all agree that it would be best to eliminate special-purpose bodies, it would never be possible in the real world. Through the remainder of this book, we shall see many reasons why special-purpose bodies of one sort or another will always be with us.

RESOURCES

Special-purpose bodies are no longer merely a seemingly obscure aspect of local government. They are receiving increasing attention from scholars of multi-level governance, especially specialists in the politics of international organizations such as the European Union. For an important article that refers to 'general-purpose jurisdictions' (such as municipalities) as 'Type I Governance' and 'task-specific jurisdictions' (special-purpose bodies) as 'Type II Governance', see Liesbet Hooghe and Gary Marks, 'Unraveling the central state, but how? Types of multi-level governance', *American Political Science Review* 97, 2 (2003): 233–43.

STUDY QUESTIONS

1. What obstacles, if any, are there to Canadian municipalities taking direct control over local public education? Would you support such a move? Why or why not?
2. To what extent in Canada do municipal councils have direct control over municipal police services? Do you think they should have more or less control?
3. What are some examples of federally controlled local special-purpose bodies in the area of Canada in which you live? By checking their websites, discuss what they are trying to do to promote economic development and/or enhanced quality of life in your area.
4. Are special-purpose bodies undemocratic? Why or why not?

PART II
Adapting to Urbanization

5 Urban and Rural

Part I of this book was concerned with understanding what local governments are and how they fit into the overall Canadian governmental system. Part II shifts the focus to examining how our system of local government has adapted to the increasing importance of urban areas in relation to rural areas. Invariably our cities and towns have expanded outward, a phenomenon that local government has both sponsored and often attempted to control. To begin to understand what is at issue here, we need first to know more about the differences between what is rural and what is urban, and how these differences affected the policies of local and provincial governments. We also need to know how Statistics Canada (an agency of the federal government) defines different kinds of rural and urban settlement. Such data are essential for any analysis that attempts to understand the links between Canada's systems of local government and the governance of our cities.

Approaching Urban–Rural Differences

There are two main ways of defining 'urban'. The first is demographic. According to this approach, three main population variables—size, density, and economic heterogeneity—determine the extent to which a place is urban. Relatively large numbers of people living close to each other engaged in diverse economic activity are living in an urban environment, a place ordinary people using everyday language are likely to call a 'town' or a 'city', depending on its size.[1] A labour camp where hundreds of workers are living close to each other so as to work in a mine is not a town because insufficient diversity of economic activity takes place there. Because we do not have labour camps in Canada, we can assume that all places where large numbers of people live close to each other are urban areas. Some might want to consider a place like Fort McMurray in Alberta a labour camp, because so many Canadians, some without their families, have migrated there to work in the oil sands. Although accommodation for families is very expensive in Fort McMurray, it is clearly an urban settlement rather than a labour camp. Entrepreneurs are as free as Canadians anywhere else to open businesses there—and many have done precisely that in the hopes of attracting dollars earned by oil-sands workers. In so doing they have created an urban economy, although not one that is nearly as diverse as the ones in larger cities such as Toronto, Montreal, and Vancouver.

Defining urban places simply as places in which relatively large numbers of people live close to each other is not really very helpful. The obvious questions are: How many people? How close? The answers are inevitably going to be arbitrary and subject to dispute. If we are going to use the terms 'urban' and 'rural' with any degree of demographic precision, somebody has to arrive at some basic definitions. In Canada, the job is done by Statistics Canada, and that is why we shall soon be paying attention to their approach to the problem.

But first we must acknowledge the other approach to defining what is urban. This is the socio-cultural approach, in which being urban is more a state of mind than a demographic fact.[2] According to this approach, people can be urban in orientation even if they are farmers: they can use the Internet; watch satellite television; go on southern vacations in the wintertime; send their children to college and university; and be quite at home enjoying life in a big city when they attend meetings of organizations in which they are active (churches, agricultural groups, service clubs). In short, they live a kind of lifestyle that once was available only to people who lived in cities but now is available to all citizens of advanced liberal democracies. According to this socio-cultural approach, non-urban people, on the other hand, live in traditional ways similar to their grandparents and great-grandparents, eschewing modern technology, and feeling out of place when required to go to 'the city' for such services as specialized medical care. Using this approach to defining 'urban', we should analyze degrees of urbanity by observing lifestyles or administering questionnaires.

The approach we use to defining what is urban has profound implications for determining our approach to the organization of local government. If we adopt the demographic approach, we are likely to conceptualize the needs of urban and rural areas as being quite different from each other and therefore we would likely want to have distinct institutions of local government for urban and rural areas. If, however, we accept that we will find many urban-oriented people living in relatively isolated physical locations, then the notion of having distinct systems of urban and rural local government might make little sense unless, of course, people with socio-culturally urban attitudes live in the country precisely because they do *not* want to live close to thousands of other people in a demographically urban environment. We shall return in later chapters to the important issue of how the different approaches to defining 'urban' affect policy decisions about the organization of local government.

In the meantime, a crucial point needs to be made about the difference between urban and non-urban. Urban areas require more government services, and the kinds of additional services they require are generally supplied by local governments. Imagine a resident of a condominium in downtown Vancouver and somebody else who lives on a farm in rural Manitoba. The ordinary day-to-day life of the downtown resident will be highly dependent on the following public services:

- water supply for drinking and cleansing;
- sewage treatment so that the streets and harbour are not filthy and hazards to health;
- building regulation, street lighting, and fire protection so as to feel secure in the built environment;
- frequent and visible police patrol to ensure public order among thousands of strangers;
- public transit so as to be able to move around, including journeys to and from work.

These are just some of the essential public services that city-dwellers require. If they are going to be living in a city in the first place, they likely will expect a wide range of nearby cultural and recreational amenities as well, the provision of which will almost certainly require government assistance, if not direct involvement.

Like the city-dweller, the farm resident requires public roads, but there will likely be few demands, even from farmers who might be socio-culturally urban, that the government should control noise and congestion or that it should provide cleaning and lighting for the roads. The farm will have its own well, water pump, and septic system. There may or may not be garbage collection. There will be no regular police patrol and strangers in the area would be rare, and remarked upon by vigilant neighbours. Fire insurance rates will be high because response times from volunteer firefighters will be relatively long, and their ability to fight the fire would likely depend on ready access to a nearby surface water supply. Unlike city residents, however, farmers often need governments to make special provisions for draining land, for allocating surface water for irrigation, or for ensuring that fences between properties are maintained. Such matters are relatively minor compared to the needs of the urbanite.

It is important to acknowledge that many crucial government services are equally important to all citizens regardless of where they live: medical care; income security for the old, disabled, and unemployed; national defence; large-scale environmental protection. It is no accident that policy for these governmental functions is not determined at the local level. Rural residents do require police for the enforcement of criminal law, but rural policing is based much more on response to particular incidents than on regular patrol. Public education is, of course, another government function that is now universally acknowledged to be vital for all children regardless of where they might live. Interestingly for our purposes, this is precisely why educational policy-making has become more centralized in recent decades and why school boards have commonly had their territories expanded to take in both urban and rural areas. Rural children quite properly now have access to many of the same educational facilities and opportunities as their urban counterparts, even if long bus rides are the frequent trade-off.

How Statistics Canada Determines Urban and Rural

For Statistics Canada the starting point for constructing the distinction between urban and rural is an entity called a 'dissemination block', which is a small geographical area usually bounded by streets, roads, or railroad tracks.

> If a dissemination block or group of contiguous dissemination blocks, each having a population density of at least 400 persons per square kilometre for the current census, has a minimum total population of 1,000, then the dissemination block or group of contiguous dissemination blocks is delineated as a new urban area.[3]

Areas classified as urban areas in previous censuses retain that designation as long as the area maintains a minimum population of 1,000. If the difference between the territory of the urban area and the territory of the municipality is less than 10 square kilometres, then the boundaries of the urban area are adjusted to match those of the municipality. Here are some other key factors in defining urban areas:

The distance by road between urban areas is measured. If the distance is less than two kilometres, then the urban areas are combined to form a single urban area. . . .

The resulting urban areas are reviewed and may be modified to ensure spatial contiguity where appropriate, for example, the removal of interior holes . . . [caused by such factors as] commercial and industrial districts, railway yards, airports, parks, and other uninhabited areas.[4]

According to the 2006 Canadian census, there were 895 urban areas in Canada. It is important to note that some urban areas include all or parts of a number of different municipalities; that not all municipalities contain an urban area; and that some municipalities contain more than one urban area (the single-tier municipality of Chatham–Kent in south-western Ontario contains five). In short, the delineation of boundaries of 'urban areas' by Statistics Canada is almost completely unrelated to the existence of municipal boundaries.

As far as a clear distinction between urban and rural is concerned, all residents of Canada's 'urban areas' comprise the country's urban population and all the rest are classified as rural. This means that anyone living in an 'urban area' with a population as low as 1,000 is considered by the census as urban, just as a resident of downtown Toronto is. By these standards, just over 80 per cent of Canadian residents were classified as urban in 2006.

It is not surprising that Statistics Canada has over the years added increasingly sophisticated and complicated definitions of different kinds of urban areas. Before moving on to these, however, we should look at the historical evolution of Canada's urban and rural populations. Although it is doubtless true that people's conceptions of 'urban' have changed since 1851, Statistics Canada has been able to construct the chart below only because the main features of its definitions of urban and rural have remained constant.

According to the 2006 census, there are 29 'urban areas' in Canada having populations of more than 100,000. Their total population is 18,547,222. If we were to use this measure (and nobody seems to), only 59 per cent of Canadians are urban.[5]

Census Metropolitan Areas and Census Agglomerations

The data in Figure 5.1 are the source of claims that over 80 per cent of Canadians live in urban areas. But Statistics Canada has developed other ways of quantifying Canada's urban population. An 'urban core'

Figure 5.1 Rural Population in Canada Became a Minority after 1921

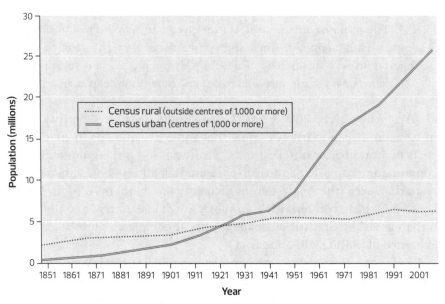

Source: Ray D. Bollman and Heather A. Clemenson, 'Structure and Change in Canada's Rural Demography: An Update to2006 with Provincial Detail', Statistics Canada Research Paper, Agriculture and Working Paper Series, Dec. 2008, Catalogue no. 21–601–M, No. 90, p. 5.

comprises the territories of all the municipalities, at least 75 per cent of whose populations are included within an urban area having a population of more than 10,000. If the population of an urban core is less than 50,000, it is the starting point for the construction of a 'census agglomeration' (CA); if it is more than 50,000, it is the starting point for a 'census metropolitan area' (CMA). Collectively, CMAs and CAs are referred to as 'large urban centres' (LUCs). Municipalities are added to urban cores to create LUCs as a result of calculations deriving from commuter flows that are determined from questions asked in the previous census about place of work. If more than 100 commuters in a municipality are near an urban core and if 50 per cent of the employed labour force in that municipality work in the urban core, then that municipality is added to the LUC. A municipality is also added if it attracts more than 100 commuters and more than 25 per cent of its employed labour force lives in the urban core.[6]

If, when these calculations are applied to an urban core of more than 50,000 and the resulting population of the core and municipalities added is not more than 100,000, then the area remains as a CA rather than becoming a CMA. CAs can be merged with CMAs as a result of these calculations. In such a case, the urban core of the merged CA is referred to as a 'secondary urban core'. If the population of an urban core in a CA falls below 10,000, then the area no longer exists as a CA. Once an area becomes a CMA, however, it remains so regardless of what happens to its population. Table 5.1 shows the population of all the LUCs with populations of more than 100,000 as determined by the 2006 census. One of the obvious difficulties with the table—resulting from the practice of treating CMAs as permanent—is that, because the Toronto, Oshawa, Barrie, Hamilton, St Catharine's–Niagara, and Kitchener CMAs are contiguous, it is difficult to use CMA population data to obtain a full picture of the territory and population of the entire Toronto metropolitan region. We shall return to this issue later in the chapter.

Degrees of Urban Connectedness in Rural Areas

We have already seen that all areas in Canada not classified as urban are considered rural. By the standards used for defining urban, 20 per cent of the Canadian population is rural. But it is important to note that in 2006, 35 per cent of these rural residents actually lived within the territory of LUCs. This percentage has grown significantly over the years, as shown in Figure 5.2 on page 78.

Because of their proximity to urban cores (i.e., urban areas of at least 10,000 people) all the rural people living in LUCs have ready access physically to some form of urban life. In fact, as we know from the definition of LUCs, a significant number of them are likely commuting to work in urban cores.

Any resident of Canada not living in an LUC is classified by Statistics Canada as 'rural and small town' (RST). Note that RST includes people who live in urban areas with populations between 1,000 and 10,000. Interestingly, the number of such people in 2006 was almost equal to the number of rural residents included within LUCs. The result is that, whether we use the 'urban area' versus 'rural' or the LUC versus RST classifications, the result is the same: 80 per cent of Canadians are in the urban category.

Statistics Canada also measures the commuting links of residents of municipalities that are not included within LUCs. If more than 30 per cent of the employed labour force of a municipality commute for work to an urban core, then residents of that municipality are classified as being in a strong metropolitan-influenced zone (MIZ). If the number is between five and 30 per cent, they are in a moderate MIZ. If more than zero, but less than 5 per cent, it is a weak MIZ. Where there are no commuters to an urban core, the municipality is classified as being 'No MIZ'.

Table 5.1 Population Counts for LUCs with Total Populations over 100,000, 2006 and 2001 Censuses

Geographic Name	Population, 2006	Population, 2001	% change
Toronto (ON)	5,113,149	4,682,897	9.2
Montréal (QC)[a]	3,635,571	3,451,027[b]	5.3
Vancouver (BC)	2,116,581	1,986,965	6.5
Ottawa – Gatineau (ON/QC)	1,130,761	1,067,800[b]	5.9
Calgary (AB)[a]	1,079,310	951,494[b]	13.4
Edmonton (AB)	1,034,945	937,845	10.4
Québec (QC)[a]	715,515	686,569[b]	4.2
Winnipeg (MB)	694,668	676,594[b]	2.7
Hamilton (ON)	692,911	662,401	4.6
London (ON)	457,720	435,600[b]	5.1
Kitchener (ON)	451,235	414,284	8.9
St Catharines – Niagara (ON)	390,317	377,009	3.5
Halifax (NS)	372,858	359,183	3.8
Oshawa (ON)	330,594	296,298	11.6
Victoria (BC)[a]	330,088	311,902	5.8
Windsor (ON)	323,342	307,877	5
Saskatoon (SK)	233,923	225,927	3.5
Regina (SK)	194,971	192,800	1.1
Sherbrooke (QC)	186,952	175,950[b]	6.3
St John's (NL)	181,113	172,918	4.7
Barrie (ON)	177,061	148,480	19.2
Kelowna (BC)	162,276	147,739	9.8
Abbotsford (BC)	159,020	147,370	7.9
Greater Sudbury / Grand Sudbury (ON)	158,258	155,601	1.7
Kingston (ON)	152,358	146,838	3.8
Saguenay (QC)	151,643	154,938	-2.1
Trois-Rivières (QC)	141,529	137,507	2.9
Guelph (ON)	127,009	117,344	8.2
Moncton (NB)	126,424	118,678[b]	6.5
Brantford (ON)[a]	124,607	118,086[b]	5.5

Table 5.1 continued

Geographic Name	Population, 2006	Population, 2001	% change
Thunder Bay (ON)	122,907	121,986	0.8
Saint John (NB)	122,389	122,678	–0.2
Peterborough (ON)	116,570	110,876[b]	5.1
Chatham–Kent (ON)	108,589	107,709	0.8
Cape Breton (NS)	105,928	109,330	–3.1

[a] indicates that the population count excludes data from one or more incompletely enumerated Indian reserves or Indian settlements.

[b] indicates that the area of the LUC changed between 2001 and 2006. Population counts from 2001 have been changed to reflect the population of the area in 2006.

Source: Adapted from Statistics Canada, at: <www12.statcan.ca/census-recensement/2006/dp-pd/hlt/97-550/Index.cfm?TPL=P1C&Page=RETR&LANG=Eng&T=201&S=3&O=D&RPP=150>.

Although patterns vary somewhat by province, for Canada as a whole only just over 1 per cent of the population live in No MIZ. The population in the other three categories (making up just under 20 per cent of Canada's total population) is split roughly equally but, significantly, the strong MIZ category is growing fastest.[7] In short, people who live in Canada's rural areas are becoming increasingly reliant on urban areas for employment, which means that the population in rural areas is becoming more concentrated in areas closer to urban cores.

The Greater Golden Horseshoe

As we noted earlier, six CMAs in the Toronto area are contiguous. Because the rules used by Statistics Canada prevent the merger of CMAs, the Toronto CMA simply does not capture the entire territory and population of the area that we usually think of as the Toronto city-region. The boundaries of the 'Toronto urban core' abut the boundaries of the Oshawa CMA to the east and the Hamilton CMA to the west. Under current rules, these boundaries will not change, whatever happens to the commuting patterns of residents of these CMAs into Toronto. Statistics Canada recognized this problem in 2001 when it presented data from an area it called the Extended Golden Horseshoe, which takes in a territory roughly equivalent to that of the six CMAs. At the same time, it presented analyses of data from three other major urban regions: Montreal, Vancouver, and the Calgary–Edmonton corridor.[8] But none of these three areas is nearly as complex as the Extended Golden Horseshoe, mainly

Figure 5.2 Percentage of 'Census Rural' Population Living within CMAS and CAS

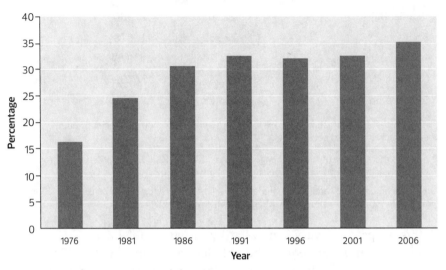

Source: Ray D. Bollman and Heather A. Clemenson, 'Structure and Change in Canada's Rural Demography: An Update to 2006 with Provincial Detail', Statistics Canada Research Paper, Agriculture and Working Paper Series, Dec. 2008, Catalogue no. 21–601–M, No. 90, p. 9.

because of the absence of contiguous CMAs. In any event, Statistics Canada did not update these data with results from the 2006 census.

In 2006, the government of Ontario officially defined a similar area as the Greater Golden Horseshoe (GGH). We shall explore it further, not just because it provides a good picture of the reality of Canada's largest city-region, but also because it is the territorial basis for the most ambitious foray by any Canadian province into the complex field of large-scale urban and regional planning.

The 2006 populations of its municipal component parts (as shown on Figure 5.3) are listed in Table 5.2. Because the total population of Ontario in 2006 was 12,160,282, this meant that 66.2 per cent of Ontario's population lived in the GGH.

The Ontario government has enacted two major laws designed to control the future use of land within the GGH. The first was the Greenbelt Act, 2005. It essentially prevents all new urban development in the designated Greenbelt area shown in Figure 5.3. Much of this land, especially the Niagara Escarpment, had already been protected by previous legislation. But the new Greenbelt clearly encircles Toronto with a view to preventing continuous urban sprawl and to providing ready access to the countryside for urban residents.

Figure 5.3 Greater Golden Horseshoe Showing the Greenbelt and Boundaries of the Toronto CMA

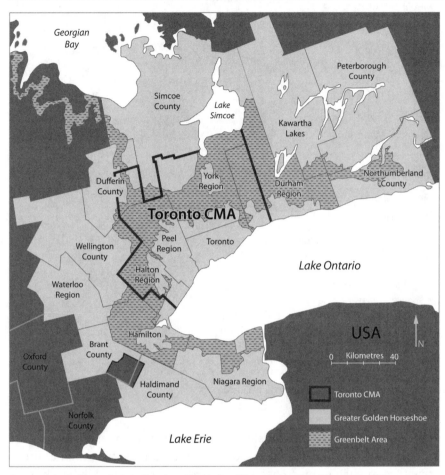

Source: Adapted from Andrew Sancton, *The Limits of Boundaries: Why City-Regions Cannot Be Self-governing* (Montreal and Kingston: McGill-Queen's University Press, 2008), 29.

The companion legislation was the Places to Grow Act, 2005. This legislation, by granting the government enhanced authority to plan for new growth and infrastructure, potentially applies throughout Ontario. Under the terms of the Act, in 2006 the government proclaimed the Growth Plan for the Greater Golden Horseshoe.[9] This plan lays down procedures by which an expected 3.7 million new GGH residents will be accommodated by 2031. The main theme is intensification. By 2015, 40 per cent of all new residential development will be required to take place within established built-up areas. The plan also designates some

Table 5.2 Population of the Municipal Units of the Greater Golden Horseshoe

Municipal Unit	Population
City of Toronto	2,503,281
Region of Peel	1,159,405
Region of York	892,712
Region of Durham	561,258
City of Hamilton	504,559
Region of Waterloo	478,121
Region of Halton	439,256
Region of Niagara	427,421
Simcoe County and Barrie	422,204
Wellington County and Guelph	200,425
Peterborough County and Peterborough	133,080
Brant County and Brantford	125,099
Northumberland County	80,963
City of Kawartha Lakes	74,561
Dufferin County	54,436
Haldimand County	45,212
GGH Total	**8,048,993**

Source: Statistics Canada, *2006 Census of Canada*.

established communities outside the Greenbelt as areas for expansion and sketches out plans for new transportation and environmental infrastructure to enable this to occur in an orderly and sustainable fashion.

These initiatives from the Ontario government merit our attention because they illustrate two important facts about Canada's largest metropolitan region:

1. Because the concept of the CMA is no longer useful in defining the territory of Toronto's built-up area and its area of economic influence, the province has determined its own definition of the area, the GGH.
2. Because almost two-thirds of Ontarians live in the GGH and because planning for its future infrastructure is so crucial to the province's economic future, the government of Ontario has taken direct charge of large-scale planning within the GGH.

Table 5.3 Provinces (except Ontario) Listed According to Extent Population Is Dominated by Largest CMA or CA in the Province

Province	Population	Largest CMA/CA	Population	% of Total Population
Manitoba	1,148,401	Winnipeg	694,668	60%
British Columbia	4,118,487	Vancouver	2,116,581	51%
Quebec	7,546,131	Montreal	3,635,571	48%
Prince Edward Island	135,581	Charlottetown	58,625	43%
Nova Scotia	913,462	Halifax	330,594	36%
Newfoundland and Labrador	505,469	St John's	181,113	36%
Alberta	3,290,350	Calgary	1,079,310	33%
Saskatchewan	968,157	Saskatoon	233,923	24%
New Brunswick	729,997	Moncton	126,424	17%

Source: Statistics Canada, *2006 Census of Canada.*

As we shall see, these actions by the Ontario government are potentially of great importance for understanding the role of local government in Canada because they suggest the possibility that in the future provincial governments might be the most important institutions in determining the outward physical growth of our largest cities.

CMAs and Provinces

If there is any possibility that developments in Ontario will be replicated elsewhere, then there will have to be similar examples of a single city and its region dominating the provincial population. For other provinces, the largest CMA in the province is the best indicator of such dominance because there are no examples outside Toronto where CMAs are contiguous.

Table 5.3 shows the populations of each of the other nine provinces, together with the population of its largest CMA (or CA in the case of Prince Edward Island). The provinces are listed in order of the extent to which the population is dominated by that of the largest CMA.

Anyone with even the most elementary understanding of Canada's urban geography will be able to understand most of the reasons why this list takes the form that it does. Except for the last three provinces on the list, all the others are dominated by one city. The extent of the domination roughly reflects the general level of urbanization within the province. Three Atlantic provinces (PEI, Nova Scotia, and Newfoundland

Figure 5.4 Rates of Population Growth in the Calgary–Edmonton Corridor, 1996–2001

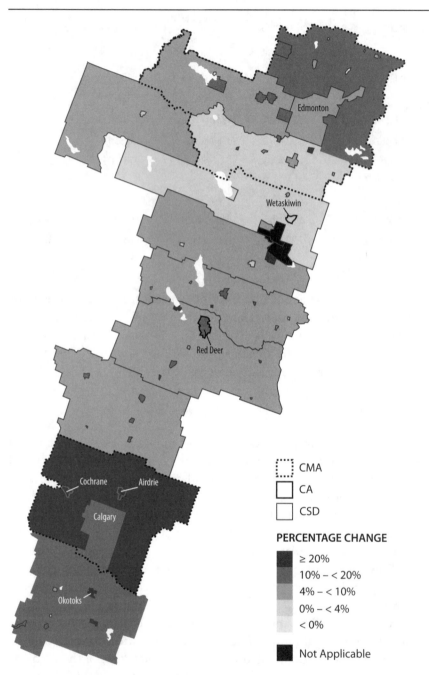

Source: Adapted from <http://geodepot.statcan.ca/Diss/Highlights/Page9/Cal_Edm_e.jpg>.

and Labrador) are at the bottom of the group of provinces that have only one clearly dominant city because, relative to other provinces, their populations are dispersed in small towns and rural areas. This applies especially to New Brunswick, which is at the very bottom of the list. It has no one dominant city. In addition to Moncton, the Saint John CMA (2006 population of 122,389) and the Fredericton CA (85,688) vie for supremacy. This factor, along with tensions between north and south and French and English, ensures that New Brunswick is not an easy province to govern.

Alberta and Saskatchewan merit special attention. They are the only two provinces with two major competing CMAs. In neither province is the provincial capital the largest, in part, perhaps, because electoral pressures have caused successive provincial governments to ensure that provincial largesse has been distributed more or less equally between the two cities and therefore between northern and southern portions of the province. Although, as we have already noted, Statistics Canada in 2001 considered the Calgary–Edmonton corridor to be one of Canada's four 'major urban regions', there is little real evidence it is becoming an integrated metropolitan area. If it were, one would at least expect the two cities to be growing towards each other. In fact, as the map in Figure 5.4 shows, in the last five years of the twentieth century, Edmonton's area of highest growth was to its north, not in the southern corridor on the way to Calgary.

If the governments of Alberta and Saskatchewan were ever to become as directly involved in large-scale urban planning as the government of Ontario is for the Toronto area, they would have to do so in a very careful and even-handed manner for each of their two major metropolitan regions. Such a path would be fraught with difficulty, which makes it unlikely that either province will follow it any time soon. Instead, they have tried to structure municipal institutions in such a way that local authorities can carry out this task in each region. To varying degrees, this has been the path followed in other provinces as well. Such initiatives have taken quite different forms and have met different levels of success. Analyzing them is an important objective of the remaining chapters in this part of the book.

Causes of Growth in Canada's Largest CMAs

Clearly, the proportion of Canadians living in urban areas, especially in the largest CMAs, has been increasing dramatically for many decades, and this trend is by no means unique to Canada. An important feature of the well-known process of globalization has been a massive movement of humanity in the developing countries from the countryside to the city. Urban life has attracted rural migrants not because it offered instant wealth in orderly residential neighbourhoods, but because urban opportunities even in makeshift housing on the edges of huge Third World cities seemed superior to a lifetime of subsistence agriculture in an economically stagnant countryside. Recent growth in Canada's cities has not been the result of internal migration from rural areas. In Canada, and other developed countries, this process accompanied industrialization, which began in Canada in Montreal in the second half of the nineteenth century.[10]

Globalization involves a massive increase in world trade, much of it fuelled by low-cost manufacturing in Third World cities that sucks people from the countryside. This trade is in turn financed and managed not by national governments but by major banks and transnational corporations, most of which have tended to concentrate in established financial centres whose relative importance in the world has dramatically increased—New York, London, and Tokyo being the prime examples. A key feature of globalization is the way in which it constructs linkages among urban economies throughout the world that apparently bypass the traditional rules and regulations imposed by national governments. The main objective of powerful international entities such as the World Trade Organization is to decrease the capacity of national governments to impose national rules and regulations respecting international trade.

What does all this have to do with Canadian local government? The answer is complex. First, it makes us pay more attention to cities. Anyone concerned with Canada's international competitiveness (which effectively means the future quality of life for Canadians) must be concerned about how our major cities will fit in the global network.[11] Can Toronto's banks be major players in international finance? Can Montreal build on its obvious potential as a bridge between Europe and North America? What will Vancouver's role be in the network of Pacific cities? Will hydrocarbons remain important in the world economy such that Calgary and Edmonton become major international cities as Alberta's resources become increasingly crucial for global prosperity?

When we refer to cities in this context, we are clearly not referring only to the central municipalities of Toronto, Montreal, Vancouver, Calgary, and Edmonton. We are referring at least to the CMAs, and possibly to the GGH and the entire Calgary–Edmonton corridor. With some exceptions that we shall explore in the next few chapters, there

Table 5.4   Selected Population Characteristics of Canada's Census
Metropolitan Areas with Populations over 500,000, 2006

CMA	% Visible Minority	Foreign-born	Aboriginal Indentity
Toronto	42.9	45.7	0.5
Montreal	16.5	20.6	0.5
Vancouver	39.6	41.7	1.9
Ottawa–Gatineau	16.0	18.1	1.8
Calgary	22.2	23.6	2.5
Edmonton	17.1	18.5	5.1
Quebec	2.3	3.7	0.6
Winnipeg	15.0	17.8	10.0
Hamilton	12.3	24.3	1.3

Source: Statistics Canada, *2006 Census of Canada.*

are no municipal governments that correspond to these areas. In any event, municipal governments do not have jurisdiction over many of the matters that directly relate to a city's international competitiveness. For example, the city of Toronto can do nothing about the regulation of the banks and other financial institutions whose headquarters are so important for its economy. It is true that municipalities, through their control over the built environment, can take some action to make their cities more attractive or less attractive to creative entrepreneurs,[12] but they cannot bring the ocean to Winnipeg or ski hills to Toronto. Just because globalization has caused cities to become more important in the global economy, it does not necessarily follow that municipal governments will become more important.

But globalization has had another profound impact on large Canadian cities. Globalization has caused new patterns of international migration that have brought in waves of new immigrants. Just as rural migrants flocked to cities in developing countries, many who met with some success in these cities have foreseen even greater opportunities in developed countries. As birth rates fell in these countries, and as their citizens showed less willingness to take on many of the less pleasant service jobs in big cities, the doors for immigrants opened. Canada was no exception. The result has been a dramatic change in the ethnic makeup of large Canadian cities.[13] Table 5.4 shows the high proportions of foreign-born and visible minorities in the Toronto and Vancouver CMAs, and some of the relatively low proportions elsewhere, especially in Quebec

City. The table also shows the percentage in each of these CMAs who responded to the 2006 census questionnaire by stating that they identified with at least one Aboriginal group (North American Indian, Métis, or Inuit). Especially in western cities such as Winnipeg and Edmonton (and Saskatoon and Regina), this percentage has been increasing significantly in recent years as Aboriginal people move to the city for similar reasons as rural-to-urban migrants in developing countries.[14]

Much more could be written about the changing demographics of Canadian cities. For example, increasing evidence indicates that downtown areas of the largest Canadian CMAs are becoming residential areas for the wealthy[15] and that lower-income city-dwellers are moving to the inner suburbs where housing is generally cheaper. All of these factors are profoundly important for understanding the contextual background for the study of urban politics, which is the focus of Part III of this book.

Conclusion

Local governments do not exist in isolation from the urban and/or rural environments in which they are located. Indeed, as we have seen, whether an area is urban or rural in its essential characteristics is a major factor in determining the nature and extent of public services that its local governments are expected to provide. Observers frequently and rightly claim that Canada is becoming increasingly urban and that this process has profound implications for government at all levels. In order to understand such claims, we need to know about the various demographic measures used by Statistics Canada to classify different kinds of urban and rural areas. In the Toronto area, however, Statistics Canada has been unable to adapt its traditional census classifications to the full territorial extent of the sprawling city-region. That is why, in this chapter, emphasis was placed on the Greater Golden Horseshoe, a territory defined by the Ontario government. Three other provinces—Manitoba, British Columbia, and Quebec—also contain dominant metropolitan areas. In the future, we shall have to observe carefully to see if each of these provinces follows Ontario's example and becomes the lead player in large-scale planning for the major metropolitan area in the province.

Meanwhile, all provinces—including Ontario—have structured their systems of local government to take account of the differences between rural and urban and to provide mechanisms to enable these systems to adjust to various patterns of urbanization. This is the subject of the next three chapters.

RESOURCES

The Canadian census—conducted every five years—is an exceptionally valuable resource and students of local government should know
how to use it. The most recent census was conducted in 2006. For basic
population data for many of the census areas outlined in this chapter,
see: <www12.statcan.ca/census-recensement/2006/dp-pd/hlt/97-550/
Index.cfm?Page=INDX&LANG=Eng>. To obtain a wide range of data
for individual communities in Canada, use the 'Community Profiles'
at: <www12.statcan.ca/census-recensement/2006/dp-pd/prof/92-591/
index.cfm?Lang=E>. In 2010 the federal government unexpectedly
announced that it will no longer be compulsory for randomly selected
Canadian citizens to answer the more detailed (long-form) census questionnaires, thereby casting doubt on the future accuracy of data (such
as those relating to place of birth and Aboriginal identity) derived from
these questionnaires.

STUDY QUESTIONS

1. Is it possible to live in the countryside and to have an urban lifestyle at the same time? Explain your reasoning.
2. What do we mean when we say that 80 per cent of the Canadian
   population is urban and 20 per cent is rural?
3. Explain the differences between the Toronto CMA and the Greater
   Golden Horseshoe. Do you think one is superior to the other in defining the real nature of the Toronto area? Explain your reasoning.
4. What have been some of the impacts of globalization on large
   Canadian cities? Has globalization bypassed smaller places?

6 Annexations

This chapter is about how the boundaries of urban municipalities—cities, towns, and villages—are adjusted to accommodate urban expansion. It focuses primarily on how this process has occurred incrementally, traditionally, and locally rather than being the result of major interventions by provincial governments. Such interventions and reorganizations will be the focus of Chapters 7 and 8.

Both municipal annexations and amalgamations are considered here. The distinction between 'annexation' and 'amalgamation' is somewhat technical, and not always of great significance in the real world, but it needs to be acknowledged. An annexation takes place when a municipality absorbs *some* of the land under the jurisdiction of an adjoining municipality. An amalgamation is when two or more municipalities come together such that the territory of all of them is placed under the jurisdiction of a single municipality. According to this technical and legal distinction, if a municipality of one million people comes together with a municipality of five hundred, the result would be an amalgamation. But in everyday language—even among municipal professionals—we would be much more likely to state that the larger municipality 'annexed' the smaller than to say that they 'amalgamated' with each other. In the real world, the large annexes the small and equals amalgamate.

Most of the focus in this chapter is on 'annexations', even if the events described technically were amalgamations. This is because we shall be using the language used at the time by the participants in the process. The first section of the chapter looks at municipal annexation in general by discussing a hypothetical urban settlement. Then we move on to important Canadian case studies in Montreal, Edmonton, London, and Calgary.

The Expansion of a Hypothetical Urban Settlement[1]

We saw in Chapter 1 that municipalities in Canada have been created in the past either as the direct result of a local initiative approved by the province or as a direct result of action initiated by the province itself. For the purpose of this hypothetical example, it does not much matter how the municipality came into being. Our starting point is a city incorporated as a municipality. This means, among other things, that it has defined boundaries. Forward-thinking local officials would have done everything possible to ensure that the boundaries included rural land beyond the built-up area so that there would be room for expansion within the municipality. Most businesses and residents within any town or city have always favoured at least moderate growth. Businesses want growth to expand profit-making opportunities and residents generally favour growth because it enhances property values and provides job opportunities for future generations. Eventually economic growth will mean that all the land within the municipality's boundaries becomes built up. What happens then?

It is conceivable that city authorities will do nothing and that whoever has jurisdiction over land use in the adjoining rural area will prohibit further growth there. In this unlikely situation, further growth is virtually impossible: the city is stymied. In the short term, property values might increase because of the scarcity of urban land and buildings, but in the longer term the area is likely to slip into obscurity as other nearby cities absorb new growth. A much more likely possibility is that the rural authorities will allow urban growth adjoining the city boundaries. Such action raises all kinds of questions, many of which are of great practical importance today in many communities across Canada. What kind of urban infrastructure will be available in the rural area and who will pay for it? How will urban residents and businesses in the rural municipality get along with the farmers? Will it be cheaper to live and do business in the rural area and, if so, will the urban municipality experience an exodus? Will city officials resent their neighbour's growth, or will they help facilitate it so that the area as a whole can continue to expand? These questions all relate to 'fringe development' in rural municipalities and they are the subject of considerable concern to policy-makers in all provinces.

Another possibility is that the city would attempt to annex land from the rural municipality either before or after the fringe development occurs. If it happens beforehand, affected property-owners (including farmers) are likely to be favourable because annexation by an urban municipality is almost sure to raise the value of their land in anticipation of almost certain development. If it happens afterwards, affected property-owners might be opposed if they sense that annexation to the city will cause taxes on their property to increase.[2] Depending on how easy it is to incorporate municipally, property-owners on the urban fringe might attempt to create their own new suburban municipality in an effort to prevent annexation. In any event, officials in the rural municipality are unlikely to favour either annexation or suburban incorporation, at least not unless their municipality gets some form of financial compensation. The central government (provinces in Canada) needs some kind of procedure to determine if and how annexations and new incorporations are to occur. In Canada such procedures have involved inter-municipal negotiations, referendums, administrative tribunals, and provincial legislation. We shall examine examples of these various procedures in the cases that follow later in this chapter.

Even efficient and fair procedures for annexations do not solve all of the problems. For example, if a rural municipality continually loses land to an urban neighbour, there come a time when its own viability is in doubt. At that point someone will have to decide if all of it should be absorbed by the city, even if that means including a large and continuing agricultural area within the urban boundaries, or if the rural remnant should be attached to some other rural municipality. Another problem that can emerge is that two urban areas can keep expanding through annexation such that they eventually become contiguous. In these circumstances, it is unlikely that one will be able to annex future land for growth from the other.

This discussion has shown how urban areas can evolve in such a way that they contain many separate municipalities.

- Adjoining rural municipalities might have become urban over time.
- New urban municipalities might have been established within a former part of a rural municipality.
- Two previously distinct urban areas might have grown into each other.
- All or some of these processes might have occurred simultaneously.

Since the mid-nineteenth century, many politicians, civil servants, academics, and sometimes even real-estate developers have observed such phenomena with growing concern. They refer to the tendency for increasing numbers of municipalities within a single urban area as 'fragmentation', and they have worked hard to reverse the trend by advocating some form of 'consolidation' of municipalities. If annexation has not been possible or desirable, they have promoted other consolidationist alternatives, to be discussed in the next two chapters. Before then, however, we shall look at important Canadian examples of locally generated annexations and amalgamations.

Montreal

The city of Montreal was first incorporated in 1833, but the charter expired in 1836 and was not immediately renewed because of the political turmoil that resulted in the Rebellion of 1837. A new charter for the city was granted by the governor general of the United Province of Canada in 1840, when the city's population was 31,000.[3] The city's boundaries encompassed only the area bounded roughly by Mount Royal and the river, and Atwater and Papineau streets. In the first few years after incorporation much of this land remained rural. By 1845 there were nine other incorporated municipalities on the island of Montreal, all rural parishes. But, as industrialization in Montreal took hold, much of the urban development actually took place outside the city's official boundaries. By 1881 there were 27 other municipalities on the island, most of which were villages that had been incorporated by local initiative after the Quebec legislature approved new laws facilitating the incorporation process. Two of the new municipalities were towns: Lachine and Saint-Henri.[4]

The Annexation of Maisonneuve

Between 1881 and 1921, 51 new municipalities came into being on the island of Montreal, but many lasted only a few years before agreeing to be annexed by the city of Montreal. The first of dozens of such annexations occurred in 1883, when most of the urbanized part of the town of Hochelaga joined Montreal. The last was Maisonneuve in 1918. In the interval, Montreal absorbed all or parts of 31 other municipalities, increasing its territory by a factor of five. The annexations invariably occurred because property-owners in the annexed areas, believing they would be better off financially within the city, agreed to it. In most cases their municipalities were virtually bankrupt.[5]

Maisonneuve was the most dramatic example.[6] Its financial difficulties were actually the result of a major scam. One contemporary Montreal opponent of the annexation objected because city taxpayers would end up holding Maisonneuve's massive debt: 'The bunch of "get rich quick" artists that undertook the exploiting of Maisonneuve bought farm land, blocked them out into city streets, had sewers built, water mains laid, permanent pavements and sidewalks installed, out of the civic treasury through miles of vacant land, with not a house erected thereon.'[7] In addition to a city hall, market, and fire station, the 'get rich quick' artists also used money borrowed on behalf of Maisonneuve to buy land for a huge park at inflated prices from provincial politicians (the park later became the site of the stadium for the 1976 Olympic Games, when another round of municipal indebtedness began). Immediately after Maisonneuve joined Montreal in 1918, it accounted for 5 per cent of the city's population, 3.5 per cent of its taxable property, and 16 per cent of its debt.[8]

Maisonneuve's unfortunate story unfolded in the general absence of provincial regulation relating to land development, municipal indebtedness, and conflicts of interest. Developers used municipalities that they controlled in order to borrow money from lenders who assumed that they would eventually be repaid by the municipal taxpayers if the development was financially successful or by the city of Montreal if it was not. Until 1918, the city was anxious to annex whatever land it could on the grounds that a bigger municipality would eventually be more beneficial to its property-owners than a smaller one surrounded by bankrupt suburbs. The problem was that this policy eventually became financially unsustainable, even for an otherwise prosperous municipality such as Montreal. The city ended up absorbing the financially troubled suburbs, while those that were financially successful, such as Westmount, Outremont, and Mount Royal, remained independent. Nevertheless, according to the 1921 federal census, the city of Montreal included 78 per cent of the population of the metropolitan area (i.e., the CMA, although it was defined differently then). In the absence of further annexations, and with suburban municipalities growing at a faster rate than the city, this percentage had been reduced to 54 by the time of the 1961 census.[9]

'One Island, One City'[10]

In 1960, the city's charismatic young mayor, Jean Drapeau, began a campaign to annex all of the island's municipalities to the city of Montreal. His vision was 'One island, one city'. This was just one of his many grandiose schemes, which included the building of Montreal's subway system (the Métro), Expo 67, and the 1976 Summer Olympics. Knowing that most suburbs would resist his plan, Drapeau tried to get the Quebec government to amend the legislation relevant to annexation so as to enable the Montreal city council to decide on an annexation without the approval of the other municipality. The only check on the city would be that any of its proposed annexations would have to be approved by the Quebec Municipal Commission, a quasi-judicial administrative tribunal charged, among other things, with sorting out inter-municipal disputes. The existing legislation required the approval of both councils and approval by a majority of voters in a referendum in the municipality that was proposed to be annexed. The Quebec government refused Drapeau's request for a change in the procedures.

Drapeau tried again in 1963. This time the province agreed that, if the city could convince the council of a suburban municipality to agree to annexation, it would go ahead unless a designated number of citizens requested a binding referendum. If, however, the suburban council refused the city's request, the issue would go straight to the Quebec Municipal Commission for a decision. Under this system Montreal annexed two suburban municipalities, one of which, Rivière-des-prairies on the eastern tip of the island, was not contiguous with the rest of the city. In 1968, the municipality of Saint-Michel, which had been under the supervision of the Quebec Municipal Commission due to municipal corruption, was also annexed after a favourable referendum and the passage of a special Quebec law. Finally, in 1982, residents of east-island Pointe-aux-Trembles voted for annexation. In each of these cases the annexed suburbs had been in grave financial difficulty. Their residents agreed to annexation because the city of Montreal agreed to take over their municipality's debts. Like his predecessors decades before, Mayor Drapeau had added territory to his city, but at considerable financial cost. The city's territory was not further extended until 2002, a development that will be discussed in Chapter 8.

Edmonton

Edmonton was incorporated as a town on the north bank of the North Saskatchewan River in 1892. Strathcona was incorporated as a town on the south side in 1899. Strathcona was the terminus of a CPR spur line from Calgary and was the area's main rail link until the Grand Trunk Pacific railway (now part of Canadian National Railway, or CN) arrived in Edmonton in 1905. In 1907, Strathcona was chosen by the provincial government as the site for the new University of Alberta. In 1905, Edmonton was chosen by the federal government to be the capital of the new province of Alberta. As both the capital and the location of the station for the east–west rail link, Edmonton had won the battle for supremacy over its southern neighbour. 'There was virtually no opposition'[11] when Strathcona amalgamated with Edmonton in 1912. This and other amalgamations and annexations that occurred until 1917 increased the city's size from 7.2 square miles to 41.2.[12] There were no further increases in territory until 1947. Between 1947 and

1980 there were 19 separate annexations adding 55,474 acres to the city's territory.[13]

The Annexation Battle of 1979–80

On 22 March 1979, the city of Edmonton launched the most dramatic local annexation initiative in Canadian history. On that date the city applied to Alberta's Local Authorities Board (LAB):

> to annex completely two adjacent municipalities (the City of St Albert and the County of Strathcona) and significant portions of two others (the County of Parkland and the Municipal District of Sturgeon). The application, if approved, would have increased the City's area from 79,962 to 547,155 acres and its population from 482,500 to 568,286 (1978 data). Subsequent hearings before the LAB (from September, 1979 through July, 1980) consumed 106 days of testimony, witnessed the filing of 299 exhibits and produced 12,235 pages of transcript. The City alone produced more than 30 expert witnesses before the Board: 183 witnesses were heard in all.[14]

Writing just after the hearings were finished, one of the expert witnesses for Strathcona County stated that:

> The Edmonton annexation case will have been the longest, probably the most complex and certainly the most costly adversary process in Canadian local government history. A conservative estimate of the direct cost only, as represented by payment by involved municipalities to consultants and lawyers, will exceed $4 million![15]

The city's aim was to establish itself as the single municipal government for the entire metropolitan area (81 per cent of the CMA population of 657,057 lived within the city in 1981).[16] Its expert witnesses advanced a wide array of arguments in claiming that its policy would lead to better land-use planning, more effective use of urban infrastructure, and economies of scale in the provision of many municipal services. On the other side, witnesses presented evidence from elsewhere, especially the United States and Britain, to counter these assertions. There was much squabbling among the lawyers as to what qualified as 'evidence'. Two of the city's expert witnesses later observed:

> Despite the fact that the issues before the Board were of a nature that could not be 'proved' in the judicial sense much of the subsequent

proceedings developed in an adversarial manner. This involved attempts to discredit city witnesses; to make them 'prove' by way of evidence or personal knowledge matters that were common knowledge; and generally to attribute to the City undesirable motives governing its pursuit of annexation.[17]

One of the 'undesirable motives' probably was the frequent claim that all the city was really interested in was taking control of 'refinery row', located just to the east of Edmonton's eastern boundary in Strathcona County. In its written argument to the LAB, the city stated:

> The single and obsessive objective according to which Strathcona has managed land use since the early 1950's is to preserve the unearned, windfall industry which happened to locate within their boundaries in the early 1950's.[18]

The reference to 'windfall industry' is to the oil refineries. Property tax revenue from this area was so lucrative that both sides in the dispute were willing to spend large sums of money to defend it (Strathcona) or gain access to it (Edmonton).

The LAB's decision was released in December 1980. The decision was almost completely congruent with what the city asked for, thereby taking a very broad view of the virtues of annexation:

> We see annexation as an essential tool in fashioning the planned development not only of the annexing authority, but the region to which it contributes in giving a lifestyle. In the past years, this tool has been put to limited purpose. It has been looked upon as a means of satisfying the annexing authority's immediate need for land, or of a developer to bring land within the City . . . . No adequate consideration has been given to using the tool as an instrument designed to further regional development other than on a narrow sectional basis . . . . We have looked at 'annexation' as a tool designed to achieve not only land for immediate use, but also to achieve jurisdictional power to plan and control growth in the region in which the City is located.[19]

Nobody was happy with the report. The targets of the annexation were bitterly disappointed. But even supporters of annexation stated that 'Certainly students of metropolitan development will be disappointed at the absence of any detailed analysis as the basis for the recommendations.'[20] The lack of explanation was justified on the grounds that the less detailed the analysis, the more difficult it would be that opponents could find grounds for appealing the board's decision to the courts.[21]

In any event, the provincial cabinet had the legal authority to override an LAB decision. Faced with massive opposition from residents of Edmonton suburbs, this is exactly what it did. In June 1981 Edmonton was allocated 86,000 acres of new land, much of it undeveloped in Strathcona County to the northeast of the city. Some of it was not even included in the LAB allocation but had been purchased by the city through Royal Trust, presumably so as to prevent windfall gains to private landholders.[22] The city gained a slice of refinery row, but much of it was left in Strathcona County. The key political point was that the annexation affected relatively few suburban residents. To this day the city of St Albert remains independent of Edmonton, as does Sherwood Park, a residential suburb within Strathcona County. In 2006 the population of the city of Edmonton made up 70.6 per cent of the total population in the Edmonton CMA.[23]

In the end the decision about the Edmonton annexation was very much a political compromise. The city got some of it wanted, but the suburbs kept almost all of what was most important to them. Such a compromise required the skill of the politician, not the skill of the planning consultant, the lawyer, or the expert witness. All of the resources expended at the LAB were in vain. Since 1980, an annexation proposal of this size has never been argued before a Canadian quasi-judicial administrative body. As we shall see in Chapter 7, relations between Edmonton and its suburbs remain strained.

London, Ontario

London separated politically from Middlesex County and became a single-tier city in 1855. It has remained so ever since, not being directly affected either by the implementation of two-tier regional government systems in the 1960s and 1970s or by the municipal 'restructuring' sponsored by the Harris government in the late 1990s and early 2000s. Since 1855, however, its boundaries have constantly been expanded through annexations, both large and small. In the early 1960s and early 1990s respectively, large annexations allowed London to avoid the dramatic changes that affected many other Ontario cities later in each decade. In this discussion of London's annexations, we shall refer only to those of 1885, 1961, and 1993, focusing most on the last. But each has something special to teach us about municipal annexation.

London East

London (not Edmonton) was Canada's first major oil-refining centre and the original headquarters of the Imperial Oil Company. This was a result of its good rail connections and its proximity to the oil fields of Lambton County, where Canada's first oil discoveries were made in the 1850s. Significantly, in the 1860s London's first refineries were built in London township *outside* the city's then-eastern boundary (Adelaide Street) adjacent to the Great Western Railway (now part of CN). Timothy Cobban has argued that such a location was chosen to escape 'the regulatory reach of city council'[24] because refineries then and now are perceived as obnoxious neighbours for urban residents. Nevertheless, as the refineries grew, service industries and workers located nearby, all outside London's boundaries. Cobban reports that:

> In March 1872, London council announced its desire to annex 'that portion of ratepayers in the vicinity of Refiners in Township of London,' and went about it gently, striking a committee to hold meetings with the refiners in the hopes of 'procuring their assent.' That assent was not forthcoming, and, despite frequent reports of 'progress' from the committee's chairperson, the annexation movement faltered.[25]

Meanwhile, the number of complaints from residents within the city boundaries about noise and noxious odours from the refineries continued to grow.

In 1874 the response of the refiners was to take steps to incorporate their area so as 'to put an end to these repeated attempts at "forcing the suburb into the city"'.[26] The village of London East became a legal entity on 4 January 1875. In 1880 four of the refining companies in London East merged to form Imperial Oil. But, despite all this apparent success, all was not well in London East. Cobban describes what happened in the autumn of 1884 when the railway's car works caught fire:

> The city's fire brigade was summoned, as was customary for large conflagrations in London East, for the suburb had no professional fire service of its own. The twenty-man fire brigade raced to Adelaide street, the city's boundary, with teams of horses pulling boiler pumps, hose carts and ladder wagons, but there they waited for either a $100 indemnity fee from London East or the Mayor's special permission to proceed, as per their instructions from city council. When neither materialized, they eventually crossed the boundary anyway. Once they finally arrived

at the fire, they discovered that that the nearest water hydrant held no water. Although the suburb had laid a network of water mains and fire hydrants two years earlier, it had not been able to secure its own water source, and had been refused in its attempts to purchase access to the city's water system. By the time the fire brigade secured a source of water, the car works had been engulfed for two hours. Hours later, it had burnt to the ground, destroying $200,000 worth of the railway's plant and equipment and displacing its four hundred employees.[27]

The next year London East agreed to annexation on the condition that the city would not force the removal of the refineries as long as they stayed in their original area. In any event, by 1883 most of London's refining operations had moved to Petrolia,[28] where they stayed until 1898 when Standard Oil purchased Imperial and moved the refineries to Sarnia.[29]

London East was no more, but it had been the centre of petroleum manufacturing in Canada for two decades. There was no longer any reason for it being a separate municipality—and it had proven incapable of doing what urban municipalities are supposed to do, such as to provide water and protect property.

Victory at the OMB

Prior to 1993, London's biggest annexation occurred in 1961. It had been a long time in the works, as London had been trying to take control over land being developed outside its boundaries throughout the 1950s.[30] In particular, it coveted a heavily industrialized area to the east on Oxford Street on the way to the airport, land now partly occupied by 3M and General Dynamics; land to the south connecting the city to the newly constructed Highway 401; and to the north the land occupied by the University of Western Ontario. City officials also were concerned that population growth was much greater in the surrounding townships in Middlesex County than in the city and that two in particular—London and Westminster—could themselves become rival urban centres. In 1958 the London city council approved a bylaw calling for the annexation of 24,000 hectares from four adjoining townships, an amount of land that would increase its territory by a factor of more than seven. About one-sixth of the land in the townships had already been developed. In accordance with the province's then legal requirements for municipal annexation, the 1958 bylaw was referred to the OMB. A three-member panel held hearings on the matter in London for seven full weeks at various times between April and December 1959. Ten different lawyers representing 14 different organizations and individuals were given formal standing. In May 1960, the panel released its 38-page decision in which it awarded the city 12,220 hectares, or about half what it had asked for, all from the townships of London and Westminster. The annexation was ordered to take effect on 1 January 1961. While the city had requested sufficient land to enable it to plan the outward expansion of the urban area over a 25-year period, the OMB awarded an amount that 'contains all the present development which is part of the London community as well as lands adjacent or proximate where the further development envisaged in this decision can be expected to take place within a reasonable time in the future.'[31]

The members of the OMB panel clearly believed that their function was to determine the structural arrangements that promoted 'the greatest common good'. They explicitly rejected the view that municipalities themselves had interests that merited consideration:

> Many opinions expressed as to desirable municipal boundaries seem based on a hypothesis that a municipal corporation is much the same as a mercantile corporation. Indeed, many submissions made at the hearing and particularly many of those made in opposition to annexation seem to assume that municipal corporations possess certain vested interests and rights which they are entitled to assert and retain against the whole world, as it were. The Board is of the respectful opinion that any claim of this nature made by a municipal corporation must be regarded only in the light of the best interests of all the inhabitants of and other ratepayers in the whole area in question.[32]

This is an important statement, because it clearly expresses the view—to become much more prevalent in Ontario and other provinces later in the decade and beyond—that annexation issues were not about short-term disputes between municipalities but rather about making public policy for urban areas. The notion that municipal corporations did not 'possess certain vested interests and rights' in this context would have been shocking indeed to the people who established the first municipal corporations in medieval England (see Chapter 1).

As far as participation by interested members of the public was concerned, the OMB decision makes reference only to a 'very large number of petitions', all of which expressed a fear that annexation would cause 'an increase in taxes'.[33] Board members were obviously skeptical about the petitions, because they note that 'it was impossible to determine the circumstances under which a great many if not most of the names were obtained. . . . [I]t is not surprising to find a substantial and even spirited response to any petition circulated for the purpose of keeping taxes down.'[34] The decision also notes that there were no expressed objections 'by petition or otherwise' from any ratepayer within the city and that the Board 'has neither the duty nor the right to permit the wishes of a part only of those concerned to outweigh its findings of what is clearly in the best interests of all the inhabitants and ratepayers in the whole area.'[35] There can be no doubt that OMB panel members were effectively saying that their job was to represent the interests of the silent majority. This is as close as they came to being concerned with the role of the public in a process that was otherwise dominated by lawyers, experts, and developers.

A brief passage in the decision relates to the position of the local federation of agriculture. Federation members objected to having their farms placed under the jurisdiction of a municipal government concerned with urban, rather than rural, administration. They were especially concerned about high levels of urban taxation. By not granting the city's full territorial demands, the Board effectively agreed with the federation's position. In a position contrary to that adopted by the province in the 1990s, the Board stated that '[n]o farmlands should be included except those within the area of the present urban development and those that will be so developed within a reasonable time.' It then wryly predicted that owners of such land would not object, because 'they will very probably be able to sell their land for subdivision before long in any event.'[36]

The 1960 OMB decision on London's annexation is a well-reasoned, comprehensive document. In retrospect, it served the city well. Had the annexation not taken place in 1961, London would have had imposed on it a two-tier regional system of the kind implemented in other Ontario cities a few years later, systems to be described in the next chapter. But the virtues of the *process* involved in the 1961 decision are less obvious. Even the OMB panel members themselves referred to the hearings on the London annexation as 'lengthy, very costly, and dislocating'.[37]

Arbitration

By the late 1970s, there had been many other examples in Ontario— notably in Barrie—of protracted OMB hearings on annexation. Perhaps because it was clear by this time that no new two-tier regional governments would be established, the issue of improving boundary-adjustment procedures had become a priority. In 1979, the Ontario government established a pilot project in the city of Brantford and Brant County to settle a local boundary dispute through negotiation rather than by quasi-judicial hearings conducted by the OMB. The experiment was successful. It resulted in the passage of the Municipal Boundary Negotiations Act,

1981, a law designed to reduce drastically the role of the OMB and to replicate the Brantford experience in other parts of the province.

By the early 1980s officials in London were again complaining that they were running out of land for industrial development. But nothing happened until 18 November 1988 when the city informed the Ministry of Municipal Affairs that it wanted to 'proceed as expeditiously as possible under the provisions of the Municipal Boundary Negotiations Act, 1981' to annex 'certain lands from the Township of London and the Town of Westminster'.[38]

The first stage of the process involved investigation by a ministerial 'fact-finder' who reported on issues relevant to the three municipalities involved. But the conclusion, reiterated in a cover letter from the Minister of Municipal Affairs, stated that 'the area affected is much more extensive than identified by the City in its proposal and the issues must be approached in a more comprehensive manner.'[39] This ministerial declaration, made in what would be the last few months of the provincial Liberal administration, was probably the most significant decision made in the entire process—and it had nothing to do with either fact-finding or negotiations.

Negotiations among the parties went nowhere, in large part because the province's 'chief negotiator' kept insisting on 'comprehensiveness'. In 1992, the NDP Minister of Municipal Affairs departed from procedures outlined in the Act and appointed an 'arbitrator', promising that he would implement whatever the arbitrator recommended. However, the arbitrator was given restrictive terms of reference stating what must be recommended:

[t]hat there be a government structure comprised of elected people and based on the principle of representation by population, with responsibility for at least planning and servicing to cover the area reasonably anticipated to be within the City of London's area of major influence for at least twenty years, including:

- future urban areas dependent upon London-centred infrastructure
- London Airport
- sufficient lands adjacent to the Highway 401/402 corridor.[40]

The arbitrator was John Brant, a local businessperson. He held 11 public meetings in London and the surrounding area in early 1992. The public hearing process seemed to be an enormous success. Meetings were well attended and well reported in the local media. Brant went to great pains to have everyone feel relaxed and he seemed genuinely open to all the ideas presented, especially if they came from 'ordinary citizens'. Herein lay a serious problem: his terms of reference did not allow him to be open to all ideas, especially to those of the vast majority of presenters who wanted to keep things roughly as they were.

The arbitrator's report was released in early April 1992. It contained 21 discrete recommendations, which 'can only be considered in their entirety: they are completely inter-related and balanced to provide an optimal opportunity for the entire area. They must be implemented as though they were one.'[41] On the crucial subject of the city boundaries, Brant allocated to London 26,000 hectares from the four adjoining municipalities. The town of Westminster was to be eliminated.

In a newspaper interview a few weeks later, Brant reflected on the arbitration process. When asked if he was surprised about the overwhelmingly negative public response to his report, he stated:

> There was a large number of people who were anxious that London not expand or that London's expansion be minimized. Those people had hoped to persuade me to break my mandate. . . . People are coming back to me and saying 'you didn't hear us, you didn't listen.' The truth of the matter is that they didn't read the terms of reference. . . . The nice thing about the process was that the terms of reference were always clear. . . . I never really challenged the terms of reference. . . . I didn't have any problem with the terms of reference.[42]

Brant was also asked about the relative importance of what he heard at the public hearings, compared to 'the material . . . received outside the public process'. His answer: 'If I had to pick a number, it would be a 50–50 impact.'[43]

From the minister's point of view, the whole purpose of the arbitration process was to relieve him from having to make a decision about which people in municipalities surrounding London held very strong views. But, because the arbitration process he initiated had no legal status, its results could only be implemented by legislation. As soon as the minister started talking about the legislation, different groups—including a backbench MPP from his own party who represented much of the area to be annexed—started to lobby for their preferred approach. It soon became evident that Brant's decisions would not be implemented 'in their entirety'. Indeed, a whole new debate had begun. It took eight months after Brant's report was released for this debate to be completed. Nevertheless, on 1 January 1993, the town of Westminster ceased to exist and London had its new boundaries.

Almost 20 years after the annexation, the land around the intersection of Highways 401 and 402 still has not been developed. On 12 January 2009, the local daily newspaper reported that London's senior provincial cabinet minister was proposing that federal and provincial infrastructure money be used to build a new sewage treatment plant in the area to enable industrial development. There was no indication that this was a project for which annexation had been enacted in 1992! The 1992 London annexation had ramifications for Ontario as a whole. As we shall see in Chapter 8, when the Progressive Conservatives led by Mike Harris were elected to office in 1995, they soon developed procedures whereby one person would be sent into an area to decide on municipal amalgamations. These procedures were a direct result of lessons learned from the arbitration experiment in London in 1992. One of the lessons learned was that it was better to authorize one person to make a final binding decision so that additional legislation would not be needed.

Calgary

Calgary, located at the confluence of the Bow and Elbow rivers, developed as a significant urban settlement after 1874, when the CPR chose it as a townsite and maintenance repair depot.[44] More than any other city in Canada, its territory has grown as a result of a long series of incremental annexations,[45] the latest occurring in 2007. The general pattern has been for developers to buy land in adjacent rural municipalities and, when they are ready to develop, to request annexation by the city so as to obtain access to water supply and sewer systems.[46] The Local Authorities Board (LAB), a body discussed earlier this chapter with reference to Edmonton, was charged by the province with reviewing annexation agreements and, in cases of dispute, resolving them.

With only a few exceptions, Calgary's outward expansion has not been hindered by the presence of other incorporated urban settlements, because the adjacent land was largely unsettled and primarily used for ranching. The notable exceptions were Bowness and Montgomery to the west and Forest Lawn to the east. All were absorbed by Calgary in the early 1960s. The process merits our attention.

Aftermath of the McNally Report

The first point to note is that Calgary's expansion at this time was inspired partly by the report of a provincial Royal Commission in 1956 headed by Frederick McNally that was charged with investigating problems of metropolitan growth in both Edmonton and Calgary. The McNally report favoured a single municipality for the entire urban area in both cities, but implementation of this principle turned out to be much easier in Calgary than in Edmonton because the latter was more of a farming area and had fewer surrounding urban settlements. McNally specifically recommended that Calgary absorb its three urban neighbours and that its total territory be expanded from 40 square miles to 105.[47] The provincial government in Alberta never undertook to implement the McNally recommendations, but they clearly influenced the behaviour of many of the important players. The city of Calgary took great comfort from the fact that McNally was endorsing its long-standing annexation strategy, even if the same report severely criticized some of its haphazard planning processes.

In 1958, Calgary applied to annex valuable land between it and the town of Forest Lawn (population 4,000). The town responded by applying to annex the same land itself. By 1961, the city had consolidated various annexation proposals in different parts of the city and they were all heard together by the Board of Public Utilities (predecessor of the LAB) in 1961. In its decision, the Board stated: 'The essential question . . . is not as to whether Calgary should be allowed to annex Forest Lawn but rather which municipality should be allowed to annex the territory common to both applications.' Observing that Calgary was better suited to this end, the Board recommended annexation of the disputed land, and added the town of Forest Lawn as well on the grounds that it had no future otherwise. The other annexations to the north, south and northwest were accepted without opposition.[48]

Forest Lawn was a working-class suburb on the east side of Calgary. Bowness and Montgomery were struggling suburban towns to the west, both without water and sewer services at the time of the McNally report. Max Foran has described their fate:

> The City annexed the Town of Montgomery in 1963. In approving the application initiated by the Town through resolution and petition [by its council], and supported by the City, the Local Authorities Board described the community of 5,200 as a logical extension of Calgary's residential area. In the years following the McNally Commission the Town had installed its own utilities that had been connected to the City before the annexation was processed. The City had done well. In October 1963, the Town of Bowness voted 1003 to 397 for annexation to the City. Though not overly happy with the financial implications, the City did not oppose the bid. . . . With the annexation of Bowness and its population of 10,000 the City had expanded its area to 154 square miles.[49]

Dispute with Rocky View

One of the most recent annexation disputes has been among the nastiest and, unlike most in Calgary, it did not result in the city gaining more territory. In 2004, the city launched another round of annexation initiatives. The most contentious affected the Municipal District of Rocky View (MDRV, now Rocky View County) to its north. Prior to 1995, Calgary could influence urban development in neighbouring municipalities because it dominated the area's regional planning commission. But these commissions were abolished by the province in 1995 and since then there has been little the city could do to restrain its rural neighbours except to refuse to provide its own infrastructure to facilitate rural development. In the early 2000s Rocky View approved the development of a commercial megaproject in East Balzac (the 'retail/racetrack development' on Figure 6.1) and a meat-packing plant (Ranchers' Beef) between Calgary's northern city limits and the town of Airdrie. The meat-packing plant had been opposed by residents of the area within the city where the plant's owners originally wanted to locate. In the spring of 2006, to provide a sewage system for the area, Rocky View:

> completed construction of a 42-km wastewater pipeline from Balzac to Langdon following a route deliberately skirting the city's northern and eastern perimeter. At [a cost of] $40 million, the pipeline was seen by many as economically inefficient, as it duplicated existing capacity that could be provided at a small fraction of the cost. Moreover, to pay for the pipeline, MDRV would actively promote new development on the city's fringe, a plan, according to Calgary's mayor, that promoted environmentally unsound 'rural sprawl' and unduly constrained the city's long-term planning capability and growth corridors.[50]

When Rocky View's original plans for obtaining a piped water supply for the area collapsed, city politicians assumed they could withhold city servicing of the area until Rocky View agreed to the annexations desired by the city. But Rocky View devised another solution:

> The Western Irrigation District (WID) (one of 13 districts in a quasigovernmental network managing the distribution of water for irrigation in southern Alberta) agreed to sell a portion of its abundant licence to MDRV [Rocky View] in return for a $15 million upgrade to its canal system. As the WID draws its water from the Bow River at Calgary, the twinning of the wastewater pipeline with a freshwater line could

Figure 6.1 Calgary Region Showing the Wastewater Pipeline and Adjacent Municipal Districts

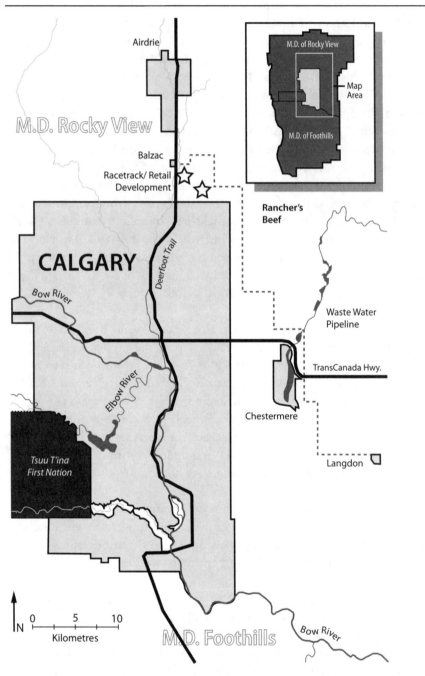

Source: Adapted from Geoff Ghitter and Alan Smart, 'Mad Cows, Regional Governance, and Urban Sprawl: Path Dependence and Unintended Consequences in the Calgary Region', *Urban Affairs Review* 44, 5 (May 2009): 623. Reprinted by permission of SAGE Publications.

proceed as originally planned. The (lack of) availability of water for development, however, has been permanently embedded as a factor for all future development in the region.[51]

If nothing else, this issue demonstrates how closely annexation disputes can relate to important issues about urban sprawl and the environment.

In any event, like most North American cities, the city of Calgary now contains important fringe development outside its municipal boundaries. Furthermore, its current boundaries are coming closer and closer to non-contiguous urban municipalities, in the same way that they approached Forest Lawn, Bowness, and Montgomery in the 1950s. Such places as Airdrie, Crossfield, Cochrane, Chestermere, and Okotoks are growing even faster than Calgary itself. The more Calgary grows, the more its neighbouring municipalities will grow and the more they will become integrated into the urban area that is focused on Calgary as the central city. The strategic choice that Calgary faces is whether it should work co-operatively with these urban governments or whether it should absorb them as part of a continuing commitment to include all of the CMA within its boundaries. If it chooses the latter course of action, future annexation battles will be considerably more difficult than those it has won in the past. If it chooses the former, Calgary's inter-municipal issues and problems will start to resemble those of other major metropolitan areas in Canada and elsewhere,[52] problems we shall address more fully in the next two chapters.

Conclusion

For Canada's biggest cities, it is unlikely that we shall ever see many more locally driven annexations, except perhaps in Edmonton and Calgary. For most large Canadian cities, their respective provinces have stepped in and imposed their own solutions to problems of urban expansion. Even in Edmonton and Calgary, the most recent annexation battles have demonstrated the costs and perils of arguing an annexation case at a quasi-judicial tribunal and of attempting a local settlement through negotiation. In the much smaller city of Barrie, Ontario, in 2009, attempts at a mediated local settlement of an annexation issue failed, causing the Ontario government to step in with a legislated solution, the Barrie–Innisfil Boundary Adjustment Act, 2009.

But in hundreds of smaller towns and villages across Canada, annexation remains the most common way for urban municipalities to expand their boundaries to accommodate urban development. All provinces have attempted to develop mechanisms for enabling small-scale annexations that are both fair and not unduly costly for the participants. Everyone wants to provide opportunities for all the arguments to be advanced and considered, but no one (except lawyers and consultants) wants to replicate the Edmonton annexation hearings conducted by the Alberta LAB in 1980. Whatever desirable mechanisms have been developed, there is always the possibility that a local annexation process will break down and that someone will appeal to the province to settle the issue with legislation. In some provinces (e.g., Ontario), such legislative interventions have been quite common; in others (e.g., British Columbia), local municipalities are generally left alone to work out their differences. In any event, when it comes to structuring municipalities so that they can both guide and respond to urban expansion, provinces have ways of responding other than relying exclusively on annexations. It is to these other responses that we now turn.

RESOURCES

If you live in a town or a city, go to its website, public library, or municipal archives and try to obtain a map showing how the municipal boundaries have expanded since the town or city was first incorporated. See if you can determine the procedures used to make the changes and whether or not they caused much political conflict at the time. Sometimes there is still evidence within town and cities of municipal boundaries that were eliminated by annexation many decades ago. For example, there can still be quite different types of development on each side of the old boundary. Try to find examples of such evidence. If you are familiar with an urban area that is bisected by municipal boundaries, try to explain how they have survived and what impact they appear to have on the nature of urban development in the two municipalities.

STUDY QUESTIONS

1. How did developers make money in Maisonneuve prior to its amalgamation with Montreal?
2. Do you agree with the claim by the OMB in its 1960 London decision that municipalities do not have interests that need to be considered in boundary disputes? Explain your reasoning.
3. What was wrong in your view with the Alberta LAB process in relation to the Edmonton annexation dispute in the late 1970s and early 1980s?
4. What might prevent Calgary from continuing to annex indefinitely?

7 Two-Tier Metropolitan and Regional Governments

We learned in the previous chapter that in most places annexations cannot go on forever. Eventually, the boundaries of the central city run up against incorporated suburbs or other urban municipalities that can sometimes be as old as the central city itself. Residents of such places are not likely to agree to be absorbed, unless, of course, their own municipalities have become virtually bankrupt and are unable to provide the services that the central city can. In the absence of any intervention by the provincial government, the resulting situation will be one in which there is a single built-up urban area comprising a central-city municipality surrounded by a number of independent suburban municipalities. For many analysts of urban governance, such a situation is a problem, one that is often referred to as the 'metropolitan problem'. For others, a multi-municipal-urban area is desirable.

The first objective of this chapter is to understand the nature of the disagreement between these two positions, one of which we can label as the 'consolidationist' position, the other as 'public choice'. The disagreement goes far beyond Canada. In the real world of Canadian municipal government, however, the consolidationist position has predominated. For most of this chapter we shall be examining two-tier systems of urban municipal government that have been championed by consolidationists. Their position has been that, in the absence of continuous annexation, an alternative solution to governing the entire urban area is to establish a metropolitan level of municipal government on top of the existing municipalities to provide a level of government that can address problems facing the whole area.

Some consolidationists actually prefer two-tier metropolitan systems to large, single-tier systems resulting from annexations because the retention of local municipalities provides for an element of local control, which might be much needed in a very large urban area. Others see two-tier systems as a second-best solution because they add to the complexity of municipal government. This latter view was clearly the approach taken by the McNally Commission in Alberta in the 1950s when it stated its preference for continuing annexation in Edmonton and Calgary rather than following Ontario's example of establishing a two-tier metropolitan system for Toronto, a process that we shall carefully examine in this chapter. The 'public-choice' approach has rarely been articulated in Canadian debates about organizing the municipal government of our large cities. It did, however, receive some attention in debates in the 1990s when, as we shall see in the next chapter, provincial governments in eastern Canada enacted large-scale municipal amalgamations to create single-tier systems for large urban areas.

After examining the differences between consolidationists and advocates of public choice, the chapter will then focus on the emergence of two-tier systems of urban government in Canada. These systems have taken quite different forms at different times, so much so that sometimes the distinction between single-tier and two-tier systems appears to break down. This has been especially true with the creation of regional districts in British Columbia, metropolitan communities in Montreal and Quebec City, and new institutional arrangements for the Edmonton and Calgary regions.

Consolidationists versus Public Choice

Consolidationists believe that each metropolitan area needs a municipal government capable of making decisions on at least some of the municipal issues facing the entire area. For our purposes in this discussion, 'metropolitan areas' corresponds to the Canadian 'census metropolitan areas' (CMAs) discussed in Chapter 5. In the English-speaking world, consolidationists first articulated their positions in the nineteenth century with reference to the governance of large cities in Britain and the United States, especially London and New York. An upper-tier London County Council was established in 1888.[1] In 1898 in New York 15 cities and towns and 11 villages in five separate counties were bought together, after local approval through referendums, to create a single city with five distinct boroughs.[2] The arguments justifying these institutional changes are basically the same as those used today to justify similar proposals. There are four main arguments:[3]

- *Efficiency*. Some, if not all, municipal services benefit from economies of scale. This means that the more people served by a particular municipal service, the cheaper it will be to deliver a single unit of that service. To the extent that there are economies of scale in municipal services, they can be provided more efficiently with municipal governments that are larger.

- *Planning for infrastructure and environmental protection.* Metropolitan areas need public infrastructure such as roads, fixed-rail transit systems, water and sewage systems, major recreational facilities, etc. Although it is quite conceivable that individual municipalities could provide these for themselves, a metropolitan area requires co-ordinated infrastructure development so roads and transit systems connect with each other and one municipality's sewage does not pollute another's water supply. A single municipal authority is required to provide such co-ordination.

- *Equity.* People who live in the same metropolitan area should have roughly the same level of municipal services, regardless of the financial resources of the particular municipality in which they live. Consequently, there should be a single municipal authority providing all or some of these services itself or, at a minimum, it should channel financial resources from richer areas to poorer areas to provide at least a degree of equalization.

- *Economic development and promotion.* Global investors in new enterprises have hundreds of potential locations. Metropolitan areas are in competition with each other for such investment. Investors do not care about municipal boundaries but they do care, for example, what the Vancouver metropolitan area has to offer compared to Seattle. Individual municipalities within the same metropolitan area should not each be promoting their own advantages on the international stage. A single municipal authority is required that can act on behalf of the entire area.

Although the relative importance of each of these arguments has varied from time to time and place to place, in one form or another each is almost invariably present in any debate about the organization of municipal government in metropolitan areas. As we shall see, however, changes in the real world are not usually brought about as a result of abstract debates. Usually, some form of crisis or precipitating event causes any significant change in the pattern of municipal organization.

The consolidationist position is built on at least two major assumptions:

1. Central governments (provinces in Canada) are unwilling or unable to step in themselves and attempt to solve whatever policy problems result from having more than one municipality in the same metropolitan area.

2. Having multiple municipal governments in the same urban area creates only problems, and not advantages.

This second assumption is the main target of those who favour the public-choice position.

In its urban setting,[4] public choice has its origins in the 1956 academic article written by Charles Tiebout, which we discussed briefly in Chapter 2. The key insight of Tiebout's article is that multiple municipalities in a metropolitan area can be seen as being like competing private firms, each one providing its own distinct mix of goods and services at its own price levels. Rational consumers can pick the one that provides the mix they prefer at the price they prefer. Multiple competing municipalities are beneficial for consumers in the same way that multiple competing grocery stores are beneficial. Food is just as essential for urban life as the services provided by municipalities. But in our market economy some people end up shopping in bargain stores with poor-quality products and others use their money to patronize specialized gourmet stores. For Tiebout, municipalities were similar. Residents who did not like the services on offer in their municipality could 'vote with their feet' by moving to another one, just as high-income people shop at more expensive grocery stores if they experience poor quality at the cheaper ones. (Many people, of course, such as the poor and the elderly, are not in a position to vote with their feet, just as they often are not in a position to buy expensive groceries or, for that matter, to access less expensive grocery stores.) In this way, residents not only could get what they most wanted—and could afford—in local services but the services likely would be provided efficiently, because a municipality that provided poor services at high cost would end up with no residents at all and everybody working for it would be out of work.

It is not difficult to see some of the obvious flaws in Tiebout's approach:

1. Tiebout did not take into account that most people decide where to live because of proximity to their work, or their partner's work, or because of the location of other family or loved ones.
2. Even if work and family were not an issue, most people do not keep careful track of levels of municipal services and taxes in various municipalities so are unlikely to maximize their choices in the way Tiebout suggests.
3. Even if residents possessed all the necessary information, the costs of moving homes are such that they would be unlikely to do so merely to obtain marginal gains in municipal services in relation to tax levels.

Academic debates have evolved around each of these points.[5] The details need not concern us here. But, at a bare minimum, the 'Tiebout hypothesis' suggests that we should pay more attention than consolidationists do to the virtues of providing an element of choice to residents of large cities.

Public-choice scholars challenge the view that only big governments can solve big problems; they generally conclude that big governments often make big problems worse. In urban settings, their approach is in direct conflict with that of the consolidationists. Often, public-choice scholars provide empirical evidence to undermine the consolidationists' most cherished views. For example, they discovered that, for a great many municipal services, there were few economies of scale and that, for some, diseconomies of scale set in at relatively low population levels. They attributed their findings to the fact that larger municipalities generated more layers of management, stronger unions demanding higher wage levels, and a decreased ability to adapt service levels to exactly what residents desired.[6]

Public-choice scholars also discovered that consolidationists had underestimated the likelihood that small governments would work together and with private contractors to overcome the disadvantages of smallness. When large infrastructure was needed, public-choice scholars looked to central governments and/or multi-municipal special-purpose bodies to step in. As far as equity issues were concerned, they argued that larger central governments were best-suited to redistribute income and resources from the rich to the poor. Finally, public-choice scholars have simply not taken seriously the view that potential investors in a metropolitan area will be positively influenced by the existence of a single government, one of whose roles is to attract their attention. The public-choice view is that investors know what they are looking for anyway and, like consumers, are going to appreciate having a choice of municipalities in which to locate.[7]

Before moving on to look at real-world accomplishments by Canadian consolidationists it is important to re-emphasize that, until very recently, the public-choice perspective has hardly been present in Canadian debates about municipal organization in urban areas. People who have resisted consolidationist solutions have only rarely articulated views that have explicitly, or even implicitly, echoed public-choice perspectives. Consequently, they have often appeared as stubbornly resistant to change or as unprincipled defenders of privilege. But during many of the institutional changes to be discussed in this chapter, consolidationists dominated the debates because two-tier solutions in themselves were relatively non-controversial—they involved adding a level of municipal government, not amalgamation. From the 1950s to the 1970s—before today's high levels of pessimism about the ability of governments to solve problems—the idea of adding a level of municipal government in metropolitan areas seemed like a sensible, pragmatic response to complex problems caused by rapid urban growth.

The Municipality of Metropolitan Toronto

In her definitive account of 'the political dynamics of urban expansion in the Toronto region', Frances Frisken observed:

> Until the early part of the 20th century, Toronto grew by annexation in the same way as many other North American cities, taking in small municipalities or suburban districts that are still well known by their original names (for example, Yorkville, the Annex, Parkdale, North Toronto, Moore Park). In 1912, however, City Council ruled out further annexations, having decided that the costs of providing services to annexed districts exceeded any benefits they might bring to the city. Council held firmly to that position in the face of later requests for annexation from the suburbs of York and East York, which viewed annexation as a way to secure better services, particularly those offered by the Toronto Transportation Commission.[8]

Early proposals for a two-tier form of metropolitan government emerged at the same time as annexation was losing its appeal,[9] just as they did in Montreal.[10]

By 1949, with uncontrolled and rapid urban development taking place all around its borders, especially in the rural townships of Etobicoke, North York, and Scarborough, the Toronto city council reversed its position on annexation, voting 19–2 to annex all of its adjacent suburbs. All of the suburbs objected, but only Mimico proposed an alternative: a special service board to provide major regional infrastructure. In 1950, Premier Leslie Frost referred both Toronto's and Mimico's proposals to the OMB for resolution.[11]

In January 1953 the OMB chair, Lorne Cumming, announced that he was recommending a compromise solution: the creation of a two-tier federated form of municipal government comprising the city of Toronto and 12 surrounding municipalities.[12] A few months later the Ontario legislature enacted this proposal and on 1 January 1 1953 the Municipality of Metropolitan Toronto came into being. Its main initial functions were to build new arterial roads and water supply and sewage systems. One of the arterial roads was the Gardiner Expressway, named for the very successful first chair of the Metro Council, Fred Gardiner. In 1957, a Metro police service was created and later most municipal social services costs were moved to the Metro level. Costs were paid for by each municipality in proportion to its share of total taxable property assessment within the boundaries of the new Metro system. In 1954, this meant that the city of Toronto was paying 62 per cent of the cost. Despite its heavy financial commitment to Metro and despite the fact that it comprised 57 per cent of Metro's population, the city was given only 12 of the 24 seats on Metro's governing council. In its early years, there can be little doubt that the main purpose of the Metro system was to use the city's resources to finance new infrastructure in the suburbs.

By 1963, the city's shares of Metro's taxable property assessment and population had declined to 44 per cent and 38 per cent, respectively, but it still held half the seats on Metro council. Greater violations of the principle of representation by population could be found among the suburbs. North York, with a population of 308,000, was still allocated only one seat; so was Swansea, with its population of 9,000. In the same year, Premier John Robarts appointed H. Carl Goldenberg of Montreal to review the entire Metro system. In 1965 the Goldenberg commission recommended that the 13 municipalities be consolidated into four and that each be represented on the Metro council in proportion to its population. In 1966, much of the report was implemented, except that six consolidated lower-tier municipalities were created (Toronto, York, East York, Etobicoke, North York, and Scarborough) instead of four.

The most important structural change within Metro since 1966 was the reorganization of Metro council in 1988. In 1977 a Royal Commission headed by the former Ontario Premier, John Robarts, recommended a council composed of the mayors of the six constituent municipalities and 27 councillors directly elected from specially designated Metro wards. Each of the 27 Metro councillors would also sit on the local council of his or her respective lower-tier municipality. As a result of yet another study on the same issue in 1986, the direct election of 28 Metro councillors was implemented in 1988. Under this scheme, local mayors still sat on Metro council but Metro councillors had no role on lower-tier councils.

As we shall see in the next chapter, Metro was abolished in 1998. In its early years, however, there can be little doubt that it was a huge success. It attracted the attention of students and practitioners of urban governance from around the Western world. In London, England, the boundaries of the old LCC had never been extended and it was now more like a central-city government than a metropolitan one. Metro Toronto was a unique two-tier metropolitan federation of the type that many consolidationists had been advocating for years. As Frisken notes, both domestic and international observers 'were virtually unanimous in concluding that Metro had accomplished its principal objective: to speed up the provision of infrastructure to support suburban population growth and industrial expansion.'[13]

By the late 1960s, however, Metro obviously had become less effective. Not much new suburban infrastructure was needed, because Etobicoke, North York, and Scarborough were already largely built out (and, as we shall see in Chapter 10, development companies were by this time expected to build and/or pay for most of the new infrastructure, anyway). In addition, increasing political conflict existed within Metro council between representatives of the city of Toronto and the suburban members, some of which related to the refusal by the new suburban majority on the council to help finance the rebuilding of old infrastructure in the inner city. But the most serious conflict revolved around the desire of the suburban majority to build a new network of expressways to allow better suburban automobile access to downtown. The proposed north–south Spadina Expressway was to be the first link in the network, and construction south of Highway 401 began. But city politicians (backed by very strong citizens' groups) resisted. In 1971, the new provincial Premier, Bill Davis, announced legislation to overturn Metro's (and the OMB's) decision on the matter, famously stating, 'If we are building a transportation system to serve the automobile, the Spadina Expressway would be a good place to start. But if we are building a transportation system to serve people, the Spadina Expressway is a good place to stop.'[14] As a result of provincial legislation, the expressway (now known as the Allen Road) ends at Eglinton Avenue rather than cutting through inner-city neighbourhoods on its way to a proposed new east–west expressway that also was killed.

If Metro was to maintain its mission to plan and finance new suburban infrastructure, its boundaries would have had to have been extended. But suburban municipal politicians beyond Metro had worked out their own ways of planning and financing infrastructure and, as we shall soon see, the Ontario government facilitated their desires to remain free of Metro by providing them with their own two-tier regional governments. By the time the Ontario government provided for direct election to Metro council in 1988, Metro simply did not have that much to do, a fact reflected in the lack of serious competition for Metro seats in the municipal elections that followed. Those who were elected (or sometimes acclaimed) were reduced to squabbling with lower-tier councillors about who was to be blamed for whatever was going wrong. Ten years later, Metro was no more. By this time there were few who would mourn its loss.

The Metropolitan Corporation of Greater Winnipeg

In the late 1950s there were 19 separate municipalities in metropolitan Winnipeg, with about half of the population living in the central city. Area-wide special-purpose bodies dealt with water supply, sewage, public transit, and regional planning. In 1960, the Progressive Conservative government of Manitoba, led by Duff Roblin, introduced legislation to bring these special-purpose bodies together into a new multi-functional metropolitan government, the Metropolitan Corporation of Greater Winnipeg. In some respects Metro Winnipeg, which began its work in 1961, was modelled on Metro Toronto. But the Manitoba government provided for a Metro council quite different from the original one in Toronto. There were to be only 10 members and all were to be elected to serve only on the Metro council. The law also provided that each Metro electoral district had to include parts of at least two separate municipalities. All these stipulations were designed to ensure that Metro councillors were loyal primarily to the objectives of Metro itself, rather than to those of the constituent lower-tier municipalities.[15]

The man who was director of planning for Metro Winnipeg from its creation until 1967 has provided this fascinating comparison of the metro systems in Winnipeg and Toronto:

> Unlike the Metro Toronto system, there was no direct link with the councils of the area municipalities through the membership of their mayors and some of their councillors on Metro Council. Throughout its life the Metro government was repeatedly faced with real or imagined accusations of disregarding the municipal problems and points of view. Furthermore, when the original metro–municipal conflicts arose, these quickly became public issues and were debated in the news media. This minimized the possibility of negotiated settlements of issues such as happened in Metro Toronto's committee rooms. Advocates of 'open-ness' in local government may argue that the public conflict caused by the Winnipeg system was beneficial in that it made sure the public was aware of, and could participate in, the resolution of the metro–municipal issues; on the other hand, the protagonists quickly assumed firm positions on issues making negotiation and compromise much more difficult.[16]

Metro Winnipeg successfully modernized much of the area's infra-structure and ended the practice of dumping untreated sewage into the

Red and Assiniboine rivers. It also adopted a metropolitan plan that guided the area's urban development for many years after it had been abolished.[17] But the political conflicts between Metro and local politicians, especially Winnipeg's popular long-time mayor, Steve Juba, were too damaging. When the NDP was elected in Manitoba in 1970, one of its first major acts was to merge Metro and its constituent municipalities into a 'unicity'. We shall examine this process in the next chapter.

Regional Municipalities in Ontario

As we briefly noted in Chapter 1, the territory of southern Ontario was divided into counties in the nineteenth century, all of which until the late twentieth century were upper-tier units of rural government. When an urban area in southern Ontario became large enough to be classified as a city, it became separate politically from the county of which it was a part and became a single-tier municipal government. In our discussion of annexations in London, Ontario, we noted that London has been a single-tier municipal government since it became a city in 1855. When Metro Toronto was created in 1953, the city of Toronto became the first city in Ontario's history to be part of a two-tier system of municipal government. From 1969 to 1974, 10 two-tier regional municipalities were created in Ontario and all involved establishing at least one city as a lower-tier government within the system. Ontario's regional municipalities were clearly modelled on Metro Toronto. As we saw in our discussion of Metro Toronto, by the late 1960s the number of its constituent municipalities had been reduced from 13 to six, and policing and social services had become Metro responsibilities. When each of the regional municipalities was established, these reorganizations that had been accomplished incrementally in Metro Toronto were carried out all at once. Indeed, the rearrangement of lower-tier municipal boundaries by the province was often more controversial than the establishment of the regional municipality.

Stewart Fyfe has provided us with an excellent listing of the main elements initially common to all or most of Ontario's regional municipalities.

1. An upper-tier unit is created for the large urban centre and its hinterland. The old county boundaries have commonly but not universally been followed.

2. There is a reduction in the number of local municipalities, mainly by consolidation, together with large annexations, to give the urban centre more control over its hinterland.

3. The council is composed of members of local councils . . . and

roughly in accordance with population. The chairman is appointed by the province for the first term, following the Toronto precedent. Thereafter he [or she] is to be chosen by the council, following the county model and that of Toronto also.

4. The regional municipality is responsible for public health, police, regional planning, arterial roads, sewage disposal, bulk water supply treatment, garbage disposal, capital borrowing, welfare [social services], and regional parks . . .

5. Local municipalities are responsible for local planning, roads, parks, local sewers, water distribution, garbage collection, fire protection, street lighting, and tax collection.

6. The regional municipality is financed by a requisition on the local municipalities, in proportion to their share of the total [property] assessment.[18]

Table 7.1 lists Ontario's regional municipalities, showing their dates of coming into existence and abolition (if applicable) and the most populous municipality (in 2006 or at time of abolition) within each.

Regional municipalities were never very popular, in part because they were created at a time of considerable inflation and many residents attributed greatly increased tax bills to their creation, and, in part, because of

Table 7.1 Regional Municipalities in Ontario, Showing Year of Implementation and Abolition (If Applicable) and Name of Largest City

Regional Municipality	Years	Largest City
Ottawa–Carleton	1969–2000	Ottawa
Niagara	1970–	St. Catharines
York	1970–	Markham
Peel	1973–	Mississauga
Halton	1973–	Oakville
Waterloo	1973–	Kitchener
Hamilton–Wentworth	1973–2000	Hamilton
Sudbury	1973–2000	Sudbury
Durham	1973–	Oshawa
Haldimand–Norfolk	1974–2000	Nanticoke

Sources: Stewart Fyfe, 'Local Government Reform in Toronto: 1853–1973', in R. Charles Bryfogle and Ralph R. Krueger, eds, *Urban Problems*, rev. edn (Toronto: Holt, Rinehart, and Winston, 1975), 360; Statistics Canada, *2006 Census of Canada*. Abolition dates derive from Ontario's Fewer Municipal Politicians Act of 1999, which is described in Andrew Sancton, *Merger Mania: The Assault on Local Government* (Montreal and Kingston: McGill-Queen's University Press, 2000), 154–9.

the upheavals caused by the lower-tier boundary changes. Throughout their existence debates have continued about exactly how they should be structured, many of these debates mirroring those already discussed for Metro Toronto and Metro Winnipeg. Over time, most took on more functions than they were originally assigned, especially relating to water supply and sewers. In any event, in 1999 the Ontario government introduced legislation to abolish four of them: Ottawa–Carleton, Hamilton, Sudbury, and Haldimand–Norfolk. The legislation will be briefly discussed in the next chapter.

All of the remaining six regional municipalities are within the territory of the Greater Golden Horseshoe (see Chapter 5). The existence of Peel, York, and Durham immediately adjacent to Metro Toronto was one of the factors that prevented the extension of Metro's boundaries in the 1970s and 1980s, hence preventing it from continuing as a genuine government for the entire metropolitan area. Dissatisfaction with regional municipalities remains in these areas, but most residents seem to prefer the status quo to either of the two main alternatives: complete amalgamation (which is what happened in the other regions in 2000) or becoming part of some form of extended Metro Toronto, an option that did seem a real possibility in the 1990s (as we shall see in the next chapter) but which is now off the table.

Rather than review in detail all the debates and manoeuvrings about how each of the remaining regions should be structured politically, we shall simply review in Table 7.2 the current state of affairs. In all cases, voters (rather than lower-tier councils) elect all regional councillors; similarly, mayors of all lower-tier municipalities are members of their respective regional councils. But the table shows that, in Waterloo and Niagara, the mayors are the only lower-tier elected officials serving at the regional level; in the other four regional municipalities most mayors are joined by members of their own councils. Only in Waterloo and Halton are the regional chairs (who are best understood as regional mayors) directly elected. Elsewhere, regional chairs are elected by members of regional council. If a person elected chair is a member of regional council, he or she gives up whatever other position to which they have been elected.

The table also shows that, except in Durham, the largest municipality in each region is generally under-represented on the basis of their respective shares of each region's population. This is in part caused by the fact that even the smallest municipality always gets at least one representative, however small its population. But there is also a general bias against giving any one municipality too much power within the region. This has been especially true with respect to Mississauga within Peel, and the issue has been the cause of one of the most serious challenges this century to an Ontario regional municipality.

Mississauga and the Regional Municipality of Peel

The creation of most regional governments in Ontario was preceded by a 'review' conducted by an expert on local government. Thomas J. Plunkett was assigned to review the local government structures in Peel and Halton counties, the fastest-growing areas in the Toronto region. Plunkett's report was the most radical of any of the reviews conducted in the 1960s. He proposed a single-tier 'urban county of Mississauga' that would replace all existing municipalities in the southern parts of Peel and Halton counties and another large rural unit covering the northern parts. Although the report made perfect sense in terms of patterns of suburban development, it was opposed by virtually all of the local politicians and developers. After much delay and debate, the Ontario government announced in 1973 that there would be two regional governments in the area, one for Peel and one for Halton.[19]

The boundaries of the old counties were left almost untouched, but the constituent parts were dramatically restructured. The most controversial of these was the creation of the new city of Mississauga within Peel. It was formed by the amalgamation of the town of Mississauga (formerly Toronto township) with the towns of Port Credit and Streetsville. One of the fiercest critics of the amalgamation was the mayor of Streetsville, Hazel McCallion. In 1978, however, she was elected mayor of Mississauga and has held that post ever since, notwithstanding the fact that in 2010 she was 89 years old.[20]

Table 7.2 Features of Ontario's Six Regional Municipalities

	Number of Lower-Tier Municipalities	2006 Population	% Population in Largest Municipality	Number of Regional Councillors Excluding Chair	% of Councillors Assigned to Largest Municipality
Waterloo	7	478,121	42.8	15	33.3
Niagara	12	427,421	30.9	30	23.3
Halton	4	439,256	37.7	20	35.0
Peel	3	1,159,405	57.7	24	50.0
York	9	892,712	29.3	20	25.0
Durham	8	561,258	25.2	25	32.0

Sources: Statistics Canada, *2006 Census of Canada*; websites of the various regional municipalities.

After 2000 (when the constituent parts of Ottawa–Carleton regional municipality were merged together to create the new city of Ottawa), Mississauga became the most populous city in Ontario to be part of a two-tier system. Starting in 2001, McCallion launched a campaign to separate Mississauga from Peel. McCallion's biographer sets the stage with these words:

> The Region of Peel hardly seems like a monster, with its soft-spoken chair, its low-profile bureaucrats, and a lack of controversy over day-to-day operations. But if it is not a monster, it could be portrayed as a monstrosity—a wasteful tier of local government on whose council Mississauga is grossly under-represented. Smaller cities like London, Guelph, and Barrie are 'separated' cities. They do not groan under an upper-tier government. Why should Mississauga?[21]

In 2002 a citizens' task force created by McCallion recommended that the Peel regional municipality be phased out over a five-year period to be replaced by a lighter co-ordinating body for a larger Toronto region. Twenty thousand residents returned a form to Mississauga city hall supporting the mayor's position that Peel region should be abolished.[22] Despite McCallion's strong pressure, the provincial Liberal government (elected in 2003) refused to act, knowing that any move to split up Peel would throw 'wide open the debates across the province on all sorts of municipal grievances, separatist aspirations, de-amalgamations, annexationist proposals, and maybe even schemes not hitherto contemplated'.[23]

Then, McCallion announced her alternative: that Mississauga should at least be fairly represented on the Peel council. At the time the mayor and all nine councillors comprised Mississauga's representation on the 21-member council, which then elected a chair as a twenty-second member. In April 2006, the Ontario government announced that it would introduce legislation expanding the Mississauga council to 11 members plus the mayor and that all would continue to sit on a Peel council of 24 members, who would then elect a chair. McCallion declared victory.[24]

Conclusion to Ontario's Regional Governments

In the early 1970s, two-tier regional governments in Ontario were seen by experts as significant institutional reforms in urban governance. Many expected that they would eventually be established throughout the southern part of the province and that single-tier separated cities would become relics of the past. But the process was halted in the mid-1970s in the wake of much local political opposition.[25] Four were abolished in 2000. Four of the six that that remain (including Peel) are in the immediate orbit of the amalgamated city of Toronto, anomalous survivors of the dramatic municipal amalgamations of the late 1990s. The regional municipalities of Niagara and Waterloo are more removed from Toronto's core but as they are still in the Greater Golden Horseshoe, both exist in complex municipal environments with a number of significant urban municipalities as their reluctant members. Mayor McCallion's efforts to bring change to Peel are likely to be replicated elsewhere.

Urban, Regional, and Metropolitan Communities in Quebec

After the city of Montreal's financially disastrous annexation of Maisonneuve in 1918 (described in Chapter 6), the Quebec government established a Montreal Metropolitan Commission. Its main purpose was to force wealthier suburban municipalities to subsidize poorer ones, which Montreal was no longer willing to annex. Although a few inter-municipal functions were added later, it never became a wide-ranging metropolitan government such as those established later in Toronto and Winnipeg. The same can be said for its successor, the Montreal Metropolitan Corporation, established in 1959.[26]

The Montreal Urban Community

The late 1960s was a time of considerable political instability in many cities in the Western world. Among Canadian cities, Montreal was especially affected by street violence, largely because of linguistic and political tensions between French and English and separatists and federalists. Between June 1968 and October 1969, two Montreal police officers had been killed and more than 250 injured. Notwithstanding the perils for the Montreal police, they were paid less than those in Metro Toronto. In the aftermath of Expo 67, city officials claimed they could not afford to match Toronto's police salaries. On 7 October 1969 the Montreal police launched an illegal work stoppage that lasted for 16 hours before Quebec's legislature approved a law, obeyed by the police, which forced them back to work. During this brief interval there were nine armed bank robberies, 30 other armed robberies, and 494 complaints involving almost a million dollars of damage, much of it from looting. Federal troops and Quebec provincial police were moved into the city. Meanwhile, Montreal's suburban municipalities were protected by their own police services, whose members stayed on the job.[27]

Montreal officials soon agreed to meet most of the financial demands from the police union. Their strategy was to convince the provincial government to force the suburbs to help them meet the cost. They pointed out that, because Metro Toronto had a unified police force that covered the relatively peaceful suburbs as well as the downtown, it was able to reduce per capita costs compared to the city of Montreal. One of them stated: 'Montreal's police department is effectively the shield which protects all of the Island of Montreal. Justice would almost be restored if the costs of all police services were shared by all citizens of the island.'[28] The city's strategy was successful. Starting in 1970, the island of Montreal had a new metropolitan government, the Montreal Urban Community (MUC), the main purpose of which, initially, was to share policing costs.

The legislation establishing the MUC also gave it the authority to take action on such matters as regional planning, air pollution, traffic control on main arteries, public transit, the supply of drinking water, the treatment of sewage, and the disposal of garbage. Over the years it acted on many of these matters, most notably to build a primary sewage treatment plant to stop the practice of releasing the city's untreated sewage directly into the St Lawrence River. But policing remained its primary focus. In 1970 and 1971 all the municipalities kept their own police services but shared costs on the basis of each municipality's share of total MUC property assessment. Not surprisingly, total police costs rose dramatically. The situation was like a group of 30 diners going to a restaurant and agreeing that they would split the bill in proportion to the value of each diner's home. Even the person with the most expensive home is likely to do better by ordering the most expensive items on the menu, because that is what others—especially the people living in cheap homes—are likely to do. Starting in 1972, all the police forces were unified and the Montreal Urban Community Police Department was created.[29]

The MUC existed from 1970 until 2001, when the 28 municipalities in the MUC were amalgamated. During its existence battles between the city and the suburbs were constant. The main problem was that the city of Montreal comprised more than half the population of just under two million and the suburbs varied in size from almost 100,000 (Montreal North) to just over 1,000 (Senneville). Representatives of the various municipalities on the MUC council were given multiple votes in accordance with population (one vote for each 1,000 people represented) and all decisions required a double majority of both city and suburban votes. The system was very complex, and few MUC residents had any idea of how their metropolitan government actually worked. Various attempts to restructure the boundaries of the constituent municipal units (similar to what happened in Metro Toronto in the 1960s) foundered on linguistic issues: few politicians wanted to merge French and English municipalities or to create a large English one in the western part of the island. The result was that all boundaries were left alone.[30]

Elsewhere in Quebec

An urban community for the Quebec City area and a regional community for the Outaouais (now Gatineau) were established at the same time as the MUC, probably because the main opposition party in the Quebec legislature at the time (the Liberals) agreed to speedy passage of the MUC legislation if Quebec City and Hull benefited from the same assistance from their suburbs as did the city of Montreal. Unlike the MUC, the lower-tier municipalities within these upper-tier institutions were consolidated, from 26 to 13 in Quebec City and from 32 to eight in the Outaouais.[31] Like the MUC, these institutions ceased to exist at the end of 2001.

In 1979, provincial legislation was approved that abolished Quebec's 71 upper-tier rural counties (similar to Ontario's) and replaced them with 95 municipal regional counties (MRCs). The main difference between the old counties and the MRCs is that the latter have responsibility for regional planning and, for this purpose, separated cities became part of the MRC in which they were located. In some respects, therefore, they are similar to regional governments in Ontario, the main difference being that they are not responsible for nearly as many municipal functions and therefore have much smaller budgets. As shown in Table 1.1, there are now 86 MRCs in Quebec.[32]

Metropolitan Communities in Montreal and Quebec

There are two 'supra-regional authorities' in Quebec. These came into existence in 2002 for areas very similar to the CMAs for both Montreal and Quebec City, meaning that the territories they cover are much larger than their predecessors, the Montreal and Quebec urban communities. But their functional responsibilities are much less. They have nothing to do with policing but they do have responsibilities relating to regional planning, waste disposal, regional parks, co-ordination of public transit, economic development, regional infrastructure, and cost-sharing for public housing.[33] An unusual feature of these entities is that the mayors of Montreal and Quebec City are automatically the chairs of the governing councils of their respective metropolitan communities, which means that their leadership functions extend beyond their own municipal boundaries. However, neither of these supra-regional entities has yet had much impact and very few residents have any reason to be aware of them.

Some of the territories of these two metropolitan communities are also under the jurisdiction of MRCs. Residents of such areas are faced, therefore, with three tiers of municipal government, the only place in the country where this is the case. As we shall see in the next chapter, the arrangements for municipal government within the former territory of the MUC are even more complex.

Regional Districts in British Columbia

Between 1965 and 1967 the British Columbia government implemented a system of regional districts for the entire province, including those areas not contained within incorporated municipalities. The 27 regional districts in British Columbia differ from regional government in Ontario in the following ways:

- The district's governing body is called a 'board of directors' not a 'council'.
- Some members have multiple votes depending on the size of their municipalities.
- Member municipalities can opt out of many district functions, but no districts have any responsibility for police or social services.
- Districts provide different functions for different areas within their boundaries, especially for unincorporated areas.
- All municipal representatives on district boards of directors, including the chair, are elected members of municipal councils; and districts were created without changing any existing municipal boundaries, i.e., there was no simultaneous lower-tier consolidation.

In short, the creation of regional districts was much less disruptive to the traditional pattern of municipal government. Although there have been some calls for direct election to the boards of directors of regional districts,[34] the provincial government has never moved towards implementing such a change, presumably because of the lack of municipal support for such a move and a concern about the jurisdictional conflicts that would likely ensue, as they did in Metro Winnipeg and Metro Toronto.

Metro Vancouver

Until 1967, inter-municipal services in metropolitan Vancouver were handled largely by special-purpose bodies. Two of these were continued as the Greater Vancouver Sewerage and Drainage District and the Greater Vancouver Water District, but their operations were essentially combined with those of the Greater Vancouver Regional District (GVRD), now known unofficially as Metro Vancouver. Its territory 'essentially corresponds'[35] to the Vancouver CMA. Unlike two-tier metropolitan and regional governments in Ontario, the GVRD has actually expanded its boundaries since its inception. The fact that peripheral municipalities, prior to their application for full membership, have already been part of the GVRD for a limited number of functions (as Abbotsford is now for parks) is no doubt part of the explanation. The governance arrangements for Metro Vancouver are complex, as shown in Table 7.3.

More so than for any other metropolitan area in Canada, planning documents for Metro Vancouver are obsessed, for understandable reasons, with protecting the natural physical environment and with maintaining a 'livable region'. In the mid-1970s the GVRD adopted its *Livable Region Plan* (LRP). The plan's main objective was to prevent urban sprawl by minimizing commuting. More jobs would be created in regional town centres so people could live closer to where they worked.[36] In 1990 the GVRD adopted an updated version of the LRP called *Choosing Our Future*, which was replaced in turn in 1995 by the *Livable Region Strategic Plan*.[37] Unlike regional governments in Ontario, regional districts do not have the authority arbitrarily to impose planning objectives on municipalities; their influence is accomplished by persuasion and, ultimately, by various forms of mediation and arbitration. Probably because many residents of Vancouver seem profoundly worried that continued economic growth might destroy their remarkable natural environment, they seem to have injected a greater sense of urgency into their regional planning than residents of other Canadian metropolitan areas. Metro Vancouver might not have much formal authority, but its planning activities spark considerable public involvement.

The Vancouver CMA is Canada's third most populous (2.12 million in 2006). The population of the city of Vancouver is only 580,000. The suburban city of Surrey is not far behind at 400,000 and there are 19 other independent municipalities. In short, at least by Canadian standards, the metropolitan area is municipally fragmented. Nevertheless, looking at Vancouver's governance system as a whole, it is hard to imagine a mechanism that could better combine local self-government with the existence of an institution that can provide a degree of metropolitan leadership as well as a framework in which municipalities can voluntarily co-operate with each other. Metro Vancouver's governance arrangements have lots of problems, but compared to problems found elsewhere in Canada and in other countries, they are minimal. Other metropolitan areas have much to learn from Vancouver.

Table 7.3 Board of the Greater Vancouver Regional District, 2009

DIRECTOR	RD	SD	WD
ABBOTSFORD:			
Mayor George Peary	4		
Councillor Moe Gill	3		
ANMORE:			
Vacant	1		1
BELCARRA:			
Mayor Ralph Drew	1		1
BOWEN ISLAND:			
Councillor Peter Frinton	1		
BURNABY:			
Mayor Derek Corrigan	4	4	4
Councillor Sav Dhaliwal	3	3	3
Councillor Colleen Jordan	4	4	4
COQUITLAM:			
Mayor Richard Stewart	3	3	3
Councillor Brent Asmundson	3	3	3
DELTA:			
Mayor Lois Jackson	5	5	5
ELECTORAL AREA A:			
Director Maria Harris	1	1	1
LANGLEY CITY:			
Councillor Gayle Martin	2	2	2
LANGLEY TOWNSHIP:			
Mayor Rick Green	5	5	5
LIONS BAY:			
Mayor Brenda Broughton	1		
MAPLE RIDGE:			
Mayor Ernie Daykin	4	4	4
NEW WESTMINSTER:			
Mayor Wayne Wright	3	3	3
NORTH VANCOUVER CITY:			
Mayor Darrell Mussatto	3	3	3
NORTH VANCOUVER DISTRICT:			
Mayor Richard Walton	5	5	5
PIT MEADOWS:			
Mayor Don MacLean	1	1	1

Table 7.3 (continued)

DIRECTOR	RD	SD	WD
PORT COQUITLAM:			
Mayor Greg Moore	3	3	3
PORT MOODY:			
Mayor Joe Trasolini	2	2	2
RICHMOND:			
Mayor Malcolm Brodie	5	5	5
Councillor Harold Steves	4	4	4
SURREY:			
Councillor Linda Hepner	5	5	5
Councillor Marvin Hunt	5	5	5
Councillor Judy Villeneuve	5	5	5
Mayor Dianne Watts	5	5	5
TSAWWASSEN:			
Chief Kim Baird	1		1
VANCOUVER:			
Councillor George Chow	5	5	5
Councillor Heather Deal	5	5	5
Councillor Raymond Louie	5	5	5
Councillor Andrea Reimer	4	4	4
Mayor Gregor Robertson	5	5	5
Councillor Tim Stevenson	5	5	5
WEST VANCOUVER:			
Mayor Pamela Goldsmith-Jones	3	3	3
WHITE ROCK:			
Mayor Catherine Ferguson	1	1	

The 2009 Board consists of 37 Directors representing 21 Municipalities, one Electoral Area, one treaty First Nation, and one Municipality that is a member of the GVRD for the parks function. These Directors are members of your Municipal or First Nation council who have been appointed to the Board by their respective councils.

The number of directors appointed to the Board depends on the population of the Municipality, Electoral Area, or First Nation. As well, directors are allowed one vote for every 20,000 people in their Municipality, Electoral Area, or First Nation, up to a total of five votes. The number in each of the three columns refers to the number of votes allocated to each of the directors for each of the three boards.

RD: Greater Vancouver Regional District
SD: Greater Vancouver Sewerage and Drainage District
WD: Greater Vancouver Water District

Abbotsford is a member of the GVRD for the parks function only.

Source: <http://www.metrovancouver.org/boards/Pages/directors.aspx>.

Regional Partnerships in Edmonton and Calgary

In the previous chapter we noted the importance of municipal annexations for the recent territorial expansion of both Edmonton and Calgary. More so than Calgary, the Edmonton area faced significant inter-municipal issues, in part because of bad feelings that survived the annexation battles of 1979 and 1980. These issues were exacerbated in the late 1990s after the Alberta government abolished the province's regional planning commission in 1994 as an economy measure and as a means to promote local economic development by making individual municipalities almost completely responsible for land-use issues.[38] In 1998 the Alberta government appointed a former provincial treasurer, Lou Hyndman, to review the governance arrangements for the entire Edmonton area.

Edmonton

Hyndman's final report is an important document for local government in Canada because it did *not* focus on *structural* change and was less consolidationist than any official government report on the subject of municipal organization in metropolitan areas. In his report Hyndman wrote:

> Many different approaches were considered as part of this Review. Of the many options available, partnerships are the best option for this region. Partnerships involve networking, negotiation, and mutual investment for mutual gain. The old style, centralized approach with command and control from the top is not the way to govern our region. . . .
>
> Over the last four decades, this region has developed as a 'community of communities', offering a range of residential and business choices that is unusual in comparison to most metropolitan areas in Canada. This is a strength of the region and it should be respected.
>
> A standardized 'one size fits all' approach to the delivery of services in the region simply will not work. Citizens and their municipal leaders want choices. Those choices must include being able to choose among the diverse neighbourhoods and communities in the region. . . . Choices in how services are delivered in the region must also be considered. These could include municipal collaboration, co-operation or integration, service boards, agencies and commissions, private companies, volunteer associations, or any combination of these options.[39]

Nevertheless, Hyndman did recommend that a 'Greater Edmonton Partnership' be established comprising all 21 municipalities in the area, each of which would have voting strength roughly equivalent to its relative share of the total population.[40] Such an institution was essentially the continuation of the Alberta Capital Regional Alliance (ACRA), a voluntary inter-municipal body that had been in existence since 1995. Rather than legislating for the new body, the Alberta government simply encouraged ACRA to continue.[41]

In October 2006, however, the city of Edmonton withdrew from ACRA, claiming that it had proven incapable of addressing important regional land-use issues that had implications for the fair sharing of fiscal resources in the region. In January 2008, provincial legislation replaced ACRA with the Capital Region Board (CRB), a planning body that 25 municipalities in the area were compelled to join. The Board is presided over presently by a provincially appointed chair. Provincial regulations authorized by the legislation provide that each member municipality has a single representative with one vote. However, any decision must be supported by the representatives of at least 17 municipalities representing at least 75 per cent of the total CRB population. If a municipal representative is absent or abstains from a vote, then the representative's vote is considered to be affirmative. This latter provision prevents members from blocking action by boycotting votes. The CRB approved the *Capital Region Growth Plan: Growing Forward* in April 2009 and now meets regularly to approve planning strategies of member municipalities before they become legally enforceable and to respond to various provincial requirements for regional planning decisions.[42] Although the CRB delivers no real services to residents, it does have significant planning authority with the potential to shape the future of the region. Whether it will evolve into a multi-functional upper-tier regional government is still unclear. In any event, developments subsequent to Hyndman's report in 2000 suggest that his faith in voluntary partnerships was misplaced.

Calgary

ACRA served as a model for the Calgary Regional Partnership (CRP) that began operations in 2001. While ACRA was breaking down, the CRP provided itself in 2008 with decision-making rules for land-use planning issues that could not be resolved by consensus. Here is its own description of these rules as described in the Calgary Metropolitan Plan that it adopted in June 2009:

[F]or any binding decision the following will need to occur:

1. A vote that contains a majority of the region's population; and
2. A vote that contains at least two thirds (12 of 17) of the CRP membership. . . .

Given that the City of Calgary represents over 85% of the CRP's population, any positive decision would require Calgary's consent. However, the two-thirds super majority requirement, or 12 of the current 17 members of the CRP, strikes a reasonable balance between respect for local autonomy and the ability to act in the broader regional interest. This decision making model provides a check in that Calgary would need the support of 11 other communities to carry a vote forward. Therefore, Calgary cannot impose its will on the region, but neither can regional decisions be made without Calgary's support. This is an important policy trade off considering the influence that Calgary carries within the region.[43]

The following items, however, would still require unanimous consent:

- Changes to the CRP's decision rules.
- Changes to the legal or statutory authority of the CRP or a member.
- Expansion of the CRP's membership.[44]

The Plan clearly is aimed at requiring member municipalities to follow its provisions so that the province would not have to directly intervene as it did in Edmonton. It tackled many controversial issues, including annexation:

Annexation continues to be an important tool in managing growth for municipalities. The CMP recognizes and supports the potential for annexation in identified urban growth areas based upon municipal growth rates, long-term land needs, and other strategic interests, in accordance with the requirements as set out in the Municipal Government Act.[45]

Despite its strong move into regional planning, the CRP still claims that it is not a 'level of government'. The following appears on its website:

Q: Is the CRP another level of government or bureaucracy?
A: No. We are an inventor and incubator. We facilitate co-operative partnerships on common regional issues. Although members are part of a larger region and partnership, they also continue to protect their individual uniqueness as unique communities.[46]

In the previous chapter we examined the tensions between the city of Calgary and Rocky View County. These tensions contributed to the decision by Rocky View in September 2009 to withdraw from the CRP. The county's reeve (mayor) said that 'concerns centre on tying regional servicing to proposed densities of communities; inclusion of annexation provisions when annexations are already covered under the Municipal Government Act; and a Calgary Regional Partnership voting structure that takes away municipal autonomy.'[47] Rocky View's decision was another blow in Alberta to the notion that municipalities in a metropolitan area can work together to achieve common goals voluntarily.

Conclusion

In this chapter we have observed a wide range of two-tier systems. At one extreme is the Corporation of Metropolitan Winnipeg (1961–71), governed by a 10-person council, all of whom were directly elected from districts that included territory from at least two different municipalities. At the other end of the scale are the voluntary regional partnerships in Edmonton and Calgary. Metro Winnipeg was abolished primarily because of the intense political conflict between the two levels. The voluntary partnerships in Alberta were plagued by the voluntary departure of key members, causing Edmonton's to be replaced by the province and Calgary's to be severely threatened. The record of other two-tier systems has been shaky as well: Metro Toronto could not survive more than 10 years (1988–98) of direct elections to Metro council and Ontario's other two-tier regional systems have faced both political turmoil and outright abolition. In Quebec, urban and regional communities survived for about 30 years (1970–2001), only to give way to much weaker metropolitan communities.

The only success stories have been the regional districts in British Columbia, including Metro Vancouver. Municipal membership is compulsory, but municipalities can opt in or out of most services that they provide; boundaries are fixed, but territories of particular services are not; all municipalities are represented on the boards of directors, but votes are weighted to account for population differences; regional planning is an important function, but local municipalities retain significant planning autonomy; the province is not afraid to step in on important policy issues (transit, for example), but it does not try to rearrange municipal boundaries. These are the kinds of policies and practices that have enabled regional districts to survive and prosper for a period of more than 40 years. They are Canada' success stories in two-tier metropolitan and regional government.

RESOURCES

Canada's longest-lasting, most successful example of a multi-functional metropolitan government is the Greater Vancouver Regional District, now known as Metro Vancouver. It has an impressive website that is worth thorough exploration. See: <www.metrovancouver.org/Pages/default.aspx>.

STUDY QUESTIONS

1. What is 'the metropolitan problem'? What are the main differences in how consolidationists and adherents of public choice approach this 'problem'?
2. Why and how was the Municipality of Metropolitan Toronto originally created? What were its main successes and why, in your view, was it less successful in its later years?
3. What, in your view, are the reasons why the Greater Vancouver Regional District (now known as Metro Vancouver) has lasted longer than other two-tier urban governments in Canada?

8 Amalgamations and De-amalgamations

In Chapter 6 we were concerned with the outward expansion of city boundaries, the process usually known as annexation. Chapter 7 was about how some provincial legislatures established two-tier systems of urban government that were usually alternatives to continuous annexation, although the establishment of urban two-tier systems in Ontario was generally accompanied by the consolidation of lower-tier governments as well. This chapter is about the most dramatic form of provincial intervention in urban governmental arrangements: the passage of laws that amalgamate urban (and sometimes adjoining rural) municipalities with each other to create a much larger single-tier urban government. In western Canada, the most dramatic example of such an amalgamation occurred in Winnipeg in 1971 when a 'unicity' replaced the Metropolitan Corporation of Greater Winnipeg. But most of the Canadian legislated amalgamations occurred in the 1990s and early 2000s. Such action in turn sparked demands for de-amalgamation, a process that in Quebec actually was implemented. Contrary to what is sometimes claimed, there was no worldwide movement for municipal amalgamations during this period, although significant amalgamations took place in parts of Britain, Australia, New Zealand, Greece, and Denmark.[1] Even in Canada, legislated amalgamations were restricted to the eastern provinces. In British Columbia, governments of various political persuasions made it clear they would not force amalgamations. However, Abbotsford and Matsqui were amalgamated in 1995 after voters in both municipalities approved the process in referendums.[2] The first involuntary municipal amalgamation occurred in Windsor, Ontario and, because it was a precedent for all that followed, it deserves our attention.

The Windsor Precedent

The first case in Canada of a municipality being amalgamated with another against the expressed will of its council and residents occurred in Windsor, Ontario, in 1935. The only scholars who have reported on it are Larry Kulisek and Trevor Price and the following description of the case is based on their account. Kulisek and Price call the Windsor case 'a decisive development of provincial policy'[3] and they are absolutely right. They describe the pre-1930 situation in Ontario in these words:

> municipalities had considerable scope to initiate services, respond to their citizens' needs and to seek authority for changes. While the process recognized the legal authority of the provincial legislature to approve changes, the initiative lay with the municipalities, which were building up their budgets and their administrative capabilities.
>
> In such key issues as the establishment of municipal boundaries and the changing of structures of government, the initiative also lay at the local level. Before amalgamations and annexations could occur it was necessary for local plebiscites to be held and for majority approval of those in the affected areas to be given. . . .[4]

It is startling to turn to the footnote accompanying this last sentence and to see that authority for it is attributed to the 1937 Harvard University master's thesis of Bora Laskin entitled 'The Ontario Municipal Board'. Laskin was to become one of Canada's most distinguished jurists, eventually serving as Chief Justice of Canada.

In 1917, in the midst of an unprecedented urban development boom in the area, various municipalities, including the city of Windsor, asked the provincial legislature to establish the Essex Border Utilities Commission (EBUC). The province obliged and the EBUC ended up creating an integrated water supply system for the area, taking over some aspects of area-wide planning, creating a district health board and operating hospitals, and taking over some parks that served district-wide needs.[5] In short, the EBUC seems to have evolved from an inter-municipal special-purpose body to an early variety of a multi-functional metropolitan government. It is important to note, however, that its creation was initiated by the local municipalities, not by the Ontario government. Notwithstanding the existence of the EBUC, local business elites in the 1920s promoted municipal amalgamation but, because it was not approved by referendum in all the affected municipalities, it was not implemented.

The Windsor area was especially hard hit by the Great Depression. By 1933 all the municipalities in the area except Walkerville, which had been the most adamantly opposed to annexation, were effectively bankrupt and under the financial supervision of the province. In 1934, a new Liberal government was elected in Ontario. David Croll, a former mayor of Windsor, was appointed as the province's first Minister of Municipal Affairs.[6] He sponsored legislation to establish a Windsor Finance Commission and to amalgamate the four central municipalities, including Walkerville, into a new city of Windsor. The legislation was introduced with no local consultation. It was announced on 11 April 1935 and was approved in its final form on 16 April, there being virtually no debate in the legislature apparently because it was introduced right at the end of the session.[7]

Walkerville had the most to lose since its debts were less than the others in relation to its tax base and it had not defaulted on interest payments up to 1934. Walkerville feared that its tax assessment would be increased to help pay for the debts of weaker municipalities and that its own services would deteriorate to a lower uniform level, once all services had been merged in a new Windsor. Walkerville put great emphasis on pride of place, which had been heightened by the fact that its name was carried worldwide on Canadian Club whisky produced by Hiram Walker Ltd.[8]

Walkerville residents fought the legislation in the courts, all the way to the Judicial Committee of the Privy Council in London, England, at that time Canada's highest court of appeal. The residents advanced the ingenious argument that the amalgamation legislation was really about bankruptcy, a subject under federal jurisdiction. By amalgamating municipalities to stave off bankruptcy, the residents argued that the provincial legislature was somehow invading federal jurisdiction. Everyone knew, however, that the main objective of the Walkerville residents was to protect local autonomy and that the arguments about bankruptcy were the slender legal reed to which they could attach their real concern. They claimed that:

> Quite apart from its many financial inequities both the act itself and the methods used in securing its enactment . . . were so un-British in character that it had become imperative . . . to take action in order to preserve (community) rights, if the long tradition of British justice and fair play is to be maintained in this country.[9]

The residents lost at all levels, with each court declaring that provincial legislatures had the unfettered authority to alter municipal structures in whatever way they wanted. In 1939, the Judicial Committee upheld the amalgamation legislation by stating that, 'It is not only the right . . . but it would appear to be the duty of the provincial legislature to provide the necessary remedy, so that the health of the inhabitants and the necessities of organized life should be preserved.'[10] As we shall see, recent judicial rulings on related matters in Canada have been remarkably con-sistent with the rulings made decades before with respect to Windsor, even though the Windsor case has not appeared in the judgements.

If Walkerville had been on the other side of the Detroit River in the United States, it could have appealed to American law and convention respecting the right of many municipalities to 'home rule', that is, the right to determine their own municipal structures and procedures. But home rule, as we saw in Chapter 3, never emerged in Canada, in large part because there are no written provincial constitutions in which its provisions can be embedded. In the absence of home rule the residents of Walkerville had no legal ammunition with which to fight, especially when the enemy was a former mayor of Windsor backed by a disciplined majority in the provincial legislature.

The effect of the Windsor precedent in Canada is far from clear. It must have had a considerable impact on Canadian municipal experts at the time, but, whatever the impact was, it seems not to have been recorded. In the first major university textbook on Canadian municipal government, published in 1954, K. Grant Crawford wrote only one sen-tence about the Windsor amalgamation: 'On occasion the province may take action [with respect to boundary changes] as was done in Ontario in 1935 when the cities of Windsor and East Windsor and the towns of Walkerville and Sandwich were amalgamated by provincial statute.'[11] In any event, by the 1960s, no one seemed to be arguing in Canada, as Bora Laskin was in 1937, that any form of provincial action to change munici-pal boundaries and structures customarily required local consent; nei-ther did anyone justify unilateral provincial action on the basis of what had happened 30 years before in Windsor.

In 1965 in Quebec, the provincial legislature merged 14 municipali-ties on Île-Jésus (immediately to the north of the Island of Montreal) to create the new city of Laval, with a population of 170,000. Most of the affected municipalities were opposed, but there were no claims that the provincial legislature was acting beyond its jurisdiction.[12] In 1967 New Brunswick merged the city of Lancaster with the city of Saint John. In 1970 Ontario amalgamated Port William and Fort Arthur to create the new city of Thunder Bay. Much more significant, however, was the cre-ation a year later of Winnipeg's unicity.

Winnipeg's Unicity

The municipal amalgamation in Winnipeg was brought about by a newly elected Manitoba New Democratic Party (NDP) government led by

Premier Ed Schreyer. The new government wanted to end the inter-municipal bickering, promote fiscal equity, and provide new mechanisms for citizen involvement in municipal government. The general theory was that the former administrative operations of Metro Winnipeg and its 12 constituent municipalities could be combined and centralized to create a powerful and effective bureaucratic machine that could be harnessed to solve the city's many problems, especially in the core. Financial resources for this purpose would be generated by the centralization itself and by the fact that the tax bases of the wealthier suburban municipalities would henceforth be shared.

Fortunately for students of municipal reorganization, the NDP government hired consultants to assist them with the process, and these consultants wrote a book about their experience.[13] One of its most fascinating parts is an account of the discussion and conflicts that went on within the Manitoba cabinet about 'the relationship between citizens and the proposed new city government'.[14] Some ministers advocated radically new mechanisms for citizen involvement and others were more interested in maintaining traditional forms. For a brief period of time, one of the consultants was James Lorimer, a Toronto-based activist and publisher, who submitted a paper calling for local community councils or corporations to be established within the unicity structure. Lorimer's paper proposed four potential responsibilities for such bodies:

1. To draw up and administer a community plan, to control land use densities and development within their locality;
2. To influence overall policies regarding other functions of local government;
3. To instruct the elected representatives sitting on the central city council as to what position to take up in that forum; and
4. Limited fiscal power to establish a mill [tax] rate to raise the funds necessary to pay for a limited staff, including social animators, whose task would be to reach out into the community for the involvement and participation of a large number of residents in the government of the city.[15]

Sidney Green, a convinced amalgamationist and a member of the cabinet committee developing the policy, rejected the Lorimer proposals. In a letter to a cabinet colleague he wrote:

> I believe that any attempt by the provincial government to implement . . . [Lorimer's] proposals will put us further behind relative to the reorganization of municipal government. . . . Specifically, I do not

believe that neighbourhood councils should have authority in the area of planning or development, nor do I believe that that they should have a residuary, albeit limited, fiscal power.

It is my view that the process of community involvement is one that must be created by the structure of the government itself and then by the political activities which are inspired as a result of intensified political interest. It is not artificially created by social animators.[16]

Green's position won out, a fact that explains why Lorimer was only briefly a consultant on the project. The conflict between Lorimer and Green was important. It happened in 1970, a time when enthusiasm for direct citizen involvement in government was at its peak. Lorimer was in the process of establishing himself as a prominent spokesperson for increased urban democracy. He was consulting for an NDP government that appeared outwardly sympathetic to his position. If ever there were a chance that Canadian municipal government would take a radically different path, this was it. But, in the end, the Manitoba NDP implemented a municipal amalgamation that was hardly radical. As we shall see later in this chapter, it was in Montreal 30 years later that more radical ideas for decentralization in an amalgamated city were actually implemented—and not as a result of an explicit plan to enhance citizen participation.

Unicity started in 1972 with a municipal council having 50 members and a mayor. The idea was that a large council elected from small single-member wards would give a wider variety of people a chance to be elected. But there were many complaints about its unwieldy size, and it has been progressively cut to its current size of 15. Each councillor sits on a community committee with other councillors from his or her area of the city. Initially, the legislation required that there be 13 community committees, but now no such legislative requirements remain. In any event, these committees could never make final decisions, even for their own areas. Still more problematic were the initial legislative requirements that each community committee be advised by a residents' advisory group to be elected annually at community meetings. Because these advisory groups were charged with advising committees that in turn had no decision-making authority, residents soon lost interest. There is very little about Winnipeg's current arrangements for citizen participation in municipal government that make it different from any other large Canadian city.

A frequent complaint from those concerned with social problems in Winnipeg's core was that the unicity council directed most of its resources to developing the suburbs. This was not surprising, since most of the voters in the amalgamated city lived in the suburbs. Fortunately for Winnipeg, its federal politicians, especially Lloyd Axworthy, were adept at attracting federal investment to the core. The tri-level agreement on Winnipeg's 'Core Area Initiative', first negotiated in 1981, has been especially important.[17]

When unicity began in 1972, its territory included 99 per cent of the population of the Winnipeg CMA. In 1992 a Progressive Conservative provincial government allowed the rural area of Headingley in the west of the city to secede and establish a new rural municipality.[18] This was just one of many factors that caused the city's share of total the CMA population to decline to 91 per cent by 2006.[19] Municipalities that are economically connected to Winnipeg are growing faster than the city of Winnipeg itself. As a result, in 2005 the Manitoba legislature approved a law to establish the Capital Region Partnership comprising the city of Winnipeg and 15 surrounding municipalities.[20] Even as a unicity, Winnipeg still has a metropolitan problem.

The Early 1990s: Newfoundland, Prince Edward Island, and New Brunswick

The 1990s were to bring a dramatic increase in legislated municipal amalgamations. The movement was barely noticeable in Newfoundland and Prince Edward Island, picked up steam in New Brunswick, and captured national attention with a huge amalgamation in Halifax in 1993. This activity in Atlantic Canada turned out to be a prelude to later events in Ontario and Quebec.

St John's, Newfoundland

The St John's Metropolitan Area Board was in existence between 1963 and 1991. Its main mandates were 'to control and administer the [unincorporated] fringe areas' and 'to provide a general control of development and growth in the Metropolitan Area'.[21] In 1978, it was given control of a provincially owned regional water supply system. At no time, however, did this Board have any jurisdiction within the territory of incorporated municipalities. During the 1970s and 1980s various proposals for the establishment of a form of two-tier government in the area emerged, but none was implemented.

Effective 1 January 1992 the provincial government enacted a significant municipal reorganization within the St John's CMA. Its main effect was to abolish the Metropolitan Area Board and to reduce the number of municipalities from 18 to 13. The city of St John's absorbed the municipalities of Wedgwood Park and Goulds and most of the area previously under the jurisdiction of the Board. For the city, this effort was of dubious benefit. In a 1996 position paper, the city stated:

> The Goulds and Metro Board lands are, for the most part, rural in nature with sprawling lineal urban developments. Upgrading infrastructure in these areas to a standard comparable to that in St John's will require a major infusion of funding. As the Province did not provide the necessary transition funding for capital works, and with development frozen until adequate infrastructure can be provided, these areas are seen more as a financial responsibility than an asset for the City.[22]

Also effective 1 January 1992, the city was given jurisdiction over the area known as Southlands, previously part of the suburban city of Mount Pearl. It was clear from the beginning that this particular transfer was a form of provincial compensation to the city. Because it was an expanding, serviced, suburban subdivision, tax revenues from it would grow over time. But what makes St John's especially important is that the 1992 reorganization charged the city with new regional responsibilities. Instead of establishing an upper-tier regional government, the city became responsible for providing the following services outside its boundaries within various parts of the wider region: public transit, solid-waste management, water supply, fire protection, and secondary processing of sewage.[23] The amalgamations were relatively minor, but the increased regional responsibilities for St John's were significant.

Charlottetown and Summerside

As befits Canada's smallest province, amalgamations in Prince Edward Island were modest. In 1994, the legislature approved the City of Summerside Act and the Charlottetown Area Municipalities Act. To create the new city of Summerside, the province amalgamated five distinct areas, three of which were incorporated as municipalities. In the Charlottetown area the province created three new or enlarged municipalities (Charlottetown, Stratford, and Cornwall) where there were once 18 municipalities and two unincorporated areas. In 2005, a close observer of PEI politics wrote:

> By creating three municipalities in the Charlottetown urban area, the province left unresolved the issues of effective urban planning and service delivery. Stratford, with a population of fewer than 6,500, and Cornwall, with a population of fewer than 4,500, are relatively small and, therefore, pressure for further rationalization is likely to arise.[24]

So far, nothing has happened. Meanwhile, the populations of the cities of Summerside and Charlotteown in 2006 were 14,500 and 32,174, respectively.

New Brunswick

In 1992, the provincial government in New Brunswick launched what appeared to be an ambitious program of municipal amalgamations. The city of Miramichi was created from 11 communities (including Newcastle and Chatham) in 1995[25] and four communities were amalgamated with Edmundston in 1998.[26] However, what did *not* happen in New Brunswick's two largest cities, Moncton and Saint John, is more interesting. In the case of Moncton, one of the suburban municipalities, Dieppe, has a French-speaking majority. Merging it with Moncton was seen as an assault on minority rights and was avoided. Because Dieppe was left alone, the English-speaking suburb of Riverview also was left undisturbed, and the three communities then worked on ways to increase inter-municipal co-operation.[27] In Saint John the provincial government at one stage declared itself committed to an amalgamation of almost the entire CMA. But it backed away when it became convinced that spreading the pension plan of the city of Saint John to suburban municipalities would cost taxpayers more than any amalgamation might save. Instead, it reduced the number of suburban municipalities from eight to three and created new regional institutions covering the metropolitan area.[28]

Cape Breton and Halifax

After receiving a report from his Task Force on Local Government, Premier Donald Cameron of Nova Scotia (a Progressive Conservative) announced in late 1992 that municipal amalgamations would go ahead in both Cape Breton and Halifax. But in May 1993, he was replaced as Premier by the former mayor of Dartmouth, John Savage (a Liberal), who proclaimed during the election campaign that amalgamation of the four Halifax municipalities was 'a crazy idea'.[29] In mid-1994, Savage sponsored legislation to amalgamate eight municipalities in the industrial part of Cape Breton (including Sydney, New Waterford, and Glace Bay) so as to create the single-tier Cape Breton Regional Municipality.[30]

In July 1993, the Savage government received the Interim Report of the Municipal Reform Commissioner for Halifax County, a document commissioned by its predecessor and prepared by C. William Hayward.[31] The report is a landmark document in the history of

Canadian municipal government. For the first time ever, a person charged with making recommendations about municipal amalgamation analyzed the budgets of the affected municipalities, and for each item declared how much money would be saved 'due to restructuring', i.e., by amalgamation. In the fiscal year 1992–3, Hayward estimated total spending for the four municipalities (Halifax, Dartmouth, Bedford, and Halifax County) to be $439.6 million. Savings resulting from amalgamation were stated as $9.8 million or 2.2 per cent of the total. It would be unfair to suggest that the Hayward report paid no attention to non-financial issues. There were claims that a unitary system would be 'more responsive, [that] accountability . . . [would] be improved, [that] planning . . . [would] also be more effective, [and that] [s]ounder financial decisions, particularly for capital spending, should also result.'

Hayward did acknowledge two potential difficulties. The first was that '[i]n larger municipal units citizens may view their governments as distant and inaccessible.' His solution was to provide for a network of 'community councils, community committees, community advisory committees and citizen advisory committees'. He briefly discusses the Winnipeg experience with such bodies, listing seven different reasons why they have not worked. He concludes the discussion by writing: 'The intention is to provide a way for citizens to have a greater say in the way services are provided, in what services are provided, and in the form the community will take. At the same time, whatever advantages can be obtained from a larger unit are kept. The result should be accessible and responsive government at the least cost.'

The second problem was the new municipality's sheer territorial size, especially the difficulties posed by the existence of a very large, sparsely populated rural hinterland. Here Hayward makes a telling admission: 'Those who look simply at numbers and conclude that the rural areas will be outvoted and ignored are overlooking the way the democratic process works. Councillors, like any other elected persons (absent party discipline), will support the concerns of others in an attempt to generate support for their own pet projects.'

Despite Premier Savage's initial declared opposition to amalgamation, he reversed his position in October 1994 as part of an overall strategy to reduce government spending and to promote economic development. The government's new policy caused the four affected municipalities to sponsor their own consultants' study of the proposed amalgamation. The consultants' report generally accepted Hayward's findings about cost savings, but pointed out that they would roughly be

cancelled out by increases in expenditures caused by 'policy harmonization' and 'service levelling'. By May 1995, the legislation establishing
the Halifax Regional Municipality was approved. There was relatively
little difficulty in the legislature because the main opposition party, the
Progressive Conservative Party, was in government when the whole process was started. The Halifax Regional Municipality (HRM), comprising more than one-third of Nova Scotia's population and more than 10
per cent of its territory, includes six community councils as part of the
package. Each of the 24 council members belongs to one. The community councils operate with small budgets and have limited authority to
make decisions about local matters, including zoning changes, as long
as they are consistent with overall HRM policies.

The Halifax amalgamation took place 15 years ago. Unlike the other
amalgamations in Atlantic Canada it created a major Canadian municipality. In 2006, there were 372,679 residents of the HRM, making it
the thirteenth most populous municipality in the country (between
two suburban municipalities: Surrey, BC, and Laval, Quebec). Most
residents of the urban part of the HRM are no doubt quite reconciled
to its existence and can hardly remember the inter-municipal squabbling among the city, the county, Dartmouth, and Bedford. Rural
residents still grumble about being overlooked and forgotten by their
urban counterparts, even though they are almost certainly better off
financially than they would have been without the amalgamation.[32]
Numerous accounts[33] suggest that the HRM has cost more money than
it has saved. Transition costs associated with the amalgamation were
$26 million; Hayward had predicted $10 million. In a comprehensive
study of the effects of amalgamating police services within the HRM,
James C. McDavid concluded that costs went up (in real-dollar terms),
and that there were fewer total police officers, lower service levels, and
no real change in crime rates.[34]

Since amalgamation the HRM has resolved long-standing disputes
about a regional landfill site and established a state-of-the-art compost-
ing facility. Benefiting from extensive federal and provincial grants, it
has also built a sewage treatment plant so as to stop the dumping of raw
sewage into Halifax harbour. Although the plant has suffered serious
operational difficulties, these can hardly be blamed on the amalgamation. Halifax has been relatively prosperous over the past 15 years, but
this cannot be attributed to amalgamation, either. It seems due much
more to the development of offshore natural gas and to the ongoing tendency of large organizations to choose the Maritimes' largest urban area
as the location of centralized office functions.

Ontario

The most significant changes in the history of Canadian local government occurred in Ontario in the 1990s. Amalgamations were a major part of the story, but there were also major changes to provincial–municipal funding arrangements and to the operation of the property tax system.[35] The fact that so much was going on at once has made it difficult to analyze the individual effect of any particular change. Some analysts believe that this strategy was part of the government's intention to provoke so much change all at once that 'politics as usual' would fundamentally change in some way that could only be better, at least for the provincial government. Others tended to see a more carefully crafted set of changes: the province would download its costs to municipalities; these extra municipal costs would be paid for by savings from amalgamations and/or by a property tax system that was fairer and more conducive to economic growth.

We need not concern ourselves with the inner workings of Ontario's provincial government. We need only to understand that the Progressive Conservative government elected in 1995 and led by Premier Mike Harris achieved office by tapping into an apparently profound public dissatisfaction with high deficits, high taxes, and perceived government waste.[36] Two-tier governments, with their perceived 'overlap and duplication', appeared to be a significant part of the problem. Much more so than the federal Conservative Prime Minister Brian Mulroney, who left office in 1993, Harris was committed to following in the footsteps of Margaret Thatcher in Britain and Ronald Reagan in the United States, both of whom had dramatically reduced the size of government in their respective countries. In the pages that follow, it is important to remember that the actions of the Harris government with respect to municipalities were only a part of its attempt to implement its overall plan, known as the Common Sense Revolution (CSR). But, as we shall see, sometimes only a minimum of common sense was evident in what it did.

The Harris government sponsored three major pieces of legislation that caused municipal amalgamations:

- The Savings and Restructuring Act, Schedule M, 1996
- The City of Toronto Act, 1997
- The Fewer Municipal Politicians Act, 1999.

Each will be discussed in turn.

The Savings and Restructuring Act, Schedule M, 1996[37]

Municipal amalgamations did not clearly appear on the Harris government's public agenda until 29 November 1995, the day on which Bill 26, the Savings and Restructuring Act, was first made public. Schedule M of Bill 26 defined municipal restructuring in terms of various forms of annexation and amalgamation; established a procedure for municipalities to arrive at locally agreed restructuring arrangements; and provided for the appointment, in the case of local disagreement, of a commissioner who would have the power to impose new boundaries and structures within the affected area. This innovation had much more to do with the 'arbitration' experience in London a few years earlier than with anything contained within the CSR. Significantly, Schedule M did not apply within two-tier regional governments or restructured counties, presumably because they had already been 'restructured'. In any event, nothing in the CSR prepared the way for all the amalgamations that would follow. By early April 1997, more than a year after the Bill 26 procedures had been in place, relatively little action had been taken with respect to municipal restructuring. The minister had approved 21 plans, which, in total, had reduced the number of municipalities by 50 (out of a total of 815). After this time, the pace of municipal submissions quickened, in large measure because of what had happened when the first commission appointed under the terms of Schedule M ordered the amalgamation of the city of Chatham with all municipalities within Kent County.

Chatham–Kent

The Chatham–Kent case deserves attention, not just for its influence on subsequent municipal behaviour, but also because it has been the most dramatic and extensive of all the restructurings carried out under the provisions of Schedule M. From April 1996 until January 1997, local politicians in Kent County—located halfway between London and Windsor in southwestern Ontario—had debated every conceivable alternative form of structure, from abolishing the county to merging all county municipalities into one. The only option that failed to win any degree of support was the idea that a complete merger should include the city of Chatham. On 22 January 1997, a member died of a heart attack on the floor of the county council while defending the county's continued existence. A week later a majority of members boycotted the next meeting, which was the last opportunity to arrive at a local decision. Seven municipalities had already asked for a commission to be appointed but the Minister of Municipal Affairs, Al Leach, had postponed action until it was clear that local agreement was not possible.

When he appointed a one-man commission on 6 February 1997, Leach prescribed that the area in question include both the city (population 43,000) and the county (66,000). This was probably the single most important decision in the entire process—and it was clearly taken by the government, not the commissioner. After issuing an initial report in which he had narrowed the choices—to a two-tier system including the city or a one-tier system including the city—the commissioner, Peter Meyboom, reported on 28 April that he had chosen the one-tier option. He acknowledged that only one of the 23 affected municipalities, the township of Tilbury East, supported his choice.

The commissioner's decision sparked predictable statements of outrage from various municipal politicians—but after a few days the storm passed. Part of the explanation for the lack of dissent is that both politicians and administrators realized they soon would be jockeying for position in the new structure and no one wanted to diminish his or her chances by arguing that it was illegitimate. Another reason is that the Toronto megacity battle was going on at the same time and, in comparison, Chatham–Kent seemed insignificant. But, unlike Toronto, amalgamation in Chatham–Kent did not require an act of the legislature; it merged entities (the city and the county) that were not previously linked for local government purposes; and it included a city, a large town (Wallaceburg, with a population of 12,000), and various less-populous towns, villages, and rural townships.

The real lesson from Chatham–Kent is that amalgamation was accepted, even though it was not popular. Residents demonstrated remarkably little public concern about the loss of their local governments as a result of one person's decision. It almost appeared that people in the area felt they deserved a form of punishment or strong medicine because their municipalities had behaved badly by not restructuring themselves before a commissioner was brought in. Remarkably, the government's claims that the appointment of a commissioner was a response to local wishes and that it was not responsible for the content of his decision seem to have been accepted. The fact remains, however: never before in Ontario (or in any other liberal democratic jurisdiction, it seems) has one person had the authority—and used it—to so dramatically alter an established system of local government.

'Voluntary' Amalgamations

From April 1997 on, Chatham–Kent became the horrible example that no one else wanted to follow. Counties scurried to get on with restructuring so they would avoid a commissioner telling them what they had to do. For many, the main object was to devise a plan that would not involve becoming linked with a populous urban centre whose residents could dominate the local political process. Ironically, if all the parties involved were convinced that no one in their group would request a commissioner, the urgency to take action was greatly reduced. This probably explains why some areas acted and others did not.

Prior to the passage of Bill 26, there were 815 municipalities in Ontario. Except for the creation of the megacity in Toronto, all of the municipal restructurings approved by the Harris government prior to 1999 were brought about under the provisions of Bill 26. As of 23 August 1999, the Harris Conservatives had caused the number of municipalities in Ontario to be reduced by 229 (28 per cent) and the number of elected municipal officials had shrunk by 1,059 (23 per cent). Some of the amalgamations were clearly defensive: assessment-rich townships merged with each other so that they could avoid pressure to share their assessment with poorer neighbours. The general pattern, however, was that villages or towns merged with neighbouring townships, despite long-standing local views that they were best kept separate due to significantly different needs for municipal services. The basic trade-off was that the village or town shared its richer tax base in return for political dominance (through representation by population on the new council) and for new room for urban expansion. Most of these amalgamations came about as a result of a fear that, if they were not done voluntarily, the Ontario government would step in and force amalgamations, possibly with less desirable partners.

Kawartha Lakes[38]

The city of Kawartha Lakes was the result of Commissioner Harry Kitchen's deliberations about the municipal structures of Victoria County, including the town of Lindsay. It came into existence on 1 January 2001 with a population of about 69,000. Unlike the situation in other government-forced Ontario amalgamations, the main citizens group opposing the merger, Voices of Central Ontario (VOCO), became even more active after the merger. VOCO gathered petitions with 11,000 signatures asking that the merger be undone and it conducted its own referendum in which 96.5 per cent of 6,209 voters expressed a preference to undo the amalgamation by returning to the previous system of municipal government.

During a visit to Kawartha Lakes in October 2001, Ontario's then opposition leader, Dalton McGuinty, stated that Ontario Liberals believed that past amalgamations could be reversed by a local referendum if there were a substantial demonstration of public support for the holding of such a referendum. He stated that the petition campaign in Victoria County 'has clearly met that threshold'.

On 15 April 2002 Ernie Eves succeeded Mike Harris as the Conservative Premier of Ontario. On that day Premier Eves appointed Chris Hodgson, the MPP for Kawartha Lakes, as his new Minister of Municipal Affairs. We do not know whether or not Eves took into account the fact that Hodgson for two years had been under intense pressure from his constituents to do something about Commissioner Kitchen's decision to create the city of Kawartha Lakes. In any event, as Minister of Municipal Affairs, Hodgson was in a position to act. With little or no publicity outside his own constituency, Hodgson agreed in November 2002 to put a 'minister's question' about demerger on the ballot in Kawartha Lakes at the time of the municipal elections in November 2003. He stated that the threshold for success would be the same as in any democratic election: 50 per cent plus one of the ballots cast. After a brief local debate about the wording of the question, Hodgson decided that it would be: 'Are you in favour of a return to the previous municipal model of government with an upper-tier municipality and 16 lower-tier municipalities?' A few weeks later—long before the date of the referendum—Chris Hodgson retired from politics. By the time the referendum actually took place, Dalton McGuinty was Premier.

The first and only government-sponsored de-amalgamation referendum in Ontario was held in November 2003. The campaign in Kawartha Lakes was hard-fought. Opponents of de-amalgamation warned of new costs and despaired at wiping out all the work that had been done in creating the new municipality. They especially highlighted fears that some of the smallest urban settlements could not afford by themselves to provide water to their residents because of the tightened provincial requirements for public water supply systems. With a turnout of 48 per cent of eligible voters, 16,802 voted Yes and 15,918 voted No. According to the rules of the game, the electors had approved the dismantling of the city of Kawartha Lakes. But nothing would happen unless the McGuinty government took action.

Clear victories for the Yes side were apparent in southern townships closer to Peterborough and Toronto and in the town of Bobcaygeon. Not surprisingly, the No side won by approximately 3,000 to 1,000 votes within the old county seat of Lindsay, the largest urban community in the municipality. Outside Lindsay, the decision to dismantle Kawartha Lakes was clear. The count was close only because voters in Lindsay supported the amalgamation, just as their council had supported the original plan to bring in a commissioner.

At the same time as the referendum, voters in Kawartha Lakes elected a mayor who supported de-amalgamation and a council that was also narrowly in favour. After their election, they attempted to convince the McGuinty government to implement de-amalgamation on the most favourable terms possible. But the process was ended by a letter from the Minister of Municipal Affairs dated 18 February 2004 in which he simply stated that the government 'will not be implementing the de-amalgamation of the city of Kawartha Lakes at this time.' The minister closed by stating that he would be open to considering other proposals for municipal restructuring. Despite its referendum, Kawartha Lakes was now in the same situation as every other merged municipality in the province: de-amalgamation was theoretically possible, but no one had any idea how it could or should be carried out. As we shall see later in this chapter when discussing amalgamations in Quebec, the de-amalgamation movement there turned out to be much stronger.[39]

The Megacity in Toronto

The largest and best-known municipal amalgamation in Canadian history came into effect on 1 January 1998 when the constituent parts of the Municipality of Metropolitan Toronto were merged to create a new city of Toronto. The amalgamation was the result of a separate piece of legislation applying only to Toronto. It is absolutely clear that, prior to their election in 1995, the Harris Conservatives had no intention of creating what was to become known as the 'megacity'. Their original intention was to eliminate the Metro level of government, but in the final analysis they could not figure out what to do with the municipal services for which Metro was responsible. Amalgamation eliminated such a concern because all municipal services within Metro's territory would henceforward be delivered by the same municipality. Other possible reasons for establishing the megacity were to swamp the left-wing voting majority in the old city of Toronto with more right-wing suburban voters in Etobicoke, North York, and Scarborough[40] and/or to enhance Toronto's global competitiveness.

Saving Money[41]

The government itself focused on saving money. On 23 November 1996—about three weeks before first announcing his megacity policy—Municipal Affairs Minister Al Leach commissioned a study to assess the financial implications of the amalgamation. The results were made public on 16 December. The next day, as part of his announcement, Leach made the following statement: 'Yesterday, our government released a study prepared by management consultants KPMG. It showed that over the first three years of its existence, a unified City of Toronto would save $865 million, then $300 million annually from then on.'

There are five important points to be made about this statement:

1. Although Leach acknowledged that 'it's not just about money', financial savings were unquestionably the main justification for the policy. Other references to 'developing a central core in the GTA and Ontario that is competitive and strong and has international presence in the world market' and to 'sweeping away artificial barriers' were not developed. For example, there was no consultants' study—or any other kind of justification—relating to the claim that the global competitive position of Toronto businesses would be improved as a result of amalgamation.

2. The KPMG study was much more tentative in its conclusions than Leach suggested. Commenting on the study the day before, Ron Hikel, a KPMG partner, stated: 'It's possible that the amalgamation could produce significantly lower savings than we have talked about, or even a negative result, a net increase in expenditures.'

3. The study referred to two types of savings: those that would result directly from the amalgamation ($82 million to $112 million annually) and those that would result from 'efficiency enhancements' ($148 million to $252 million annually). There was no necessary connection between amalgamation and the suggested 'efficiency enhancements'. Indeed, some of these enhancements related to services that already were amalgamated, such as the police service.

4. The study made no reference to the potential for increased costs due to the harmonization of service levels and collective agreements.

5. Leach made no reference to one-time transition costs, which were estimated by KPMG at between $150 and $220 million.

A month later, at the beginning of the second-reading debate in the legislature on the bill to create the megacity, Leach was still referring to the KPMG study as an important justification for his action. It should be noted, however, that his language had become more cautious: 'There are literally dozens of studies that have looked at municipal restructuring in the greater Toronto area. That includes a study done by KPMG that showed that amalgamation in Metro Toronto can save taxpayers up to $865 million over the next three years and $300 million thereafter . . . .'

As the protracted debate proceeded, government spokespeople tended to make fewer references to the KPMG study, but they kept referring to the elimination of duplication and overlap and the creation of more private-sector jobs. Saving money was supposed to be a result of eliminating duplication and a cause of private-sector job creation. By the government's own standards, savings from megacity were absolutely crucial. This is precisely why so much effort was expended while the provincial Conservatives were still in office (until 2003) to attempt to show that the megacity was indeed saving money.

During 1998, megacity residents noticed very few changes in how municipal services actually were delivered. This was because, except at the management level, nothing much changed. City workers simply carried on as before, without being integrated with respect to their day-to-day operations. It was largely because there were so few changes that most residents seemed to believe at first that amalgamation was a success. Those who had predicted chaos from the megacity were manifestly wrong.[42] In 1999, noticeable change began, but it was gradual and relatively well managed. In subsequent years, each new annual municipal budget seemed to bring some new financial crisis or other. The usual pattern was for the province to come up with some form of last-minute rescue plan.

In the immediate aftermath of the amalgamation, various attempts were made to demonstrate its beneficial financial effects. More than 10 years later it is clear that the city of Toronto has many financial problems, but it is impossible to trace them all to the amalgamation or to claim that they would have been absent had there been no amalgamation. Probably the most definitive statement about the financial effects of the amalgamation was made in April 2003 when the Toronto City Summit Alliance, a coalition of over 40 civic leaders from the private, voluntary, and public sectors in the Toronto region, argued that Toronto needed 'a new fiscal deal' in part because 'The amalgamation of the City of Toronto has not produced the overall cost savings that were projected. Although there have been savings from staff reductions, the harmonization of wage and service levels has resulted in higher costs for the new City. We will continue to feel these higher costs in the future.'[43]

Opposition to the Megacity
Although initial polling by the government suggested that the public supported amalgamation,[44] public opinion quickly turned negative. The Harris government enjoyed significant political support in Metro's suburban municipalities, but residents soon expressed dissatisfaction with the prospect of being joined with the city. Various polls and informal referendums demonstrated considerable levels of discontent.

But the most surprising and flamboyant opposition came from within the city of Toronto, especially from a group called Citizens for

Local Democracy (C4LD) led by community activist and former Toronto Mayor John Sewell. C4LD held open weekly meetings throughout most of 1997, organized street protests, and attempted to form links to amalgamation opponents in the suburbs. But C4LD was primarily committed to defending the central city's 'progressive' municipal policies concerned with protecting inner-city neighbourhoods against disruptive development, providing free recreation programs to all residents, and supplementing local social services with additional municipal services for the poor. Suburban opponents of amalgamation had little interest in such objectives; one of the reasons they feared amalgamation was the prospect of having to use their tax contributions to finance what they considered 'frills' and 'extravagances'. But C4LD and suburban opponents could at least agree that forcing the amalgamation was undemocratic in that it denied local citizens the ability to make their own decisions about their local institutions. Such a political agenda could not attract much in the way of support from poor and working-class residents or from Toronto's many recent immigrants, and even C4LD remained primarily a middle-class movement.[45] Nevertheless, the relatively brief existence of C4LD remains hugely important for any student of Canadian urban politics because it dramatically demonstrated that large numbers of citizens can be so committed to their municipality and its policies that they will commit huge amounts of time and resources to defending them. The emergence of C4LD was certainly a big surprise for the Harris government.

C4LD and the lower-tier municipalities of Metro Toronto challenged the amalgamation legislation in the courts, arguing that it violated political rights that were implicit in the Canadian Charter of Rights and Freedoms. Creating a new Yiddish word in the context of the Toronto debate, Justice Stephen Borins of the Ontario Court's General Division ruled that the provincial legislature was fully entitled to enact municipal amalgamations. He stated that the arguments he had heard in his court were political, not legal. 'It may be', he wrote in his decision, 'that the government displayed *megachutzpah* in proceeding as it did, and in believing that the inhabitants of Metro Toronto would submit . . . without being given an opportunity to have a real say in how they were to live and be governed.' Nonetheless, 'the *Charter* does not guarantee the individual the right to live his or her life free from government *chutzpah* or imperiousness.'[46] The Ontario Court of Appeal upheld Borins's decision.

Community Councils
During the legislative debates and the court case, the government placed considerable emphasis on the fact that the ward boundaries for the new

council would not cross the old municipal boundaries and that the territory of each of the old municipalities would be served by a 'community council' comprising the members of the city council for that territory. Although the community councils were given no decision-making authority, the government claimed they would be important mechanisms for local views to be channelled to the new amalgamated municipalities. In many important respects this was true. The new council ended up with such large agendas that almost all recommendations from community councils about local zoning changes were accepted without debate. One of the operational problems was that the community council of East York was responsible for only about one-sixth as many people as the one for the old city of Toronto. After the passage of the Fewer Municipal Politicians Act in 1999 (to be discussed in the next section), the number of community councils was reduced to four (Toronto and East York, Etobicoke and York, North York, and Scarborough). But they can hardly be considered as particularly 'local' because the number of residents that each covers is larger than the number of residents in all but a handful of the most populous Canadian municipalities. More important than the boundary changes was a legislative change in 2006 that allowed the Toronto city council to delegate some decision-making authority to community councils. Significantly, however, community councils still cannot make final decisions on zoning changes; nor can they levy any form of local tax.

Political Developments in the Megacity
The megacity's first municipal election was in the autumn of 1997. The mayor of North York, Mel Lastman, an apparent political ally of the Harris Conservatives, defeated Barbara Hall, the mayor of the old city of Toronto, to become the first mayor of the megacity. Most of the newly elected councillors supported Lastman, who did a good job in steering the new institution towards stability and acceptance but a bad job in making the kind of drastic changes that would have been needed to capture dramatic cost savings. Lastman was re-elected in 2000. But in 2003, David Miller, a left-leaning councillor from the central city, won the mayor's job after Lastman retired. Like Lastman, he was generally supported by a majority of councillors and he, too, was re-elected (to a four-year term) in 2006. The great irony, of course, was that from 2003 to 2010, the amalgamated city of Toronto was governed by a left-leaning mayor and council, a prospect that had seemed impossible to the many supporters of C4LD in 1997. Not only did the megacity policy not save money, it was not even successful in producing a permanent

conservative majority on the new city council. It is hard to imagine how the Toronto amalgamation could have been less successful in meeting its apparent objectives.

The Fewer Municipal Politicians Act

After the passage of Toronto's amalgamation legislation in 1997, the Ontario government still faced some difficult municipal issues. There was much dissatisfaction with two-tier regional government. After receiving reports from four 'special advisers' (who were like the commissioners in Chatham–Kent and Kawartha Lakes but without final decision-making authority), the Minister of Municipal Affairs announced that each of the regional municipalities of Ottawa–Carleton, Hamilton–Wentworth, and Sudbury would be amalgamated on 1 January 2001 into one new city: Ottawa, Hamilton, and Greater Sudbury, respectively. The Regional Municipality of Haldimand–Norfolk, comprising six lower-tier municipalities, was to be reorganized at the same time into two single-tier counties, Haldimand and Norfolk. The same legislation reduced the size of the Toronto city council to 45. The government could rightly claim that the various components of the legislation eliminated the positions of 203 municipal politicians, an accomplishment that was designed to appeal to the notion that any reduction in the number of elected politicians must be beneficial.[47]

Unlike the amalgamation in Toronto, the creation of the new cities in Ottawa, Hamilton, and Greater Sudbury meant that many small villages and large tracts of rural and sparsely populated land became united with densely populated urban areas, resulting in significant political tensions. The rural residents have successfully argued for more representation on the new councils than their numbers warrant so that their political influence will not be completely swamped by the urbanites. The granting of such extra representation causes urban councillors to claim they are being discriminated against. In 2009, at least one urban councillor in Ottawa was arguing that the amalgamation issue should be revisited while some rural residents were arguing for secession. There was similar rural discontent in Hamilton and Greater Sudbury.

Conclusions from the Ontario Experience

Between 1996 and 2001 the number of municipalities in Ontario was reduced from 850 to 445.[48] After 2001, neither the Conservative government nor its Liberal successor has had any interest in pursuing municipal reorganization in any form. The relatively brief frenzy of amalgamations at the end of the 1990s has had a profound influence on

Ontario municipal government, but it is difficult to point to any significant improvements. One of the most sympathetic assessments comes
from David Siegel:

> The new municipalities cover larger areas, thus improving fiscal equity
> across the entire area and improving the ability to deliver certain ser-
> vices such as land-use planning, public transit, streets and roads, and
> economic development. Hardly anyone believes that the new system
> saves money as was hoped, but the larger municipalities have larger
> budgets and are therefore able to hire more highly qualified people.
> Surveys in some municipalities, though, have indicated that citizens
> have seen no change in the quality of service delivery.[49]

But the lack of any positive achievements from municipal amalgamations
in Ontario did not stop Quebec from pursuing the same course of action
in the early 2000s.

Quebec

Municipal amalgamations have been on the political agenda in Quebec
since the mid-1960s. Between 1961 and 2000 the number of municipalities in the province was reduced from about 1,750 to just over 1,300.[50]
But the biggest changes took effect in 2001 and 2002. Unlike Ontario,
they were initiated in large measure by the mayors of larger cities, especially Pierre Bourque of Montreal, who urged the provincial government
to follow Ontario's example and legislate the amalgamation of suburban municipalities to the central city. The central-city mayors were convinced that such amalgamations would be financially beneficial to their
residents in that suburbanites would be required to pay a greater share of
central-city costs. The amalgamations resulted from two laws approved
by Quebec's National Assembly in 2000. The first, Bill 124, authorized
the Minister of Municipal Affairs to amalgamate municipalities not contained within the census metropolitan areas of Montreal, Quebec City,
and the Quebec portion of the Ottawa CMA. The second, Bill 170, specified amalgamations within these CMAs and established metropolitan
communities for Montreal and Quebec City (discussed briefly in the
previous chapter). In addition to Montreal, which is the main focus of
this section, the laws also had the effect of amalgamating neighbouring
municipalities with Quebec City, Longueuil (on the south shore of the
St Lawrence across from Montreal), Hull, (now known as Gatineau),
Chicoutimi (now known as Saguenay), Sherbrooke, and Trois-Rivières.

Numerous other amalgamations took place involving rural areas, small towns, and villages.

The Montreal Amalgamation[51]

In 1999, Mayor Pierre Bourque of Montreal was already working hard to accomplish his objective of amalgamating all the municipalities on the Island of Montreal into a new city of Montreal. The suburbs—francophone and anglophone alike—were resisting. The political dynamics were almost identical to what they were when Mayor Drapeau of Montreal launched his similar campaign in the 1960s. The main difference was that, at the level of the Quebec government and in the anglophone municipalities, there was a heightened sense of the linguistic implications. For the Quebec government, the concern was that an amalgamated city of Montreal would have only a razor-thin francophone majority and could conceivably be captured politically by declared non-sovereignists, even by partitionists who could threaten to have Montreal separate from a newly independent Quebec. For the anglophone suburbs, the concern was that, under the provisions of Quebec's Charter of the French Language, their territories would lose their bilingual status if they were absorbed by a city whose majority was French-speaking. In the mid-1960s, sovereignty, partition, and language laws were not serious political issues. In the late 1990s they were.

But these issues could not be raised by mainstream politicians, francophone or anglophone, provincial or local. This is why they do not appear in any official reports, including the Bédard report on municipal fiscal issues,[52] a report that favoured a drastic reduction of municipalities on the Island of Montreal, but not total amalgamation. The unspoken linguistic problem with any such proposal is that it involved, at a minimum, the merger of some francophone-majority municipalities on the West Island into a new and populous anglophone-majority municipality. In practical political terms, this simply was not possible.

The point, of course, is that total amalgamation seemed equally impossible. This was confirmed in June 1999 when both Premier Lucien Bouchard and Louise Harel, the Minister of Municipal Affairs, explicitly rejected the plan espoused by Mayor Bourque. Premier Bouchard was quoted as saying, 'One island, one city—that's not in the picture for us. But one knows, meanwhile, that one cannot leave the situation just as it is.'[53] A modest reorganization, such as one that would bring the inner suburbs of Westmount and Outremont into the city of Montreal, might have made sense to those who wanted to bolster the social and economic strength of the central city, but it would have been seen by many as an arbitrary and stopgap measure that could be achieved only at a huge political cost.

By September 1999, the option of complete amalgamation was back on the table. As with Premier Harris in Ontario when he had promised to do something about municipal structures in the Toronto area, the option of amalgamation re-emerged for Premier Bouchard after his own outer suburban MNAs rejected the option of a strong, directly elected authority for the entire Montreal region. In April 2000, at the same time as it released its White Paper on municipal reform,[54] the government appointed chairs of advisory committees for municipal structures in Montreal, Quebec City, and the Outauois area. For Montreal, the chair was Louis Bernard.

Bernard's report was made public on 11 October 2000. Although the report called for the creation of a single city of Montreal covering the entire Island, it also noted that it was important 'to preserve the tie between the citizens and their immediate political environment, to reinforce the feeling of being attached to the place where one lives and to favour the development of social and cultural diversity.' Bernard also made reference to the need to 'preserve the cultural and historical heritage of diverse communities'. Nevertheless, the report made no explicit reference to language.[55] There was no evidence that Bernard consulted anyone other than municipal officials.

The report created a crucial political challenge for Montreal's larger suburban municipalities, especially the anglophone ones, because it went much further to accommodate suburban demands than anyone had predicted. Bernard proposed the creation of 27 boroughs, each to have a council that would have the authority to manage a significant range of local services and to levy a tax on property within the territory of the borough to pay for these services. Boroughs that were formerly autonomous suburbs could even maintain responsibility for negotiating collective agreements with their unions, a provision that enraged the existing unions within the city of Montreal. Never in Canadian municipal history had a serious proposal for an amalgamation been accompanied by such a high degree of political and financial decentralization. Indeed, the most compelling criticism of the Bernard plan was that it effectively involved the creation of a three-tier system of local government for the Island of Montreal: the newly created Montreal Metropolitan Community (MMC) covering the entire metropolitan area (see Chapter 7); the new city of Montreal covering the Island; and the 27 boroughs.

The Bernard report caused a split within the Montreal suburban municipalities. Unlike many mayors of francophone-majority suburbs, the mayor of Westmount, Peter Trent, announced that he was completely opposed to the Bernard plan, the main reason being that suburban municipalities would lose their separate corporate existence.[56] He believed that whatever autonomy the proposed boroughs began with would inevitably be eroded as the amalgamated city of Montreal became established. On 15 November 2000 the government announced the content of Bill 170. Boroughs were not given any authority to levy taxes or to enter into collective agreements. It appears that Premier Bouchard decided he could not take on both union and suburban opposition at the same time.[57] When suburban municipalities such as Westmount objected to the Bernard report just as strenuously as the unions in the city of Montreal, it was not surprising that Premier Bouchard opted to gain at least some significant political support by satisfying the unions and limiting the autonomy of the boroughs. Nevertheless, even without any authority over taxation and collective agreements, the boroughs were given more legal authority over local services than similar bodies that were established after amalgamation in other Canadian cities, including Halifax and Toronto.

The language issue emerged in a much more public way at the same time. The government announced that boroughs formerly within anglophone municipalities would retain their bilingual status under the Charter of the French Language. This policy required in the West Island that the territories of francophone municipalities be grouped together to form a single borough, even though their territories were not contiguous. Furthermore, the section of Bill 170 concerning Montreal opened with the declaration that 'Montreal is a French-speaking city.' Taken together, these various provisions indicated how carefully the government had balanced the various linguistic imperatives it faced, both from within the Parti Québécois and from the anglophone minority.

The government's careful handling of the language issue demonstrated that its imperatives were actually more important than the amalgamation itself. In many respects the very existence of the boroughs is merely a mechanism to work around the language issues that the amalgamation created. But why did the Bouchard government choose the amalgamation option in the first place? One answer, as we have seen, is that the alternative of creating a new, stronger metropolitan authority was not acceptable to its own core supporters in the outer suburbs. Just as Harris amalgamated Toronto in order to be shown to be doing something to address an apparent crisis of governance in the province's largest city, so did Bouchard amalgamate Montreal. Bouchard had the added justification that he was merely following Ontario's example.[58] Unlike Harris in Ontario, Bouchard and his colleagues pointed to the desirability of equalizing taxes and services across the new city.

The first elections for the new council of the amalgamated city of Montreal were held in November 2001. Notwithstanding his great success in promoting the amalgamation, Mayor Bourque lost his bid for re-election to Gérald Tremblay, a former provincial Liberal cabinet minister whose support was based mostly in the amalgamated suburbs.

The De-amalgamation Movement[59]

In October 2000, during the time when the legislation for amalgamation was dominating Quebec's political agenda, the opposition Liberal Party held a policy convention. One of the resolutions, approved with little deliberation or fanfare, committed the party to a policy of allowing referendums in the territories of amalgamated municipalities so that residents could de-amalgamate and re-establish their former municipalities. A few weeks later, party leader Jean Charest was wildly cheered at a large anti-amalgamation rally in the Montreal suburb of Pointe Claire when he restated his party's commitment to implementing a de-amalgamation process.

From December 2000 until March 2003, de-amalgamation was not on the agenda of Quebec politics. At one point, the Liberal critic for municipal affairs was quoted as saying that his party 'would not be unhappy' if the issue went away. Unnamed aides to Mayor Tremblay stated that 'senior Liberals have told them privately any provincial demerger framework law would either exclude Montreal or fix the details so as to make demergers highly unlikely.'[60] There was no mention of de-amalgamation in the official Liberal platform released in September 2002. Focus instead was on the myriad complications of merging multiple bureaucracies. In many ways the Montreal amalgamation was far more difficult than Toronto's. In Montreal more than four times as many municipalities were involved. More important still was the fact that, within the borders of the old city of Montreal, the amalgamation involved decentralization to boroughs that had never existed before,[61] a factor that was totally absent from the Toronto restructuring.

Most former suburban politicians had either withdrawn from local politics completely or had become part of the power structure of the amalgamated municipality. The main exception was Peter Trent, the former mayor of Westmount. Because de-amalgamation was the only mechanism for restoring Westmount's corporate existence, he had become a fervent advocate. In mid-January 2003, he took the initiative, on behalf of various anti-amalgamation citizens' groups across the province, to hire a retired judge, Lawrence Poitras, to write a report about the feasibility of demergers. The report was released on 17 March 2003, five days after the beginning of the provincial election campaign that brought Jean Charest to power. On the first day of the campaign Premier Bernard Landry had attacked the Liberal position by stating that, 'Just having such an idea disqualifies them from having the ambition to govern Quebec.'[62] The combination of the unprovoked attack by the PQ on the idea of municipal de-amalgamation and the release of the Poitras report ensured that de-amalgamation would be an important issue during the campaign.

The Poitras report said little that was new. It did point out that, unlike Ontario, Quebec had actually experienced a few cases of de-amalgamations, notably affecting Buckingham in 1974, Gatineau in 1988, Côte-Nord-du-Golfe du Saint-Laurent in 1989, and Bonne-Espérance in 1993.[63] It claimed that inter-municipal services for de-amalgamated municipalities could be provided by a combination of special-purpose agencies and inter-municipal agreements.[64] The combination of Landry's initial attacks and the release of the Poitras report forced Charest to take a position. The same day that the Poitras report was made public Charest stated that he was still committed, during the first year of his mandate as Premier, to providing a mechanism for citizens to decide on de-amalgamation, even though he personally would not campaign for or against. Charest won the election. De-amalgamation was clearly an important issue as the Liberals unexpectedly won seats in areas where opposition to amalgamation was strong, such as in Saguenay.

Making De-amalgamation Possible

Once Mayor Tremblay of Montreal became convinced that the new Charest government was going to provide for de-amalgamation referendums, he decided he had to be able to present a viable case for keeping the amalgamated city together, so he requested that the Quebec National Assembly approve legislation (Bill 33) to allocate still more authority to the boroughs and to have their mayors (i.e., the chairs of the borough councils) directly elected. Defenders of the original amalgamation, such as the former mayor of Montreal, Pierre Bourque, objected on the grounds that borough decentralization had gone so far that the original purposes of the amalgamation were being undermined. Nevertheless, the Charest government effectively gave Tremblay what he asked for.

Formulating its legislation for the de-amalgamation process proved much more difficult. The decisions that had to be made were numerous.

What would trigger a de-amalgamation referendum? How much support for de-amalgamation at the referendum would be necessary for it to be implemented? How would it be implemented? Who would pay for what?

The most important and difficult set of questions involved the nature of the subsequent relationship between any de-amalgamated municipality and the municipality from which it separated. The government decided that many common services, including firefighting, would be under the jurisdiction of an 'urban agglomeration council' that would bring together representatives of both the central municipality and the de-amalgamated ones. Exactly how such a council would work was not determined until long after the de-amalgamation referendums took place.

The government's legislation stated that, for a de-amalgamation referendum to take place, 10 per cent of eligible voters within the territory of a former municipality would have to sign a petition requesting such a referendum. This happened within 87 former municipalities that formed parts of 29 amalgamated municipalities. The referendums were held on 20 June 2004.[65] For a de-amalgamation to be approved, 50 per cent of the votes cast representing 35 per cent of the total eligible voters had to be affirmative. This threshold was met in 31 former municipalities that were part of 12 different amalgamated municipalities. Fifteen of the affirmative decisions for demerger were within the amalgamated city of Montreal. The de-amalgamated municipalities regained their corporate identity on 1 January 2006.

Municipal Complexity in De-amalgamated Montreal

Montreal's 15 de-amalgamated municipalities have roughly the same functions and structures as they did prior to 2002, with the important exception that they are no longer responsible for firefighting. The city of Montreal, however, is now quite radically different than it was prior to 2002. The most important difference is that it now comprises 19 boroughs. These boroughs are *not* distinct corporate entities; they remain part of the municipal corporation of the city. The territory of each borough comprises one or more electoral districts of the city, each of which has a directly elected mayor who also sits on city council. All but one (Outremont) of the boroughs has at least one other city councillor on its borough council and some have four. Because each borough council must have a minimum of five members, 40 borough councillors also are elected to serve only at that level. In total there are 64 members of the Montreal city council, including the mayor of Montreal, who also serves as the mayor of the downtown borough of Ville-Marie, and the 18 mayors of the other boroughs.[66] The borough councils have the same functional responsibilities as the de-amalgamated municipalities, but they cannot levy their own taxes without the agreement of the city council. In actual practice, boroughs rely on city council for an annual grant of funds. Boroughs can hire personnel, but such personnel are employees of the city and are subject to the city's collective agreements.

Municipal functions within the city that are not the responsibility of the boroughs are the corporate responsibility of Montreal and are administered by its employees, but decision-making with respect to these functions is the responsibility not of the Montreal city council but of the agglomeration council. The only remaining functions of the Montreal city council are to allocate funds to the boroughs and to make decisions about the position the city will take with respect to issues coming before the agglomeration council. The mayor of Montreal appoints 15 of Montreal's city councillors to the agglomeration council and 15 representatives come from the de-amalgamated municipalities. Votes are weighted according to population, so city representatives have 87 per cent of the total votes. The result is that de-amalgamated municipalities have virtually no power with respect to functions under the control of the agglomeration council. They simply have to pay their share of the costs based on their relative share of property assessment within the agglomeration.

Conclusions from the Quebec Experience

In the aftermath of the amalgamations and de-amalgamations of the early 2000s, there were 1,139 municipalities in Quebec,[67] down only marginally from the number at the beginning of the millennium. In 2003, when the Charest government took office, the MMC was in place, anchored at the centre by the city of Montreal, which included all of the Island of Montreal, comprising 27 boroughs having significant local authority. The MMC is still there, but 15 municipalities have de-amalgamated from the city, and the political authority of the Montreal city council has been fragmented, both by the establishment of the agglomeration council and by the strengthening of the remaining 19 boroughs. How are we to assess these changes? The easiest response is to conclude that what has happened is a complete disaster. De-amalgamation has meant nothing in practice; amalgamated municipalities have been needlessly dismembered; and the resulting system of inter-municipal relationships is both incomprehensible and hopelessly undemocratic. But there are other possible interpretations.

First, it is no small accomplishment that the Charest government, unlike the McGuinty government in Ontario, followed through on its promise to create a mechanism for de-amalgamation. The process was accepted as legitimate by the de-amalgamation activists, who worked hard to collect signatures to trigger referendums and then, in some cases at least, to win them. Second, the government did absolutely nothing to harm the post-amalgamation fiscal position of the central cities, including the city of Montreal. De-amalgamated municipalities escaped neither old nor new fiscal burdens. What they regained was the undisputed authority to tax their property-owners to pay for local services at whatever rate they desired.

With respect to arrangements for the agglomeration council and the strengthened role for the boroughs, we can at least conclude that the Charest government has been innovative. Who would have thought 10 years ago that a single Canadian municipal corporation could have three distinct levels of political decision-making authority (borough, city, agglomeration), including 19 directly elected mayors? And that, superimposed on all this, would be another layer of metropolitan government. Such a system exists not only in Montreal, but in Quebec City and Longueuil, as well.

Conclusion

Provincially imposed municipal amalgamations in Canada seem to have come in waves. The precedent was set in Windsor in 1935; more followed from the mid-1960s to the early 1970s, the most important being the creation of the Winnipeg unicity in 1971; and from the early 1990s to the early 2000s the eastern Canadian provinces experienced an intense period of amalgamations, with Toronto and Montreal being the most important examples. But since 2002, there have been no forced amalgamations, and Quebec has experienced de-amalgamations. What can we learn from this strange chronology?

Odd as it may seem, waves of imposed municipal amalgamations are probably best thought of as fads. One jurisdiction starts for reasons peculiar to its own particular circumstances. Then, others follow, fearing that they might somehow be falling behind. In Canada, this particular fad has been weak in the provinces west of Manitoba, although some have argued that rural Saskatchewan is in dire need of municipal consolidation.[68] British Columbia seems to have escaped the fad altogether, perhaps because its regional districts have dealt effectively with inter-municipal services and disputes since the late 1960s. In any event, it would surely be difficult to demonstrate that the people of British Columbia are somehow worse off than other Canadians because their provincial legislature has not imposed municipal amalgamations.

At some point in the future, when a new generation of politicians know little about our last wave of municipal amalgamations, some will trot out arguments about the need to save money, enhance economic competitiveness, or ensure equality in urban tax levels and services. They will propose municipal amalgamations as a solution. Hopefully, citizens will demand to examine carefully the experience of the 1990s and 2000s. What will the policy-makers of the future conclude?

RESOURCES

For an entertaining and instructive video by Ryan Young about how citizens of Sainte-Anne-de-Bellevue reacted to their village's forced amalgamation with the city of Montreal and how they were successful in the de-amalgamation referendum, see *The Village Resists*. The video can be ordered from: Vision 9 Productions, 25 Lamarche, Sainte Anne de Bellevue, Quebec, H9X 2A9, (514) 457–9758.

STUDY QUESTIONS

1. What is the significance of the Windsor amalgamation in 1935?
2. Is it possible to combine a large, amalgamated city with increased opportunities for small-scale decision-making and citizen participation? Explain your reasoning.
3. In what ways, if any, do you think amalgamation makes a city better able to compete for new economic development?
4. Do you think Premier Charest of Quebec was wise to have kept his promise to allow for a form of municipal de-amalgamation? Do you think Premier McGuinty of Ontario should have done the same thing? Explain your reasoning.

PART III

Politics and Management in Canadian Urban Government

9 Municipal Politics, Councils, and Elections

M uch of the material in previous chapters has been about the struc-tures of local government: why they exist; what they do; how they have changed. Because the Constitution of Canada places 'municipal institutions' under provincial jurisdiction, any student of the structures of Canadian local government has to know a great deal about decisions made by provincial legislatures. So far, we have paid more attention to what provinces have decided than to how municipal councils work. In this part of the book we change our focus and begin to look at what actually goes on within municipal politics. We shall not be able to ignore provinces altogether, however, because they are responsible not just for deciding about the functions and boundaries of municipal governments, but also for making the basic rules of the game for municipal politics. We need to know about these rules in order to understand Canadian municipal politics. But understanding politics at any level involves far more than understanding formal rules. We have to understand informal rules and conventions and, more important still, we have to understand how certain people acquire power to get things done or to prevent other people from doing what they want to. This part of the book, therefore, is primarily about power in Canadian municipal government. Chapter 9 is introductory as it outlines some of the important factors involved in understanding Canadian municipal politics, councils, and elections.

Municipal Politics and Political Parties

The formal source of power in municipal government is the municipal council, the members of which are elected. Later in this chapter we shall be examining how these elections actually work in Canada. But, before getting caught up in these important details, we need to know something about how Canadians (and people in other democratic countries) have conceptualized municipal politics over time.

Municipal Politics as a Reflection of Social Elites

Anyone who has ever lived in a small town knows that many community decisions are made not in open meetings of official organizations such as municipal councils but in private, informal get-togethers of a few local notables. To the extent that this really is the case in whatever size of town we might be studying, the formal rules of municipal government are of very little importance, because everyone understands that what happens in municipal councils is a mere rubber-stamping of decisions that have already been made elsewhere. Often, the really powerful people in small towns are elected to municipal councils. If they are, their power in the community does not derive from being a municipal councillor but from being part of the small informal group that decides things. If they do not run for local office, they are not any less powerful, because real decisions are not made in the municipal council anyway.

This way of viewing power in local communities was given considerable credence in the mid-twentieth century by various American sociologists who studied 'community power'. One of the most famous of these studies looked at how local decisions were made in Atlanta, Georgia. The author discovered a small and powerful elite that, indeed, effectively made most of the important local decisions, whether such decisions were formally within the purview of the municipal council or not.[1] 'Community power' studies generated huge controversies in American political science,[2] some of which we shall address in subsequent chapters.

The most comprehensive study of power in a single Canadian small town was written by David M. Rayside in 1991. It focused on Alexandria, in eastern Ontario. This is what Rayside had to say about community power in Alexandria:

> Because Alexandria's town council is preoccupied with avoiding controversy, and because initiatives for change often come from outside municipal government circles, understanding power and influence over community affairs requires complex analysis. Earlier in the area's history, political, social, and economic hierarchies coincided more clearly, and locating a single set of notable figures with influence in a variety of domains would have been relatively straightforward. . . . In late twentieth-century Alexandria, influence over community affairs in some ways still seems concentrated in a small and relatively cohesive

circle of associates, in ways that parallel the findings of much of the community power literature. In other ways, though, influence seems dispersed, hardly located within the town at all, let alone within a small circle of notables.[3]

Much of Rayside's book is aimed at showing how governmental and corporate institutions outside Alexandria were increasingly making the most important decisions for the community. This is a theme largely neglected in the American literature, in part because it was written decades earlier before such centralizing forces gained so much strength, and perhaps because American state governments have been more careful about intruding on local decisions. In any event, Rayside gives us few reasons to study small-town politics in Canada: no one wants to launch local political conflict and important decisions for the town are made somewhere else besides.

In the early days of major Canadian cities, provincial governments established municipalities and left them relatively free to decide local issues for themselves. But cursory glances into the backgrounds of the kinds of people who tended to get elected to municipal councils suggest that service on a municipal council for a community's elite was not unlike service today on the board of a local art gallery or symphony orchestra. Election to municipal councils was 'arranged' for the right people; being a member was very much part-time and continuing with one's normal business activities was completely normal. For such people, making decisions about city business was in large measure simply an extension of their other business activities.

In Canada's major cities today membership on municipal councils is most assuredly not dominated by social and/or economic elites. The presidents of the big banks are unlikely to appear as participants in Toronto's municipal election campaigns; the same is true in Calgary of the big energy companies. Sociologists would say that this is a sign of functional specialization and role differentiation, a characteristic of all complex urban societies. But Marxist sociologists (and political scientists) would be quick to point out that such specialization and differentiation do not prevent the major economic forces in society from *controlling* decisions apparently made by democratically elected politicians. In the next chapter, we shall examine a variant of this general claim: that because the main economic role of Canadian urban municipal governments is to control urban development, these governments are really controlled by urban developers. But, whatever we might think of the general validity of Marxist analysis in the early twenty-first century, we must in our analyses of municipal decision-making keep in mind the possibility that governmental structures and elections might not be very important, because economic forces—some difficult to observe and to understand—might be the key determinants of local political outcomes. A related possibility, explicitly stated by Rayside, is that important decisions for most local communities are made somewhere else by big corporations or by central (provincial or federal) governments.

Municipal Politics and National Parties

By the mid- to late nineteenth century, a larger proportion of adult males had been granted the vote and political parties had become increasingly important in mobilizing voters. In Europe, working-class voters were mobilized primarily by parties on the left: Marxist or social democratic. In North American cities, where there were usually many recent immigrants, parties often mobilized votes through 'urban political machines'.[4] The key characteristic of such machines was that their organizers (or 'bosses') promised material rewards—often, jobs—in return for votes. In the United States, a huge literature is devoted to these urban political machines, much of it attempting to determine whether their levels of obvious corruption were justified by the great social gains experienced by the ethnic groups (especially the Irish) who benefited from their newly found political power.

Bosses of American urban political machines were key figures in national political parties—usually the Democrats, but not always. As recently as 1960, the boss of Chicago's Democratic machine played a key role in the election of John F. Kennedy to the presidency of the United States, perhaps by dumping a few crucial ballot boxes into Lake Michigan instead of having them tilt Illinois towards Kennedy's opponent, Richard Nixon. By promising electoral support for state and national political candidates, urban bosses could gain more resources (jobs, contracts, projects) for their own supporters. Regardless of their national importance, these bosses maintained considerable local autonomy. In Europe, however, socialist parties tended to run candidates at all levels of government and candidates for local office often had little room to manoeuvre in addressing local issues.

Some examples of urban political machines and of socialist parties in local politics crop up in Canada but, compared to elsewhere, they have been minimal. On the other hand, and more so than perhaps in any other democratic country, Canadian municipal politics is generally not influenced by national political parties. Again, unlike most federations, Canada has political parties at the federal and provincial levels that—except for the New Democratic Party (NDP)—are structurally separate from each other. Because municipalities are under provincial jurisdiction, we might at least expect *provincial* parties to be involved in municipal politics, but little evidence suggests that is the case. To understand why, we must know about the reform movement that transformed the politics of North American cities over a hundred years ago.

The Era of Municipal Reform

By the second half of the nineteenth century, large cities in North America had become unhealthy, dirty, and corrupt. The urban reform (or Progressive) movement was about cleansing cities, in every sense of the word. The movement marked the beginning of professional social work, urban planning, public health, public libraries, and serious attempts to promote temperance and honest and efficient municipal government. This last concern is most relevant to our focus. With regard to municipal government, reformers wanted to rid the cities of political machines, most obviously by minimizing the role of political parties in municipal politics. They proposed various institutional reforms to achieve this objective, some of which will be examined later. For the current discussion, we need only consider their desire to have small city councils composed of members elected not for their party qualifications but for their potential to make policy decisions based on the overall best interests of the city. Reformers wanted the administrative apparatus of the city to be taken from party hacks and turned over to trained professionals headed by a city manager, someone with special skills in co-ordinating and controlling a wide range of city services in accordance with modern administrative practices.

The North American reform movement had strong support in Canada, especially in the largest cities of Montreal and Toronto.[5] As other cities grew larger, especially in western Canada, reform influence spread there as well. For our purposes in this section, the most important effect of the reform movement was to convince most Canadian urban municipal voters that political parties served no purpose in municipal politics because they introduced political factors into decisions that should be based only on sound business-like and technical principles. One of the best-known reform maxims was that 'There is no political way to pave a road.' In pre-reform times, it was assumed that road-building was the lucrative privilege of the supporters of whoever was in power. One of the great reform accomplishments was to convince most people that contracts for roadwork (and other municipal activities) should go only to those who can best balance quality and price. A hundred years ago, decisions to build particular roads were generally assumed to be good decisions; now decisions about building particular roads are almost always subject to genuine political debate. In short, it remains the case that there is no political way to pave a road; the only way to get approval to build a road is through a political process, usually in a municipality.

Because of the ongoing influence of the reform movement, most candidates and voters in municipal politics seem to value the non-partisan approach. They do not want political parties of any kind to be overtly involved in municipal elections even though parties often play important roles that are generally invisible, except to the most careful of observers. Especially in smaller cities, it is common for successful candidates to proclaim their independence from all parties and their attachment to making decisions in accordance with 'sound business principles'. Few of the candidates who make such declarations are aware that they are in fact parroting the talk of anti-party reformers from over a hundred years ago.

Local Political Parties in Canada

An important student of American urban politics, Paul Peterson, has suggested that political parties that exist solely at the municipal level cannot be sustained because the issues are not sufficiently important.[6] In national politics parties are formed and sustained around major political issues such as war and peace, free trade, and social class. The media pay close attention to what the parties do and individual voters form relatively long-lasting party attachments of varying degrees of intensity. Such factors generally do not exist at the municipal level. The main political cleavage in municipal politics is often between pro-development and anti-development groups, but such a division seems incapable of generating ongoing party allegiances, perhaps because people's attitudes to development tend to be affected by where it is taking place (near or far from home) or the state of the local economy at any particular point in time. In any event, two major Canadian cities—Vancouver and Montreal—provide evidence to suggest that, in the Canadian context at least, Peterson might be wrong.

Vancouver

In the 1936 Vancouver municipal election, candidates from the Co-operative Commonwealth Federation (CCF, predecessor of the current NDP) won three of eight seats on the city council. As we have seen, the idea of socialists running for municipal office was not unusual, especially during the Depression. But their success caused local Liberals, Conservatives, and business people to come together in 1937 to form the Non-Partisan Association (NPA). By the end of the decade the CCF 'was spent as a municipal force'.[7] The NPA—a political group that runs candidates in municipal elections committed to keeping party politics out of municipal government—has been a dominant force in Vancouver politics ever since.

In the late 1960s, two other local parties formed: the Committee of Progressive Electors (COPE) and The Electors Action Movement (TEAM). COPE was clearly on the left of the political spectrum; TEAM was in the centre. In 1968 TEAM's candidate for mayor, Art Phillips, won the election. When Mike Harcourt was mayor as an independent between 1980 and 1986, he was generally supported on council by TEAM. Harcourt later became leader of the provincial NDP and Premier of British Columbia, but TEAM faded away. Gordon Campbell was the NPA mayor of Vancouver from 1986 to 1993 and the Liberal provincial Premier since 2001. He resigned as premier in early November 2010, although he will stay on until a successor is chosen sometime in 2011. COPE controlled the Vancouver city council from 2002 to 2005, with its leader, Larry Campbell (whose previous work as city coroner inspired a TV show, *Da Vinci's Inquest*), as mayor. But COPE could not survive the stresses of governing. Larry Campbell decided not to run again and was appointed to the Senate in Ottawa as a Liberal. Politically moderate members of COPE split away to form Vision Vancouver, which took control of the Vancouver city council in 2008 when its leader, Gregor Robertson, became mayor. The most recent NPA mayor of Vancouver was Sam Sullivan, 2005–8.

Montreal

In 1954, the Civic Action League, a citizens' group committed to cleaning up corruption in Montreal, decided to run candidates for municipal office. Its mayoral candidate was Jean Drapeau. To everyone's surprise, Drapeau won his election, but the League did not win control of the council. In 1957, Drapeau was defeated by Sarto Fournier, a Liberal senator who also had the support of Premier Maurice Duplessis. When Drapeau ran again in 1960 he created his own Civic Party that was totally under his own personal control. With Drapeau as mayor, it controlled Montreal city council for 26 years, thereby becoming the most successful municipal political party in Canadian history. During that time Montreal built its subway system (the Métro) and hosted Expo 67 and the 1976 Olympic Games. The Civic Party effectively ceased to exist when Drapeau decided not to seek re-election in 1986.

Since that time three separate municipal parties have held majorities on the Montreal city council: the Montreal Citizens' Movement (MCM) led by Mayor Jean Doré (1986–93);[8] Vision Montreal, with Mayor Pierre Bourque (1994–2001); and Montreal Island Citizens' Union, Union Montreal since 2007, with Mayor Gérald Tremblay (2002–). The MCM was a left-leaning party that had opposed Mayor Drapeau for many years. After losing the 1993 municipal election, it went into a period of decline before merging with Tremblay's party in 2001. Mayors Drapeau, Bourque, and Tremblay constructed their own parties in order to win the mayor's office and a majority on city council. In 2009 Vision Montreal chose a new leader and candidate for mayor in Louise Harel, the former Parti Québécois Minister of Municipal Affairs who had sponsored the legislation for amalgamation in Montreal. Although she failed to defeat Mayor Tremblay, she certainly perpetuated Vision Montreal as a strong opposition party and as a defender of a strong and centralized city of Montreal. Union Montreal, on the other hand, supports the decentralized borough system that Mayor Tremblay implemented in a fruitless attempt to prevent de-amalgamation in 2004.

Provincial Support for Municipal Parties

Quebec and British Columbia are the only provinces whose municipal election laws provide for the existence of municipal parties, although in the latter they are referred to as 'elector organizations' or 'slates'. The BC law even governs contests to seek nominations from elector organizations or slates and the Quebec law provides that party candidates rely exclusively on party fundraising and expenditures, half of which is refunded by the municipality for all candidates (including independents) who receive more than 15 per cent of the total vote. Quebec law also provides that both 'government' and 'opposition' parties in municipal councils of cities with populations over 50,000 receive municipal funding for staff and research.

But, as we have seen, even such provincial support does not guarantee the stability of municipal political parties. If anything, all it guarantees is that different municipal politicians at different elections will try to create their own temporary parties in order to benefit from various provisions of the law, such as getting the party name on the ballot or (in Quebec) receiving public subsidies for election campaigns. The most stable municipal political parties in Canada have been the NPA in Vancouver, which is committed to keeping political parties out of municipal politics, and the Civic Party in Montreal, which lasted no longer than its founder's career as mayor. Arguably the NPA is stable because its members share ideological interests in defeating attempts by NDP supporters to control

the Vancouver city council. Perhaps Vision Vancouver will be more successful in unifying such people into a cohesive local party on the left
of the political spectrum. In Montreal, it is interesting to note that the
2009 municipal election saw a former provincial Liberal cabinet minister (Mayor Tremblay, leader of Union Montreal) being challenged by a
former Parti Québécois cabinet minister (Louise Harel, leader of Vision
Montreal). Their respective areas of strong support in the election certainly reflected the areas of strength of their respective former provincial
parties. Perhaps the Quebec provincial party system has already taken
over the municipal party system in Montreal. We shall be in a position to
know better after the next Montreal election in 2013. In any event, it is
likely that the only way we shall obtain stable municipal political parties
in Canadian cities is to import provincial parties in one form or another.

Whether or not there are political parties in municipal councils is a
key question in the governance of our major cities. Many (including no
doubt those in the NPA in Vancouver) will agree with the reformers of
more than a hundred years ago that parties have no place in municipal
government and that municipal councils should be more like boards
of directors of large businesses than like provincial or federal legislatures. Others look enviously at the political coherence and predictability provided by a Prime Minister or Premier backed by a disciplined
majority party and wish that such a state of affairs could be replicated
in municipal government, as it has been for much of Montreal's recent
history.[9] But the problem here, of course, is that many citizens do not
want city governments that seem as remote and centralized as a majority government in a parliamentary system. How could ordinary citizens
mobilize to convince such a government to change its mind on important issues about local development, for example? Some would point to
Mayor Drapeau's Montreal as the horrible example of how strong local
parties eliminate meaningful local participation. Others will point to
Drapeau's accomplishments and conclude that we need parties such
as his to enable municipal leaders to achieve ambitious goals. As we
confront various issues in this and later chapters relating to city governance, the desirability or undesirability of municipal political parties
will never be far from the surface.

Size and Structure of Municipal Councils

Councils are the formal decision-making mechanisms for municipalities. How they are structured is important both for municipal elections
and for the process of decision-making. Provincial legislation ultimately

determines how municipal councils are structured, but this same legislation often allows municipal councils to make some structural decisions themselves. In this section we shall be less concerned with the sources of legal authority for structural decisions and more concerned with the nature and implications of the various structural alternatives. There are three main variables in studying council structures:

- size;
- representation by wards or at-large or some combination of both;
- committee system.

It is important to realize that these three variables are interconnected with each other and, to a lesser extent, with the existence or not of municipal political parties. In the 'parliamentary' model of municipal councils, which has historically been present in Britain and other European countries, we expect to find political parties in large councils where members are elected by wards (i.e., electoral districts) and in which much important business is carried out by council committees. In the 'reformed' or 'council-manager' model, found in many American smaller towns and suburbs and in some Canadian ones, we find the absence of political parties, small councils elected at-large (i.e., all members elected from the entire municipal territory), and no committees. As we shall see, however, municipal councils in most major Canadian cities do not fit neatly into one model or the other.

Council Size

When we consider the universe of municipal councils in Canada, we must not forget that there are not only single-tier municipalities but also the two supra-regional authorities in Quebec and 86 regional or upper-tier municipalities in Quebec, 30 in Ontario, and 27 in British Columbia. Listed in Table 9.1 are the populations and sizes of the councils for the two supra-regional authorities, the two largest regional ones, and the 10 largest single- or lower-tier ones (all numbers include the mayor and/or presiding officer).

There are two ways to assess council size. The first has to do with the number of people per councillor. By this measure, the supra-regional and regional authorities listed here are irrelevant, because all of their members are elected to serve also at the lower tier. In other words, the existence of these authorities adds nothing to the total number of councillors in the area. For those concerned only with the costs of having councillors, it would seem that, in theory at least, it would be better to have more people per councillor than fewer. In this regard, Calgary

Table 9.1 Sizes of Canadian Municipal Councils

	Population	Number of Councillors	Residents per Councillor
Supra-regional			
Montreal Metropolitan Community	3,600,000	28	
Quebec Metropolitan Community	727,000	17	
Regional			
Metro Vancouver	2,116,581	37	
Regional Municipality of Peel	1,159,405	25	
Single- or lower-tier			
Toronto	2,503,281	45	55,628
Montreal**	1,620,693	65	24,934
Calgary	988,193	15	65,879
Ottawa	812,129	24	33,838
Edmonton	730,372	13	56,174
Mississauga*	668,549	12	55,712
Winnipeg	633,451	16	39,591
Vancouver*	578,041	11	52,549
Hamilton	504,559	16	31,535
Quebec City**	491,142	38	12,925

*Indicates municipality is a lower-tier municipality in a two-tier system.

**Indicates the municipality is part of a supra-regional authority. Number of council members does not include councillors serving only at the borough level.

Sources: Websites of the relevant municipalities and the *2006 Census of Canada*.

is the most efficient council in the country, with each member serving an average of almost 66,000 people. Although Ontario's Progressive Conservative government in the 1990s led by Mike Harris took great pride in reducing the total number of municipal politicians in the province, there is no inherent virtue in having fewer elected municipal politicians rather than more. Even if cost is the only criterion—and it surely cannot be in a democratic society—it is likely that individual councillors serving large numbers of residents (as in Calgary) will require more support staff to do their job, thereby raising total costs associated with elected officials. The exact cost of councils in various municipalities can be subject, in theory, to empirical investigation, but obtaining comparable data across municipalities is difficult, if not impossible. In any event, contrary to common public perceptions, the costs attributed to councils are never more than 1 per cent of municipal operating budgets, and usually considerably less, so whenever concerns about such costs are expressed, they are inevitably exaggerated.

People concerned with the quality of representation, rather than cost, will probably believe that it is better to have fewer people for each member of council. This argument was advanced by the opponents of the Toronto amalgamation during the court case that challenged the legislation, but as we saw in the previous chapter, the judge effectively stated that such concerns were none of the court's business because provinces had great freedom with respect to municipal institutions. In any event, Toronto's ratio of people to councillors is lower than that of Calgary, Edmonton, and Mississauga. In order to have low ratios, councils must either be very large, as in Montreal and Quebec City, or municipal populations must be small, which is the case in the vast majority of Canadian municipalities.

The second way to assess council size is in relation to effectiveness of decision-making. This is far from easy, because there is no objective way to determine effective decision-making. In principle, however, we can likely agree that the process involves an opportunity for all points of view to be expressed and listened to by all the people who actually make the decision. A very small council in which everyone thinks the same way is not likely to be effective, unless it is the council for a very small municipality in which all the residents think the same way. For large cities, such a state of affairs is impossible. A large non-partisan city council (Toronto's, for example) might enable all points of view to be expressed, but with 45 members and meetings that go on for days there is much frustration among members and often little listening. That is why there have been frequent proposals for change, many of which involve taking steps to reduce council size, to encourage the creation of municipal parties, and/or to enhance the leadership capacity of the mayor (to be discussed in Chapter 11).

Montreal and Quebec City both have large councils and political parties. As in parliamentary systems, the parties help structure the debate so that meetings can often be relatively short. Parties with a clear set of policies have a good chance of implementing them, in part because there are few ways of stopping them. Much of the real debate, however, occurs within the parties and behind closed doors so, in comparison with other cities, citizens often have only a limited understanding of what is really going on. Vancouver has political parties and a small council but, as we shall see in the next section, this is primarily because it and other BC municipalities have at-large elections.

The most common arrangement in Canadian municipalities is to have non-partisan councils with memberships between about seven and 25. Councillors sit around a table, often shaped like a horseshoe, with the mayor presiding. In this setting they interact directly with each other and occasionally convince their colleagues to change their minds on the basis of new information and new arguments. Although there might be factions on the council, voting alliances usually shift from issue to issue. Such meetings can be very messy, with much confusion about wordings of motions and implications of various courses of action. But decisions get made and some get reported in the local media. More than any other venue in the Canadian governmental system, a relatively small non-partisan municipal council is a place to watch representative democracy in action. Much of what goes on in public in federal and provincial legislatures is political theatre and has little to do with decision-making. In these systems, real decisions get made in party caucuses and in cabinets, but such meetings are not open to the public or the media. Openness of municipal council meetings is an important issue and will be discussed below.

Wards versus At-Large Elections

It generally is agreed in democratic societies that elections should determine who holds public office, but much disagreement prevails about how the electoral systems should work. For example, in Canadian federal and provincial politics, numerous proposals are put forward to switch from a system in which legislatures are composed of individuals who obtain the most votes in particular electoral districts to one in which multiple members are elected from much larger districts in accordance with the relative strength of the various parties. The problem with the current system is that, if a Liberal wins each district with 51 per cent of the vote, Liberals will occupy all the seats in the legislature. The problems with the alternative system are that there are no longer distinct local members, and party organizations attain considerable power in determining who gets elected. In the general absence of parties in municipal politics in Canada, there is no way that the second system—proportional representation—could be implemented. But that has not stopped frequent searches for better systems.

In Canadian municipal government electoral districts are generally known as wards. Most large municipalities (except in BC) are divided into wards and in most cases the one candidate at an election who gets the most votes is declared the councillor for that ward. But in some municipalities more than one member is elected from each ward. In these cases, voters in each ward have as many votes as there are councillors to be elected. If two are to be elected, the top two vote-getters are the winners.

Three main questions associated with drawing ward boundaries are:

- Should they be relatively equal in population?
- Should they attempt to encompass particular 'communities of interest' and, if so, which ones?
- Who draws the boundaries and when?

Population

The idea that wards should have roughly equal population would appear to be self-evident in a democracy, where the objective presumably is to make everyone's vote in a given municipality roughly equal in weight. There can be debates about whether the measure of ward size should be population or number of eligible voters. Some parts of particular municipalities might harbour relatively higher numbers of people too young to vote or recent immigrants who are non-citizens.[10] In most cases population is the measure, justified on the grounds that the person who is elected has to represent all residents, not just those who are eligible to vote.

In the last decade in Ontario, however, the effects of some municipal amalgamations have caused the issue of equal populations of wards to be revisited. The problem is that some amalgamated municipalities have large areas of rural land in which relatively few people live. Prior to amalgamation, such people were used to governing themselves in their own rural-based municipalities. After amalgamation, they found themselves swamped by urban voters with little interest in rural issues. The rural people felt the least that could be done for them was to establish rural wards with smaller populations. When Ottawa refused to do this in the early 2000s, rural residents appealed to the Ontario Municipal Board. In a 2003 decision, the OMB overturned a city bylaw establishing wards that generally mixed rural and suburban areas. In the decision, the OMB stated:

> The evidence supports the contention that the City of Ottawa does contain rural communities with historical economic and social differences. Rural concerns are not always understood in the context of urban policy and rural concerns often require a special understanding of rural issues. Members of council elected by urban voters may not always have the experience or the willingness to represent rural points of view. One-dimensional representation will eventually be harmful to the local economy.[11]

The end result was the establishment of three rural wards whose average population was 34 per cent lower than the average for the city as a whole.[12] Such an arrangement would be illegal in Quebec because legislation relating to municipal elections provides that: 'the number of electors in an electoral district must not deviate by more than 25 per cent from the average for municipalities with less than 20,000 inhabitants. This percentage is 15 per cent for municipalities with over 20,000 inhabitants.'[13]

Communities of Interest

The OMB decision on the Ottawa wards recognized that rural areas comprise communities of interest that should have their own wards. But how are communities of interest determined in urban areas? First, it should be recognized that, however they are defined, urban communities of interest are unlikely to have populations of similar size, so it is unlikely they could each ever have their own ward. If different neighbourhoods have to be put together or split, how should it be done? One way is to build wards along major arteries leading into the core area, thereby creating 'pie-shaped wards'. Another way is to unite areas of similar social class or ethnic backgrounds. The latter approach is more commonly accepted. In a recent decision about wards in London, Ontario, the OMB stated:

> It seems obvious to the Board that a pie-shaped Ward system could be inequitable based upon 'communities of interest' because in each Ward there are more votes in the outer suburban areas. A possible result could be that suburban 'communities of interest' are overprotected by City Council to the detriment of other 'communities of interest.'[14]

Who Decides and When?

Municipal councils generally are responsible for drawing ward boundaries but, as we have seen above with respect to Ontario, some form of appeal from council decisions usually exists, which is entirely appropriate because incumbent councillors do have a special interest in how the boundaries are drawn. In Quebec, municipal councils are required to review the boundaries every four years prior to a municipal election. In other provinces, including Ontario, councils are not required to regularly review boundaries. As a result, wards can become quite unequal in population over time without the council taking any action at all. Ontario citizens can appeal to the OMB to take action, but such appeals are rare.

At-Large Elections—Vancouver

Reformers a hundred years ago wanted to get rid of wards. They thought that ward councillors were largely incapable of looking at the interests of the city as a whole and meddled too much in administrative matters affecting their wards. Similar criticisms are made today,[15] which explains why some continue to extol the virtues of at-large municipal elections in which all councillors are elected by all voters in the entire municipality. There is no reason why ward and at-large elections cannot coexist. Indeed, this is exactly what happens in Thunder Bay, Ontario, where five councillors (and the mayor) are elected at-large and seven more are elected from each of seven wards.

A strong case can be made against at-large elections. Indeed, the United States Supreme Court has struck down local at-large electoral systems on the grounds that they can submerge the electoral strength of racial minorities. If a racial minority made up 40 per cent of the population of a city and if they were concentrated in a particular area (which is usually the case), they could easily end up with no council representatives if the majority voted as a bloc against minority candidates. But such a possibility has not prevented British Columbia from legislating a municipal electoral system in which at-large elections are the default option for all municipalities. No municipality has opted for wards.[16] The issue has been particularly controversial in Vancouver and merits our attention.

Vancouver's history with at-large elections is a fascinating story, told well by Thomas R. Berger in the opening pages of his 2004 report on electoral reform in Vancouver. The following account closely follows Berger's.[17] After incorporation in 1886, Vancouver voters elected a mayor and 10 councillors, all at-large. But the third bylaw passed by the council established a five-ward system for the next election in which two councillors were elected from each ward. Except for a brief 'interregnum' from 1920 to 1923 when the city experimented with a form of proportional representation, Vancouver operated with a ward system until 1936, although the number of wards was occasionally increased. Starting in 1916 only one member was elected from each ward. In 1935 both business groups and the CCF (not an unusual alliance among reformers) convinced the provincial government to hold a referendum on an at-large system for Vancouver. With only a 19 per cent turnout, 69 per cent of voters supported the change and the city has had an at-large system ever since.

After World War II the at-large system became deeply unpopular with left-leaning citizens who watched the NPA dominate elections and saw few residents of the poorer east side of the city get elected to city council. In a referendum in 1973, 58.9 per cent of voters rejected a return to a ward system. In 1978, 51.7 per cent approved such a change but the commission charged with implementation designed such a complex new system that the council refused to approve it. Not surprisingly, the city held another referendum in 1983 and a ward system was approved by 57 per cent of the voters. By this time, the issue had become extremely polarized between left and right, with conservatives seeming to believe that wards were a kind of Communist plot. In any event, the (conservative) Social Credit Premier, Bill Bennett, decided that he would only approve of a ward system if 60 per cent voted in favour and this requirement was written into law. In a referendum in 1988, 56 per cent voted in favour of wards but, in accordance with the law, nothing happened. By 1996, the 60 per cent rule had been repealed, but Vancouver city council drafted 'a confusing multi-question referendum that produced a 59 per cent majority in favour of retaining the at-large system, with a 54 per cent margin favouring wards if the existing system were to be changed.'[18] Once again, nothing happened.

In his 2004 report (p. 40), Berger recommended a 14-ward system with one councillor from each ward. He pointed out that west-side residents were much more likely to vote than east-side residents (39.2 per cent and 31.5 per cent, respectively in 2002). With a ward system a lower turnout rate would not affect the ability of east-siders to obtain their own representation, but with an at-large system it did. Another referendum was held in October 2004 and this time there was a 54 per cent majority in favour of retaining the at-large system. Analysis of results by polling district suggests, not surprisingly, that the wealthier west side voted in favour of the at-large system and the poorer east side voted for wards. Polls near the centre of the Indo-Canadian community supported wards (as one would expect from a geographically concentrated minority group) but polls where many Chinese Canadians lived were against.[19] Wards remain an important issue for some voters but most elected officials, including the Vision Vancouver members who control the council, do not seem enthusiastic about taking it up yet again. In no other Canadian city—and possibly in no other major world city—have issues about the nature of the municipal voting system been so important in local politics.

Committee Systems

Most municipal councils, especially larger ones, establish a network of council committees to facilitate their work. Council committees are different from special-purpose bodies because the former are made up exclusively of councillors and they have no legal authority to make any decisions unless they have explicitly received delegated authority from the council as a whole. They also must be distinguished from citizens' advisory committees, whose members usually are appointed by council from among ordinary citizens to advise on particular topics. Council committees are usually one of two types: standing and special. Standing committees are permanent, although membership might change relatively frequently. They are charged with reviewing particular kinds of agenda items (roads, land-use planning, corporate services, etc.) before they are decided on by council as a whole. In larger municipalities, standing committees are especially suitable as a mechanism to hear delegations from the general public prior to decision-making. As the name implies, special committees are established for a particular purpose and cease to exist when the purpose has been accomplished.

Some councils establish executive committees that, because of their leadership responsibilities, will be discussed in Chapter 11. At the opposite extreme is a 'committee of the whole', which is nothing more than the whole council meeting under relaxed rules of order. Committees of the whole are used by many councils whenever they want to engage in extended and informal discussions of a particular topic. They are also often used by councils—especially by councils that do not have standing committees—as a mechanism for hearing delegations from citizens. Because all committees must report formally to the council, committees of the whole present the unusual spectacle of a group of people reporting to itself.

Strange as it may seem to some, committee systems can be controversial. Experience with committees in some municipalities in the past suggests that, if councillors stay on particular standing committees for a long time, they can come to think that they (rather than staff) are actually meant to be administering the service or function, rather than advising the council as a whole about policy decisions that need to be taken. This has been a particular concern in rural areas, such as in Ontario counties, where councils can sometimes be large and administrative staff relatively weak. Sometimes councillors can get so wrapped up in the business of their particular committee that they simply do not pay much attention to other issues facing the council, assuming that members of other committees are looking after other business. To the extent that this pattern exists, no one is looking after the interests of the municipality as a whole.

Reformers in the early twentieth century were particularly concerned about the toxic combination of powerful standing committees and ward councillors whose sole focus was on their own wards. For such people, membership on the roads committee, for example, was simply a mechanism for getting better roads in their own wards. This problem is just one of many reasons why reformers favoured small councils, at-large elections, weak committees, and highly qualified staff. As we have seen, the city of Vancouver fits this model. Its council does have standing committees, but all members are on all committees. The committees serve mainly as mechanisms to hear delegations from the public, not as potentially independent sources of decision-making power.

In large cities with large city councils, such as Toronto, committees are essential. Without them, items of municipal business would never be properly considered because each of the thousands items before council each year could not possibly be fully debated by the full council. As it is, agendas are very full because all recommendations from standing committees need to be approved by the full council before being implemented. At least, council members with minimal interest in particular items know that the items likely have been properly reviewed in the appropriate committee.

Openness of Meetings and of Votes in Municipal Councils

Unless provincial statutes state otherwise, municipal councils can make their own rules about the extent to which their meetings will be open or closed to the media and the public.[20] Many provincial statutes originally included provisions stating that regular council meetings were to be open to the public but that the council could decide to go *in camera* (into a closed meeting) at its discretion. Such discretion was necessary. If, for example, the council were deliberating about how much money it would be willing to pay for a parcel of land, a public discussion would disadvantage the municipality in any negotiations with the seller. In extreme cases, however, some councils have used their discretion to form a committee of the whole, discuss virtually all items of business *in camera*, and then rubber-stamp the decisions after the committee reports to the open council meeting. Such action has caused much media and public discontent, causing provincial legislatures to approve various laws to tighten the rules. Ironically, any provincial cabinet that formulated such legislation prior to its introduction in the legislature would meet in private, so the public would not know the original positions of the various ministers on such matters. Legislatures have little difficulty meeting in public because, prior to debates, the government and even the opposition have already worked out their positions. Unlike municipal councils, legislatures rarely have to make decisions about ongoing negotiations with private bodies or individuals.

In most provinces it is now extremely difficult for councils to meet in private unless they explicitly declare that they are dealing with such matters as commercial transactions, labour relations, personnel issues affecting identifiable individuals, or the receipt of legal advice. Laws about open meetings generally extend to informal meetings or to 'retreats' in which councillors might be expected to plot long-term strategy in a relaxed atmosphere away from the media and the public.[21] In short, municipal councils are required to carry out their public business in public. Although enforcement mechanisms vary from province to province, there must now be very few municipal councillors in Canada who are not aware of the legal requirements for openness.

Open meetings imply that the voting decisions of individual members of council on items of council business also are public. Sometimes, tracking down councillors' voting records is difficult. Most decisions in most councils are made without any vote—they are deemed to be approved because no one objects. If all such items were included in any analysis of council votes, there would be little variation among members because the vast majority of all votes cast would be affirmative. For other matters, however, votes in many councils are taken by an informal show of hands, and no record is kept unless a councillor requests a recorded vote. If the recorded vote is taken orally, then members at the end of the roll call can take account of others' votes as they decide what to do. Electronic voting prevents such a problem and leaves a clear record about who has voted for what on every issue about which there is disagreement. Municipal decision-making will be more transparent and open when all councils have adopted such technology.

Is Being a Municipal Councillor a Full-Time Job?[22]

In principle, every municipal councillor can decide how he or she wants to do the job. In a small municipality, where remuneration is negligible, a councillor with lots of time and independent financial resources could work on municipal business all the time. In large municipalities, where councillors might get paid around $100,000 annually (not counting budgets for office supplies and staff support), a councillor could still carry on a private business, only showing up for the occasional meeting at city hall. Re-election, of course, would be unlikely because attentive media would soon note the slacking off. The point here is that there is really no job description for a municipal councillor. Even within the same municipality, councillors take radically different approaches to their jobs, which is not necessarily a problem—variety among democratic representatives is not wrong.

But councils do have to make decisions that affect the nature of the job and therefore the kind of people who run for municipal office. Such decisions are of particular importance in mid-sized cities, where expectations of municipal councillors might be ambiguous. One such decision seems very simple on the surface: when to schedule official meetings of council and its committees. If meetings are regularly held in the daytime, the implication is that being a councillor prevents regular full-time employment. The attendant implication is that remuneration should be relatively high, unless it is assumed that council membership really is being reserved for retirees, autonomous professionals (e.g., lawyers in private practice), or people with independent incomes. But what does a 'relatively high' income mean? For a recent university graduate, the prospect of earning $80,000 a year as a councillor might seem enormously attractive; the attraction might be considerably less for a 40-year old accountant with three children and a mortgage.

For reformers who wanted to minimize the role of traditional politics in municipal government, the favoured policy would be to hold evening meetings and pay councillors relatively little. The expectation would be that councillors would stay clear of details and show up at council meetings only to make decisions on matters presented to them by their highly qualified staff of municipal professionals. Attractive as such a model might seem, it runs into difficulty when residents expect councillors to respond immediately to requests for help with neighbourhood issues or when the local media uncover improper actions by trusted municipal staff. In fact, the pressure in municipal government is towards making the position of councillor closer to full-time rather than to part-time. In many cities, councillors are expected to attend meetings at city hall in the day and meetings with residents in the evenings. The job becomes more than full-time and not suitable for people with young families even if remuneration is exceptionally high.

As the job of councillor becomes closer to full-time, municipalities as organizations become much more complex. The old reform-style model of a professional staff working in isolation from politicians—except at times of formal meetings—becomes totally out of touch with reality. In our major cities today, councillors are interacting with staff at all levels all the time. In places like Toronto, members of councillors' personal staffs are interacting with municipal staff all the time, often asking officials to bend normal practices to meet the needs of particular constituents. Thus, the management function in municipalities often becomes more difficult than in private companies—where members of boards of directors have nothing to do with mid-level managers—or in federal or provincial governments—where individual legislators hardly have more influence on public servants than members of the general public. We shall return to this issue in Chapter 12.

Whether full-time or part-time, municipal councillors must pay close attention to increasingly stringent rules about conflicts of interest. In general, they must not participate in decision-making concerning any matters in which they or their immediate families have a pecuniary interest. As recently as July 2010, a judge presiding over an inquiry into possible conflicts of interest in Mississauga had reason to restate the fundamental nature of the problem, regardless of what particular provincial statutes might say. He wrote:

> Members of City Council are entrusted by those who elect them to act in the public interest. Optics are important. In other words, members of a municipal council must conduct themselves in such a way as to avoid any reasonable apprehension that their personal interest could in any way influence their elected responsibility. Suffice it to say that members of Council (and staff) are not to use their office to promote private interests, whether their own or those of relatives or friends. They must be unbiased in the exercise of their duties. That is not only the common law, but the common sense standard by which the conduct of municipal representatives ought to be judged.[23]

In small communities especially, prominent business people can have a personal interest in just about anything. Therefore, many public-spirited citizens find the idea of being a municipal councillor unappealing. This observation is not to suggest that we should tolerate conflicts of interest but rather attempts to explain why we get the kind of councillors that we do. Not only is the job of municipal councillor becoming increasingly full-time, it also is becoming increasingly a lifelong, full-time career. Municipal elections are of crucial importance.

Municipal Elections: Terms of Office, Turnout, and Minority Representation

Municipal election dates and terms of office are set by provincial law. Unlike parliamentary systems, municipal leaders cannot call elections when it suits them or when the majority of council disagrees with the mayor (as in a vote of no-confidence). Even when a member of council dies or resigns, councils often appoint a replacement rather than go through the trouble and expense of holding a special election. Provincial legislatures frequently make adjustments to laws for municipal elections. In recent years a general trend has been to lengthen municipal terms of office, usually on the principle that, if federal and provincial legislatures are normally supposed to be elected for four-year terms, a similar term should be appropriate for municipalities. In the past, terms have been as short as two years, leading to claims that municipal councillors could never focus on the long term because they were always either preparing for an election or recovering from one. Terms of office for municipal councils are now four years in all provinces except BC, PEI, Saskatchewan, and Alberta, where they are for three years. In rural Saskatchewan, however, two-year terms are still the norm.[24]

Despite much wringing of hands and increasingly visible advertising campaigns to convince people to vote, turnouts at municipal elections generally are low. Occasionally, when a particularly contentious issue is at hand or when a mayoral campaign involves well-known opponents, turnout of eligible voters in cities is over 50 per cent, but 30 to 40 per cent is much more the norm. Evidence from Ontario in the 1980s and 1990s suggests that the smaller the municipality, the higher the turnout is likely to be.[25] A telephone survey conducted shortly after the municipal election in St Catharines, Ontario, confirmed what most observers of Canadian municipal elections have always assumed: older people claim to have voted at a higher rate than younger people and homeowners are more likely to claim to have voted than tenants.[26] More surprisingly, the same survey found that levels of education were not a factor affecting voter turnout (although the authors of the study apparently did not control this factor for age, and we know that younger people generally are better-educated than their elders) and that people not born in Canada are more likely to claim to have voted than those born in the country. However, these data are questionable because 63 per cent of respondents in the supposedly random survey claimed to have voted in the 2003 election, but the actual turnout was only 30 per cent.

The harsh reality is that we know very little about municipal voting behaviour in Canada. One of the few things we do know, however, is that in non-partisan elections, incumbents have a huge initial advantage because, at least, voters tend to know who they are.[27] Unless they have misbehaved badly, incumbents tend to get re-elected, a factor that greatly encourages the phenomenon of the career municipal politician described above. When an incumbent decides not to run, competition for the 'vacant' position can be fierce, although in Toronto a practice seems to be developing whereby retiring councillors attempt to pass on their seats to the most senior members of their respective personal staffs, a factor that goes even further to suggest that paid involvement in municipal politics in major Canadian cities can last throughout an entire working life.

Many people are rightly concerned about the representation of women and minorities on municipal councils. Ample evidence shows that women and minorities are under-represented,[28] although someone should try to figure out why, between 2006 and 2010, nine of 12 members of Mississauga's municipal council were women and why none were from visible minorities, despite large numbers of visible minority residents in that city. For students of municipal government, the most important question is whether women and minorities are better represented on municipal councils than they are in federal and provincial legislatures. Fortunately, a recently published collection of essays has addressed precisely this question. The editors point out that:

> a variety of studies published over a decade ago empirically demonstrated a higher proportion of women serving on municipal councils, at a particular moment in time, than in federal or provincial legislatures. Typically, this was explained by two factors: the reluctance of parties to run female candidates, particularly in their 'safe seats'; and the greater affinity women were deemed to have for 'politics where we live', in hometown urban government.[29]

But the new study suggests the opposite: women in Montreal, Toronto, Hamilton, Winnipeg, Regina, and Vancouver were better represented in the early 2000s at the federal and provincial levels than at the municipal level. The situation for visible minorities was more ambiguous, but clearly showed no 'municipal advantage'. The authors explain this in part 'by the renewed effort of federal and provincial political parties to run women and minority candidates'.[30] The corollary would seem to be that women and visible minorities should do better in cities in which there are municipal party systems. Such is not the case in Montreal and Vancouver. Presumably, successful parties in these cities are not as committed to the cause of electing women and visible minorities as are successful federal and provincial parties.

Financing Municipal Campaigns

Running a serious campaign for municipal elected office in cities costs money. Office space and equipment need to be rented; lawn signs and brochures printed; media spots purchased; pizza delivered to volunteers. Sometimes candidates also will pay for public-opinion polling and engage in other sophisticated campaign operations. In past decades no one seemed to care much where the money for such expenses came from, although it always has been against the law to offer outright bribes to councillors to buy their support for council votes. As we shall see in the next chapter, many have been concerned since the 1960s that people who are reliant on municipal policy decisions to make a living—developers, builders, contractors, owners of taxicab licences, etc.—can become too powerful if they can spend sufficient sums of money to get some candidates for municipal councils elected and to prevent the election of others.

A recent report published by the BC government summarizes the general state of affairs in Canada in early 2010 relating to the regulation of municipal election campaign funding:

> BC's rules are largely uniform across the province, except for certain procedural matters for which a local government may adopt a bylaw. Alberta, Saskatchewan, New Brunswick, PEI, Yukon, Northwest Territories, and Nunavut do not have any provincially mandated local government campaign financing rules. Alberta and Saskatchewan allow local governments to establish their own bylaws regarding campaign financing, so if campaign financing rules exist at all, they vary from community to community. New Brunswick allows municipalities to impose expense limits and contributions limits by bylaw. Manitoba, Quebec, Ontario, and Newfoundland and Labrador require some form of disclosure of campaign contributions and often expenses as well. Those four provinces also have contribution limits and restrictions, though only Ontario and Quebec also have expense limits.[31]

It is important to note that Quebec provides tax credits for contributions to municipal election campaigns and requires municipalities to reimburse 50 per cent of the electoral expenses of a party or a candidate who receives at least 15 per cent of the vote. Manitoba and Ontario allow municipalities to provide rebates to people who make contributions to municipal election campaigns. Quebec and the city of Toronto[32] prohibit contributions from corporations and trade unions.[33] The municipal bylaw in Calgary for election financing contains no requirements other than that all donations of over $100 be publicly reported. From such reports we can read that Mayor David Bronconnier raised $673,616 for his re-election campaign in 2007, including one donation of $20,000 from a contracting firm.[34]

Recent work by Robert MacDermid at York University on campaign funding in Toronto-area municipalities during the 2006 elections demonstrated the importance of contributions from the development industry. In 2006, one-third of the amount of money donated to candidates who were elected to the Vaughan city council came from development companies. One-quarter came from individuals associated with the development industry.[35] Starting in 2010, contributions from corporations and trade unions will be illegal in Toronto. Presumably some of their funds will be replaced by increased donations from related individuals, although limits on individual donations remain at $750 for each candidate and $5,000 in total for each municipality. This still provides development interests with considerable opportunity, even in Toronto, to fund municipal elections. Opportunities elsewhere, except in Quebec, remain much greater. Reasons for their intense concern with municipal politics will be explored in detail in the next chapter.

Conclusion

Municipal councils in Canada are where municipal issues are decided. More so than any other decision-making body in Canada, their work is done in public. Their public meetings generally provide much evidence to citizens that councillors are divided, that they are influenced by powerful groups, that they are highly reliant on staff advice, and that sometimes they do not even fully understand what they are doing. People often think that changing municipal structures and procedures will bring about miraculous cures: smaller councils or larger ones; ward systems or at-large elections; stronger or weaker committees; higher salaries or lower salaries for councillors; shorter or longer terms of office; public subsidies for municipal campaigns or more emphasis on individual contributions. Unfortunately, little, if any, evidence suggests that one alternative or the other leads to better outcomes. This is because no one can agree on what constitutes a better outcome. One person's idea of a success story is another person's disaster.

Nowhere is this more evident in municipal politics than in relation to land development, the key item of municipal business everywhere in Canada. For developers, municipal councils are doing a good job when they approve developments quickly and predictably so as to enhance employment and provide housing and commercial building that enables various local economies to prosper. For many others, especially environmentalists, councils that routinely approve development proposals are pathological in the extreme. Such battles are what municipal politics is largely about. Rather than pursuing further the various issues relating to the structure of municipal councils, it is important that we turn to the politics of urban land development.

RESOURCES

By consulting the website of the municipality in which you reside (or the website of the provincial Directeur-général des elections if you are in Quebec), find out who the candidates were for each elected office, what the turnout for the election was, whether incumbents generally were re-elected, and whether there seemed to be a connection between campaign expenditures and votes received.

STUDY QUESTIONS

1. Should there be political parties in Canadian municipal elections? If so, what kind of parties?
2. What are the arguments for having small councils elected at large, on the one hand, and having large councils elected by wards, on the other?
3. What are the advantages and disadvantages of having full-time municipal councillors who attempt to make a career in this line of work?

10 Developers, Councillors, and Citizens

In Chapter 2 we learned that, unlike in many other democratic countries, municipal governments in Canada and the United States are concerned mostly with the built environment. In Canada, people concerned with the quality of local schools or of services for developmentally disabled adults have little need to be concerned with the actions of municipal governments. People who make a living from converting rural land into urban development are hugely interested in what municipalities do, because municipalities make many of the rules that affect their livelihoods. To a lesser degree this interest also applies to ordinary homeowners, because for many people their home is their major asset, and municipal action (or inaction) in their neighbourhoods can have a significant impact on its value. In theory, municipal policy about land development is equally important for renters who hope one day to own their own homes at a reasonable cost in a pleasing environment but, because these people do not organize themselves in municipal politics the same way that developers and homeowners do, their interests are not so often taken into account.

In this chapter we begin by examining different processes that have been used to convert rural land into urban land. Ontario—in particular, London[1]—will serve as a case study; but the evolution of the process has been roughly similar in all major Canadian urban areas except, arguably, in Quebec, where developers have not played such a major role in financing urban development. Later in the chapter we look at other issues relating to the role of developers and of citizens' groups in urban politics.

How Rural Land Has Become Urban in Ontario

Creating new urban land usually requires that a large rural property be 'subdivided' into smaller lots. For this to happen, there has to be at a minimum a governmental system for keeping track of who owns what land. In Canada such systems for 'registering' landownership are usually administered by provincial governments. In theory, original grants of land could be registered in such an office and the owner could then proceed to make purely private arrangements—including outright sale—for its disposition. Subsequent owners would rely on proof of purchase to trace their ownership back to the original grant. Such a system is fraught with uncertainty—both for owners and for governments. A prominent scholar of Canadian land-use law has pointed out that 'Because of the failure to register plans consequent upon subdivision of land for sale and because of the confusion arising in land registration, title certification and municipal administration in general, it became, over a century ago in Ontario, mandatory to register such plans in the registry office.'[2] The key point seems to be, however, that originally no attempt was made at substantive regulation. Anyone who went through the correct administrative process at the registry office could subdivide his or her land.

Because the subdivision of land, particularly in urban areas, inevitably led to new demands for such local public services as sewers and roads, municipalities were seen to have a direct interest in the subdivision process. The 1910 Ontario Registry Act 'provided that the Registrar should not register a plan of subdivision unless accompanied by the approval of the municipal council or order of a judge approving such a plan.'[3] Judges could hear appeals from negative municipal decisions. In 1918 the Ontario Planning and Development Act provided that cities, towns, and villages could declare 'urban zones' in areas up to five miles outside their boundaries and that, for such zones, they would have to approve any new subdivision. Under the same law, the Ontario Railway and Municipal Board (now the OMB) became the agency for appeals of municipal subdivision decisions.

Unfortunately for many builders and homeowners in the early twentieth century, the requirement that municipalities approve new subdivisions did not guarantee that municipalities would actually provide the necessary infrastructure at the time new homes were built. If municipalities built roads, sewers, and water supply systems before homes were built, they sometimes found that the infrastructure was unused for long periods until economic circumstances caused the home-building to happen. But if builders gambled and went ahead without the infrastructure in place, municipalities would sometimes claim that they had insufficient funds to proceed, leaving new homeowners having to access their properties through mud trails and having to make do with primitive sanitation arrangements.

Local Improvement Taxes

The Ontario Local Improvement Act of 1914 established a system whereby urban municipalities could construct new installations such as water mains, sewers, curbs, gutters, sidewalks, and paved streets and pass on the cost through a special local improvement tax levied on property owners of abutting land. Local improvements could be initiated either by the municipal council or by property-owners. If a council supported residential development in a particular area, it would initiate the local improvement process. Property-owners could initiate local improvements by petitioning the local council. If two-thirds of owners, representing half the value of the properties liable to be assessed, directed the city to act, council was forced to comply. Regardless of how local improvements were initiated, borrowing was the responsibility of the municipality. When the work was finished, property-owners were required to pay back the loan through an additional charge on their property taxes. If, in any year, insufficient funds were raised to pay the property-owners' portion of the loan repayment, the municipality was liable to make up the shortfall. To do so the council could increase each owner's assessment in the remaining years. The main features of this system for local improvements are still in place in Ontario to this day. New arrangements for financing infrastructure in residential subdivisions have been added, but the older ones have not been repealed. In most major municipalities, however, only relatively minor installations in established areas are financed through local improvement taxes. A typical example might be the building of a sidewalk where one had not existed before. Affected property-owners present the required petition; the city builds the sidewalk; and, for 20 years, the property-owners' taxes are increased accordingly.

From the municipality's point of view there was one major flaw in financing infrastructure in new subdivisions by local improvement taxes: if the properties did not sell, the developer would likely be bankrupt and the taxes would not be paid. The municipality would end up owning, at best, some vacant houses or, at worst, an entire partially completed subdivision, with roads, sewers, and water mains leading nowhere. The tax burden for financing the useless installations would shift to the taxpayers of the city as a whole. In exceptionally difficult economic circumstances, such as those experienced in the 1930s, financial disasters of this kind could push the municipality to the edge of bankruptcy and beyond.

Subdivision Agreements

The aftermath of World War II brought great pressure on municipalities to provide new housing. Notwithstanding their experiences in the Great Depression, most were willing, with federal and provincial help, to finance major expansions in trunk sewers, water mains, and major roads. In so doing, their debt levels shot upward. In such circumstances, how were the more local installations normally associated with local improvement taxes to be financed? The private developers came to the rescue. Knowing that their new houses were certain to be purchased, they (initially at least) had few reservations about entering into 'subdivision agreements' with municipalities, under which they obligated themselves to build the public infrastructure for the subdivisions according to municipal specifications and then turned them over to the municipality when the project was complete. Their costs would normally be passed on to the purchaser, who would then face higher mortgage payments instead of local improvement taxes. As residential mortgage rates are generally higher than interest rates paid on municipal borrowing, total financing costs under this system were higher. The perceived societal benefit was the removal of the constraints on subdivision production caused by real or apparent limitations on municipal borrowing capacities. The Ontario Committee on Taxation described the historical origin of subdivision agreements as follows:

> The early development of direct financing of municipal service installations has not been well documented. But it is clear that the practice of requiring developers to agree to take responsibility for providing certain services or meeting certain costs which would otherwise fall upon the municipality first gained importance in the years immediately following World War II. Among the earliest municipalities to impose such conditions were the three major recipients of Toronto's metropolitan expansion—the large townships of Etobicoke, North York, and Scarborough. Initially, the legality of subdivision agreements . . . was in doubt. These agreements none the less multiplied in a setting where, given the pace of urban growth and the demand for housing, neither developers nor municipalities were overly concerned with legal refinements.[4]

By the time the legal status of subdivision agreements was clarified in the late 1950s and early 1960s, they were being used for all major residential subdivisions throughout the province. Under this new system, there could be no approved subdivision unless the applicant had access to sufficient capital resources to finance and build the infrastructure. The result was that local speculators and small building companies were forced out by larger concerns, usually major construction companies that had begun acquiring farmland for eventual subdivision so as to ensure their own supply of developable land.

Many subdivision agreements contained provisions obliging the developer to pay 'cash imposts', 'lot levies', or 'development charges' (the term used varies by jurisdiction, but they are all essentially the same) for infrastructure costs associated with the new subdivision. Such monies could pay for improvements to major installations outside the subdivision that could be shown to be needed as a direct or indirect result of the subdivision's being built. As time went on, municipalities increasingly extended the scope of these charges such that they are now often used to help finance extensions to public transit, fire and police stations, libraries, and schools in addition to roads and parks and such hidden infrastructure as systems for water supply and sewage treatment and removal. The important point to note here is that, even more so than subdivision agreements, they have the effect of requiring that development companies be large and financially strong so that they can absorb the cost of the charges until they can sell their new homes.

In the early twentieth century, a key role for any urban municipal government was to plan, build, and finance the infrastructure that makes urban life possible. In the early twenty-first century, municipalities still plan this infrastructure. Within new subdivisions, however, it is now generally built and paid for by developers. Outside new subdivisions, the required new infrastructure is often paid for by these same developers through development charges. Buyers of new homes, therefore, are not just paying for their houses. They are paying for the infrastructure within their subdivision and some of it that is outside, which is one of the reasons why new houses are expensive. Prices of new houses help to drive up prices of older ones. Many people claim that this situation is good public policy because 'growth should pay for growth.' But there is a case to be made that, if we want it, we all should pay for growth, and if we do not want it, we should use our municipalities to prohibit it.

Subdivision agreements and development charges essentially allow developers the right to purchase growth from the municipalities that are charged with regulating it. However, they must do so within the formal land-use planning arrangements that have been legislated by the various provinces. In Ontario, the council-approved municipal document that specifies where new development is to take place is called the 'official plan'. In other provinces, equivalent documents are known by such names as 'development plans' (Alberta and Manitoba) and 'municipal planning strategies' (Nova Scotia).[5]

Stoneybrook: The Creation of a Residential Subdivision in London in the 1980s

The 69 hectares of farmland at the extreme northern periphery of the city on which Stoneybrook was built became part of London in as a result of the massive annexation of 1961 (see Chapter 6). By 1974 it had been acquired by the Matthews Group, one of London's two major residential developers. In that year Matthews applied for permission to subdivide the land in order to build approximately 570 single-family houses and 200 units of row housing.

London's planning department recommended approval but the city received dozens of complaints from existing residents on the other side of the area's major east–west arterial road. The complainants argued that the developer's plans to build three-storey row housing along the road would reduce property values in the area. Townhouses of this kind were called 'monstrosities'. It was alleged that their occupation by families with young children would lead to traffic congestion and safety problems, as well as overcrowding in the local schools. Local councillors argued that such high-density development was too expensive because it would mean increased costs for sewers, water mains, and streets.

The developer's response was that the main reason for including the row housing was so that it could act as a sound barrier for the single-family houses against the noise coming from the main road. Despite such a telling admission, the developer backed down in the face of continued local opposition. The plans were changed to provide for only 635 single-family houses. Final approval of Stoneybrook's first phase did not take place until 1979, five years after the original application. Delays were caused by the need to upgrade the nearby sewage treatment plant, to rezone the land from farmland to residential to bring it into accord with the city's official plan, to acquire the necessary approval from various provincial agencies, and to work out all the details of the servicing arrangements. However, after 1979 it was the developer who wanted to delay, because of a slowdown in the economy. During the 1980s city council granted various extensions to its original approvals. The plan of subdivision for the first phase was registered in 1982; the plan for the fifth and final phase in 1987.

Subdivision agreements between the city of London and the Matthews Group were signed for each of Stoneybrook's five phases. The agreements set out the standards for all infrastructure construction. They also specified the land that would be transferred to the city on completion, as well as the various utility easements (passageways) that would be required. While construction was underway, city engineers had the authority to make periodic inspections to ensure that work was being carried out as provided for in the agreement. It would be incorrect to suggest that the developer made all the important decisions. The city's regulations for subdivisions assured that surface water would drain to some approved, predetermined location; that roads would be suitable for use by garbage trucks, snowploughs, and buses; that underground utilities would be accessible for repair; and that at least some land would be made available for such public facilities as schools and parks.

The early advocates of land-use planning expected more. They argued that the 'community master plan', as enforced by comprehensive zoning, could shape urban development in accordance with some agreed-upon notion of an over-riding public or city interest. In this sense the complex planning apparatus of London, Ontario—and other Canadian cities—falls short. Even most planners recognize that their real task in municipal government is to facilitate the cost-effective development of our cities by major companies rather than to inspire new visions for our built environment.

The financing of infrastructure for new residential subdivisions has progressed from local improvement taxes to subdivision agreements and development charges. Whatever the virtues of the modern arrangements might be, they are not a mechanism for increased municipal control of the development process. They have been supported by the development industry—in London at least—precisely because they help free developers from municipal financial constraints. Such constraints derive from the limitations—either self-imposed or as determined by the province and/or the financial marketplace—on a given municipality's capacity to incur long-term debt. As a municipality approaches its upper limit for debt, it must begin to make difficult decisions about allocating scarce resources, in this case, funds for the building of new infrastructure. In such circumstances, the need to make these decisions empowers the municipality to shape the nature of its outward physical expansion. Such empowerment is precisely what private developers wish to avoid; hence their support for a mechanism enabling them effectively to purchase the necessary infrastructure for their own projects by paying some specified per unit charge in advance.

Apart from the developer, the Stoneybrook case underlines the role of one other important set of actors in the creation of new subdivisions: neighbouring residents. They caused the developer to eliminate row housing from the plans and make the development exclusively single-family dwellings, thereby nullifying an apparent attempt by the developer to follow provincial policy about the provision of new housing for people with moderate incomes. Local councillors appeared to do little more than pass on residents' complaints to the developer.

Nevertheless, the alignment of interests is clear. The province and the development industry favour dense development, the former because it provides more moderately priced housing, the latter because it increases profit on a given amount of land. Local residents usually oppose dense development, and their position is reflected often by their councillors, which in turn becomes the official position of the municipality. For local residents, dense development is seen as causing more noise and congestion as well as lower property values for the area as a whole. Neighbouring residents effectively want lower-income people located anywhere except near them; municipalities (especially in Ontario where municipalities are responsible for sharing the financial costs of various welfare-related services) want the same people located anywhere except within their boundaries. In order to win quick approval, developers seem quite willing to make whatever concessions are required to the municipality and neighbouring residents. This certainly seems to have been the case in Stoneybrook.

Under these arrangements, the municipality and the residents' groups advance their own financial interests while being seen at the same time to be beating down the rapacious developer. The development company still makes money; indeed, if there is a strong market for new single-family homes, it simply passes on its increased unit costs to the purchaser. Low-income people never understand the opportunities they have lost. Only the province comes out an obvious loser, a fact that no doubt explains various provincial efforts to require moderate-income housing in all new developments.

The Stoneybrook case is presented here as a typical example of subdivision development on land that the municipality had already designated for this purpose. In British Columbia, Quebec, and within the Greater Golden Horseshoe in Ontario, provincial governments are implementing quite aggressive policies to preserve agricultural land and to help prevent urban sprawl. In these places it is very difficult indeed for owners to subdivide their land for urban development. Where such provincial policies are in place we can expect conflicts about the creation of new urban land to become even more intense and to involve both provincial and municipal levels of government. Pressure for intense development on new urban land will be greater because provincial policies have caused it to become a scarcer resource. The kinds of people in Stoneybrook who successfully resisted the development of row housing across a main arterial from their own houses will not likely take kindly to being told that dense development will be coming and that there is little they can do about it. Of course, if they live near a greenbelt or agricultural land reserve they have little to worry about, except the very real possibility that their pleasant suburban lifestyles will occasionally be disturbed by noxious agricultural odours.

Shopping Malls versus Downtowns

When new residential land is created on the peripheries of urban areas, developers inevitably want to provide new shopping areas, not just for the new nearby residents but for urban and rural shoppers as well. Such is the purpose of a 'regional shopping mall' or its apparent successor, the 'power centre'. Through their land-use planning policies, municipalities play a key role in deciding where these new commercial facilities are to be located and how big they can be. These decisions are extremely important both for owners of downtown commercial property and for suburban developers of commercial property. In the absence of municipal regulation, we would doubtless have many more failed shopping centres dotting our urban landscapes. This means that owners whose land is designated for major commercial development have received a major financial benefit. Some would say it is like winning the lottery; successful developers would say that skill in understanding the details of a particular city's outward physical development is a much more important factor than luck. As we did in the last section, we shall illustrate the politics of shopping malls and downtowns by looking at a brief case study from London, Ontario. What happened in London also happened in dozens of other mid-sized Canadian cities.

Store Wars in London, Ontario

The authors of a major study of Londoners' shopping habits in 1983–4 noted that London's planning policies had always been protective of downtown interests. The central business district (CBD) was supposed to remain the dominant retail area in London and competition among shopping centres throughout the city was supposed to be balanced so that each district was well served and so that no single shopping centre was able to achieve dominance. This policy, generally adhered to, meant London had relatively more but smaller shopping centres per capita than most other North American cities and had apparently avoided the problem of downtown deterioration in favour of regional malls located in the suburbs.

By just about every conceivable measure, the study clearly demonstrated the dominance of the downtown shopping area in relation to other areas and malls within the city. Nevertheless, the authors found many reasons for concern. Respondents to their survey expressed dissatisfaction with parking, lack of protection from the weather, and various other matters related to convenience. The downtown attracted old and young shoppers, rich and poor, but, predictably, it was not so effective in attracting middle-aged, middle-income families with children.

The authors' main policy recommendations were based not so much on their survey data as on their interpretations of possible future developments. They note that 'while estimates vary somewhat as to exactly how much space is actually coming into the London market over the next five years, we believe the order of magnitude of all reasonable estimates is far beyond what London can support through growth in population or buying power.'[6] This reason was mainly why they concluded that the downtown 'is faced with a crucial testing period which we believe will determine the long-term viability of the central business district in London.'[7] Much of the rest of this section is about what happened during this 'crucial testing period'. First, however, we must examine why and how so much additional suburban shopping space was approved in the early and mid-1980s.

The first approval for mall expansion in the 1980s involved a major Canadian development company, Cadillac-Fairview, which proposed a new shopping centre at Masonville at the extreme northerly edge of the city's territory and near the new Stoneybrook residential subdivision. Apart from the usual neighbouring residents' concerns about increased traffic, the proposal was relatively non-controversial. It was understood, however, that because this was to be the first major shopping centre to serve the relatively affluent northwest area of the city, its existence would likely be a considerable challenge for downtown retailers. When originally approved in 1980, Masonville was supposed to be built in 1983. Mainly because of the recession in the early 1980s, the opening was delayed until 1985, well after the 1983–4 study of Londoners' shopping habits.

While Masonville was being approved in the north, the owners of two large shopping centres in south London announced major expansion plans and another developer proposed building a new one in the same general area. The city council approved one of the major expansions and the other ones were approved in 1982, after a significant intervention by the provincial government. When all this new suburban shopping space came on stream, the downtown was effectively finished as a major shopping destination, notwithstanding an ultimately unsuccessful effort in the late 1980s by another major developer, the Campeau Corporation, to build and operate a major downtown shopping mall. After becoming almost totally empty, this mall is now home to the main branch of the city's public library (where a major department store used to be), a call centre, the extension department of the University of Western Ontario, and various other non-retail operations. Despite significant municipal investment in the downtown in recent years, it still struggles, although new high-rise apartment buildings downtown indicate that things might finally be turning around. But the days of the downtown being a major shopping destination will surely never return.

No mass movement of citizens in the 1980s defended the downtown against suburban shopping malls. The fight was mainly among major commercial property-owners, and the ones downtown did not openly make their case in the political arena. Presumably committed to principles of open free-market competition for the retail dollar, they naively believed that stores downtown could compete with the new major regional malls. They were wrong. A major question for any student of the politics of urban development is this: Could the municipal council have prevented the decline of the downtown by refusing to approve the building of suburban shopping malls? We cannot learn the answer to this question because there are suburban shopping malls in every major Canadian urban centre and, except for the very largest of our cities, most have seen the virtual disappearance of the downtown commercial core. For many who now look back nostalgically at such downtown cores, the harsh truth is probably that they have disappeared because most Canadian urban residents decided they would rather shop in the suburbs. If this is true, we can conclude that the marketplace, as represented by developers, and local democratic politics, as represented by decisions made by elected politicians, combined to give the people what they want.

The great irony is that even the largest of regional shopping malls now are threatened by the 'power centres' anchored by 'big-box' stores, each surrounded by its own massive parking lots. The marketplace seems to have shifted again and municipal councillors have done little, if anything, to shape it. There are even fewer citizens rallying to 'save our mall' than there were to save our downtowns.

Old Buildings versus New Buildings

Developers do not restrict their attempts to make money to the suburbs. In central-city areas that have any potential for increased economic activity, developers try to turn old buildings into new buildings. Sometimes this is a long process, with the relevant land serving for many years as a parking lot. Municipal councils can regulate both demolition and building and therefore have an important role in this process. The most important form of municipal regulation relating to individual buildings is generally called 'zoning bylaws' ('land-use bylaws' in Alberta). Because zoning bylaws apply to individual properties and, therefore, directly affect the value of assets held by particular people and corporations, provinces have generally required municipal councils to demonstrate that they have acted fairly when they make a zoning change. At a minimum, this means that affected property-owners get a chance formally to express their views before the council takes action. In Ontario, property-owners can appeal any municipal zoning change to the Ontario Municipal Board (discussed in Chapter 3), and the OMB has a particular obligation to provide a fair and impartial hearing.

Municipal councillors generally want to encourage new development because it leads to higher municipal tax revenues and provides immediate employment in the construction industry. But many are also concerned about preserving old buildings, especially in places where there is great pressure for new development. The preservation of older buildings is often an important local issue. Jane Jacobs, an important writer in the twentieth century on the subject of cities, famously argues that cities need old buildings for economic growth. She notes that economic and creative innovators seldom got their start in shiny new glass-and-steel high-rises. Instead, Jacobs claims, their biggest breakthroughs inevitably are born in low-rent, old buildings that are affordable and convenient to other central-city services.[8] A city that encourages the bulldozing of such buildings, in the hope (or even the promise) that they will be replaced by new office and commercial buildings, is foreclosing potential opportunities created by genuine innovation rather than by shuffling around office locations.

A different kind of economic argument relates to the need for downtown areas to have distinct visual identities. Although it is not impossible for new buildings to provide such identities (the Sydney Opera

House in Australia is probably the world's best example), it is usually older buildings that provide a distinct sense of place. As the economic function of downtowns turns more to tourism and leisure activities and away from shopping and routine office functions, it is increasingly important that potential visitors have a reason to go to one place rather than to another. The atmosphere provided by older buildings can provide just such a reason. It is important to remember that both of these arguments for protecting older buildings—as incubators for innovation and as providers of visual identity—are based in a desire to enhance a city's economic well-being. The argument is that new development sometimes harms a city's economic prospects. When faced with proposals to demolish old buildings in favour of new development, municipal councillors are often faced with difficult judgement calls about the best course for their city's economy.

Many citizens wish to preserve old buildings for primarily non-economic reasons. They simply believe that our communities must retain links to the past so that we better understand the historical legacies left to us by earlier generations. Such people are likely to argue that preserving important old buildings trumps short-term economic concerns, but, not surprisingly, they also increasingly make use of the economic arguments referred to above. Many developers today understand that preserving older buildings is often very much in their own best interests, so there are fewer battles in Canada around this issue than there were 30 or 40 years ago. For example, neither the Montreal Forum nor Maple Leaf Gardens was demolished after the Canadiens and Maple Leafs departed these hallowed grounds for newer buildings. Both have been recycled for other urban uses, although Maple Leaf Gardens will still have a rink, to be used by Ryerson University.

Conflicts today about older buildings tend to focus on ones that are much less famous and usually badly run down. Citizens' groups concerned with preservation often argue that developers should be compelled to fix up such buildings rather than be allowed to tear them down. Much of the dispute is about the cost of repairs and who should pay. While the battles go on, buildings get more run down, a fact that strengthens the developer's case. Sometimes such buildings even burn down or get flooded, thereby ending the debate altogether. Difficult legal issues often emerge in such conflicts. How they are settled depends on the details of municipal bylaws or provincial legislation. The developers' claim usually is that property-owners should be able to do what they want with their property, especially if it is not designated as a heritage property prior to a requested demolition. They argue that, if a municipality wants to 'save' a building, it should be willing to purchase it at fair market value. Municipalities seldom agree, and search instead for compromise solutions involving the use of old facades on new buildings or even the approval of totally new buildings designed to look like old ones (the Disneyland solution).

Neighbourhoods versus 'Cataclysmic Change'

Many of the defining events in Canadian urban politics in the past 50 years have involved battles between governments or private developers intent on building major projects and neighbourhood groups that have resisted them, sometimes successfully, sometimes not. The origins of these battles go back to conflicting visions about the ideal city. Jane Jacobs articulated the conflict best in her book, *The Death and Life of Great American Cities* (1961). She began by attacking 'modernist' visions of the city that she claimed destroyed its very essence. Such visions involved central cities composed mainly of high-rise buildings and expressways that connected the centre to a ring of planned suburbs. In the mid-twentieth century, these modernist approaches to city-building were at the heart of policies aimed at 'slum clearance', whereby poor and working-class neighbourhoods would be bulldozed and replaced by high-rises or by new expressways. In the 1950s in New York, Jacobs successfully fought to protect her own neighbourhood in SoHo against plans to build an expressway that would have effectively destroyed it. Her famous book was a direct result of her experience. In *Death and Life* she articulates an anti-modernist vision of the city, in which what she calls 'cataclysmic' changes are eschewed for cautious, gradual policies aimed at preserving and upgrading neighbourhoods rather than destroying them. Contrary to conventional modernist land-use planning ideas at the time, she extolled the virtues of mixed commercial and residential uses. She explained why both high-rise apartments and sprawling single-family homes were inappropriate for cities, turning instead to the kind of structures that had been at the heart of cities for ages: rows of low-rise mixed-use structures built close to the street, often with stores at the street level and apartments above.

During the Vietnam War in the 1960s, she and her family moved to Toronto. Ironically, she settled in a part of central Toronto directly in the path of an expressway planned by Metro Toronto that would cut right through the neighbourhood. Not surprisingly, she quickly became prominent in the successful citizens' movement to stop the Spadina Expressway. Jacobs's influence was felt in cities throughout the Western world. Citizens' groups felt empowered to challenge so-called 'experts' (such as traffic engineers who designed comprehensive expressway systems for cities) and soon the experts changed their view to incorporate much of Jacobs's thinking. This change is nowhere more evident than among professional land-use planners who now learn in their university courses about the virtues of mixed uses and stabilizing and preserving traditional neighbourhoods.

Battles about expressways took place in almost all major Canadian cities.[9] In Montreal a conflict currently boils about the reconstruction of an expressway interchange originally built in the 1960s.[10] Just as plans to bulldoze entire neighbourhoods are no longer seriously advanced, few, if any, governments plan to build major new expressways in established urban areas. In fact, in Toronto, debates are beginning about the possible dismantling of the Gardiner Expressway that separates downtown Toronto from the shores of Lake Ontario. Government plans for 'slum clearance' and expressways have not been the only threats to stability in traditional urban neighbourhoods. Private-sector developers have been important as well, and remain today as forces against which neighbourhood associations are always on guard.

In the 1950s and 1960s, developers frequently engaged in what was known as 'blockbusting'. They would surreptitiously buy a few houses in a particular city block where they planned to build a new high-rise apartment building. They would then deliberately rent these properties to people whom the neighbours would consider undesirables. This would cause more people to think of selling—and the developers' agents would be right there to buy. The process would be repeated until the development company had enough land for the building, at which time it would go to the city council and ask for the land to be rezoned to allow a high-rise apartment. A justification for the request was that the neighbourhood was no longer stable!

Still, in many older commercial areas of cities, developers buy properties in the expectation that one day they will make money by building new buildings. How big those buildings will be will depend on decisions taken by the municipal council, so developers have a huge interest in who is elected as councillors. However, blockbusting in residential areas is a strategy that is unlikely to work anymore. Most city councils have made it very clear in their land-use planning policies that existing inner-city residential neighbourhoods will never be rezoned to accommodate larger buildings. Developers generally believe them—and citizens' groups act vigilantly to ensure that councillors make few, if any, concessions. Many new high-rises, especially condominiums, are still being built in our more prosperous cities. How is this possible? The answer is that, due to shifts in shopping patterns we have already discussed, and even more importantly, due to the move of inner-city manufacturing jobs to the suburbs and to other countries (such as China), our cities in recent decades have found themselves with huge expanses of under-used land. Residential developers have been quick to move in and to create new high-income neighbourhoods where dilapidated factories used to be. One result is that central parts of cities now have more residents and fewer jobs, so much so that commuting flows out of the city to suburban jobs are as great in some places as the more traditional suburb-to-city commute.

Another result is that poorer people are being pushed out of the centres of our more prosperous cities, especially Toronto, Montreal, and Vancouver. Contributing to this process is the 'gentrification' of inner-city neighbourhoods. When high-income people are convinced that blockbusting will no longer occur and that neighbourhoods are being genuinely protected by municipal governments, they have every incentive to buy houses in such neighbourhoods, even if the houses require extensive renovation. In many respects this process is a sign that things are going well for a city or a neighbourhood. Slow change in this direction fits Jacobs's prescriptions for saving cities. The problem, of course, is that over time (instead of quickly, as in slum clearance) poor people are driven from their own neighbourhoods. This is especially damaging for renters, arguably less so for owners of modest homes who find themselves receiving unimaginably high prices when they decide to sell and move away.

If most inner-city residential neighbourhoods are now safe from megaprojects, does this mean that smaller projects aimed at increasing residential density to prevent sprawl are also doomed? There are disturbing signs that this might be the case. Residents have been so successful in many places in defending their neighbourhoods that they see any attempt to build something new as an attack on neighbourhood stability. It is one thing to protest against plans for a disruptive high-rise in the middle of a quiet residential street. It is quite another to protest against one that is at the edge of a neighbourhood at the intersection of major arteries and on top of a subway stop. Most people who think seriously about cities would acknowledge that such a location is exactly where high-rise apartments should be. But nearby residents fret about shadows and increased congestion in the subway station. In the real world of Toronto city politics, this is exactly what happened concerning a proposed high-rise at the corner of Yonge and Eglinton. A scaled-back version of the building was finally approved, but the veteran local councillor who supported the development lost her seat in the 2003 municipal election.[11]

'New Reformers' and the Development Industry

During the 1960s and 1970s, opposition to slum clearance, expressways, and uncontrolled development of high-rise buildings created a new urban reform movement. In the previous chapter we examined some of the features of the 'old' reform movement: emphasis on management by experts; diminished role for politicians; at-large elections. In many ways the new reform movement was a direct repudiation of the main positions of the old one. The new reformers looked at municipal government and saw councillors who always favoured new development and municipal staff who thought that their main role was to facilitate it. In most respects these observations were accurate. Councils might comprise representatives of both business and labour, and they would often disagree about tax levels and the distribution of municipal resources, but both sides almost always agreed that new buildings of just about any kind were good for business and good for workers (especially construction workers). With respect to municipal staff, there was nothing in the professional training of engineers, lawyers, and accountants to cause them to question the need for expressways and new buildings. Prior to the general acceptance of Jane Jacobs's vision for cities, the same was true for professional land-use planners.

New reformers began to be elected in Canadian cities in the late 1960s. Like the old reformers, they generally rejected the introduction of federal and provincial parties into municipal government. New reformers, however, accepted the notion that municipal decision-making was political. But rather than being committed to 'following a party line', most new reformers believed that their greatest obligation was to open the doors of city hall to citizen participation and to reflect citizens' views in their council decision-making. As we have seen, citizens, especially in the inner city, were increasingly likely to reject expert opinion. Wherever new reformers gained a toehold on municipal councils, they caused great frustration for municipal staff, business people, and labour unions because it looked like they were opposed to 'progress'. In fact, like Jane Jacobs, whom they universally admired (especially in Toronto), they changed the definition of 'progress' from a belief in building new roads and buildings to preserving viable and diverse inner-city neighbourhoods.

New reformers were not a coherent group. They split into two broadly different camps, urban conservatives and populist radicals.[12] In Toronto, David Crombie (mayor from 1972 to 1978) and John Sewell (mayor, 1978–80) represented each of the two groups, respectively.

Crombie, known as 'the tiny perfect mayor' because of his popularity and shortness of stature, emphasized the preservation of neighbourhoods; Sewell emphasized the need for citizens constantly to challenge existing power structures. Crombie went on to become a cabinet minister in the Progressive Conservative federal government of Brian Mulroney, while Sewell has remained steadily a critic and outsider. While Crombie ended up supporting the amalgamation of Metro Toronto in 1998, Sewell, as we have seen in Chapter 8, was the main leader of C4LD, the main citizens' group in opposition.

In Vancouver, the local political party known as TEAM represented the more moderate new reformers while COPE was the more radical faction. In Montreal, both tendencies were contained within the Montreal Citizens' Movement (MCM), which is one reason why that group often seemed so internally divided. Both COPE and the MCM also received strong support from labour unions, which added another complication, given that labour unions generally desire jobs for construction workers. Recent Canadian mayors such as Glen Murray (Winnipeg), David Miller (Toronto), and Gregor Robertson (Vancouver) owe a great deal to the new reformers, but they—and other contemporary left-leaning municipal politicians—have been shaped by other forces as well.

The new reformers emerged from a general radicalism of the 1960s during which all power structures were placed under great pressure. What followed was a series of new social movements, each with its own cause: feminism, environmentalism, gay liberation, the anti-globalization movement. Each of these has had its effect on municipal politics in general and new reformers in particular. Because municipal government is especially concerned with the built environment in cities, it is not surprising that environmentalism has been of special importance. In fact, it is now extremely difficult to distinguish between the influence of the new reform movement and the influence of environmentalism on today's municipal activists. If someone opposes urban expressways, is it because of their vision of the quality of city life or because they are concerned about carbon footprints and global warming? Probably both.

City politics in Canada today still revolves mainly around issues relating to development. Some elected councillors and serious candidates for office have not really been much influenced by the new reform movement (for example, mayors Sam Katz in Winnipeg and Larry O'Brien in Ottawa), but all will say that they favour citizen participation and wish to preserve neighbourhoods. Their real objective is to promote growth and development, even if they sometimes differ from each other about how much they are willing to tax themselves in support of such growth. Councillors and candidates who have been influenced by the new reformers are much more cautious and skeptical about the benefits of development, although such people are hard to find in areas where growth has been slow or non-existent. Not surprisingly, development companies (where they are permitted to do so by law) and individuals associated with development companies will want to contribute to the election campaigns of candidates who generally favour development. Some will want to contribute to their opponents as well, especially if they are likely to be elected. In so doing, the developers are potentially purchasing good will, as well as trying to indicate to the general public that they are fair-minded and not solely intent on purchasing control of municipal councils. Many new reformers will refuse such contributions, and some of these will argue that no one should be allowed to accept contributions from developers or that public subsidies for municipal elections should replace developers' subsidies. Whatever happens, as long as Canadian municipalities remain as focused as they have been on making decisions about where and when buildings are to be constructed, developers and municipal politics will never be separated from each other.

Although it is difficult to analyze the overall impact of the new reformers, there is likely to be at least one item of agreement: new reformers have had a profound influence on how municipal governments have approached the issue of citizen participation.

Citizen Participation

Prior to the 1960s ordinary citizens were not much listened to in city government. There was a reason for the aphorism, 'You can't fight city hall.' As we have seen, most agreed that growth was good, that experts knew how to accommodate it, and that the job of municipal councils was to decide how much tax revenue could be wrung from property-owners in order to facilitate growth and provide essential services. But new reformers demanded that citizens challenging these assumptions be heard. Initially, these citizens expressed themselves through raucous public meetings, demonstrations, sit-ins, and blockades, many of which attracted considerable attention from the media. But the more successful they were, the more they were consulted before decisions were made. The most radical of the activists refused such consultations because their real objective was to expose arbitrary state action as a prelude to some form of revolution. But most genuinely wanted less drastic change, and change is what they got.

From the 1970s on, municipalities across Canada introduced a bewildering array of new participatory mechanisms, most notably mandatory public meetings and consultations prior to any zoning changes.[13] For many land-use planners, a crucially important new skill was the ability to conduct such events so that everyone would feel that he or she had been treated fairly. Depending on the strength of the anti-development forces within a particular municipal council, any substantial opposition to a proposal expressed at these meetings could be its death knell. For developers, therefore, the object of the game was to conduct their own careful and cautious consultations before submitting any formal proposal. From a developer's point of view, the best kind of public meeting was one at which no one showed up. However, as land-use planners and others became more committed to the idea that good planning required extensive public consultation, the fact that the public often seemed uninterested became a problem. Provoking public interest in small proposed changes in a particular neighbourhood was not usually difficult, but the more important and generalized an issue became (the future of downtown, strategies for investment in public transit), the more difficult it was to attract interest. Experience in Canada over the last 20 or 30 years leads to the depressing conclusion that most urban residents do not want to be intensely involved with big issues involving their municipal governments, but that they are concerned about small issues affecting their own neighbourhoods. Opposition to municipal amalgamation was perhaps an exception to this observation, although most such opposition seemed to be based precisely on the assumption that amalgamation would reduce local influence over neighbourhood issues.

Much attention has been paid to the NIMBY—Not In My Back Yard—syndrome. The observed problem here is that many citizen participants in policy-making for land-use issues seem to object to any change that is proposed for the immediate areas in which they live. Sometimes the opposition seems quite irrational. Why do people behave in this way? William Fischel, an American land economist who has also served on a local planning commission, has an answer: what most NIMBY participants are trying to do is simply to protect their most valuable financial asset (their home) against possible unanticipated outcomes that would cause a decline in its value. Homeowners buy fire insurance to protect themselves against the unlikely possibility that their house will burn down; but no insurance is available to protect them against the possibility that the value of their home will decline if there is some unanticipated consequence resulting from a modest change nearby. The natural response under these circumstances is to resist almost any change on the grounds that at least current arrangements are fully understood. Fischel suggests that homeowners would be much less resistant to change if they could be provided with some form of insurance to protect the value of their home against possible negative effects of change caused by municipal actions.[14] Unfortunately, it is extremely difficult to see how such insurance would operate in the real world, mainly because it would be almost impossible to isolate the financial effects of such changes from other factors that cause price variations in houses.

As a kind of second-best alternative to such insurance, homeowners often form neighbourhood associations (often called 'ratepayers' associations' because members wish to emphasize that they pay property taxes, to be discussed in more detail in Chapter 14). The main purpose of these associations is to do whatever is necessary to protect property values. Often they accentuate the NIMBY syndrome: if only a few members are upset about a proposal for change, they tend to get the support of the entire association so as to maintain loyalty and unity. Instead of a few objectors, the municipality finds itself facing an entire association.

Meanwhile, municipalities will urge people to participate; developers will accommodate concerns of neighbouring property-owners as best they can while still maximizing profits; and property-owners will remain vigilant. Occasionally, large numbers of people will be mobilized around a particular local issue, but the issues that attract attention are usually related to wider social movements. For example, a municipality trying to find a new landfill site might provoke environmentalists who object in principle to all new landfill sites. Occasions are now quite rare when municipalities attempt to impose changes on a neighbourhood without first making sure that there will be few, if any, objections. But when they make a mistake, they usually are quite quick to back down. The influence of the new reformers is still strong, even if not so visible as it once was.

Conclusion

Knowing about the formal functions and structures of local government is important. Such knowledge by itself is not so important unless we understand how people use these structures to try to get what they want. In Chapter 13, we shall examine the ways in which local governments spend their money, and this will provide considerable information about what makes local government so vital in the real world, especially in cities. But some of the most important things that municipalities are responsible for do not cost money: granting permission to private developers to construct buildings is a prime example. Some municipal decisions about buildings and land development can be appealed (especially in Ontario) to provincial quasi-judicial agencies, but council decisions are still usually the key stage in the approval process. Because municipalities are also responsible for arranging for the provision of the basic infrastructure necessary for new development to be viable, they are of crucial importance for anyone (including homeowners) with financial interests in the built environment. There has been considerable debate among social scientists about the extent to which the land-development industry determines the decisions of municipal councils.[15] For our purposes, we need only recognize the close connection between land development and municipal politics, and leave it to others to sort out exactly how these connections work in particular cities at particular times.

As we shall see in the next chapter, citizens usually expect municipal governments to provide leadership in securing the economic development and prosperity of their respective cities. But municipalities have only limited tools that they can use to achieve this objective. This is just one of the many reasons why being a municipal leader, especially a mayor, is such a difficult job. The basic factors needed to create wealth in a city (or anywhere else) are some combination of capital, labour, and land. Municipalities do not control currencies, nor can they regulate how money is moved around or invested, and they do not control labour—within a given country people and workers can migrate as they wish without the permission of any municipality. But municipalities do have a significant level of control over how land is used within their boundaries. This is the main reason why issues having to do with land are so important in municipal politics.[16]

RESOURCES

Explore the downtown area of the community where you live. What actions did the municipal government take to make it lively, interesting, and prosperous? What mistakes did they make? For guidance, you might want to consult Jane Jacobs, *The Death and Life of Great American Cities*.

STUDY QUESTIONS

1. Do you think developers should pay the full cost of all municipal infrastructure associated with new subdivisions? Explain your reasoning.

2. Why, in your view, did municipalities not do more to protect re-
    tail business in their downtowns from competition from suburban
    malls?

3. Would Canadian cities be better off today if there were more inner-
    city expressways? What caused the original plans of traffic engi-
    neers for such expressways not to be implemented?

4. Have you ever actively participated in a municipal political issue?
    If not, what kind of an issue would cause you to become involved?
    What form would your participation take?

11 Mayors and Local Political Leadership

In the last chapter we focused on the importance of land in municipal politics. The emphasis was on the ways in which land developers and various other interests associated with the industry are able to have considerable influence over what municipal councils actually decided. At the same time, we saw lots of evidence that developers do not always get what they want. This is because municipal councils are not simply passive mechanisms whereby developers' interests are translated into municipal policy. All developers do not share the same interests all the time, and other property-owners, especially homeowners, have their own interests that are usually strongly articulated to municipal councils. At a minimum, municipal councils have to act as referees between different powerful interests. In reality, they usually do more than this. Some council members, especially mayors, want to launch their own independent initiatives and bring about significant change within their cities or towns. This chapter is about how some mayors manage to do this and provide leadership in a complex municipal environment.

First, we need to examine the legal status of Canadian mayors and then look at mechanisms through which they can exert their influence on council. We then turn to some real-world examples of mayoral leadership. Finally, we consider the extent to which successful municipal leadership in Canada requires the construction of 'urban regimes' and look at various styles of mayoral leadership.

Legal Status of Mayors

Many contradictions appear in the office of mayor in a Canadian city. On the one hand, mayors are directly elected. More people vote directly for the mayor of Toronto than for any other office in Canada, because mayors in Canada, except in many municipalities in Newfoundland and Labrador,[1] are directly elected by all eligible voters. The Prime Minister of Canada and the premiers of the provinces, on the other hand, are directly elected only by voters in their own electoral districts. They become heads of their respective governments because they lead the party that has the most seats in the legislature. While nothing in the written Constitution mentions the offices of Prime Minister or Premier, the powers of mayors are outlined in every Municipal Act of every province in the country.

In Ontario, however, the Municipal Act refers to mayors as being 'heads of council', along with the wardens of counties and chairs of regional municipalities, positions that are similar to that of mayors. In Alberta, section 154 of the Municipal Government Act briefly outlines the responsibilities of 'chief elected officials' and section 155 states that the council can choose another title (such as 'mayor') if it so desires. In most provinces, including Alberta, the legal duties of the mayor listed in the statute are very limited, and include presiding over council meetings. Section 225 of the Ontario Act states that the role of the head of council is 'to act as the chief executive officer of the municipality', a grant of authority that seems quite impressive. But section 226.1 circumscribes the role in these words:

As chief executive officer of a municipality, the head of council shall,
(a) uphold and promote the purposes of the municipality;
(b) promote public involvement in the municipality's activities;
(c) act as the representative of the municipality both within and outside the municipality, and promote the municipality locally, nationally and internationally; and
(d) participate in and foster activities that enhance the economic, social and environmental well-being of the municipality and its residents.

Compared to the responsibilities of a chief executive officer of a business corporation, these roles are remarkably limited, especially when we consider what section 227 has to say about the role of the 'municipal administration':

It is the role of the officers and employees of the municipality,
(a) to implement council's decisions and establish administrative practices and procedures to carry out council's decisions;
(b) to undertake research and provide advice to council on the policies and programs of the municipality; and
(c) to carry out other duties required under this or any Act and other duties assigned by the municipality.

This section suggests that, although the mayor might be the 'chief executive officer', he or she does not have any direct control over the municipality's administrative apparatus. The usual practice, as we shall see in the next chapter, is for the council to appoint someone to be the head of the municipal bureaucracy (usually called a 'city manager' or a 'chief administrative officer') and for that person to be responsible to the council as a whole rather than to the mayor.

The same situation applies to mayors in other provinces. In legal terms, there are no 'strong mayors' in Canada. The strong-mayor system in the United States is one in which the mayor is directly responsible for the operation of the city's bureaucracy and in most cases has the authority personally to appoint the senior municipal officers. A strong mayor in the United States has similar powers in the municipality as has the US President in relation to the federal government. But just as the President does not sit in Congress, a strong mayor does not sit in a municipal council. If a strong mayor has political allies in the council, he might be able to control the council, but with no guarantees. The strength of strong mayors derives from their control over the administration, not over the council, although sometimes mayors have the authority to veto council decisions, at least temporarily. In a parliamentary system, on the other hand, such as we have in Ottawa and in the provincial capitals, a Prime Minister or a Premier whose party has won a majority of the legislative seats controls both the legislature and the civil service. Most mayors in Canada are weak in that they control neither the bureaucracy nor the council.

In cities with municipal parties (as in Vancouver, Montreal, and Quebec City), the mayor derives political power from being head of his or her party. Elsewhere mayors can only approximate such power if they cultivate groups of councillors to support their position on as many issues as possible, a time-consuming and often thankless task. Many mayors in the country are on the losing sides of council votes more often than on the winning side. As was noted above, in most Canadian municipalities, mayors preside over meetings and have a special role in determining the agenda, but this gives them little in the way of special advantage. Presiding over council meetings often puts mayors at a disadvantage. In order to contribute to debates mayors usually have to leave the chair and ask someone else take over. In Toronto, Montreal, and Winnipeg, the mayor no longer chairs council meetings; instead a 'speaker' or chair is chosen by the council (often on the nomination of the mayor) to act permanently as the presiding officer. In this way the mayor is freed up to act as a legislative leader on the floor of the council for whatever position he or she wants to advance.

Executive Committees

Prime ministers and premiers choose ministers, usually elected members from their own party, who collectively form the cabinet that is responsible to the legislature for the operation of the government. In Canadian municipalities the council as a whole is collectively responsible for the operation of the municipal government. There is no equivalent to a cabinet in Canadian municipalities. Some councils have executive committees. In their simplest form, such committees result from internal decisions of councils about how to organize the way they do business. An executive committee is simply another standing committee, perhaps with special responsibility for making recommendations to council on matters such as human resource policy that relate to the entire municipality. Members are chosen by the entire council in the same way as are members of other standing committees. The only distinctive feature of such committees is that they usually are presided over by the mayor.

The executive committee for the city of Winnipeg (called the 'executive policy committee') is different. In 1997, a business-oriented mayor, Susan Thompson, undertook to bring significant change to Winnipeg's political and administrative structures. Under her leadership, city council agreed to engage a well-known Canadian municipal consultant, George B. Cuff, to review the city's operations. Much of Cuff's report called for the standard nostrums of the 'new public management', which involve trying to adapt the practices of private business to the public sector, but he also addressed structural issues. Probably his most notable recommendation was to abolish the city's Board of Commissioners. Such a board was a peculiarly western Canadian structure that included a chief commissioner as chair, who was the city's senior staff member, other commissioners who headed different parts of the administration, and the mayor. In addition to acting as a kind of official management team, the Board was charged with preparing the council agenda. Cuff concluded that the existence of the Board of Commissioners caused confusion and delay and hampered transparency and accountability. As a result of Cuff's report, city council abolished the Board and replaced it with both a single chief administrative officer (CAO) and an executive policy committee (EPC) on the council. The mayor chairs the EPC, decides on the number of members (although the number cannot be more than half the size of the council, which is 16), and appoints them. Most simultaneously become chairs of the council's five standing committees. In 2010 there were seven EPC members in total, including the mayor. Although this committee is similar to a parliamentary cabinet in the sense that its members are appointed by the mayor and can be terminated by the mayor at any time, it is important to remember that members have no formal obligation to support or agree with the mayor. Another crucial difference from a cabinet is that most of its business is conducted in public. Nevertheless, the power of the mayor of Winnipeg to control the membership of the EPC makes him or her one of the most powerful mayors in Canada in relation to the operation of his or her municipal political system. Another important mayoral power in Winnipeg is the ability to appoint members of the EPC secretariat, a staff group that provides policy advice independent of the operating departments of the city administration. Finally, the fact that EPC members named by the mayor to be either the deputy mayor or the chairs of standing committees receive an increased salary ($80,000 versus $64,000 in 2010) gives the mayor additional leverage over his or her appointees.

Because the mayor of Winnipeg is not clearly and solely responsible for the administrative operations of the municipal government, Winnipeg still cannot be said to have an American-style strong mayor. Recently, such a system has been discussed as a possible mechanism for extracting the city of Toronto from its obvious structural difficulties since the amalgamation of 1998. When the Ontario legislature approved a new City of Toronto Act in 2006, it insisted that the city streamline its political and administrative structures to enhance accountability, especially by strengthening the authority of the mayor. City council decided in June 2006 that, starting in 2007, the mayor would appoint a deputy mayor and the heads of the council's standing committees, who would in turn comprise the majority on a new 13-member executive committee that is supposed to provide policy leadership to the council as a whole. These relatively minor changes met the province's requirements.

But the strongest municipal executive committees in Canada are in Quebec's major cities, especially the city of Montreal. Ever since the 1960s, Montreal's executive committee has been the main forum for municipal decision-making. Like federal and provincial cabinets, it does not meet in public, it can perform some functions without reference to the whole council, and most of its members have special responsibilities for parts of the municipal bureaucracy in the same way that cabinet ministers do. Important changes were made in 2010. In breaks with past practices, Mayor Tremblay decided to chair the committee himself and to appoint two of the 12 members from the opposition parties (one from Vision Montreal and the leader of Project Montreal). However, the new arrangement can hardly be called a coalition, because the leader of Vision Montreal, Louise Harel, remains as the leader of the opposition on the city council. The combination of a strong party system and a strong executive committee means that meetings of Montreal's city council are much more like meetings of parliamentary legislatures than of municipal councils in other Canadian cities. The corollary of this arrangement is that the mayor of Montreal is much more powerful than most other mayors.

How Mayors Become Powerful

In any political system, the strength of a leader can derive from a number of different sources. Among Canadian mayors, a very few are powerful because they are the leaders of municipal political parties that win a majority of seats on the municipal council; others derive a certain degree of strength from particular institutional powers they have, especially the power to appoint members of an executive committee. The mayor of Montreal has both kinds of powers. But no Canadian mayor is in complete charge of the municipal bureaucracy as in the American strong-mayor system. Some Canadian mayors, however, have managed to become quite powerful within their own municipalities without having any kind of extra formal authority. We need to have some idea of how they did it. We shall look briefly at the mayoral career of Stephen Juba of Winnipeg and in a bit more detail at that of Hazel McCallion of Mississauga.

Stephen Juba

Allan Levine, a Winnipeg historian, has written that 'Stephen Juba ran the city of Winnipeg as his personal fiefdom from 1956 to 1977.'[2] Although few mayors in Canada have been as successful with the electorate as Juba, his story is not unlike that of other popular mayors in other places. He seemed to have had very few skills other than to get ordinary voters to like him, a skill that is especially useful for mayoral candidates running city-wide without the declared support of a political party. Astonishingly, he won nine mayoral elections by large margins without spending more than $2,000 in total.[3] Campaigning as an independent 'man of the people' at various elections in the early 1950s, he managed to get himself elected in a multi-member constituency in the provincial legislature in 1953. There he became known for fighting for looser liquor laws and coloured margarine, both issues of considerable concern to his Winnipeg supporters. He lost his first two attempts to be elected mayor in 1952 and 1954, railing against both local socialists and the Independent Citizens' Election Committee (the ICEC, similar to

Vancouver's NPA). But in 1956 he defeated the ICEC incumbent, a prominent local business person who was a member of all 'the right clubs',[4]
and became Winnipeg's first non-Anglo-Saxon mayor. Levine describes
his early actions this way:

> As the people's champion, Juba challenged the system at every oppor-
> tunity. In 1957 he took on the Winnipeg and Central Gas Company
> and was responsible for a rate reduction. The city's merchants were
> grateful. The next was the Wolsley Tree Affair, a classic example of
> Juba's early style and showmanship. The focus of this episode was the
> fate of a ninety-five-year-old elm tree on Wolsley Street. . . . In the early
> fall of 1957, the city's public works committee—without notice to the
> residents of the area—decided to chop the huge tree down because it
> was a hindrance to traffic. But when the city's engineering department
> arrived to undertake the job, it was greeted by a band of protesting
> women who had linked arms around the tree. After one of the work-
> men started to threaten the women with an ax, the women started to
> chant for the mayor. On cue, Juba pulled up in his yellow Cadillac. Like
> a white knight he stopped the workmen and sent away the police, who
> had arrived to take the women back to the station in a paddy wagon.
>
> Juba believed that he was acting within his authority as the chief
> executive officer of the city; later the council, by a vote of twelve to
> six, supported his decision. So the mayor was the neighbourhood hero.
> But more important, this event received international press coverage
> and further endeared Juba to the public. It also showed the aldermen
> [councillors] just how smooth and powerful their mayor had become.[5]

From then on, Juba's power continued to increase. He promoted
Winnipeg at every opportunity, both inside and beyond Canada. He
fought many battles with the Corporation of Greater Winnipeg and won
most of them. When the provincial government was establishing the unicity system in 1971, he fought off its initial efforts to have the mayor indirectly elected by councillors (so as to encourage a parliamentary system
at the local level) because he knew that, although the people supported
him, most councillors did not, especially the ones from the amalgamated
suburbs. Juba easily won two elections in the unicity, but withdrew his
candidacy at the last minute in 1977, thereby snookering his main rival
from the ICEC who did not want to run against him but who was too late
to submit his own nomination papers.[6] The ICEC disbanded six years
later. For good or ill, Stephen Juba played a major role in preventing the
growth, and survival, of municipal political parties in Winnipeg.

Hazel McCallion

Hazel McCallion has been mayor of Mississauga since 1978. During the time she has been mayor its population has grown from about 300,000 to 670,000 in 2006.[7] It is now Canada's sixth most populous municipality. In theory, Mississauga's authority is limited by the fact that it is a lower-tier unit within the Regional Municipality of Peel, but in practice, as we have seen in Chapter 7, the Mississauga city council largely controls what happens on the Peel regional council. Because Mayor McCallion controls the Mississauga council, she also is the dominant politician within Peel. How has she managed to be mayor for so long and to build and retain such influence? The question is especially intriguing because she is a woman who was born in 1921. Tom Urbaniak, a political scientist at Cape Breton University who grew up in Mississauga and who has carefully observed her career, has written a compelling biography of McCallion[8] that both provides some answers and helps us better understand municipal politics in Canada's suburbs.

Urbaniak shows that McCallion uses many of the same political tactics exploited so successfully by Stephen Juba; for example, she shops at a different supermarket in Mississauga each week in order to meet more people[9] and she is quick to praise. 'Many a cleric has been dubbed "my favourite priest," many a youth leader labelled "a future mayor" or future "prime minister," many a school given the moniker "the best school in Mississauga."'[10] She also benefited from acting decisively and authoritatively soon after she became mayor when a massive train derailment and chemical spill in 1979 caused evacuations and disruptions for thousands of residents in the heart of the municipality. If all that mayors needed to do in Canada to become completely dominant within their own municipalities is simply to copy McCallion, they would do so and reap the rewards. The real strength of Urbaniak's analysis is in explaining what is unique about the political environment in which McCallion has operated.

McCallion was first elected mayor in Mississauga after pro-developer and pro-reform mayors had been discredited—the first, by too much disruption and hints of corruption, and the second, by hefty tax increases. 'What a time it was to step in. The city-wide interest groups were weak. The developers were discredited. And most of the municipality was serviced (with water and sewer) for development. The local leaders need not be beholden to anyone.'[11] McCallion managed to keep taxes down by convincing developers to pay development charges (see previous chapter) to fund new infrastructure even before it was clear that such charges were legal. McCallion understood that the developers had little choice because building homes and commercial buildings in Mississauga was a sure way to make money. Urbaniak notes that McCallion's political career prospered because she was working with a large 'suburban canvas', which meant that potential sources of conflict concerning land use could be kept isolated from each other. New subdivisions, new industrial parks, and even a new 'city centre' could be built with most existing residents suffering neither inconvenience nor higher taxes. As new residents moved in, the power of older small-town social networks declined. There was little to replace them. Local media were weak and Toronto's media paid little attention.

McCallion stepped into a political vacuum and used her great personal political skills to fill it. She protects municipal staff against political interference or outside criticism—from everybody except herself. For her, it is quite all right to become involved in administrative details, especially if it is about a matter a resident has brought directly to her attention. About her treatment of councillors, Urbaniak says this:

> Councillors also—if they showed themselves to be deferential—would be allowed to give direction on small matters: a backed-up sewer here, a sidewalk there. Although McCallion was never reluctant to take action directly, she would sometimes hand a file to a councillor and let him or her deal with it and get some credit.[12]

He notes that 'In Mississauga, the *de facto* Hazel McCallion Party has held virtually every seat on council. Even if its members had grievances against the mayor, they almost never raised them in public.'[13] Her critics outside council received little attention from anybody. To the extent that they sought publicity by making extreme statements, their efforts usually backfired because the end result was that they 'drew sympathy to her.'[14] To attack 'Hazel' was to attack the entire community, a community so disparate and loosely connected that she was almost the only symbol that held it together.

Tom Urbaniak's analysis of Hazel McCallion and of Mississauga politics provides us with a vivid portrait of a form of local politics that can probably be found only in Canada. In most parts of the democratic world national political parties dominate local politics almost completely, especially in the larger authorities. Thousands of non-partisan suburban municipalities abound in the United States, but none is more populous than Mississauga, and most have populations of only a few thousand. Urbaniak notes[15] that American urbanists have coined the term 'boomburb' to refer to growing suburbs with populations over 100,000.[16] No

American boomburb has a population anywhere near Mississauga's, and most are not as populous as Surrey, Burnaby, and Richmond in suburban Vancouver or Brampton, Markham, and Vaughn in suburban Toronto. Urbaniak suggests that, if Mississauga were in the United States, it would probably have a part-time mayor and council, a much more publicly prominent city manager, and frequent plebiscites on tax increases and bond issues that would provoke more citizen interest in municipal political issues.[17] In reality, however, we simply do not know, because there are no municipalities like Mississauga in the United States.

Before leaving Urbaniak's work and beginning a discussion of 'urban regimes' in Canada, we should note how Urbaniak thinks Mississauga is relevant to the study of urban regimes. For Urbaniak, the question was 'How did McCallion become so powerful that only she could get things done in Mississauga?' For regime theorists, the question is 'How does anyone get anything done in a municipality?' Urbaniak writes:

> Regime theorists, who have come to dominate the urban politics literature of late, see stable local governance as the product of a coalition of organized groups with resources—usually money or votes. In the most-cited case, the Atlanta of political scientist Clarence Stone, it was hard to move anything forward if you were not in with the downtown business elite or the leaders of the African American middle class. They were the coalition. They had fixed resources; they needed each other. But what if the resources were scattered? What if there is no downtown worthy of the designation? What if the voters are in disparate communities and poorly organized and relatively new to the city? What if the city is in the path of development anyway, without requiring grinding efforts to attract it? What if it already has the 'empty' space in which to put development? This is not an uncommon suburban dynamic.[18]

The dynamic might not be uncommon around Toronto and Vancouver, but the existence of large suburban municipalities containing 'disparate communities' is uncommon in the United States. If one person can be a regime, then Hazel McCallion is a regime. But rather than try to squeeze the Canadian urban political experience into American models, we need to examine American models for their relevance.

Do Canadian Cities Have Urban Regimes?

In Chapters 9 and 10 we saw that one possible conclusion from studying Canadian municipal politics is that all important decisions are determined by economic and social elites, or at least by major development interests. In the United States in the 1960s another significant approach emerged. Robert Dahl, a political scientist at Yale University, studied local decision-making in New Haven, Connecticut, the city in which Yale is located. He discovered that different groups were predominant on different issues and that the municipal council (and other local bodies) acted as a kind of referee in local controversies, making sure that no one group always won or always lost. Politicians who did not carefully weigh all the conflicting interests would likely lose the next election, so the system, in Dahl's view, was self-correcting. Dahl's 1961 book about New Haven, *Who Governs?*,[19] was hugely influential, largely because it presented American urban politics as a model for how democratic decision-making happens in the real world. We might not all participate in all the governmental decisions that affect our daily lives, as some democratic theories would suggest, but for Dahl, as long as our interests are defended by one group or another, and as long as each group is treated fairly and has a chance to win its case every once in a while, then we should all be satisfied. Dahl's version of democracy is called 'pluralist' because it works as long as many different interests are involved in the policy-making process. It has been subject to a great deal of criticism, notably that Dahl ignores reality in assuming that all interests in society actually are represented by organized groups and that all such groups are treated fairly when it comes to public decisions that are relevant to their interests. But many have criticized it as simply a defence of 'business as usual' in American politics.

Perhaps these criticisms explain why we have had no studies of Canadian urban politics adopting Dahl's methodology—studying how explicit decisions were made on a variety of different subjects—or that have arrived at pluralist conclusions. Instead, we have studies that focus on issues related to land development and that tend to see the decision-making process as one that pits citizens' groups against developers. As Urbaniak suggested, however, it is regime theory, not pluralism, that holds sway today among most students of American urban politics. Regime theory has had considerable influence in Canada, so it merits our attention.

Clarence Stone studied urban politics in Atlanta between 1946 and 1988 and discovered neither a decision-making process completely dominated by an economic elite nor a system that was genuinely pluralist. Instead, he found:

What makes governance in Atlanta effective is not the formal machinery of government, but rather the informal partnership between city hall and the downtown business elite. The informal partnership and the way it operates constitute the city's regime; it is the means through which major policy decisions are made.[20]

Stone notes that all organizations require informal arrangements in order to get things done, and that students of any kind of organization need to understand these arrangements. But a regime is 'not just any informal group that comes together to make a decision but [is rather] an informal yet relatively stable group with access to institutional resources that enable it to have a sustained role in making governing decisions.'[21] The 'stable group' that Stone found in Atlanta comprised middle-class African Americans who were able to take control of Atlanta's city government after the passage of the American Civil Rights Act in the 1960s and the downtown business elite who controlled prime real estate and crucial sources of jobs and wealth. Both groups needed each other to achieve their objectives. Businesses cannot carry on without co-operation and support from municipal governments; municipal governments can accomplish nothing if key businesses decide to leave town.

Stone's analysis of politics in Atlanta has been hugely influential, in no small measure because it suggests that politics is neither subordinate to economics nor simply the result of the particular strengths of particular interests around particular decisions. Instead, according to regime theory, elected politicians, who cannot accomplish what they want at the local level without outside support, make deliberate decisions to enter long-term alliances in order to achieve their goals. For political scientists, following Stone in studying how regimes are formed, how they persist, and how they change is truly an exciting challenge. Nevertheless, students of comparative urban politics have pointed out that regime theory might not be so relevant outside the United States, where political parties are much stronger at the local level and/or where central governments provide much more support and direction to local governments.[22] In these circumstances, local politicians can accomplish their objectives without having to form the kind of regime that Stone discovered in Atlanta.

Christopher Leo was the first student of Canadian urban politics to make use of regime theory. He did so in an article about how the Edmonton city council dealt with downtown development issues in the late 1980s and early 1990s. Like Stone in Atlanta, Leo finds a corporate urban regime in Edmonton primarily concerned with the development interests of major downtown corporations. Surprisingly, however, Leo notes that the 'ruling coalition is shifting, unstable, and always subject to attack, a common phenomenon in Canadian city politics'[23] and that, with reference to the development issues he analyzed, 'The give and take of local politics and the happenstance of local factors could have caused any or all of them to have turned out differently.'[24] What is surprising about these findings is that the existence of a regime, according to Stone, is supposed to bring stability and predictability to council decisions, but Leo is suggesting in reality the state of affairs in Edmonton was quite the opposite. To further confuse matters, Leo suggests that the corporate regime in Edmonton is 'characterized by subordination of the local state'[25] and that the dominant group on council was 'the passive faction whose only strategy was reaction to events controlled by others'.[26] What kind of regime is it that only does what particular developers want? From Leo's own description and analysis, it appears that there simply was no regime in place in Edmonton during the period he was studying.

In 2003, Timothy Cobban published an article on 'The Political Economy of Urban Development: Downtown Revitalization in London, Ontario, 1993–2002'.[27] The article analyzed a massive effort by city officials to bring new life to its downtown after a devastating series of setbacks, including the bankruptcy and virtual abandonment of the downtown mall referred to in the previous chapter. Cobban explicitly sets out to determine if the effort—which has been at least partially successful—was brought about by an urban regime. He finds no regime:

> While the list of usual suspects in urban regime analysis is at least partially evident in London (e.g., Chamber of Commerce, London Downtown Business Association, Ellis-Don Construction Ltd.), there is no evidence of a patterned, stable relationship between private interests and city council of the type that Stone suggests should be evident during development policy-making. The lack of an observable governing coalition and urban regime does not appear to be the result of interventionist senior government officials.[28]

Cobban argues that local business elites tend to become less involved in local politics in Canada than in the US because Canadian municipalities are much less reliant on borrowing from local financial institutions than American municipalities, because Canadian municipalities generally are prohibited by provincial legislation from offering tax concessions that attract business interest, and because most central cities in Canada (including London) have few, if any, competing suburban municipalities. In the US, this last factor acts as an incentive for downtown business interests to combine with the municipality to present a unified front against suburban competition. In London, the municipal government itself has to balance central and suburban interests because its boundaries take in almost the entire urbanized area.

In a rejoinder to Cobban's article, Leo argued that Cobban's definition of a regime is too narrow. He rightfully argues that 'there is and probably can be no precise determination of how much dominance and stability is required in order to justify the "regime" label.'[29] He goes on: 'A meaningful refutation of regime theory on its own terms would be a finding that there is no coalition-building taking place, that there are no prime movers in achieving particular policy objectives or that the prime movers do not negotiate strike compromises, and offer incentives to get others on board.' He then suggests that if Cobban had only pushed his analysis of the London case he would inevitably have found some kind of regime. 'On the face of it, the evidence he does present suggests there is a regime, one dominated by suburban interests, and that the weaker interests supporting downtown development compound their weakness with internecine strife.'[30]

The editor of the journal in which the Cobban–Leo exchange took place gave Cobban, as the author of the original article, the last word. Cobban claimed that, after re-analyzing his data, he found even less evidence suggesting that a regime was in place in London.

> By Stone's criteria, a governing coalition must be relatively stable (it cannot form and dissolve depending on the issue); it must have a cross-sectoral foundation (it must include representatives from both governmental and non-governmental organizations); and it must be informally governed internally (the relationships among coalition members must not be fully specified by formal government structures).'[31]

As is evident by now, much of the debate hinges on the definition of 'regime'. For Cobban, it is a relatively precise concept; for Leo it is a concept we can use to emphasize that much of what is important in political decision-making cannot be captured by formal rules of governmental institutions. Leo's case was buttressed by Stone himself, who in 2005 seems to considerably loosen his original definition of a regime by stating that 'I propose a more open-ended conception of a regime as simply the informal arrangements through which a community is governed.'[32] In any event, the Cobban–Leo exchange should be read by anyone with an interest in understanding how we can use the concept of an urban regime and how we can better understand urban decision-making.

In her 2009 book, *Municipalities and Multiculturalism: The Politics of Immigration in Toronto and Vancouver*, Kristin R. Good makes extensive use of the concept of 'regime'. She discovers a dazzling array of different kinds of regimes in almost every place she looks. Notably, however, in Mississauga there appear only to be 'potential regime participants'[33] because Mayor McCallion is so personally powerful in keeping issues related to immigrant settlement off the municipal political agenda. Good claims that:

> McCallion's leadership is reinforced by an invisible power structure that represents Mississauga's 'old guard'. Though direct evidence of this was not unearthed, some interviewees suggested that McCallion could 'punish' organizations and individuals that challenged her. One civil servant mentioned the perception that McCallion could have an organization's Peel Region grant withdrawn if it spoke out against the city. The threat of McCallion's personal disapproval divides the immigrant community and thus is a barrier to co-ordinated political pressure on the municipality. Immigrant communities fear the withdrawal of her presence at ethnocultural events.[34]

Good's tantalizing reference to McCallion's leadership being 'reinforced by an invisible power structure' would seem to be just the kind of alliance or coalition that a regime theorist would be looking for. In any event, this finding is not consistent with Urbaniak's claim that McCallion defeated 'the old guard' and does not need a regime or coalition to govern in Mississauga's 'broad suburban canvas'.

Of the many municipalities and organizations studied by Good, her description of Coquitlam in suburban Vancouver is the only one in which she makes no use of the word 'regime'. She quotes Coquitlam's mayor as telling her in an interview that 'an "old guard" governs Coquitlam with the support of small-c conservative retirees'.[35] Once again, such an alliance seems clearly to fit Clarence Stone's definition of an urban regime. To be fair to Good, the focus of her analysis is on regimes relating to 'the politics of immigration' in Toronto and Vancouver and not on regimes that govern individual municipalities. But it is surprising that she does not label coalitions that block policies for immigrants as regimes when she is so apt to find them in various political alignments that are designed to advance such policies.

The latest use of the term 'regime' in the analysis of Canadian municipal politics is simply as a rough approximation for 'ideological position of the council majority'. Hence, we can talk about a 'conservative regime' or a 'reformist regime'. Allahwalla, Boudreau, and Keil do this in a chapter entitled 'Neo-Liberal Governance: Entrepreneurial Municipal Regimes in Canada'. In this article, the authors make no attempt to define the concept or to refer to previous writing about municipal regimes. Readers learn only that Toronto had a neo-reformist regime when David Miller was mayor[36] and that under Mayor Tremblay, Montreal's regime is 'highly fragmented, service oriented, and even conformist (rather than socially transformative)'.[37]

The more loosely the term 'regime' is used, the less useful it is likely to be. If almost any informal interaction among people who are trying to get something done in the political arena constitutes at least the beginning of a regime, then conscientious political scientists are studying regimes all the time. Such an observation is not much different from Christopher Leo's position, discussed above. Recent emphasis on regimes is a useful reminder that, even if economic conditions *are* extremely important in determining political outcomes, politicians act, at a minimum, to transform economic imperatives into reality and usually do much more. Looking for regimes also prevents us from focusing exclusively on what happens within official institutions, such as municipal councils. This too is good, although hardly innovative in urban politics because the same motivation inspired the original 'community power' studies more than half a century ago.

In his work on Atlanta, Clarence Stone provided us with a genuinely innovative analysis of the way in which Atlanta's black middle class (who controlled city hall) worked together with Atlanta's downtown corporate elite (who controlled significant economic resources) over a long period of time to implement policies that benefit both groups. If we can find examples of similar regimes in Canadian municipal politics, our knowledge will be greatly enhanced. Until we do, we still must do the best we can to understand how Canadian municipal leaders, especially mayors, get things done.

Models of Mayoral Leadership

In 1978 in a book provocatively titled *The Ungovernable City*, the American political scientist Douglas Yates suggested that we need to analyze two main variables in order to understand 'mayoral leadership style'.[38] Such an analysis leads to the labels shown in Table 11.1. We have already seen that most mayors in Canada have a weak power base. Most are not leaders of strong parties; they have little in the way of formal legal power; and we have very limited evidence to suggest that any have been able to construct powerful regimes. Not much evidence exists to suggest most are especially innovative. This means that, according to the table, most can be classified as 'brokers'. Mayors who are brokers try to convince people with conflicting interests to compromise with each other so that some kind of policy can be adopted, even if it is nobody's first choice. Being a broker in a democratic society is an honourable, if not especially exciting, function. It requires lots of meetings, lots of listening, and lots of patience, much of it in informal settings. Although, as we have seen, informal ways of getting things done are associated with regimes, the art of arranging compromises is especially notable for being at the heart of Dahl's pluralist analysis: a broker has no overriding personal agenda but instead is more interested in balancing competing interests. Much of the day-to-day work of any municipal leader in Canada is about being a broker.

Occasionally we find mayors who want to bring about great change but are not politically strong enough to do so. 'Crusader' is an apt word for such mayors. Because most mayors in large municipalities have a strong appetite for self-preservation, we find few who are crusaders in this sense. John Sewell, the mayor of Toronto from 1978 to 1980, was an example. In the last chapter we noted that he was on the more radical end of Toronto's new reform movement in the 1960s and 1970s. As mayor, he clearly wanted to introduce a much more participatory culture at Toronto city hall but he spent little time rallying support within the council for his position. Sewell is still active in community causes today. He was defeated in 1980 by Art Eggleton, whose mayoral leadership style clearly fell into the 'broker' category. Eggleton is now a Liberal senator in Ottawa.

Stephen Juba and Hazel McCallion both developed strong power bases but were not particularly innovative. However, they were not traditional political 'bosses' in the sense that their power depended on granting jobs, contracts, and favours to their political supporters. The power of a traditional political boss is rooted in a political party, but both Juba and McCallion were strongly opposed to the presence of political parties

Table 11.1 Mayoral Leadership Style

	Innovative	Not Innovative
Strong power base	Entrepreneur	Boss
Weak power base	Crusader	Broker

Source: Adapted from Douglas Yates, *The Ungovernable City: The Politics of Urban Problems and Policy Making* (Cambridge Mass.: MIT Press, 1978), 165.

in municipal politics. They both built their invincible electoral strength by fusing their own political identity with that of the municipality itself. Except for the fact that he led his own personal political party, the mayoralty of Jean Drapeau of Montreal was similar. The main difference perhaps is that he personally sponsored more innovative municipal projects that literally changed the face of Montreal: the subway system, Expo 67, the Olympic Games. In this sense, he was clearly more entrepreneurial, even if the main sources of funds for his grand projects were the federal and provincial governments.

In recent years, the mayors who seem to have been both powerful and innovative are David Miller in Toronto (2003–10), Glen Murray in Winnipeg (1998–2004), and Larry Campbell in Vancouver (2002–05). None was entrepreneurial in the sense of seeking to bring business-like practices to municipal government, but they all tried hard to use their political capital as mayors of major cities to bring about significant political change. Miller and Murray were committed to a 'new deal for cities' and Campbell was a strong advocate for bringing about change in Vancouver's Downtown Eastside. They all had considerable support within their own councils, but to attain their objectives they needed support from other levels of government more than they needed to build a strong regime at home. It is likely, of course, that, had Mayor Miller been part of a regime that included the executive occupants of the top floors of Toronto's bank towers, he would have had more success than he did in convincing the federal government to allocate a share of GST revenues to major municipalities. But why would presidents of national banks want to be involved in such a battle? Unlike the corporate elite in downtown Atlanta, they simply had no reason to seek favour with their local mayor.

Nevertheless, in the mid-2000s, Miller, Murray, and Campbell made significant progress on their respective priorities, especially when Paul Martin was Prime Minister of Canada. Miller obtained modest new powers for Toronto,[39] but Murray did not get any new taxation authority from the province of Manitoba.[40] Campbell's efforts to aid the Downtown Eastside benefited from Vancouver's bid for the 2010 Winter Olympics.[41] In the final analysis, however, all three mayors might be assigned to the 'crusader' category. Campbell's municipal party (COPE) broke apart and he accepted an offer from Martin in 2005 to become a Liberal senator. Murray resigned as mayor of Winnipeg to run unsuccessfully as a Liberal candidate in the federal general election of 2004 and more recently, having moved to Toronto and won a by-election for a seat in the Ontario legislature, in August

2010 was named as Minister of Research and Innovation in the provincial Liberal government. Elected in Toronto in 2003, David Miller was in office longer than the other two but it already seems that much of his legacy—including the vehicle registration and land transfer taxes and an ambitious plan for renewing public transit called 'Transit City'—is being dismantled by his successor, Rob Ford.

Clarence Stone's book about Atlanta makes scarcely any reference to the Georgia state government. By contrast, it seems highly unlikely that a mayor of a major Canadian municipality could make progress on any significant issue without having considerable support from the relevant provincial government, and sometimes from the federal government as well. To understand how change comes about in Canadian cities we probably need to know more about intergovernmental relations than about municipal links with local businesses.

One of the often-overlooked facts about tri-level intergovernmental relations in Canada is that, at any point in time, one of the three levels is preparing for an election, conducting one, or just recovering from one.[42] The times when all three levels can work at a political level on a given project actually are quite limited. More limited still are the times when such elections produce results such that political leaders at all three levels can get along with each other and are committed to some form of significant changes.

For Toronto, one of those magic moments was between late 2003 and late 2005. In 2003, David Miller, Dalton McGuinty, and Paul Martin were elected in Toronto, Ontario, and Canada, respectively. All shared centrist or mildly left political values. All were committed to some form of activist urban agenda and, although their agendas naturally differed given the functional responsibilities of the different levels of government, the agendas were compatible with each other. After the June 2004 federal election, when Martin secured re-election, but only as a minority supported mainly by the NDP, federal support for cities actually increased. But, in late 2005, the Martin government was defeated in the House of Commons and in 2006 Stephen Harper—who did not believe in any new federal initiatives to help city governments—became Prime Minister. The magic moment was over, but not before municipalities across the country had benefited from new federal policies relieving them of the financial burden of paying the GST themselves and providing for the sharing of the federal gas tax (see Chapter 3).

Ironically, one of candidate Miller's major campaign commitments in 2003 was to prevent the building of a bridge from the city to the Toronto Island airport operated by the Toronto Port Authority, an

intergovernmental special-purpose body established by federal legislation (see Chapter 4). Prime Minister Martin cancelled the bridge and
agreed to compensate private-sector companies that had already been
awarded contracts to build it, and in this respect Miller won a major
victory. However, Martin refused to take steps to close the airport altogether.[43] Miller hoped that the cancellation of the bridge would cause
the airport to wither away, but the port authority bought a new ferry
and Porter Airlines, the airport's only commercial client, has been
hugely successful operating flights from the island to nearby destina-
tions in Canada and the United States. It appears that the island airport is here to stay. More airplanes are taking off and landing than ever
before. Miller won the battle of the bridge, but lost the war about the
future of the airport.

Miller and McGuinty each won another election and, as indicated
earlier, seemed to work well together until 2010 when Miller announced
he would not be running again. Soon after that Premier McGuinty
announced a reappraisal of his government's original decision to help
fund Miller's Transit City project and Mayor Ford later repudiated it.

Conclusion

The most significant question in political science is the extent to which
elected politicians in a democracy can act in a way that is independent
of the economic forces that help generate the wealth that enables the
system to function. If we are to find any such independent action in
Canadian municipalities we would expect it to be led by the mayors.
That is why this chapter has focused on their legal and extra-legal
powers. We have paid special attention to those few mayors who have
managed to overcome legal obstacles and to become relatively powerful within their respective municipalities. We have also reviewed
urban regime theory, the dominant approach in the United States to
understanding how local elected leaders can shape events within their
respective cities.

In order to have any chance of winning elections, democratic
politicians must promise to do things that are extremely difficult to
implement, if not impossible. Once elected, they operate under severe
constraints. This is clearly true even for the most powerful offices in
the most powerful countries in the world. How can we possibly expect
things to be different for mayors of Canadian cities? Given the immen-
sity of the constraints they operate under, it is remarkable that we

sometimes expect them to be able single-handedly to change substantially the quality of city life.

Changes in the quality of city life in Canada are rarely caused by dramatic changes in municipal policy. Such changes are ultimately caused by the cumulative impact of years of debate and advocacy about the environment, transportation, recreation, and the desirability of vibrant and diverse neighbourhoods. Although policy objectives relating to these matters are frequently trumpeted in municipal strategic plans and mission statements, it is in the dozens or hundreds of decisions that each urban municipality makes each year about sewage treatment, bus routes, and zoning that these matters really are decided. The municipal political process is important because these decisions are important. Mayors who use whatever resources and leadership skills they can muster to nudge decisions one way or another play a significant role in determining the kinds of cities we shall live in.

RESOURCES

Good biographies of politicians are fascinating because they enable readers to see how politicians' public actions relate to their personal background and experience. Tom Urbaniak's biography of Mayor Hazel McCallion of Mississauga is a fine example. To learn about the personal and political life of 'Hazel'—and to learn a lot about local politics at the same time—read *Her Worship: Hazel McCallion and the Development of Mississauga* (Toronto: University of Toronto Press, 2009). For shorter biographical essays about other mayors—Gerry McGeer (Vancouver), Bill Hawrelak (Edmonton), Grant MacEwan (Calgary), Stephen Juba (Winnipeg), David Crombie (Toronto), Charlotte Whitton (Ottawa), Jean Drapeau (Montreal), and Allan O'Brien (Halifax)—see Allan Levine, ed., *Your Worship: The Lives of Eight of Canada's Most Unforgettable Mayors* (Toronto: James Lorimer, 1989).

STUDY QUESTIONS

1. With regard to the political institutions in which they operate, what makes the role of mayor in a Canadian city different from the roles of the federal Prime Minister and provincial premiers?
2. What is a 'strong-mayor' system? Would you favour it for municipalities with which you are familiar? Explain your reasoning.

3. Explain how the concept of 'urban regimes' might be helpful in explaining how political power is exercised within Canadian cities? Describe the components of an urban regime with which you might be familiar.

4. What, if anything, do you know about the mayor of the municipality in which you live? What do you think is the basis of his or her political support? How would you characterize his or her mayoral leadership style?

12 Senior Management and Labour Unions

Without employees to advise them or to implement their decisions, mayors and municipal councils are powerless, regardless of how much support they have in their respective communities. Municipal employees implement council decisions. As we shall see, some people have argued that much municipal work should be contracted out to the private sector. But even if a Canadian municipal council accepted such advice and decided to contract out almost everything, it would still need at least some management employees to advise it about the contracts, to manage the competition for awarding them, and to monitor them once they were agreed.

In this chapter we first look at what is distinctive about the work of senior municipal managers. We then focus on the position of city manager or chief administrative officer (CAO). Next, we examine a case in Waterloo, Ontario, where there were serious administrative lapses at senior levels during the 2000s and where a public inquiry was established to discover what went wrong. Towards the end of the chapter, we consider the issues of contracting out and public–private partnerships and how municipal policy on these issues has been affected in Canada by the strength of municipal unions.

Distinctive Features of Municipal Management

As we learned in Chapter 1, municipal employees technically are not civil servants because they are not 'servants' of the Crown. They are, however, clearly part of the public sector. Statistics Canada reports that 3,559,000 Canadians were employed in 2009 in the public sector, which includes schools, colleges, universities, and hospitals. Of this number,

597,000 worked in 'local general government' (municipal government and associated special-purpose bodies, but not school boards) and another 63,000 worked in local government business enterprises. More people are employed by local general government than by either the federal government or the provincial governments collectively, but school boards and health and social service institutions each employ more people than general local governments.[1]

More so than at the federal and provincial levels, senior municipal managers tend to be functional specialists. Senior civil servants at the federal and provincial levels have usually been educated as generalists and expect that they will move around from one department to another as part of their career progression. Municipal managers often get their first municipal jobs because they were educated as engineers, land-use planners, lawyers, or accountants and then progress through the management hierarchy in the same functional specialization, although not necessarily in the same municipality. By definition, the highest management position in a municipality has no functional specialization, so people initially recruited to such positions often have only limited preparation. Generalists tend to get hired by the very smallest municipalities, which might have only one or two managers in total, or by the very largest, which can afford to hire policy analysts and research assistants in the offices of the very senior managers.

Unlike most federal and provincial civil servants, municipal managers are not responsible to a single political master, a minister of the Crown. In a strong city-manager system, department heads have the luxury of considering themselves to report only to the city manager, but in most municipalities all department heads also report to the council as a collective entity. Reporting to a group of people rather than a single person makes any manager's job more difficult, especially when various members of the governing body often differ publicly from each other in their basic objectives and priorities. In any event, even in a strong city-manager system, the city manager reports to the council as a whole, which makes the job more politically complex than that of most deputy ministers at other levels.

Finally, as we have seen in Chapter 9, municipal councils carry out most of their business in public. Much of this business involves receiving written and oral reports from senior managers. As a result, unlike their federal and provincial counterparts, the work of senior municipal managers is very much a matter of public record, not just in writing but also at locally televised council meetings where they are called on to answer questions from councillors who might not have properly read or understood their agenda material or who wish to use the manager in scoring a political point against an opponent.

The Role of City Managers and CAOs[2]

To understand the positions of city manager and CAO, we must go back to the Progressive reformers at the end of the nineteenth century (see Chapter 9). These are the same people who argued for small municipal councils and non-partisan at-large elections. They wanted as much as possible to remove politics from municipal government. In many ways, their most important municipal innovation was the 'council-manager plan', a system of municipal government in which the mayor's position became largely ceremonial, the council's jobs were to set broad policy and appoint a city manager, and the city manager's job was to do everything else. The establishment of such a position was seen as crucial for removing undue political influence from city administration, breaking the power of the urban political machines, and bringing professional management to urban government.

The first municipal 'general manager' in the United States was appointed for Staunton, Virginia, in 1908. This was 'the first municipal post with the title of manager, whereby a single, appointed official would have responsibility for the day-to-day management of the civic administration'.[3] Staunton became the ideal model for the reformers who advocated for the 'council-manager plan' throughout the United States and Canada. Sumpter, South Carolina, appointed a city manager in 1912 and Westmount, Quebec, appointed one in 1913, becoming the third council-manager municipality in North America.[4] In a pure council-manager system, the manager appoints all the department heads and is directly and solely responsible for all the management documents that flow to council, including the proposed annual municipal budget.

In 1914 the International City Managers' Association (ICMA) was formed to promote the council-manager plan. Except in the very largest of American cities, where strong mayor systems still predominate, ICMA has been remarkably successful and has extended its efforts throughout the Western world. On its website, the ICMA describes its recent history in these words:

> During the 1960s, the profile of local government began to show significant changes. Not only were there complex new problems created, but variations in organizations and structure became evident. Some cities, towns, and counties began providing for an appointed official

responsible for overall administrative affairs without adopting the council-manager plan as it was originally conceived. Likewise, the development of councils of governments and regional councils brought new and innovative structures to local government. It became obvious to ICMA that, in many cases, the positions being developed did not significantly vary from the role of the traditional professional positions provided for in the council-manager form of government.

In July 1969, the International City Managers' Association changed its name to the International City Management Association and began the process of recognizing local governments that provide for positions of professional management while retaining a form of government other than the council-manager plan. To distinguish them from those recognized as council-manager communities, these newly recognized places were designated 'general management' communities. Criteria were established for recognition and the individuals in these local government management positions were made eligible for corporate membership in ICMA. More recently, in 1986, ICMA completed the same process for recognizing state/provincial associations of local governments.

In May 1991, members voted to change ICMA's constitutional name to the International City/County Management Association, reflecting the membership of the Association and recognizing the evolution in county government professionalism.[5]

Many Canadian city managers and CAOs have been active in ICMA. In 2010, Simon Farbrother, the city manager of Edmonton, served as one of two ICMA international vice-presidents. All major Canadian municipalities now have either a city manager or a CAO, but in Quebec the position is known in English as 'director-general'. Regardless of the title used, the actual authority granted to the holder of the position varies significantly. Municipal acts in the various provinces and the relevant bylaw in each municipality can provide an outline of the legal situation, but even when all this research is done, much depends on the culture of the municipal organization and the management style of the particular individual. In any event, there are no major Canadian municipalities in which the city manager or CAO has as much authority as envisioned by the original designers of the council-manager plan.

When Things Go Wrong

Most of the time things go right in municipal administration: council receives good advice from municipal managers and makes a decision; managers then implement the decision relatively efficiently. Municipalities are human institutions, however, and things occasionally go wrong. When they do, we usually learn more about what happened than we do when things went right. The account that follows is presented not because municipal managers are incompetent or corrupt but because it is a case about which much is known and that can teach us a great deal. The case involves the city of Waterloo and a company called MFP Financial Services Ltd. MFP is actually better known for its involvement with the city of Toronto at about the same time. As in Waterloo, MFP's dealings with Toronto generated a public inquiry, lawsuits, and much public dissatisfaction with municipal managers and politicians. We shall examine the Waterloo case because, although it is far from simple, it is less complex than the Toronto one. Nevertheless, anyone whose interest is piqued by the Waterloo story, or who enjoys complicated detective stories, should read in full the Toronto report written by the commissioner, Madam Justice Denise E. Bellamy.[6] It is surely the best-written report of any Canadian public inquiry, so well-written that any attempt to summarize its contents cannot possibly do it justice. What follows here is an account based on the report of the Waterloo public inquiry headed by Mr Justice Ronald C. Sills.[7]

During 1998 the Recreation and Leisure Department of the city of Waterloo evaluated options for a new sport and recreation facility, a perfectly normal activity for any municipal government. There was general agreement about the need for the project and that the city should take on direct responsibility for it. The issue was how to pay for it. During the late 1990s there was much enthusiasm in the public sector for innovative financing mechanisms.[8] The common belief seemed to be that if a public-sector institution made the right legal arrangements with a private company, the company could gain a tax benefit as a result of the depreciation of the asset. The resulting tax gain could be split between both the public-sector institution and the company, making both winners. On the surface at least, this seemed to be the kind of arrangement that MFP Financial Services was offering the city of Waterloo for the recreation facility that was to be named RIM Park.[9]

In May 2000, senior city officials presented their financing plan to city council. The project was to cost $56.6 million, but $7 million was expected from private fundraising, of which $2 million was donated by the Research In Motion (RIM) company. Taxpayer contributions over 30 years for the funding of the remaining amount would 'be computed on an effective annual interest rate of 4.76 per cent'.[10] In September the deal with MFP was signed by the mayor on behalf of the city.[11] In May

2001, the local newspaper was reporting on the 'innovative financing' the city had obtained by making use of a 'tax loophole'. Unfortunately for MFP, it had borrowed the money it needed for the deal from Clarica, an insurance company based in Waterloo. Officials of the company reading the local newspaper story knew that the city's interest rate could not possibly be as low as reported and that there were no tax loopholes. Including an $11 million profit on the transaction for MFP, the Clarica people calculated the city's real interest rate to be 9.2 per cent.[12] Instead of disbursing $112 million in payments over 30 years, the city was in fact committed to paying $227 million. On 4 June 2001, representatives of MFP, Clarica, and the city met together and for the first time city officials learned what they had done. The judge conducting the subsequent public inquiry commented that 'It was a revelation that shook the financial foundation of the City and eroded public confidence in the persons who made the decision.'[13]

How could this happen? The first set of answers relates to financial trickery. The second set—and more interesting for students of local government—is about why and how the city was duped. On the financial side, the first point is that the low interest rate for the city was in fact only guaranteed for 180 days.[14] MFP took advantage of the fact that the city appeared only to be interested in the amount of its annual repayment obligations. To make the payments look low, MFP projected unrealistically high revenues from the facility, sufficient revenues to make the net cost to the city seem low.[15] City officials assumed that the low payments had something to do with the 'tax loophole'. They never insisted on seeing repayment numbers that related solely to the MFP financing.[16]

From an outside perspective, city officials seemed to be acting with 'an entrepreneurial spirit, reducing red tape while keeping within the context of goals and objectives set by the council'.[17] An example of 'red tape' would be the normal requirement that services of the type offered by MFP be sent to tender, i.e., the city officially announces the kind of service it needs and invites competing companies to make official bids. In the public inquiry Mr Justice Sills found that MFP told Waterloo's CAO 'that MFP would not be interested in the deal if it had to tender. MFP had the lowest possible rates and he knew it. It had other places to put its money and did not need the aggravation of a tendering process. It would take time and consume otherwise precious resources to go through the process. If the City tendered, it might lose the chance to contract with MFP.'[18]

How did they become so trusting of MFP? The answer has much to do with the CAO's 'social interaction' with MFP sales personnel prior to the signing of the contract:

> He attended an MFP client appreciation day golf tournament at Glen Abbey in September 1999 and 2000; the millennium celebration in 1999/2000; a charity function with the Toronto Raptors at the Harbour Castle Hotel in Toronto in April 2000; dinner and cocktails while watching the Symphony of Fire on Lake Ontario in June 2000; Oktoberfest in October of 2000; Reach for the Rainbow, a charity function for disabled children in November 2000; a Toronto Maple Leafs hockey game at the Air Canada Centre in November 2000; and the 'ultimate' golf trip to Florida in the spring of 2001.[19]

The CAO testified that he 'had been directed by Council to build relationships with important partners' and that his involvement with MFP 'was in accordance with this direction' because MFP 'was an important and beneficial partner'. He 'saw nothing wrong with the relationship.'[20] The judge, however, determined that, in not disclosing his 'schmoozing' with MFP, the CAO was in violation of the city's conflict-of-interest rules.

Concerning the mayor and council, the judge determined that they relied too much on advice from city management. The deal with MFP:

> was said to involve a very complicated tax play that none of the Councillors purported to understand. There should have been red flags flying all over the Council chambers, but none appeared. So confident was the Council in the abilities of City staff that no consideration was given to retaining legal or financial advice from an external or independent source.
>
> The Mayor and members of Council were very proud of what they perceived as being a high degree of skill and expertise offered by the senior staff. . . .
>
> The members of Council felt that they were entitled to rely on the information being provided by senior staff and that is what they did.[21]

The city of Waterloo subsequently sued MFP and settled for an arrangement whereby the total cost, with interest, of the project was reduced from $227 to $145 million, still $33 million more than what the city had originally budgeted.[22] This is a cost that is still being borne by Waterloo taxpayers and by users of the facility. In the 2003 municipal elections, all members of council either were defeated or did not run again. The CAO and the city treasurer lost their jobs. Nobody was prosecuted because there was no evidence that anyone acted illegally.

One of the main results of the Waterloo and Toronto experiences with MFP was the generation of more red tape. In the 1980s and 1990s there had been a great deal of emphasis in the public sector on freeing public-sector managers from restrictive bureaucratic rules so that they could emulate the entrepreneurial successes of their private-sector colleagues. After Waterloo and Toronto—and after the Gomery inquiry at the federal level[23]—rules were tightened once again to prevent the embarrassments so painfully documented in the public inquiries. The global financial collapse in 2008 has surely ended whatever credibility was left to the notion that the private sector has much to teach the public sector about management.

Contracting Out

MFP tried to make the case that it could provide municipalities with funds for major projects at a cheaper rate than municipalities could borrow the money. Rather than competing cleanly on price through an open tendering process, for example, it 'cultivated relationships', withheld information, and generally tried to bend the rules. But not all companies that provide services to municipalities behave in this way. Some provide excellent value for money. One of the main challenges in municipal management is to discover the circumstances under which contracting out is appropriate and when it is not.

The first point to make is that contracting out is nothing new. Every time a municipality consults an outside lawyer or expert, it is contracting out, because it is purchasing a service that could in theory be provided by its own employees, current or potential. Often there are extremely good reasons why special expertise is obtained in this way; it would simply be far too expensive to employ highly trained specialists in a particular issue whose special skills might only be needed once every few years. Similarly, if a municipality needs to clean the windows on a high-rise city hall, no one is likely to complain if it hires a specialized company to do the job. No one expects banks to employ window cleaners as permanent employees. Why should anyone expect municipalities to do so?

But what about the idea that municipalities should contract out almost everything they do? This idea has been seriously advanced from time to time, especially in the 1990s when confidence in the ability of governments to do almost anything was at a very low ebb. The issue is politically charged because contracting out is often seen—quite rightly in many cases—as an attack on unionized labour. If municipal workers have high wages because they are unionized, and if a private company can perform the same work at a cheaper price because its workers are not unionized, it is not surprising that unions would fight contracting out. The role of unions on this issue is something we shall return to in the next section of this chapter. In the meantime, there are other important issues to be examined in relation to contracting out.

The collection of garbage is a municipal function that causes many battles about contracting out. In 2001 James C. McDavid at the University of Victoria reported on results of a cross-Canada survey about the contracting out of garbage collection. Except in Quebec, he found that contracting out was usually less expensive, especially in smaller municipalities. Lowest costs seemed to be found in municipalities that combined public provision and contracting out, suggesting that direct competition between public and private providers placed downward pressure on costs.[24] But such findings do little to resolve the debate because McDavid did not collect data on wage levels or ages of workers. Some citizens do not want garbage collectors to be non-unionized young workers who will be let go when they age and become less physically productive. Where municipal workers are doing the job, this is precisely why municipal unions are so resistant to contracting out. In a similar study of residential recycling collection services reported in 2008, McDavid and Mueller found little difference in cost between public and private providers. Notably, private provision predominated, with 77 per cent of providers being contracted private companies.[25] As this is a relatively recent municipal service, private providers were often contracted at the beginning, before unions were able to negotiate their own role.

Water services (supply of drinking water and sewage) are considerably more controversial. In Toronto, for example, any hint of moving towards opening the door to private companies has met with immediate resistance from labour unions, environmentalists, and Canadian nationalists concerned with maintaining public control over freshwater resources. But elsewhere there has been considerable movement. Perhaps the best-known case is Hamilton, Ontario, where in 1995 the regional government contracted out the operation of all its water services to a subsidiary of Philip Environmental, a locally based company. The decision was based as much on a strategy for local economic development as it was on saving money. The idea was that the contract with Hamilton would help Philip develop a national and international presence in what looked like a fast-developing marketplace. The contract guaranteed cost savings to the city, new investment, and the continuation of the unionized jobs in the facilities. But all did not go smoothly. The city underestimated the costs of monitoring the contract. Sewage spills caused lawsuits and embarrassment all around. By the late 1990s Philip was laying off workers and those who were left were complaining of deteriorating equipment. Most significant of all, Philip Environmental, a company with many other investments, ran into financial difficulty and was acquired cheaply by a subsidiary of Enron Corporation, a company that would soon go bankrupt in circumstances that showed its whole operation to be built on financial fraud. American Water Services Canada, a company ultimately owned by a German utility, took over from the Enron subsidiary and tried to keep the contract. In anticipation of its expiry, Hamilton city council (which had replaced the regional government as a result of amalgamation) voted narrowly to put the contract out for tender, but no company came up with a proposal that was satisfactory to the city. In September 2004 the city council voted to take direct control of the operation of the water services.[26] In retrospect Hamilton's experience with contracting out can only be assessed as disastrous.

But this experience has not been universal. A great many Canadian municipalities successfully contract out the management of various parts of their water services. In Chapter 4 we saw that the inter-municipal special purpose bodies that supply drinking water to London, Ontario, contract out the management of the treatment plant and inter-municipal piping to American Water Services Canada. Since 2006, Veolia Water Canada (a French company once known as Vivendi) manages water services for the municipality of Brockton, Ontario.[27] Brockton is notable because it is an amalgamated municipality that includes Walkerton, the town where, in 2000, contaminated water supplied by a public body run by incompetents killed at least seven people and caused severe illness in hundreds more.[28]

Public–Private Partnerships

Veolia Water Canada has a different kind of arrangement with Moncton, New Brunswick. In the 1990s it designed, built, and paid for a new water treatment facility for Moncton. In return, Veolia obtained the exclusive right to sell water to the city for 20 years.[29] This arrangement is just one of many different ways in which partnerships can be worked out. Details will vary with each project, depending in large measure on what municipalities are looking for. In the case of the Moncton project, the city was looking both for specialized expertise in the design and construction of the plant and for a financing mechanism that enabled the city to avoid having to borrow large sums.

In other cases, municipalities are more interested in minimizing risk. One such example is the public–private partnership that built the John Labatt Centre in downtown London, Ontario, in the early 2000s. The arena was a crucial part of the city's plan for downtown revitalization and the land on which it was built was owned by the municipality. No private company would take on a project like this in downtown London without public backing. The city would not take on the project because it did not want to get into the highly specialized and financially risky business of building and operating an arena. In his study of London's downtown revitalization efforts, Timothy Cobban reports that:

> City council agreed in May 2000 to build the arena with a consortium whose principal partners included Ellis-Don Construction Ltd., a large construction firm with origins in London. The city's responsibilities under the agreement included providing the land for the arena and $31.72 million of the project's total capital costs. The private sector partners were required to provide $10 million, and pay the city $45.5 million over fifty years with full ownership of the arena transferring to the city at the end of the fifty-year agreement.[30]

The arena is operated by Philadelphia-based Global Spectrum Management (whose parent company also owns the Philadelphia Flyers hockey team and 76ers basketball team), which was also part of the original public–private partnership. Financially, the arena has been a huge success. The city has been criticized for structuring the partnership in such a way that the municipality does not gain directly from this success. But the whole point of the agreement was to protect the city from undue risk if it was not successful. In this sense the partnership met the city's objectives, not to mention the fact that the arena clearly has helped meet the city's revitalization objectives.

Today's city managers require a wide variety of skills in order to navigate through all the various tools at their disposal to meet city objectives. Trusting aggressive salespeople to give accurate and fair information about complicated deals—as in the RIM Park example—is clearly not the way to gather information for presentation to city council. As the judge in the RIM Park inquiry concluded, managers faced with such large and complicated deals must seek outside expert guidance. Ironically, of course, seeking such outside guidance is yet another form of contracting out.

Municipal Unions

Managers also have to deal with unions. Although unions have no particular interest in the contracting out of specialized professional work, they are highly sensitive to proposals to contract out the work that is normally done by their members. Municipal unions are important for a wide range of reasons, not the least of which is that many citizens think most about municipal services when unions threaten to strike or actually do withdraw the services of their members.

Collective Bargaining

Municipal unions have received very little attention from Canadian political scientists.[31] In 1978, T.J. Plunkett and G.M. Betts wrote a text on Canadian municipal management that briefly treated 'Employer–Employee Relations and Collective Bargaining'. Their opening paragraph is almost as relevant today as it was then:

> There was a time when local governments as employers established jobs and positions, assigned tasks, set wages, determined hours of work and other working conditions, and promoted, disciplined, and discharged staff at will without reference to their employees. But those days have long since passed in most urban communities. Yet, despite the fact that some groups of public service employees have been organized as trade union locals for more than three decades, elected and appointed officials have been slow to recognize the overall impact that unionization has had, and will continue to have, upon local government administration and practice. As a result, many municipalities still appear to tolerate employee unions as aberrations from the norm and tend to deal with them on an ad hoc basis during contract negotiations rather than develop a cohesive on-going strategy to promote effective and harmonious labour/management relations.[32]

Katherine Graham wrote a book chapter about 'Collective Bargaining in the Municipal Sector' in 1995. She claims that 'municipalities' generally narrow approach to the human resource management function was likely a contributing factor to the significant spread of unionization in the municipal public service by the 1960s, with the Canadian Union of Public Employees (CUPE) emerging as by far the most dominant municipal union.'[33] In 2010 CUPE was the largest union in Canada and municipal workers, as well as workers in health and educational institutions, remain as the main base of its membership. Graham raises two issues that appear to place municipalities at a disadvantage when bargaining with unions. Both relate to employer disunity. The first variant of the problem is that there are many municipalities and often just one strong union, CUPE. The union provides its local negotiators with considerable data about settlements in other municipalities and each local attempts to 'whipsaw' better settlements than those obtained elsewhere. Naturally, the municipalities respond by sharing information through municipal associations, but they generally do not seem as effective or united as CUPE. In many ways the most innovative management response to this problem has been in the Vancouver area where Metro Vancouver actually handles labour relations not only for its own employees but also for 15 of the 22 constituent municipalities. In 2010 it was managing over 60 collective agreements.[34]

Another source of management disunity is what is sometimes called 'multilateral bargaining'.[35] In this situation participants in the bargaining process know that it is ultimately impossible for management to remain united. Unity, or solidarity, is always a potential problem for unions as well, but except in the most unusual of circumstances local union negotiators are in complete control of the process. Negotiators for municipal management, on the other hand, know that strong elements on the local council, often including the mayor, are not always completely removed from the negotiating process, regardless of what they might say in public. Indeed, some municipal politicians are closely allied to labour interests and are particularly vulnerable to union efforts to crack open an apparently united management position. In contrast, it is rare for a union in the private sector to expect to have allies on a private company's board of directors.

A third problem for municipal management is that some contract settlements are determined by arbitration. Graham does not discuss it directly because she was writing about 'non-uniformed' municipal workers, i.e., workers who are not members of police or fire services. Regardless of the existence or strength of police boards as special-purpose bodies (see Chapter 4), municipal police officers are paid by municipalities mostly from revenues that they must raise themselves. The same observation applies to fire personnel, for whom there generally are no special-purpose bodies. Police and fire personnel have no legal right to go on strike, but they do have very strong local unions, albeit ones that are usually more limited by provincial legislation in their ability to affiliate with larger organizations like CUPE. In the event that management and union negotiators are unable to reach agreement for police and fire labour contracts, the outstanding issues are usually sent to arbitration. Concerning wage levels, arbitrators frequently award higher settlements than what other unions obtain in the absence of compulsory arbitration.[36]

One generous arbitration for one service leads to pressure for others to 'catch up'—which in turn creates higher goals for other unions to strive for. Municipal politicians complain frequently about arbitrated settlements for police and fire, but there appears little that they can do short of launching a full-scale attack on police officers and firefighters, which is not an attractive option for anyone seeking re-election.

Labour Support for Municipal Candidates

In Chapters 9 and 10 we examined some of the incentives for, and evidence of, close connections between the land development industry and municipal councillors. Incentives for municipal unions to take an active role in municipal politics are equally strong, not just because of concerns about wage levels and working conditions but also about matters of wider public interest such as contracting out and public–private partnerships. Canada has a long history of labour involvement in municipal elections, especially during the first half of the twentieth century (see discussion in Chapter 9 about the role of the CCF in Vancouver), but the most significant recent involvement of labour in municipal politics has been seen in British Columbia and Ontario in the early 2000s.[37] In the 2006 Ontario municipal elections local labour councils affiliated with the Canadian Labour Congress:

> held a series of strategy sessions, campaign manager and candidate schools, public speaking and media courses, and political organizer training sessions in 21 cities across the province. . . . This unprecedented political mobilization at the local level produced a slate of 438 endorsed candidates in 60 different municipalities. On election day, 217 labour-endorsed candidates were either elected or acclaimed to local councils or school boards in Ontario.[38]

In Guelph, labour-endorsed candidates won the mayoralty and a majority on city council. Prominent labour-endorsed mayors who were elected in 2006 were David Miller in Toronto and John Rodriguez (a former federal NDP MP) in Greater Sudbury.

To understand the unions' political objectives, it is especially important to understand what they were concerned about when they were interviewing candidates who were seeking endorsement:

> A typical interview would involve quizzing candidates about their positions on a number of contentious issues, including municipal procurement, privatization, contracting out, and commitment to public transit.

Most candidates were also asked if they had ever, or would ever, cross a picket line. Labour councils were not simply looking to endorse candidates who answered all the questions correctly. Rather, in addition to being satisfied that a candidate was committed to a labour-friendly platform, labour councils were interested in a candidate's overall credibility. After all, if a candidate had no hope of winning, an endorsement from a labour council might have had an adverse effect on the credibility of the CLC's municipal campaign overall. After labour councils interviewed prospective candidates and handed out endorsements accordingly, the CLC dispatched trained union members to carry labour's message to CLC-affiliated locals in various targeted communities.[39]

Continued labour involvement in local electoral politics will likely depend on the movement's assessment of the 2006 results.[40] Although no such assessments seem to be publicly available, it is likely that the Toronto municipal strike in the summer of 2009 will be considered of crucial importance. It was not a happy experience for anybody. David Miller's decision not to seek re-election in 2010 seemed to result from being perceived by many Toronto voters as being too favourable to the union and by union leaders as not favourable enough. Whatever his accomplishments as mayor, many residents will only remember the inconveniences brought about by the strike and by his apparent weakness in dealing with union demands. In any event, as we saw in Chapter 9, the campaign financing rules in Toronto for the 2010 election were different from 2006: neither corporations nor unions were allowed to contribute. However, such a rule has no effect on unions' rights to endorse candidates or to encourage members to support them.

Is Municipal Work a 'Safe Harbour'?

Fifty years ago, unions were successfully enabling organized private-sector workers in North America to become middle-class consumers. Public-sector unions barely existed and working for a municipal government, especially in 'outside' jobs, meant being close to the bottom of the labour hierarchy. Now, all of that has changed. Victories won by unions in the private sector have been dramatically eroded. Globalization has caused thousands of manufacturing jobs in North America simply to move elsewhere. Union leaders have faced the grim choice of watching the jobs leave or making concession after concession to try to preserve them. In the public sector, changes have repositioned unions differently: they have gone from victory to victory such that public-sector employment now offers considerable advantages in terms of wage levels, benefits, and security. As noted earlier, of the three levels of government in Canada, the local level employs the most workers, and dramatically so if we include the education and health sectors.

This means that the debate about public-sector employment really is about *local* public-sector employment. The debate is about the extent to which we should tolerate growing disparities between the public and private sectors. People with different political views and values will no doubt differ about whether the current public or private model is the one to follow. What must concern the student of the local public sector are the implications of the disparities if they persist and grow.

An American scholar, John D. Donahue, addresses this issue in his provocative book, *The Warping of Government Work*.[41] Donahue presents a great deal of evidence from the United States to demonstrate that public-sector jobs requiring relatively low-level skills (e.g., office clerks, janitors) pay significantly more than equivalent private-sector jobs, while jobs requiring high-level skills (lawyers, high-level managers) pay significantly less. As a result, employment offered by the public sector is extremely attractive for the less-skilled while it becomes increasingly unattractive to highly skilled employees. The difficulty of recruiting and retaining highly skilled persons, according to Donahue, explains the increasing tendency for public organizations to contract out much of their high-end work to consultants. The same organizations also try to contract out work performed by the less-skilled but they meet huge resistance from powerful public-sector unions. The stakes are exceptionally high for the unions because in many ways these unionized public-sector jobs represent most of the few remaining examples of the great union victories of the second half of the twentieth century.

Donahue refers to government jobs as 'safe harbours' for workers in the storm of globalization. He notes that the role of public-sector unions in American politics has become increasingly controversial:

> Anyone looking to wax indignant about aspects of American politics could work through a long list of more deserving candidates before directing their outrage towards workers banding together to defend their middle-class jobs. The main reason for discussing public-sector unions' rapid shift from the sidelines to the front lines of politics is that it so vividly illustrates how a government job has become something millions of Americans will fight to defend. This development is both a sorry commentary on the status of the middle class within the private sector, and a chronic impediment to delivering on the public sector's imperatives of efficiency, flexibility, and performance.[42]

Performance standards are crucial to understanding why municipal unions are so important in the context of the work that senior management in local government is supposed to do. In the private sector, managers can enhance efficiency by outsourcing jobs, say, to China. They are rewarded well for their work; while jobs are lost at home, prices are reduced in the big-box stores, and the capitalist system appears to be working. But the public-sector manager can do no such thing. Proposals to contract out even minimal amounts of work are resisted at every turn—understandably so, as Donahue reminds us. The public sector appears increasingly inefficient, which in turn provokes more anger both from lower-income citizens not engaged in public-sector employment and from private-sector, high-income earners who bemoan the inability of the public sector to be as ruthlessly competitive as they are.

What has all this got to do with Canada? In a careful analysis of data on union membership in both the United States and Canada, Leo Troy concludes that, although much is different about labour law and labour statistics in the United States and Canada, trends in the two countries are converging: private-sector unions are declining while public-sector unions are at least holding their own.[43] Although the issues raised by Donahue might be more acute in the United States, they are of great importance in Canada and likely to become more so in the future.

What this means is that some of the most profound issues facing Canadian society are being fought out in municipalities. We are used to hearing about the importance of municipal policies for the environment or for economic competitiveness. But if municipal government is one of the few remaining places where the less-skilled worker can obtain jobs that are relatively well paid, with decent benefits and security, what do we expect our municipalities to do in collective bargaining? To some extent at least, their role is to try to obtain concessions from the unions in order to save money for taxpayers. So far, however, they have not been very successful because CUPE and other unions have remained strong. Eventually, public resentment about the special advantages of public-sector employment might become too great for politicians to ignore. As Canadian provincial governments attempt to dig themselves out from the latest round of deficits, this might be the time when the issue takes centre stage. As we shall see in the next chapter, municipalities are not allowed to run operating deficits, so it would be ironic if provincial deficit-fighting was done on the backs of workers in the municipal, education, and health sectors. If it is, it would likely be as a result of a few provincial decisions rather than hundreds of municipal ones.

Conclusion

Municipal managers face many remarkably challenging and complex issues. Unlike federal and provincial civil servants, they do their job largely in public and for multiple political masters. They face a constant barrage of criticism for not spending taxpayers' money more efficiently, but they face overwhelming constraints when they try to take steps to do so. Over the last two or three decades, they have been pressured to be innovative and entrepreneurial while at the same time they were not supposed to upset vested interests, especially unions. The contracting out of municipal work to private companies has been prescribed by many as a way to bring the discipline of the private sector to public services. But, as we have seen in this chapter, Canadian experiences with contracting out have not always been positive, and they usually come about only after great political conflict. Although contracting out clearly leads to a reduction in the total number of municipal employees, it does not eliminate the need for competent municipal managers. In fact, it likely *increases* the need because, in order to ensure that it reaps any efficiencies, the municipal government needs to know as much about what is going on with the contract as the contracting company does.

Collective agreements are among the most important constraints on municipal managers. Too often these agreements have been seen simply as the public-sector equivalent of private-sector collective agreements. But the political dynamics of labour relations are much different in municipalities and the stakes have become much higher. There has been almost no academic research on collective bargaining in Canadian municipal government. We have emphasized how so much municipal business is carried out in public; but collective bargaining is done behind closed doors, and so are councils' deliberations about their bargaining strategies. How are final decisions made about negotiating positions that might provoke a strike or about concessions that might bring one to an end? What is the role of the politicians, especially those who are known to have the political support of the unions with whom the municipality is negotiating? For citizens who want to know how their municipal governments work and what their significance is to the functioning of our wider society, these are the kinds of questions to which we should have some answers. Unfortunately, we do not.

In the final analysis, decisions about the remuneration and treatment of municipal workers depend on societal values expressed by municipal councillors who are elected by voters. But these values are affected by scarce resources. We cannot give everyone what he or she wants.

RESOURCES

For contrasting views about the merits of privatization and contracting out, see the websites of the Canadian Council for Public–Private Partnerships at <www.pppcouncil.ca> and the 'privatization watch' conducted by the Canadian Union of Public Employees at <http://cupe.ca/privatizationwatch?list=articles&date=2010>.

STUDY QUESTIONS

1. What makes the job of city manager or CAO of a major Canadian municipality different from that of a senior civil servant in the federal or provincial governments?
2. Would you favour the contracting out of the management and operation of the water supply system in your municipality? Why or why not?
3. Should municipal workers doing similar jobs as those available in the private sector be paid more? Explain your reasoning.

PART IV
Financial Issues

13 Budgets, Grants, and User Fees

'Follow the money' is common advice to any investigative reporter trying to find out what is going on in complex organizations. Often such advice is directed at tracking down various forms of corruption or conflicts of interest. But it applies just as well to understanding government at any level. The serious student needs to understand how public funds are used and where they come from. The aim of this chapter is to enable such an understanding with respect to Canadian local government. We look first at the various sources of information about Canadian local government finance and how we can best make use of them. Next, we use some of these sources to analyze the purposes of Canadian local governments' expenditures. Then, we review the sources of local government revenues, emphasizing grants from other levels of government and user fees and reserving a full discussion of the municipal property tax until the next chapter. Finally, we discuss the financing of water supply systems as a case in point about the politics of user fees and government grants.

It must be emphasized that this part of the book is not meant to be a text for financial managers. It should be readily understandable to people without technical knowledge of accounting and bookkeeping. It presents material that one hopes municipal councillors and senior managers are familiar with, although many such people are more likely to know about the financial intricacies of their own municipalities rather than some of the broader issues and perspectives presented here. Even financial professionals often do not look at the wider political perspective in which their work takes place. Because this book is grounded in political science rather than in accounting or financial management, its approach to the subject should be accessible to all.[1]

Local Government Finances

All three levels of government in Canada collect data about local government finances. If one's interest is in a particular municipality, the best source is the website of that municipality because it will have the most detailed information. However, not all municipalities structure their financial information in the same way. The best way to compare financial information from municipalities in the same province is to use data collected from the relevant provincial ministry concerned with municipal affairs. Statistics Canada collects local government financial data for the entire country. These data are comparable but are lacking in detail. For example, the data from Statistics Canada can be compared by province but not across individual municipalities. Because this book addresses Canadian local government in general and aims at making interprovincial comparisons, the financial data from Statistics Canada will be most useful.

The two main kinds of financial information, each of which is available from all three levels of government, are:

1. Statements of assets and liabilities, or balance sheets. Such information is meant to convey measures of wealth or indebtedness at one particular point in time.
2. Statements of revenues and expenditures. These show the amount of money received or spent for particular purposes over a particular period of time, most often one year.

Assets and Liabilities

Statements of assets and liabilities are crucially important for businesses because they are an important way of stating how much a business is worth. They list the value of everything that the company owns and then list all the companies' debts or financial obligations. (Assets minus liabilities equal net worth; if liabilities exceed assets, the result is net indebtedness.) These statements are less important for municipalities, primarily because municipalities are not bought and sold. However, for financial professionals interested in providing funds to finance municipal debt, statements of assets and liabilities provide important information about the potential capacity of a municipality to repay its debt. Provincial legislation for municipalities in Canada requires them to comply with generally accepted accounting principles for local governments as determined by the Public Sector Accounting Board (PSAB), which is affiliated with the Canadian Institute of Chartered Accountants. Starting with

2009, municipalities are expected to include in their statements of assets and liabilities the depreciated value of their physical assets, such as roads, sewers, buildings, etc. Prior to then, unlike business corporations, the value of such physical assets was not included. Superficially, the new system will make municipalities look wealthier than they were prior to the change in accounting procedures. However, in the real world, nothing will have changed, especially because most municipal physical assets cannot realistically be bought and sold. What likely is most significant about the change is that if municipalities do nothing between the issuance of two statements (usually a period of one year) to renew or refurbish their physical assets, they will rightly be seen as suffering a reduction in the net value of their assets because the value of what they have will have depreciated (in the same way that a car depreciates in value each year that it is used). The expectation is that the incorporation of depreciation into statements of assets and liabilities will force municipal politicians and senior managers to pay more attention to ensuring that their physical assets are renewed at least at the same rate as they depreciate.

It is too early to tell what effect, if any, this accounting change will have on municipal financial decision-making. Canadian municipal statements of assets and liabilities for periods prior to 2009 do not include physical (or tangible) assets. Among other things, this means that their liabilities invariably are greater than their assets. Consequently, municipal statements of assets and liabilities almost always end with a statement of 'net financial debt'. Using data from Statistics Canada that includes school boards, Figure 13.1 shows that, as far as financial assets are concerned, Canadian local governments improved their position dramatically during the period 1993–2003. The figure shows that 'net financial debt' has declined. We shall return to issues relating to capital expenditures and borrowing later in this chapter.

Statements of Revenues and Expenditures

As noted previously, these statements report on the sources of revenue and the purposes of expenditures for a given period of time, usually a year. Annual municipal budgets are very similar to these statements except that the statements look to the past and budgets look to the future. Using data from Statistics Canada, we shall be focusing on municipal revenues and expenditures. The data we use in the sections that follow are for what Statistics Canada calls 'local general government', which includes municipal governments and their associated boards and commissions, but not school boards. The data include both operating and capital revenues and expenditures, which is not the usual municipal way

Figure 13.1 Net Financial Debt, Canadian Local Governments, 1976–2006

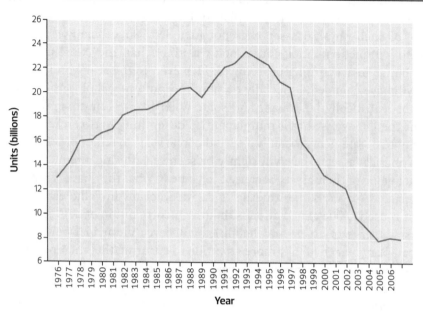

Source: Statistics Canada, CANSIM Table 3850014.

of presenting financial data. Later in this chapter we make the necessary distinctions between financial transactions for operating purposes and those for capital. For now we need only note that, although legislation in all the provinces prevents municipalities from running operating deficits, it is possible for them to spend more than they take in for any given year, if capital expenditures are included.

Municipal Expenditures

Table 13.1 shows the main categories used by Statistics Canada to classify all government expenditures, together with the amounts spent by Canadian municipal governments on each category in billions of dollars for 2008.

It is clear from these figures that municipal expenditures are dominated by roads and public transit (transportation and communication), water supply and sewage (environment), and police and fire services (protection of people and property). Although total expenditures for social services, housing, and health are modest, even these relatively small amounts are misleading because most of these expenditures are made by Ontario municipalities. In 2008, Ontario municipalities incurred more than 95.5 per cent of all Canadian municipal expenditures on social

Table 13.1 Expenditures by Local Governments in Canada for 2008 ($ billions)

Issue Area	Amount
Transportation and communications	15.8
Environment	12.8
Protection of people and property	12.1
Recreation and culture	9.1
General government	7.2
Social services	6.7
Housing	2.8
Debt charges	2.4
Health	1.9
Resource conservation and industrial development	1.5
Regional planning and development	1.4
Education	0.2

Source: Statistics Canada, CANSIM Table 3850024.

services; 66.3 per cent of expenditures on housing; and 79.8 per cent of expenditures on health.[2] In other provinces (except Quebec for housing), municipalities have little or no financial responsibility for these categories of government services.

Municipal Revenues

Statistics Canada divides municipal revenues into two main categories: own-source and transfers. Transfers are payments from the federal and provincial governments; own-source revenues include all money that the municipalities generate. Over the last 20years the data show that own-source revenue has been increasing at a significantly faster rate than revenue from transfers. In 2008, Canadian municipal governments raised almost $58 billion from their own sources and received almost $16 billion from transfer payments.[3]

Own-Source Revenues
The two main kinds of own-source revenues are 'property and related taxes' and 'sales of goods and services'. All of the next chapter will be devoted to issues relating to the property tax, because it is of crucial importance to understanding municipal government and politics in

Figure 13.2 Transfers to Canadian Local Governments, Capital and Operating

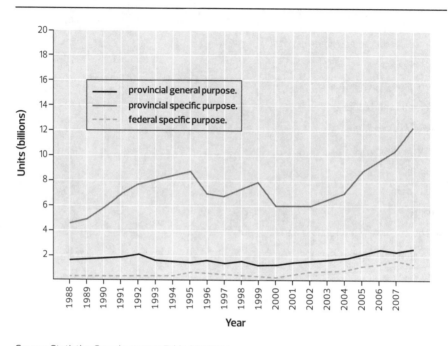

Source: Statistics Canada, CANSIM Table 3850024.

Canada. A discussion of the politics behind the pricing and selling of municipal water ends this chapter. Water is the most important commodity that Canadian municipalities sell. For our purposes now, all we need to know is the relative importance of the two main varieties of municipal own-source revenue. In 2008, municipalities raised $36.5 billion from property-related taxes and $16 billion from the sale of goods and services. The ratio between the two has barely changed over the last 20 years.[4]

Transfers

Statistics Canada reports on three main categories of transfers to municipalities:

1. provincial grants for a specific purpose (conditional grants);
2. provincial grants for general purposes (unconditional);
3. federal grants for a specific purpose.

There are no federal grants to municipalities for general purposes. The total value of each of the three types of grants over time is shown in Figure 13.2.

Although Figure 13.2 shows federal grants to municipalities increasing in recent years, the federal line is somewhat misleading because it does not capture some federal grants destined for Quebec municipalities, especially funds from the federal gas tax (see Chapter 3) that are channelled from the federal government through the Quebec government before being passed on to Quebec municipalities. It should also be noted that more than 70 per cent of the provincial specific-purpose line is made up of grants from the Ontario government to Ontario municipalities,[5] mostly for required municipal expenditures on social services, housing, and health. The main conclusion to be drawn about transfers to Canadian municipalities outside Ontario is that they are relatively unimportant. They are important in Ontario only in relation to government functions generally not performed by municipalities in other provinces.

Municipal Budgets

Adopting the annual municipal budget is often the most important function performed by a municipal council in any given year. The budget is a complex document, even in relatively small municipalities. In larger ones it can be hundreds of pages long, and almost impossible for the outsider to comprehend. Figure 13.3 is a helpful introduction.

Figure 13.3 How the Municipal Budget Works

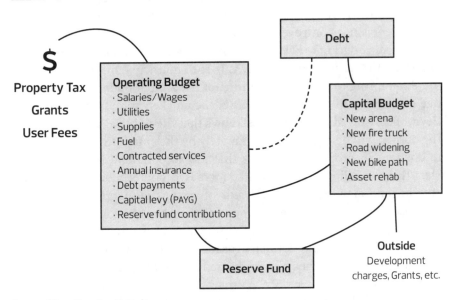

Source: City of London, Ontario.

The first point to note is that there are really two budgets, one for operating expenses and one for capital. They are linked by debt payments and reserve funds. One of Canada's foremost experts on municipal finance, Harry Kitchen, acknowledges that '[t]he use for municipal purposes of the term "capital" varies somewhat from municipality to municipality' and that '[s]ome types of expenditure defy ready classification.'[6] New construction clearly is a capital expenditure and so is a major rehabilitation of, say, a municipal arena or city hall; routine maintenance is not. Buying land and purchasing new vehicles are capital expenditures; the purchase of routine office supplies is not. As noted previously, provincial legislation prevents municipalities from budgeting for operating deficits. Municipalities are allowed to borrow to finance capital costs, but such borrowing is generally regulated by the relevant provincial government. It is important to realize that although federal and provincial governments in Canada make budgetary distinctions between capital and operating costs, they are rolled together when budgetary deficits or surpluses are reported. Only at the municipal level are such clear distinctions made between budgets for operating and capital expenses.

Huge academic literatures relate both to how public-sector budgeting works and how it should work. Regardless of innumerable plans to make budgeting decisions more rational and comprehensive, the process remains fundamentally political, in that elected officials make decisions about controversial items based on their own political instincts and calculations rather than on the basis of elaborate assessments performed by their staffs. However, most of what is contained in most governmental budgets is not controversial at all; it simply reflects the continuation of ongoing programs that no one much wants to change, or even can change. This status quo certainly is true of municipal budgets.

Attempting to find the beginning of the annual budgetary process is like attempting to determine whether the chicken comes before the egg. Everyone involved in the process knows that the political acceptability of the budget will be determined ultimately by the extent to which it results in changes to property tax levels that are acceptable to the voters who elect the councillors. If it looks like increased tax revenues will be available in the following year, the heads of various municipal departments will discover new projects and programs that they cannot live without. If funds look scarce and they wish to protect their own positions, they will not be foolish enough to launch crusades for new expenditures. Despite the fact that staff budget proposals are invariably adjusted to suit political reality, the formal part of the process begins with such requests. The requests are collected by senior municipal financial officials and reviewed by the city manager or CAO. The degree of involvement by councillors or council committees at this stage varies from place to place. In municipalities with strong city managers, it will be kept to a minimum. In any event, the proposed operating and capital budgets are formally released either by the municipal administration or by a council committee. They are then discussed and debated by council committees and/or the full council and are approved, usually with relatively minor changes. In most years in most places there is public controversy about a few particular aspects of the budgets; rarely does that process provoke significant discussion about major policy choices.

As suggested in Figure 13.3 on page 271, many aspects of the operating budget are determined by prior commitments. In particular, a municipality must meet its scheduled payments on accumulated debt. Although payment for the original project that caused the debt counts as a capital expense, the actual debt repayments are in the operating budget because they are recurring financial obligations. Similarly, ongoing municipal commitments for salaries of councillors and many staff members, as well as ongoing maintenance and other expenses, cannot possibly be avoided. In times past (and still today in very small municipalities) each municipal department would have an operating budget comprising the kinds of items shown in Figure 13.3: salaries, supplies, utilities, fuel, etc. Most proposals over the years to make budgeting more meaningful and effective have involved replacing such 'line items' with budgets relating to particular objectives. Thus, a municipal recreation department would budget instead for declared objectives, such as providing a certain number of supervised swimming-pool hours, so many places in sports programs, and specified programs in disadvantaged neighbourhoods. The theory here is that, if politicians want to cut or expand the department's budget, they do so by adjusting the levels of service as proposed in the budget. In reality, however, not all departmental costs can be allocated to particular programs. In any event, most policy-makers really do want to know how much money particular units are spending on such line items as salaries, supplies, and travel. Most budgets now include information about both program costs and line items, which is a contributing factor to their size and complexity.

In addition to providing for debt repayment and for ongoing expenses, operating budgets often make direct contributions to the capital budget for particular projects ('pay-as-you-go', just like using extra available cash to pay for a new car rather than borrowing money to pay for it) or to reserve funds (which, as the name implies, are like special savings accounts individuals might establish to enable a special purchase at some time in the future). Sometimes, provincial legislation or regulations require that municipalities establish particular reserve funds for particular purposes and specify a formula for determining the payments into the fund and the circumstances under which the funds can be withdrawn. Other reserve funds are completely voluntary, and some are designed to cover unusual and unforeseen operating costs, such as a winter requiring unusually high costs for snow removal. If a reserve fund is voluntary, then nothing stops a municipal council from 'raiding the reserves' to finance normal operating costs when times are tough—a well-known technique for avoiding sudden and dramatic tax increases in a particular year, but if practised regularly this completely negates the purpose of having reserve funds in the first place.

Most municipalities are financially cautious. They establish reserve funds for some purposes, the proceeds of which they may invest in short-term securities so as to generate additional income for the fund. Simultaneously, they borrow money for other projects at a fixed rate for a term that roughly matches the expected life of the project. This leads to the common municipal practice of borrowing money for some purposes and investing it for others, not unlike a couple who choose to borrow money for a home (mortgage) and at the same time put aside savings by investing in bonds for their retirement. Figure 13.1 on page 268 shows the net financial debt of Canadian local governments. It shows the amount by which the local governments' outstanding debt surpasses the value of their financial assets. Compared to their federal and provincial counterparts, Canadian local governments are in excellent financial shape. Complaints from citizens about local indebtedness are often misplaced. Such complaints usually do not take account of the value of reserve funds. More importantly, no serious financial analyst suggests that borrowing to acquire capital goods is a bad idea; quite the contrary. If we only construct a new facility with money we have already saved, current taxpayers are effectively subsidizing future users of the facility. This situation is quite different from one in which the federal government runs a deficit to pay for current operating costs, in which case future taxpayers are subsidizing current ones.

During the Great Depression of the 1930s, many Canadian municipalities effectively went bankrupt because they could not repay loans that had been taken out to construct new infrastructure that turned out not to be needed. Because municipal bankruptcies negatively affected the creditworthiness of the provinces in which they were located, all provinces eventually took action to prevent reckless municipal borrowing. Furthermore, as we saw in Chapter 10, municipalities in most provinces (but not so much in Quebec) eventually required developers to construct and pay for municipal infrastructure within new subdivisions, thereby passing the cost and risk from themselves to developers and eventually on to homeowners. Like all governments and corporations, the credit-worthiness of municipalities is evaluated by credit-rating agencies, the same ones that failed in their task in 2008 with respect to many large American financial institutions. Municipalities with high credit ratings can borrow money at lower rates than municipalities with low credit ratings, but high credit ratings most often are achieved by not having to borrow money; consequently, the benefits are often overstated, especially by financially conservative municipal politicians. High municipal credit ratings also are achieved by having diverse and stable local economies. Money loaned to a municipality with such an economy is almost certain to be paid back, which is not necessarily likely for an isolated one-industry town where the one industry is in danger of shutting down. The potential financial risks in such situations explains why, in some new one-industry towns, the main industry has no choice but to build much municipal infrastructure itself.

Figure 13.3 shows that capital budgets also receive funds from development charges. The evolution of these charges was described in Chapter 10. They involve property-owners (usually developers) being required to pay a municipal charge for each lot on which new buildings are constructed. The idea is that the revenue from these charges will be used to finance the additional municipal capital costs associated with the new buildings. That is why the revenue from these charges is shown in Figure 13.3 as being connected with the capital budget rather than the operating budget. In reality, most revenue from development charges goes into reserve funds before being spent directly on municipal capital acquisitions.

Multi-year planning for budgeting is always desirable, especially in relation to capital spending. In any well-run municipality, capital budgets carefully outline the sequencing of new capital projects, both for financial and engineering reasons. For example, if a road needs to be widened or reconstructed, it makes sense to renew underground piping at the same time, thereby saving both money and disruption. Of course, the need for some capital projects cannot always be determined in advance (rebuilding destruction caused by a natural disaster, for example) and everyone has to acknowledge the right of municipal councillors to depart from a pre-established capital plan if political priorities change (voters electing councillors pledged to building a new performing arts centre that had been rejected by a previous council). Multi-year planning is always subject to change.

Ordinary citizens generally care little about the intricacies of capital and operating budgets, reserve funds, and credit ratings. What they generally want are the highest possible level of services and facilities in their municipality with the lowest possible level of property taxes and user charges. As we saw in Chapter 2, balancing these conflicting demands is one of the main reasons why we have elected local governments in the first place. During the budgetary process council members are placed under the most pressure surrounding these issues. Often they are criticized for attempting to cut too deeply, such that services considered important by many people are felt to be under threat. More often they are criticized for allowing levels of user fees and property taxes to become too high.

User Fees

Even if it were desirable, it is not possible to finance all government services by user fees. Services that cannot possibly be financed by user fees are what economists call 'public goods'. When a public good is provided, it is available to everybody whether some people want it or not: the good cannot be divided, and it cannot be consumed. Classic examples of public goods are street lighting and defence against external threats. The only way to finance these services is through compulsory taxation. If we tried to charge citizens for these services, some would rationally conclude that they need not pay because, once provided, the benefits of the service cannot be denied to anybody. The end result likely would be that everyone would end up with a lower level of street lighting or of defence than what they really wanted.

At the core of any economic analysis of government is the provision of public goods because private markets simply cannot provide them at the optimal level or develop a mechanism whereby they will be financed. Debates about exact definitions of public goods can become quite silly (Can we dispense with public police forces by expecting people to provide their own bodyguards?) and we need not explore all of their intricacies. There can be little doubt that local governments provide real public goods that could not possibly be financed by user fees. Clearest examples are goods like snow removal, safe and comfortable public spaces, and measures to prevent the spread of disease by infected rodents. An almost universal temptation is to add to this list by including such expensive items as education and health care. It is completely possible to charge fees for these services and even to have them provided by private entrepreneurs, so these goods are not public goods, although powerful grounds exist for having governments provide them or at least contribute to the costs of their provision. The grounds relate to the 'positive externalities' that accrue to us all from an educated population and to a sense of fundamental fairness and equity (prevalent in most societies) that people should not die or suffer as a result of being unable to afford medical care. Services like health and education are called 'merit goods'; they are not public goods in the sense described above but they are so important to the well-being of our societies that governments take action to make sure that the appropriate people receive the required level of services. Precisely because these services are not public goods, it is usually relatively easy for citizens to purchase additional (or different) levels of the service if they so desire. As we have seen in Chapter 4, local governments in Canada are heavily involved in the provision of basic levels of public education through school boards.

As we also saw in Chapter 4, some goods cannot be provided efficiently by competing private suppliers. Distribution systems for water, sewage, natural gas, and electricity are prime examples. In an unregulated environment, one supplier soon will become dominant in a given territory because it is simply too expensive (and disruptive) for competitors to build competing systems. In the absence of regulation, the dominant supplier can make huge profits by taking advantage of the 'natural monopoly' that inevitably results. Governments either take over these services themselves or tightly regulate the private monopoly suppliers. In particular, they regulate the 'tolls' that these suppliers levy. The goods in question frequently are referred to as 'toll goods'. Canadian local governments are heavily involved in some toll goods, especially water supply and sewage. The ways in which Canadian municipalities levy charges for these particular goods will be explored more fully in the next section of this chapter.

Roads and public transit are toll goods as well. It is practically impossible to have competing private road systems within the same territory. Competing private bus and taxi companies are more feasible, but competing private fixed-rail systems within a single city are just as improbable as competing road systems. The big issue at the local level for roads and public transit is the level of the toll. Historically, toll roads in Canada were quite common, but almost all road tolls were abolished over time, in part because the collection of the tolls added to traffic delays. As we all know, changes in technology now make it possible for road tolls to be charged without causing traffic to stop. A 'congestion charge' is now levied on all private motor vehicles entering central London in England and there is much talk about the desirability of such a charge in Canada's largest cities. It is bound to be a major issue in urban politics in the years ahead. The mirror image of this debate is taking place with respect to public transit. Public transit systems were initially self-financing, with most operated by private companies. Now, they are municipally operated in Canada (except TransLink in Vancouver). Yet, no one argues for higher tolls (or fares) so that these systems can become totally self-financing. For environmental reasons, and to ease roadway congestion, the much more common argument is that government subsidies for public transit should be increased.

In certain circumstances municipalities also provide private goods, ones that are also commonly provided in the private marketplace. For example, they might operate golf courses, which will be at least partially in competition with private ones. Municipalities owning convention centres or community halls likely will be in competition with local hotels. Usually, the municipal facility has the greatest capacity and is designed to attract large meetings whose delegates will stay overnight in local hotels. However, in order to maximize business, municipal facilities are sometimes tempted to go after smaller events as well, which puts them in direct competition with meeting facilities in hotels. Invariably, municipal competition in an otherwise private marketplace becomes a local political issue. A common solution is for the municipality to adopt a business strategy for these facilities aimed at avoiding direct competition with local business rather than maximizing municipal revenue. Other local taxpayers will then claim that municipalities cannot operate businesses very well!

Only a tiny portion of municipal revenue from the sale of goods and services derives from goods and services that are also provided privately. Most such municipal revenue comes from goods and services for which municipalities are the only or the dominant supplier. The initial decision that a municipality must make about financing a particular service is whether to charge user fees at all. For many services, as we have seen, such fees are not technically possible. For others, such as roads, fees might now be technically possible, but are, for the moment at least, not politically possible. And, for others, such as garbage collection, debate in many communities still rages on.

Advocates of user fees for garbage collection make the plausible argument that they will cause residents to be more careful about the amounts of garbage they leave at the curb. This reasoning loses some of its force if the amount of garbage each household throws out is not carefully measured. Weighing garbage and recording where it comes from will likely add to the cost of collection. Selling tags for bags solves this problem, but encourages people to stuff each bag as full as it can get.

If tags are priced to cover the complete cost of collection and disposal, including all costs associated with the life cycle of a landfill site, they could become high enough to cause some people to try to dispose of their garbage illegally, thereby causing more costs and undermining the original purpose of adopting the user fees in the first place. To make the issue even more complicated, in most municipalities, owners of commercial and high-rise residential buildings must arrange and pay for their own garbage collection, often from private companies, and they receive no relief from property tax for themselves paying for a service that single-family homes usually receive as part of their overall package of tax-supported municipal services.

Once a municipality has decided to charge user fees for a service, it faces difficult issues about how to set the price. In private businesses, the obvious strategy is to set a price for a service that will, over a given period of time, maximize the financial position of the business. Municipalities do not have such a luxury. The political constraints on maximizing profits from such private services as municipal golf courses and reception rooms are fairly obvious. But there are obvious constraints on the pricing of toll goods as well. For example, if municipalities decided to maximize their revenues by charging as much as they could get away with for the supply of piped water, they could make a great deal of money. In fact, no municipal council would agree to such a strategy, because it would lead to howls of outrage, both from businesses that use large amounts of water and from poverty activists who would rightly claim that no one should be denied drinking water in a country such as Canada because they are unable to pay for it. Even if municipalities decide to charge only for the 'real cost' of a service, they still face difficult issues.

The first issue pertains to knowing the real cost of all aspects of providing a service, which is basically an accounting problem that is not insurmountable. The more difficult issue relates to the difference between 'average-cost pricing' and 'marginal-cost pricing'. Average-cost pricing is easy to understand. The municipality simply takes the total cost of providing the service, divides it by the number of anticipated number of users, and the quotient is the price. In the real world, this is often what is done in an attempt to set a price based on full-cost recovery, and there is nothing wrong with such an approach. Potential problems arise if the service involved requires major capital investments, such as sewage treatment plants. If a large plant with surplus capacity has already been built, then the 'marginal' cost of treating additional sewage will be less than the average cost. The municipality and the consumer both will be better off if the pricing is based on the marginal cost. If, however, taking in additional sewage will require the building of a new treatment plant, average-cost pricing will be too low because it will not generate enough revenue to cover the cost of a new plant. In this case, the municipality can only cover its costs if it adopts marginal-cost pricing. Harry Kitchen points out that calculating the marginal cost of providing service for each single additional user is impossible. Instead, public officials can approximate marginal-cost pricing by dividing 'all of the additional costs associated with providing an increased level of service by the number of additional users. Each user is charged the average of the incremental total costs.'[7]

A variant of this approach is 'peak-period pricing'. Public transit systems are stretched to the limit during rush hours and have surplus capacity at other times of the day. Higher charges during rush hours discourage people from travelling at that time if they have a choice, thereby reducing the need for extra capacity. To the extent that people still use the system at rush hour, extra funds are generated that add to the system's capacity. All these considerations could go by the wayside, however, if the overall public policy objective is to get commuters out of their cars during rush hours. If this is the paramount objective, it might not be such a good idea to raise public transit fares for precisely these journeys. The optimal pricing of local public services is far from being a strictly technical or mathematical issue.

Harry Kitchen joins most other economists in being a great advocate of user fees, where they are technically feasible, on the grounds that such fees lead to the most efficient use of society's resources. In the Canadian context, Kitchen argues that their use in local government should be extended not only to the services already discussed but also within certain aspects of municipal recreation programs, public libraries, and police and fire services.[8] A common objection to extending user fees within such services as recreation programs is that the cost will fall disproportionately on the poor, who would likely have to pay a higher share of their total income for municipal recreation than rich people would. In the language of economics, such charges would be 'regressive'. Kitchen responds to such a concern by stating that 'This claim . . . is about as relevant as the claim that the prices of milk and movie tickets are regressive.'[9] He and other economists suggest that, if society is concerned that poor people need more money, it is more efficient to have central governments increase personal transfer payments to them and let them decide to how to spend it rather than to provide subsidized local services to everybody, whether they really want them or not.

Financing Water[10]

Providing safe and clean piped drinking water and removing dirty water and sewage are arguably the most important functions carried out by urban municipalities. Important as these functions are, they do not meet the technical definition of a 'public good' because it is easy to exclude people who do not pay. In fact, water and sewage are examples of toll goods because there can be only a single network of pipes for each function in a given territory. Toll goods can be provided by private companies. As we saw in Chapter 4, Canada's first urban water supply systems were owned and operated by companies holding franchises issued by municipal councils. In the early days of communal water supply, the provision of a constant water pressure to city-owned fire hydrants was at least as important as piping water to private purchasers. The level of domestic water rates was closely linked to the terms of the deal concerning the fire hydrants as worked out between the city and the company.

After decades of local wrangling and after approval by ratepayers and the Ontario legislature, the Toronto city council finally purchased that city's private water supply system in 1872.[11] In other cities, private ownership was not an inevitable first step. The Hamilton city council built its own system in the 1850s after it became evident that private entrepreneurs were not interested.[12] In London, Ontario, a private water company was formed in 1854 but it went out of business the following year after its one source of water had completely dried up; the pond on which it relied was fed only by surface drainage.[13] London's first functioning system was built by the municipality and began operations in 1879.[14] Similar stories can be told for virtually every city and town in the country: private water companies may have started water supply systems, but they eventually became municipal. Sewage systems have always been municipally owned and operated.

Municipalities—and other levels of government—face many decisions about how to finance these systems. They comprise three main issues:

1. financing by general tax revenues or by usage;
2. if financing by usage, what kind of rate structure to adopt;
3. the role of subsidies for capital investments.

Financing by General Tax Revenues or by Usage

The almost universal consensus among economists and environmentalists is that water consumption should be paid for by user fees. Their position is that, if households and businesses pay for the water they consume, they will pay more attention to conservation and municipalities will receive more accurate signals about how much water is really needed. This is important not just for water policy, but for energy policy as well: considerable amounts of electricity are needed to purify water and to move it around at desirable pressures. Without water meters, however, conservation programs become much more difficult because there is no financial incentive for individual consumers to conserve. In many communities in Canada water meters have never been installed, or they have not been installed for individual units in multi-family buildings. The issue is whether or not continued investment in meters is necessary.

The main objection to charging people for the use of water is that it is not a commodity that people normally can choose to do without; because it is required for sustenance and sanitation, everyone should be entitled to whatever is required for these purposes. However, no one who adopts such a position argues that people have a right to unlimited amounts of water for unessential purposes, such as watering lawns or washing cars, or that businesses that use water for industrial processes should not pay for what they use. A rare argument against metering has been advanced in Quebec, where in 2006 only 16.5 per cent of residences had water meters while the percentage for Canada as a whole was 63.1.[15] A Quebec government commission charged with investigating a wide range of issues relating to water claimed that, unless costs for water were much higher than they are in Quebec, there is little evidence that user charges reduce consumption.[16] The commission concluded that:

> Although trends in opinion largely favour user charges, the Commission does not think it would be wise to insist cities put in place such a measure. The costs of investment and planning as well as the social costs of such a measure (fees beyond the capacity of some to pay; the difficulty of allocating costs to tenants in multi-family dwellings; the risks to hygiene) cast doubt on its universal effectiveness. From the standpoint of the argument of equitability (each paying for his own consumption) the Commission discerns confusion between the terms 'equitable' and 'equal'.
>
> 'Equitability' should be thought of in the sense of solidarity. In some places, where municipal policy already provides for user fees, it is no longer appropriate to intervene because a form of consensus, both of understanding and acceptance, has already been achieved locally. But in these cases we should prohibit municipalities from disconnecting residents from the water supply because of failure to pay their bills

and provide other means (emergency funds, or other strategies) of resolving difficulties.[17]

A much more common view was expressed in 2005 by an Ontario 'expert panel' on 'water strategy':

> The benefits of conservation programs and price signals are largely lost unless customers are metered. But metering does not benefit just water services. Customers benefit too, through the assurance that they are paying only for the amount of water that they use. Metering also reminds them of the cost of waste.
>
> When meters are installed, consumption drops: Environment Canada's Municipal Water Use and Pricing survey shows, for example, that residential per capita water use is consistently lower for metered municipalities across all size ranges.[18]

There is no metering for sewage. However, many municipalities establish a sewage charge on the basis of metered water consumption,[19] thereby creating a further incentive not to use water because the price increases dramatically. In the case of water that is not returned via the sewage system (lawn and garden watering, car washing), the user pays for sewage treatment anyway.

Different Kinds of Rate Structures

Most municipalities that charge for water on the basis of usage employ a 'constant unit rate'; the amount charged per unit is the same no matter how much is used. But there are good arguments for varying the rate depending on usage. Municipalities that use a 'declining block rate' charge less per unit as volume used increases. The obvious argument against this approach is that it appears to encourage consumption but, as Kitchen points out, 'a declining block rate system may be appropriate if it is small customers who are responsible for the inefficient water use in a system, since by charging a higher price to the small customer than the large one it gives the small customer a greater incentive to conserve water.'[20]

'Increasing block rates' work in the opposite way. Costs per unit increase as consumption increases:

> This pricing tool may be appropriate for residential customers who as a customer class are the main cause of peak demand [summer lawn watering], and for industrial users if limitations on the availability of water

justify shifting the cost burden to largest users. It should be possible to set the price differences from block to block in a way that would give the customer a clear and strong economic incentive to conserve water.[21]

A 'humpback block rate' involves higher unit rates for increased use for relatively low-volume users, so as to discourage consumption by residential users, and lower unit rates for high-volume industrial users to whom providing water is relatively cheap on a unit basis because of the very high volumes. Other rate variations involve changing the rates according to the time of year or 'excess-use' rates that apply to everyone when volumes consumed exceed a prescribed threshold.[22] All of these rate structures, except the 'constant unit rate', have the potential to reflect a form of marginal pricing, although decision-makers might not necessarily explicitly justify their decisions using this vocabulary. In other words, a municipality with excess capacity for supplying water will likely want to use a 'decreasing block rate', while one that has limited current capacity is more likely to adopt a rate structure that acts more strongly to reduce consumption in peak periods. Deciding on rate structures for water consumption is one of the more important financial actions that municipal councils take.

Subsidies for Capital Investments

Economists who urge that water use be metered and paid for as a commodity invariably believe that the price should reflect the full cost of providing the water (and the sewage treatment if such costs are meant to be included in the water charge). Full-cost pricing means that the price must cover capital investments. It is obvious, however, that consumers should not pay for the cost of a new treatment plant in their water rates during the year that the plant is constructed. One of the important functions that accountants and other financial experts perform is figuring out how to spread out these costs fairly over the lifetime of the investment. The task can be difficult, but the challenges are far from insurmountable.

Water purification and sewage treatment plants, together with their associated pipeline networks, are key features of any country's physical infrastructure. In the last few decades in Canada there has been a great deal of attention paid to claims that such infrastructure is deteriorating faster than municipalities can reinvest in it, and that federal and provincial governments should provide increased grants to municipalities for infrastructure renewal.[23] Since the financial crisis of

2008, national governments in many advanced industrial democracies (including Canada) have allocated large sums of money for 'shovel-ready' infrastructure projects to provide jobs and ameliorate the effects of the recession. It appears that many people support such programs while simultaneously believing that consumers should pay the full cost of water and/or sewer systems through user charges. But holding both these beliefs at the same time is not consistent. Subsidizing the costs of water infrastructure through grants means that metered consumers are not paying the full costs of water.[24]

On its Infrastructure Canada website the federal government states that 'Investments in water infrastructure, supported by improved metering and effective pricing, will help reduce water consumption and protect fresh water supplies', and that its water infrastructure programs:

- Improve the safety, management, reliability and efficiency of Canada's drinking water treatment and distribution systems;
- Increase the number of households with access to safe drinking water that meets or exceeds the *Guidelines for Canadian Drinking Water Quality*;
- Improve protection and management of drinking water sources;
- Improve conservation of water.[25]

The same website lists hundreds of capital grants throughout the country for various water-related infrastructure projects. Each dollar spent on such projects reduces the likelihood that Canadians will pay the full cost of the water they are using.

An important Ontario government report written in 2005, before the latest round of grants, described the problems with capital subsidies:

> The sad reality . . . is that over-generous grants actually caused many of the problems in Ontario's water sector today. These are still with us in the form of plants that were built or enlarged unnecessarily and municipalities struggling to operate plants that are too big for their customer base. The impact on attitudes has been equally damaging; numerous municipalities appear to be delaying important work that needs to be done to move to full-cost recovery because of an expectation that senior government grants will solve their problems.[26]

In many cases, this is exactly what happened in the years that followed.

With respect to how the pricing of water should be affected by capital grants, the same report stated that 'When looking at replacing large assets, even if an existing system was largely paid-for with senior government grants, the only prudent assumption in setting prices is that the municipality will one day have to pay for replacements through its own revenues.'[27] However, a municipality that priced water high so as to build up its reserves to replace an existing plant would weaken its own potential case later on that it needed new rounds of grants to replace the subsidized infrastructure that had run its course. As noted in the Ontario report, 'Municipalities such as Perth and [Greater] Sudbury that have, admirably, acted without benefits of grants to maintain their systems properly are understandably concerned that others who were less forward-thinking will be rewarded with catch-up money.'[28]

Despite the recommendations of economists and rational policy-makers, it is difficult to see how this problem can be avoided. Federal and provincial governments could proclaim that there will be no new capital grants for water infrastructure, but it is unlikely they would be believed. Meanwhile, some municipalities, especially in Quebec, will continue on without water meters and will not even pretend to charge residents and businesses on the basis of their actual use of water. Others will claim to do so, but will remain on the lookout for capital grants so that they do not really have to. Others will charge the full price for water and add on surcharges for the cost of sewage. Most will stumble along with some combination of all these different approaches, with municipal councillors only addressing the issues in a serious way when something appears to be going wrong.

There is a reason, however, by which such a hybrid approach can be justified, even for those who generally advocate full-cost pricing. Water supply systems, as we have seen earlier, are not in place solely to provide water for residential and business consumers. They are also necessary for fighting fires. Even if humans did not need water for drinking and sanitation, municipal fire departments would require readily available supplies of water. For such purposes, municipalities are an important consumer of the same commodity that they produce. Having water available for fires is close to being a public good, for which user fees are not possible. In these circumstances, it is easier to appreciate the strength of arguments made in Quebec that, because we need water pipes in the ground to fight fires anyway, it makes no sense to have consumers pay the full cost of the system based on the amount of water they consume.[29] Such a view, surprisingly, is echoed by the Ontario expert panel, which is otherwise highly favourable to full user-pay systems. The panel states that it:

does not assume that the indirect costs to the water system that make it suitable for firefighting—oversizing mains, building storage capacity, adding hydrants and keeping pressure at a high enough level—should automatically be included in water rates. There is a good argument that firefighting is a service to property, not a water or a wastewater service, and therefore the general tax base should pay the excess costs of water systems that result from firefighting needs.[30]

Taking all these factors into account, it is hardly surprising that the pricing of water is a highly complex matter.

Conclusion

Most of the material presented in this chapter, especially perhaps Figure 13.1, might lead readers to believe that Canadian municipalities are in fine financial shape. Indeed, much evidence supports such a position. Municipal balance sheets appear to be strong and some municipal infrastructure—even if it needs more maintenance that it has often received—has surplus capacity. Some of the important services municipalities provide can be financed by user charges and almost everyone seems to agree that such financing, which by definition is not a form of taxation, is economically efficient. Furthermore, there is much potential for increased reliance on user charges, especially with respect to road pricing in our big cities.

But an uncomfortable truth remains. The taxes Canadians pay on property are among the highest in the world, thereby adding significantly to the cost of housing and to the cost of doing business. Students of Canadian local government need to know as much as possible about property taxes, the subject of the next chapter.

RESOURCES

On the website of the municipality in which you live or in which you have a particular interest, seek out information concerning the most recent municipal budget. Having read this far in this book, you probably already know more about Canadian municipal government than most newly elected councillors. Imagine yourself in this position and try to determine the extent to which you think you could make intelligent decisions about the budget on behalf of the people who elected you. Think about what additional information you might like to have and how it could be provided.

STUDY QUESTIONS

1. What does the 'net financial debt' of a municipality mean? Why do you think the net financial debt of Canadian local government went down between 1993 and 2005?
2. What is the difference between a municipality's operating budget and its capital budget? How are the two connected?
3. Should major municipal arterial roads be paid for by tolls? Explain your reasoning.
4. Do you favour full-cost pricing for water? Explain your reasoning. Why do you think that federal and provincial governments continue to provide subsidies for capital costs related to municipal water supply and sewage systems?

14   The Property Tax

The property tax is of great importance for Canadian local governments because it is the main source of their revenue. It is also of obvious importance to anyone who owns property, because paying the tax is a significant cost, sometimes so significant that it causes people to sell a property that they would otherwise like to keep. But the property tax is important for renters as well, both for people who rent their residential accommodation and for people who operate businesses in rental property. Tracing the impact (or 'incidence') of the property tax is a major concern of urban economists that has practical implications for public policy. All we need realize at this point is that the property tax is not merely a technical or financial issue that concerns municipal administrators and large property-owners. It is important to everyone. We all notice those few extra cents in sales tax that are added to our every purchase. But there are some aspects of how property taxes work that likely have far more direct impacts on how we actually live our lives.

In this chapter we first explore how municipalities in a given year determine how much property tax revenue they need. We then look at how this overall amount gets translated into a charge on individual property-owners. Although relatively simple in principle, this process becomes much more complex as it is implemented in the real world, and the resulting complexities are the subject of the third section of this chapter. Finally, we compare the advantages and disadvantages of the property tax with other proposed municipal taxes.

How Much Property Tax?

We saw in the previous chapter that much of the annual municipal budgetary process is ultimately determined by the expected impact of proposed expenditures on future property tax levels. But let us briefly forget this real-world intrusion and assume unrealistically that municipal budgets are set solely on the basis of what municipal councillors want to spend. If this were the case, the process would comprise three distinct phases:

1. A set of calculations about all desired operating expenditures, including payments for debt charges and reserve funds. In many municipalities some of these expenditures will be requisitions from special-purpose bodies (or upper-tier municipalities) that municipalities are required to pay.
2. A set of calculations concerning all of the incoming revenue from all non-property-tax funds. In the last chapter we saw that the most important of these are user fees and transfers from other governments.
3. The amount by which the result of the first set of calculations exceeds the result of the second is the amount of funds that the municipality has to raise from its own taxes, which in Canada are almost exclusively property taxes.

Compared to the budgetary processes of other levels of government, this process, although it requires many calculations and assumptions, is relatively simple. There can be no decision about whether or not the budget will project an operating deficit (or surplus) because municipalities are required to adopt balanced operating budgets (always including expenses for debt charges and contributions to reserve funds). Usually, decisions about the mix of various kinds of tax increases are irrelevant because the property tax is the only one available. As we saw in the previous chapter, municipalities have to decide from time to time about whether particular services (garbage collection, roads) should be paid for by user charges or property tax revenues, and they have to make difficult decisions about levels of user fees. But once such decisions are made, the property tax generally will be the mechanism whereby shortfalls will be covered.

As previously indicated, decisions about how much property tax revenue is needed in a given year are never as clear as the three-stage process described above would suggest. Municipal councillors know that if they approve a new subsidized recreation program, property tax will be increased. They sometimes know that if they assume new recreation programs will be fully paid for by user charges, then there might be insufficient demand for the program. A decision about the program's fate, not surprisingly, is never made solely on the basis of the program's inherent virtues. Often decision-makers have to consider all three stages of the process at once. Another factor that councillors have to consider is whether or not the municipality is growing. If there is much new growth and therefore many new buildings to be taxed, then perhaps increases in the total amount of property tax revenues needed to balance the budget are not a major problem, unless the growth itself generates new municipal operating expenditures, which it usually does. But if the municipality is not growing, increased demands for property tax revenue will be difficult to meet.

As we move ahead, let us assume that the municipal budgetary process is at a point where all three stages described above have been completed. How are these decisions translated into tax bills for individual property-owners?

Determining Tax Payable for Individual Property-Owners

The amount of tax payable for each individual property-owner is determined by the assessed value of the property and by the property tax rate set by the council. Each of these factors is discussed in this section.

Unlike income taxes or sales taxes, property taxes are not levied as the direct result of any transaction. They are levied annually on the property-owner even if the owner does absolutely nothing other than to continue to own the property. Until about 50 years ago, property taxes in many provinces were levied on *all* personal property, including cars, artwork, jewellery, furniture, etc. But taxes on the value of all property were exceptionally difficult to collect because it was impossible for any government accurately to determine who owned what and how much it was all worth. It is much easier to tax 'real' property—buildings and land. As discussed in Chapter 10, municipal governments know who owns each parcel of real property because the land registry is public and available to all. Without the ownership being recorded at the registry, the owner has no proof that he or she owns the land, so there is no way that an owner can escape the tax on real property, other than simply not to pay it. In the absence of payment over a specified period of time, the municipality can confiscate the property for non-payment of taxes. Unlike sales taxes and income taxes, it is virtually impossible to escape paying property taxes—which makes it a very attractive tax from the viewpoint of any government.

The only circumstance in which property-owners might rationally walk away from their properties by not paying their taxes is if the value to them of the property is less than the total amount of taxes owing.

This can happen if the difference between the taxes payable and the outstanding mortgage is greater than the value of the property. Such a circumstance can occur when lenders make unwise loans at a time when property values are declining (which is exactly what happened in the US prior to the 2008 financial crash). It can also happen when industrial property is found to contain toxic pollutants from previous industrial activities. Sometimes the costs of the required treatment of such 'brownfield' sites are greater than the projected value of the property after the cleanup. In these circumstances, municipalities can be stuck with a property that has a negative value. Provincial laws, however, have made it much more difficult for industrial polluters to avoid liability in this way.

Assessment

The biggest problem with the property tax is determining, for tax purposes, how much a property is worth. Taxes on sales or incomes are easier because there is much less room for dispute about how much was paid for a particular item at a store or how much income a person received from his or her employer. If a particular property has been sold recently, the amount paid is usually recorded in the land registry and is a matter of public record. But, as we all know, many properties are held by the same owner for decades, so direct information about their current market value is simply not available.

One way to solve this problem is to base the assessed value for tax purposes on some factor other than its current value. Many such factors have been used in the past, and most have been deficient in one way or another. We shall return to some of these factors when we look later at possible ways of reforming property assessment. Let us assume for now that the assessment of property is to be done on the basis of its market value, which is generally the case in all Canadian municipalities. Market value is easy to calculate if a property has been recently sold or if similar properties in nearby locations have been recently sold. But many properties do not fall into these categories, an extreme example being the CN Tower. It is very difficult to determine its market value in any given year unless it was bought and sold. Similar problems arise for thousands of industrial and commercial properties, not to mention unusual residential properties. In the case of some industrial properties, it is not even clear where the building ends and large-scale equipment begins, especially if the building is built around the equipment. Disputes about such matters are highly technical and help line the pockets of lawyers and consultants, but they need not concern us here. For residential properties, in-ground swimming pools are generally considered real property, while above-ground ones are not.

It is obviously difficult for any government to assess the approximate market value of each property within its jurisdiction. There is lots of room for conflict and disagreement between property-owners and the assessors, but such disputes place property-owners in a conflicted situation: normally—and especially when they want to sell—they want everybody to consider their properties to be highly valuable and worth more than they paid for them; but, when it comes to property assessment for tax purposes, they want the government to consider the value of their properties to be as low as possible. Assessors keep extensive data relating to sales of different kinds of properties in different locations. They also keep track of applications from property-owners for building permits. If owners add space to their house or extensively renovate, they are likely to see the assessed value of their property increase. This leads to a significant criticism of one of the impacts of the property tax: it discourages owners from upgrading buildings or, at a minimum, it discourages them from applying for the required permits, which are designed to force all builders to meet the appropriate zoning and building code requirements.

The assessment of property for tax purposes is carried out by the provincial government in all provinces except Alberta, Manitoba, Ontario, and Quebec. In Ontario it is performed by a municipally owned and financed corporation, the Municipal Property Assessment Corporation (MPAC). In Newfoundland and Labrador and in Saskatchewan responsibility for assessment varies depending on location.[1] All provinces have in place mechanisms to allow property-owners to appeal the assessed value of their properties. For owners of multiple properties, or of especially valuable ones, the outcomes of such appeals can be very important. For individual homeowners, such appeals can be frustrating and expensive but sometimes the occasional victory seems to make it all worthwhile.

Rates

When the assessment process is complete within a municipality for any given year, the municipal council can then set its tax rate. In its simplest terms, the rate is the total amount of money a municipality needs to raise from the property tax divided by the total assessed value of all the properties within its boundaries. For any individual property-owner, the amount of tax payable in a given year is the product of the rate and the assessed value of his or her property. A typical example in Canada would be a home assessed at a value of $300,000 having to pay tax at a rate of

.015 (1.5 per cent), leading to an annual tax bill of $4,500. Such a calcu-
lation should illuminate two simple truths.

(1) If everybody's property value doubles, and if the assessment process captures the increase for everybody, then the municipality can cut
its rate in half and still raise the same amount of money. Despite a common view that that this is unlikely to happen, in fact, it generally does.
Municipalities cannot leave the rate the same while property values generally increase because, for everybody who does not sell property in that
year the increase in property values is simply a gain on paper. Unless
property-owners remortgage their houses at the higher value, they do not
magically have new resources with which to pay property tax increases.
This is different from income taxes where the more one makes, the more
one can pay, because the income-earner actually has more financial
resources as his or her income increases. It is true, of course, that some
people make a great deal of profit when they sell a property, but if or
how to tax that profit has nothing to do with the property tax. (This is
an income tax matter. Gains on the sale of a property used as a main
residence are not subject to income tax in Canada; gains on the sale of
all other properties are.)

(2) If assessments change at the same rate for everybody in a given
year, such changes are unlikely to have any appreciable impact on the
amount of property taxes they pay because rates likely will change
inversely to changes in property values. Therefore, people should not be
concerned if the assessed value of their property goes up by 10 per cent
while everybody else's is going up by the same rate. They do have cause
for concern, however, if the assessed value of everyone else's property
goes down by 10 per cent and theirs stays the same. In such circumstances, the municipal council will have to raise the rate by 10 per cent
simply to maintain the same revenues and the person whose property
maintained its value would be facing a 10 per cent tax increase. Such
an example reinforces the idea that the interaction between rates and
assessed values means that property owners need to pay attention not
simply to the increase or decrease in the assessed value of their property
but how it is changing *in relation to the assessed value of other properties.*

To consider another important matter in analyzing property taxes,
let us assume that a house worth $300,000 in one municipality is worth
$600,000 in an analogous location in another municipality. Such an
assumption is totally realistic, because we all know that house prices
vary dramatically from city to city, between Winnipeg and Vancouver,
for example. If house prices are generally twice as high in Vancouver

as in Winnipeg, it certainly does not follow that the costs of providing municipal services will be twice as high in Vancouver. In fact, there is no reason to expect such costs to be much different (except perhaps for snow removal). Assuming market-value assessment in both cities, we should therefore expect property tax *rates* to be lower in Vancouver, perhaps by half, because the rates apply to a much larger average assessment. But this is of little practical consequence because the total taxes paid by owners of similar houses would be roughly similar in each city. If we were to measure the property tax burden in terms of the ratio of tax paid to value of houses, it would seem as though Vancouver homeowners were subject to a relatively low tax burden, but such an outcome results solely from the fact that housing prices are higher in Vancouver. If we want to measure relative property tax burdens among different cities, we should not do so by looking at houses of similar value. We should compare houses of similar size, quality, and relative location.

So far we have assumed that municipalities charge a single tax rate on all properties. In fact, this is not generally the case. Many provinces allow municipalities to vary the rate among different 'classes' of property.[2] Examples of classes of property are: single-family residential, multi-family residential, commercial, industrial. In general in Canada, owners of single-family residences have received the best deal from municipalities, presumably because they comprise the most voters in any municipal election and councillors have the greatest immediate incentive to please them. However, these same councillors are usually under pressure to attract investment and jobs, so one would think that they would want to lower rates on industrial properties. Recently, provincial governments seem to have become more sensitive about industrial property tax rates and, in some cases, have required municipalities to narrow the gap between industrial and residential rates. In provinces such as Quebec, where municipalities have not been allowed to vary the rate among classes of properties, residential property-owners have become very upset when their taxes go up and taxes on industrial properties go down solely as a result of more rapid increases in residential property values.

Despite the fact that the property tax is in many ways an ideal mechanism for financing many municipal services, there are some significant problems and issues that must be understood by anybody who wants to understand the main financial issues facing Canadian municipalities. The most important of these issues are addressed in the sections that follow.

Alternative Assessment Systems

Despite the use of different names, all provinces base their assessment system on the perceived market value of properties at the time of assessment.[3] But such systems are always controversial, in part because property-owners object to having their assessment go up if they make improvements to their house. If they bought expensive artwork instead, they would not have to pay an annual tax based on the value of the art. The way around this problem is to base the assessment on the perceived value of the land, rather than on both the land and the building(s). Such a system is called site-value assessment. It has been used in the past in parts of Ontario and western Canada and is still in use in some countries of the British Commonwealth.[4] Such a system has many virtues, especially for those who want dense urban development to combat urban sprawl. No one would use developable land as a parking lot in a downtown core for very long if they were paying the same property taxes as the owner of a high-rise building next door. The idea that taxing land—and land alone—is the most suitable form of taxation is associated with Henry George, a nineteenth-century American political economist whose views are still supported today by a disparate band of environmentalists, libertarians, and egalitarians.[5] The most obvious problem with this scheme is assessing the value of land without the buildings that are on it. Assessment problems are even greater than with market-value assessment.

A quite different kind of assessment system is known as unit-value assessment. In this system, there are no subjective judgements by assessors. Assessment is based solely on the amount of land owned and the size of the buildings that are on it. The two factors can be combined using whatever arithmetical formula might be desired by the taxing authority. By encouraging small living units on small lots, this system is attractive for environmental reasons. However, if implemented, it would likely have some strange distributional effects. Compared with market-value assessment, relatively small homes on small lots in highly desirable areas of cities would likely see significant tax decreases, while larger homes on larger lots lived in by larger families in peripheral suburban areas would see tax increases. Making such a change would not be appealing to any provincial or municipal politician.

It is possible, of course, to combine aspects of these different systems by using complex formulas. But the more complex the formula, the less likely it will be understood. The great virtue of market-value assessment is that it is readily understood. From the point of view of the government, another advantage is that dissatisfied property-owners must argue that their property is worth less than the assessor says it is—not an attractive proposition for those who treasure their real estate. We are not likely to see departures from market-value assessment in Canada anytime soon.

Exempt Property and Grants-in-Lieu of Taxes

The federal and provincial governments cannot tax each other.[6] Because municipalities derive their authority from provincial legislatures, it follows that municipalities cannot tax federal property. It also follows that municipalities cannot tax provincial property unless the provincial legislature specifically allows such taxation. Provincial legislation also prevents municipalities from taxing provincially funded institutions such as hospitals (except in New Brunswick) and colleges and universities.[7] But federal and provincial buildings and institutions consume municipal services. For some, they pay user charges like anybody else. But they also rely on municipal roads and police and fire services, for which there generally are no user charges. In order to compensate municipalities for the provision of these services, the federal and provincial governments pay what are called 'grants (or payments)-in-lieu of taxes', an attempt to cover municipal costs resulting from their operations. It is important to note that ultimately the federal and provincial governments decide how much to pay, not the municipalities. Nevertheless, Statistics Canada, when compiling the local government financial data used in this book, considers grants-in-lieu of taxes to be municipal own-source revenue derived from 'property and related taxes' rather than considering them to be forms of transfer payments. Total municipal revenue from grants-in-lieu has hardly budged since 1988 and comprises less than 4 per cent of total municipal spending.[8]

Provincial legislation generally excludes places of worship and charitable institutions from having to pay municipal property taxes. In these cases municipalities are effectively providing their services free and are therefore providing a form of subsidy. Decisions about which properties qualify for the exemption generally are made provincially. But municipalities can decide to make grants to local organizations that are deemed to be serving some kind of public purpose, so they could make grants to cover property taxes. The problem for the organizations, however, is that such grants would need to be approved annually, while a property tax exemption is much more permanent. Compared to other forms of property, farmland is subject to less property tax in all provinces except Newfoundland and Labrador and Prince Edward Island.[9]

Over the course of Canadian municipal history the most controversial property tax exemptions have related to railroads and to manufacturing.

In the mid- and late nineteenth century, municipalities competed desperately with each other to attract railroads. One way they did this was to offer incentives, both outright financial grants and exemptions from paying property tax. Such policies soon extended to investors in manufacturing plants, whose factory outputs often were needed to make the railroads profitable. If only a very few municipalities granted tax exemptions, little harm was done. In fact, to the extent that the exemptions caused new jobs to be created in a particular place—stimulating other kinds of property investment, including residences and retail outlets—they might well have led to an increase in local property tax revenue. However, problems resulted when most, or all, municipalities started doing the same thing. No municipality was better able to compete for investment in these circumstances and all have lost property tax revenue from businesses.

Precisely because of this 'race-to-the-bottom' dynamic, provinces eventually eliminated the ability of municipalities to offer such exemptions.[10] If any tax exemptions were to be offered, provinces tended to want to make the offers themselves. However, with the rise of globalization in the late twentieth century, many municipalities found it difficult to compete with other jurisdictions around the world, especially in the United States, that still had considerable freedom to attract footloose capital investment by offering a variety of tax holidays.[11] Various kinds of special economic zones have been established within cities around the world to attract businesses by making tax concessions. Although there have been occasional demands that Canadian provinces should move in the same direction, little has come of them. Canadian municipalities can do very little, if anything, to exempt businesses from paying property taxes.

In Canada the more common complaint is that home-owning voters have offloaded an unfair property tax burden onto local businesses, particularly since businesses generally cannot make use of many municipal services, notably garbage collection. Provincial policy within Ontario and in the city of Vancouver has been explicitly aimed at phasing in more equal treatment of businesses.[12] This has painful consequences for municipal councillors because it means that, in any given year until the phase-in is complete, residential tax-rate increases are higher than the average increase that the municipality requires to balance its budget.

Who Pays?

In legal terms, we know who pays the property tax: the registered owner of each property. But to determine the real impact of the property tax, it is important to have some idea about who really pays in practice. For example, our views of the property tax are likely to be quite different depending on whether we think the owner of a low-rent apartment building pays from his/her own funds or whether we think the owner simply passes on the cost of the tax to the tenants through rents. What really happens depends on a great many factors: the state of the rental market; the potential mobility of renters; whether we are looking at the short or long term.[13]

If few housing alternatives are available, and if renters with short-term leases are not in a position to move, then it is likely that the property-owner could easily pass on any tax increases to the tenants. But let us imagine an alternative situation, with a number of similar apartment units in different buildings on both sides of a municipal border and frequent movement by tenants out of the buildings. Due to factors other than the level of municipal services provided, the annual property tax rate (as a percentage of the market value of the building) increases in the first municipality at a rate faster than the second. What happens here? Clearly the landlord in the first municipality cannot charge significantly higher rents, because he or she will end up with few or no tenants. Because rents must remain roughly equal in both municipalities, the landlord pays. This will have the effect of driving down the value of the buildings in the first municipality. As a result, someone buying these buildings at their reduced prices will actually make the same amount of profit (other things being equal) as the landlord in the second municipality. In these circumstances we say that the differences in the property tax levels are 'capitalized', because the differences in levels affect the value of the different properties in the marketplace. When property tax differentials are capitalized, they are not being passed on to tenants; instead, they are absorbed by property-owners. Even assuming high vacancy rates and mobile tenants, however, we must be careful in drawing conclusions. If property taxes were increased to provide accessible recreational facilities to a nearby apartment building, tenants would be willing to pay more in rent and the tax increases could be passed on. In this case, the value of the property would not go down as a result of higher taxes because the higher taxes would be producing a direct benefit to the property in question, and ultimately to the renters.

The issue of who really pays property taxes is important for provincial public policy in Canada because almost all provinces have some kind of scheme to provide property tax relief to low-income homeowners. In Ontario and Quebec, renters are eligible as well.[14] Data from the 1990s show that, for homeowners, the lower the gross family income, the higher the percentage of such income that is absorbed by the property tax. In British Columbia in 1992 the poorest (bottom decile) home-owning families spent 12.55 per cent of their income on property taxes. In Newfoundland and Labrador, the richest (top decile) spent only 0.79 per cent on property taxes.[15] Economists refer to a tax as 'regressive' when it absorbs a higher proportion of poor people's income than that of rich people. The relief schemes for property tax in various provinces are designed to soften the regressive nature of the property tax. Especially targeted are home-owning senior citizens. After paying off their mortgages and reaching retirement, some are forced to consider selling their family home because of high property taxes. Various schemes are now in place to reduce the likelihood of such forced sales, because no politician wants to be held responsible for senior citizens having to leave their homes because of the burden of high property taxes.

If property taxes on rental units really are passed on to renters, then schemes for property tax relief are manifestly unfair if they apply only to low-income homeowners. This is precisely why determining the incidence of the property tax is such an important practical policy issue. In Ontario, the provincial government assumes that 25 per cent of residential rents are spent on property taxes, and renters are treated as though they were homeowners for property tax relief purposes.

Other Demands on the Property Tax

In Chapter 4 we noted that some special-purpose bodies are able to make a direct charge on the municipal treasury. Whatever they decide they need in a given year, municipalities are required to pay, subject only to some form of provincial appeal mechanism. In these cases, such costs are integrated directly into the municipal budget and there is no reason for those who pay property taxes to know about them unless the municipality decides to launch some kind of publicity campaign about costs that it cannot control. But there is another mechanism whereby a special-purpose body can raise local funds: it can itself set a tax rate on the value of assessed property and charge the tax directly, even if the municipality might still collect the tax on its behalf. This is the way elected school boards in Canada traditionally have raised local funds to finance local schools.

In 2010 only school boards in Manitoba and Quebec have the authority to levy their own property taxes. However, there are provincial property taxes (mostly for educational purposes) in all provinces except Quebec and Nova Scotia, which is the only province whose municipalities do not have to share the property tax base with any other entity. In Manitoba, cities share it with school boards and the province. In the

last few decades, provincial governments have acted to restrict or eliminate the taxing authority of school boards because of concerns about
intra-provincial equity and because there was evidence that school
boards—responding to constant pressure for increased expenditures on
education—were 'crowding out' municipalities from the property tax
base.[16] Provinces that levy taxes on property for educational purposes
are generally committed to decreasing the level of such taxes over time,
so that much of the pressure on municipalities caused by crowding out
is easing. Nevertheless, as many municipal politicians search tax sources
that add to the property tax, it is surprising that they do not also stress
that, in all provinces except Nova Scotia, they do not even have exclusive
access to the tax most often considered their own, the property tax.

Alternatives to the Property Tax

As we noted in Chapter 3, Canadian municipalities in the past in some
provinces have had access both to the sales tax and to income taxes. But
the last vestiges of such access were abolished in Quebec in 1964. More
recently, especially in the early 2000s, Canadian municipal leaders made
a valiant effort to widen their taxation opportunities. Again, as we saw in
Chapter 3, in 2007 Toronto was successful in obtaining the authority to
tax personal vehicle registrations, land transfers, public entertainment,
tobacco products, and alcohol served in bars and restaurants, but it has
so far taxed only vehicles and land transfers. In this section we examine
the case for municipal alternatives to the property tax. In order to do so,
we must first understand municipal complaints about excessive reliance
on the property tax.

Nobody in municipal government wants to get rid of the property
tax. After all, it generates impressive revenues, is virtually impossible to
avoid, and is quite closely linked to most of the main municipal functions, which usually involve property in one way or another. But the main
complaint is that it is not sufficiently 'elastic', which means that it is not
sufficiently responsive to changes in the overall economy. This is perceived as a problem by municipal officials when the economy is growing,
as it was in the early 2000s. It would appear to be much less of a problem
after the economic slowdown caused by the financial crisis in 2008.

When the economy is growing, revenue from sales taxes and income
taxes increases automatically. Politicians need do nothing but watch the
extra funds flow in as incomes increase and people buy more goods.
Although the people paying the higher taxes might complain, they do so
from a position of increasing wealth, so the political impact of the higher

taxation is minimal. But people and businesses have to pay property tax even if they are not enjoying increases in income and not purchasing anything. If the value of their properties is increasing faster than the average in their municipality, then their property tax burden actually increases even though they have no additional funds. In such circumstances, if a municipal council wants to increase the property tax rate, it will face howls of opposition, not necessarily from everybody, but certainly from those whose incomes are not increasing (seniors, for example). It is in this sense that property tax revenues are inelastic.

A related problem pointed to by critics of the property tax is that non-residents of a city who use its resources—commuters or tourists—pay nothing, at least not directly. Commuters pay income tax on the money that they earn in the city, but it all goes to the federal and provincial governments. These same commuters, as well as tourists, make purchases in the city, but again all the goods and services tax (GST) and sales tax revenue goes to the federal and provincial governments. Why should a municipality spend money to encourage job creation and promote tourism when other levels of government reap the financial rewards? Part of the answer, of course, is that municipalities do benefit indirectly. Owners of office buildings, hotels, and major stores that serve commuters and tourists pay property tax like anyone else—and they likely would not have invested in such property were they not confident that that their buildings would be profitable. But, once the buildings are built, very little of the funds generated by their occupants actually finds its way into municipal coffers.

Advocates of municipal sales or income taxes aim to fix this problem. They assume, first of all, that such taxes would be collected using the same bureaucratic apparatus that has already been established by the federal and provincial governments. The idea is that municipalities would be allowed to set their own rate that would be added to the existing rates and that funds collected from the municipal rate would automatically be turned over to the relevant municipality, just as the federal government collects provincial income taxes (outside Quebec) and turns the funds over to the relevant province. The cost of collection would be negligible, except that chain stores, which do not now have to worry about the municipality in which sales took place, would then have to contend with much more detailed reporting requirements. Municipal boundaries would become much more important than they already are, because there would often be different levels of sales and income taxes on each side, which would affect shopping and retail development decisions.

If municipal income taxes were levied by the municipality in which the worker resided, then the problem of taxing commuters would not be addressed. But if employees were taxed by the municipality in which they worked, then collection would be complicated by the need to distribute the revenue to a municipality different from the one in which he or she lived. These problems are by no means insurmountable, but they do indicate that municipal income taxes could not be implemented easily in the Canadian context, even if they do exist in many other countries.[17]

Another solution would be simply to allocate shares of federal and provincial income and sales taxes to municipalities, in much the same way that the federal gas tax is currently shared (see Chapter 3). The difficulty here is that this is not really a new municipal tax at all; it is really just a disguised form of transfer payment, which is exactly how it would be recorded by Statistics Canada. Such a new transfer program might well be desirable, but it would do nothing to solve the original perceived problem: that municipalities get little in return for any investment they make to bring in outsiders. If taxes were shared on the basis of where they were collected, however, administrative problems of the kind referred to in the previous paragraph would emerge—and municipalities would have no freedom themselves to try to influence taxpayers' behaviour or to increase their own revenues through the adjustment of their own rates.

Another possibility is a municipal tax on the occupancy of hotel rooms. Such taxes already exist in Vancouver and Montreal.[18] Although not a huge generator of revenue, hotel occupancy taxes at least directly compensate the municipality for some of the costs associated with hosting visitors. The problem, of course, is that many local businesses want municipalities to do all they can to attract visitors, and levying a tax especially directed at them does not look like a desirable policy. It is surely no accident that the tax exists in precisely the two large Canadian cities that are most attractive to visitors anyway. It is hard to disagree with Harry Kitchen, who writes: 'municipalities should be given the opportunity to implement this type of tax. Presumably, if they get it wrong and drive tourists or conventions away, they will soon correct for this error in judgment.'[19]

Conclusion

This discussion of alternatives to the property tax raises larger questions about the future role of Canadian municipalities. If they are ever to levy such taxes, mayors, councillors, and senior municipal staff will have to make some very complex policy judgements about how to maximize revenue while mixing the taxes in such a way as to optimally advance the municipality's other policy interests, such as economic development and local environmental protection. We shall address this issue of municipal policy capacity in the final chapter.

The important lessons from this chapter are paradoxical. On the one hand, everyone acknowledges that the property tax has many virtues as the main source of municipal revenue and that, whatever reforms might come in the future, it will remain as the financial bedrock of Canadian municipalities, especially now that school boards are no longer significant players in the same arena. On the other hand, there are constant complaints about the property tax: it is inelastic; unfair to low-income earners; and its burdens on individual property-owners can increase, even in years where their incomes decrease. Furthermore, the assessment system inevitably produces some results that are arbitrary, if not perverse, causing aggrieved property-owners to have to launch frustrating and worrisome appeals. Correcting a problem for one property can well produce new inequities for neighbours. With all these problems, it might seem surprising that the system survives. But it does—because most of the alternatives are considerably worse.

RESOURCES

Perhaps the most comprehensive website relating to property tax in Canada is operated by Ontario's Municipal Property Assessment Corporation. Although its emphasis is obviously on assessment in Ontario, it contains a wealth of information on many issues that are also important in other provinces. See <www.mpac.on.ca>.

STUDY QUESTIONS

1. What do members of a municipal council need to know before they decide how much property tax they need to collect in a particular year?

2. Is it possible for the assessed value of a property to go up in a given year but for the total taxes payable to go down? Explain your reasoning.

3. What are the advantages and disadvantages of charging property tax only on the value of land and not on the combined value of land and buildings?

4. What additional taxation authority do you believe Canadian municipalities should have? Explain your reasoning.

5. Pick a property with which you are familiar so as find out how property tax works in particular cases. Assessments of properties for tax purposes are in the public domain, so you can find out how to access them from the web or from the relevant municipality. Does the assessment seem fair to you? What is the tax rate on the property? How much, if any, is charged explicitly for public education, either by the province or by a school board?

15 Conclusion: Change, Importance, and Complexity

Authors commonly conclude books by claiming that their subject is undergoing great change and becoming increasingly important. Such claims are hardly surprising, because they provide excellent justifications for why a book was written in the first place. This conclusion is different in that its main themes are that continuity predominates over change in Canadian local government and that its importance, relative to provincial governments at least, has *not* been increasing in recent years. The resulting challenge, therefore, is to explain why it remains an imperative that Canadians continue to pay attention to local government.

Is Canadian Local Government Changing in a Fundamental Way?

In this section we shall be asking questions about the extent to which Canadian local government has been changing and is changing. As indicated above, the responses will generally be negative. It is important to note, however, that these questions relate to *local government*, not to questions about the nature of Canadian city-regions and their demographic makeup. As we have seen throughout this book, especially in Chapter 5, higher proportions of Canadians are living in urban areas (however defined) and higher proportions of these people are immigrants or Aboriginals. The nature of work in our cities has changed, such that there are dramatically fewer manufacturing jobs and many more service jobs, some very well-paying at the high end and others relatively poorly paid at the low end. The process of globalization is at the core of these changes. Globalization is real and it is very important. But the first question we need to ask regards the impact of globalization on local government.

Globalization, Neo-Liberalism, and Rescaling

Neo-liberalism has been described as a 'cousin' of globalization.[1] It is 'a theory and practice of running the economy in a way that frees markets from state and bureaucratic control'.[2] Globalization is connected to neo-liberalism in that, starting in the 1980s, the common prescription from international organizations and consultants for most national problems relating to governance was to advocate a reduction in regulation and taxes to stimulate the wealth-generating capacity of the marketplace. 'Rescaling' is also connected in that it is the process by which globalization and the liberalization of markets cause authority and policy to be redefined in different ways for different territories.[3] Rescaling takes place when different levels of government, or special-purpose bodies, take on new tasks. How have these processes affected Canadian local government?

The claim has often been made that neo-liberalism was responsible for the wave of municipal amalgamations (described in Chapter 8) that swept over eastern Canada in the 1990s.[4] The amalgamations themselves are clearly a form of 'rescaling' because the whole purpose of an amalgamation is to create a municipal government with a dramatically larger territory, or scale. The problem with attributing the amalgamations of the 1990s to neo-liberalism, however, is that, as we saw in Chapter 8, provincially legislated amalgamations go back to the 1930s in Canada, long before the term 'neo-liberalism' had been coined. More importantly, the amalgamations in Windsor and Winnipeg were unequivocally meant to benefit residents of poorer municipalities rather than to strengthen the operation of the private market. The same is true of the Quebec amalgamations of the early 2000s. Anyone familiar with the 'public-choice' approach to local government described in Chapter 7 will recognize that this approach, rather than the consolidationist one, best fits with neo-liberalism. Even though Mike Harris's government in Ontario clearly espoused a neo-liberal ideology, its efforts to create larger municipal governments were the opposite of neo-liberal. Is it possible that Harris and his government simply did not know what they were doing?[5]

Once amalgamation is removed from the picture, what remaining evidence is there of the neo-liberalism taking hold in Canadian municipalities? The level of trust shown to MFP, a duplicitous financial services company, by the cities of Toronto and Waterloo (described in Chapter 12) represents perhaps a hint of neo-liberal tendencies, but major cases of contracting out and privatization simply cannot be found in Canadian municipalities, certainly nothing like many of the important British and

American examples. Canadian public-sector unions and their political supporters have been extremely successful in preventing this kind of neo-liberal change.

'City–Building'

Susan Phillips, a political scientist at Carleton University, has recently pointed to two important 'intersecting agendas' that 'hold the potential for more transformative change in institutions and relationships'.[6] The first of these is what she calls 'city-building': 'the struggle being led by the big cities for new powers and revenues and more effective governance structures that better suit the reality of political, economic, and social life in Canada's metropolitan areas.'[7] Much of the 'struggle' she refers to has been described here in Chapters 3 and 11. But she was writing before the Harper government put a stop to the 'cities and communities agenda' at the federal level and before mayors Campbell, Murray, and Miller left office as leaders of the 'big cities'. When Phillips refers to 'more effective governance structures . . . in Canada's metropolitan areas', she is referring to the efforts by Alan Broadbent and others to reform Canadian federalism so that cities and their metropolitan areas acquire enhanced capacity for self-government.[8] There are many problems with these efforts, not the least of which is determining their boundaries.[9] We saw, for example, in Chapter 5 that the census metropolitan area of Toronto bears little relationship to most people's (and the Ontario government's) conceptions of the Toronto city-region and that in 2001 Statistics Canada developed new territorial definitions for the Vancouver and Montreal city-regions and for the Calgary–Edmonton corridor.

It is true that during the 1990s and 2000s, Canadian municipalities saw their legislative autonomy enhanced by many important changes to provincial legislation.[10] As described in Chapter 3, they also won important financial victories by gaining complete exemptions from the GST, by obtaining a share of the federal gas tax, and by receiving massive federal infrastructure subsidies. Important as these changes were, they did not constitute transformative change. They were part of the process of incremental change that has characterized the relationship of Canadian municipal governments to the federal and provincial governments for many decades. From the vantage point of the mid-2000s Phillips could write that 'the basic conception of municipalities has been transformed in recent years, from thinking of municipalities as being deliverers of (hard) services to thinking of them as democratic governments.'[11] But by the time the decade had ended, the evidence of real change was much less apparent. Hopefully, the historical context provided in various chapters of this book will also help readers to understand that conceptualizing municipalities as 'democratic governments' is not new and that (as described in Chapter 8) the greatest threats to such a conception in Canada actually occurred during the period Phillips was writing about: the late 1990s and early 2000s when legislated municipal amalgamations were implemented in Ontario and Quebec.[12]

'Community–Building'

The second of Phillips's two 'intersecting agendas' is 'community-building'. She acknowledges that this feature is 'less prominent so far than the city-building agenda' but she claims that 'recent processes of community-building are having an equally important impact on restructuring relationships between municipalities and citizens.'[13] Community-building, however, relies less on municipalities and more on voluntary organizations and foundations. Phillips includes under community-building the many 'place-based initiatives' that have been described and analyzed by various authors, especially by Neil Bradford.[14] There has clearly been much activity around these initiatives and they merit careful study but, as was pointed out in the Introduction, this book focuses on local government and not on all the various non-governmental organizations within cities and towns that contribute to the quality of our urban life. It could well be that we are experiencing a significant period of community-building, although it is hard to believe that it surpasses in importance the kind of community-building described in Chapter 10 that occurred when Canadian urban neighbourhoods resisted various plans for 'urban renewal' and the building of urban expressways. In any event, although Phillips describes many important community-led initiatives to solve various local problems, everything in her list could have been found in most cities 40 years ago. The evidence to support the notion that the latest round of 'community-building' in Canada has somehow opened the way to a new form of participatory community governance is minimal at best.

Why Canadian Local Government Is Important and Complex

The above discussion does not mean that Canadian local government is unimportant. But its importance derives not from how it has been affected by neo-liberalism or new forms of community governance but from the reality that it exerts democratic control over so many vital features of our built environment. This is nothing new, but reminders about the continuity of purpose in local government are necessary when there are so many claims that we are in a period when it is becoming dramatically more important. In addition, the inevitability of complexity in local government points out one of the most important ways in which local governments differ from central governments (i.e., federal and provincial governments in the Canadian context). In this section we shall review the issues relating to importance and complexity.

Importance

If we looked at the broad range of functions of Canadian local governments a hundred years ago compared to today, we would be forced to conclude that local government has become less important over the last century, especially relative to provincial governments. A hundred years ago municipalities were universally regarded as the last resort for public social assistance, but they are not now. School boards once had enormous autonomy to shape the nature of public schooling in their communities, but now most decisions about funding and curriculum are taken in provincial capitals. Although these basic facts must never be forgotten as we assess the current role of local government, we need not focus exclusively on such examples of reductions of local autonomy, especially because, in terms of social equity at least, they are perfectly justified.

As has been emphasized repeatedly, local governments have considerable control over our built environment. A hundred years ago, when a much higher proportion of Canadians lived in rural areas and small towns, controlling the built environment was not nearly as important as managing the settlement of new agricultural land, especially in the West. But the urban nature of current Canadian life means that the quality of the built environment is crucial to all of us, particularly to citizens with special concerns about the environment and the quality of urban design. Subject to broad provincial control, our municipalities determine where new suburban development will take place. Subject to much less provincial control, they determine design standards for this development and the mechanisms for financing the required infrastructure. They determine the level of public protection for old buildings and the kind of development that is allowed or not allowed in our downtowns. Many of these matters were explored in Chapter 10. Municipalities also determine where roads and streets are built, how wide they will be, how well they will be maintained, and how they will accommodate pedestrians and cyclists. Subject to federal and provincial environmental standards, they determine how our water will be supplied, how our sewage will be treated, the conditions under which solid waste will be collected, and how it will disposed of. As we saw in Chapter 12, municipalities have very important decisions to make about the extent to which the actual production of these services will be contracted to private companies and how they will be paid for.

Municipal governments, as discussed in Chapter 4, have varying levels of direct control over local police services. But even where direct municipal control is minimal (as in Ontario), local special-purpose bodies fill the gap. In every city in the country there are hugely sensitive issues about how the police relate to local residents, and there is much more opportunity than is usually acknowledged for local citizens, through the appropriate channels, to have a greater role in determining what the police do and how they do it. Unlike police, fire services are invariably under direct municipal control, but for them, too, important local decisions must be made about how their personnel are to be deployed, especially as first responders in medical emergencies.

Other local special-purpose bodies, many with few direct connections to municipalities, have significant control over ports and airports and still others are crucial for the planning and provision of regional public transit. Even health services are being decentralized and made more subject to forms of local control, although progress here is not nearly as fast as many experts had hoped or predicted.

With all these crucial attributes of urban life so vitally dependent on decisions of local governments of one form or another, why would anyone possibly suggest that either the services themselves or the local governments are somehow not important? Susan Phillips has claimed that municipalities are being transformed from providers of 'hard' services (i.e., of roads and sewers rather than of social services) to democratic governments. But the 'hard' services she refers to are crucially important for urban life and they are provided democratically. As was noted in Chapter 2, all of these hard services, in theory, could be provided directly by provincial governments without having local governments at all. Local governments ensure that decisions about these key services are made by local people who are accountable in some way to local citizens.

Anyone who thinks that making local democratic decisions about 'hard' services is easy or routine has not watched the agonies that local councils often go through in making such decisions. How much do we subsidize public transit systems to provide weekend service to people who have no other way of getting around a medium-sized city where most people have cars? Do we build a larger sewage treatment plant than we need now in the expectation that our community will grow? Do we widen an arterial road to ease traffic flow even if it means decreased property values and quality of life for residents in nearby houses? Do we maintain a policy of low industrial water rates just because a major consumer and employer threatens to leave if the rates are raised? Do we close a local school where enrolment is declining so as to redirect badly needed resources elsewhere, even if it means that a community or neighbourhood might wither and die? These are not hypothetical issues. They are faced regularly and repeatedly by municipal councillors and school board members whose levels of education and technical background are no greater than most readers of this book. And (except in some cities in British Columbia and Quebec) they have no party caucus or leader telling them what to do. Arguably, as we saw in Chapter 10, some of them are told what to do by developers and other groups associated with the property industry. But all of these factors are powerful reasons for political scientists, the media, and informed citizens to pay attention to the day-to-day business of local government rather than to write it off as boring and irrelevant.

Complexity

Understanding local government in Canada would obviously be much easier if every city and town had one municipal government that was responsible for all local functions and subject to the jurisdiction of the federal government. In these circumstances there would be no special-purpose bodies, no two- (or three-) tier systems of municipal government, and very little institutional variation across the country. As we have seen throughout this book, much of the institutional variation is caused by the fact that different provinces have different kinds of laws about local government, which is as it should be in a federation. Why have a federal system if provinces do not adopt different policies to match their particular situations? But there is also considerable institutional variation even within most provinces, caused in large part by provinces imposing various waves of institutional change, often by allowing different forms of local option and not completely eliminating what went before.

The most powerful and pervasive reason for institutional complexity at the local level relates to boundaries. Within sovereign states and constituent units of federations (such as provinces in Canada), boundaries are not now much in dispute.[15] But boundaries for cities and metropolitan areas are always in dispute. Sometimes the disputes have nothing to do with local government; people just have differing conceptions about where an urban area ends and the countryside begins. For statistical purposes these kinds of disputes are authoritatively decided by Statistics Canada when it draws the boundaries of what it calls 'urban areas', 'census agglomerations', and 'census metropolitan areas'. But Canada, more so than most countries, also has experienced ongoing disputes about municipal boundaries, disputes that received considerable attention in Chapters 6, 7, and 8. The outcomes of these disputes have left a remarkably varied collection of municipal arrangements for different metropolitan areas: from the mind-boggling array of boroughs, de-amalgamated municipalities, agglomeration councils, and metropolitan communities in Montreal and Quebec City to the relative simplicity of Calgary, a municipality that has grown outward repeatedly through annexation. Even Calgary, as we saw in Chapter 6, appears to be coming close to the end of the annexation road.

Major cities do not have simple arrangements for municipal government. The underlying reason for this is that different functions of urban government require different boundaries. Institutions for the planning of outward regional development in big cities require different boundaries from institutions that are established to run a system of inner-city neighbourhood parks. Sometimes all of these different functions are forced to coexist within the same municipal boundaries, or within the somewhat less rigid arrangements allowed by two-tier systems. But ultimate flexibility is provided by having different boundaries for different special-purpose bodies responsible for different governmental functions. The fact that both Metrolinx for Toronto and Hamilton and TransLink for the Vancouver area have their own unique boundaries for regional transit purposes is a perfect illustration of this point. That they exist, and that they are responsible for such an important function of government, indicates why the institutional arrangements for urban government are often as complex as they are.

Assessing Canadian Local Government

As we saw in Chapter 5, there is considerable evidence in Canada, especially for Toronto, that provincial governments are increasingly making the key strategic decisions about the long-term futures of Canadian city-regions. This is not bad news for local government; it is good news. It means that municipalities need not constantly be enlarged or reorganized in the vain hope that one day their boundaries will perfectly match the apparent functional requirements of our growing urban areas. It means, instead, that they can get on with the business of providing all the various services and regulations expected of them. Sometimes they will do this in co-operation with their municipal neighbours, either through various kinds of relatively informal agreements or by establishing new inter-municipal special-purpose bodies for the joint provision of particular services. Sometimes the provincial—and even the federal—government will be closely involved, requiring that municipal officials be highly skilled and knowledgeable with respect to intergovernmental negotiating. But negotiating on behalf of municipalities in the intergovernmental arena does not inevitably mean pleading for financial assistance or new taxation authority. As indicated in Chapters 13 and 14, municipalities have considerable resources to finance their own activities both by charging appropriate user fees and by levying property taxes.

How can ordinary citizens relate to local governments, especially amid the complexity that characterizes Canadian local government? One approach is for local officials to continue to try to design new ways to engage local citizens in civic participation. As suggested in Chapter 10, provoking such participation when homeowners feel threatened by a particular municipal undertaking has never been a problem. But convincing these same people to attend public meetings to discuss matters of broad local interest has always been a different matter. Perhaps the Internet, social networking programs, or other devices that have not yet been invented will one day make possible a level of local engagement that theorists of local participatory engagement have so far only dreamed about.

In the meantime, we must never forget the municipal councillors and mayors whom we elect every two, three, or four years (see Chapters 9 and 11). These mayors and councillors are at the very core of our system of local government. As already indicated, most elected municipal officials are ordinary people, sometimes frustratingly so from the standpoint of their lack of expertise. They become involved in municipal politics because they know many people (sometimes through political parties), because they have become neighbourhood leaders around a particular issue, because they have sought out a particularly visible form of community service, or because they see it as a way of making a (usually modest) income before moving on to something bigger and better and more lucrative. Whatever their motives, they are charged with balancing the professional concerns of municipal staff with the usually parochial concerns of local residents, the concerns of local employers with those of environmentalists, the concerns of those who want or need high levels of expensive municipal services with those who want low taxes and user charges. If local citizens know and understand what their mayors and councillors are doing, both within their own municipalities and within the various local special-purpose bodies and other governmental agencies with which they are connected, and if citizens vote in accordance with their evaluations of the officials' performance, then our system of local government is performing as it should in accordance with the reasons for having systems of local government.

Needless to say, the system is riddled with flaws. Voter turnout is abysmally low and many of those who do vote appear to have very little understanding of the key issues and how the candidates relate to them. A few (but by no means the majority) of the people elected to municipal office seem somehow less than ordinary and quite incapable of grappling seriously with many of the difficult issues facing municipal councils. More so than at other levels of government, there will always be proposals to fix problems of apparently unsatisfactory municipal decision-making by changing the internal structures and/or the external boundaries of the relevant municipality. Much of this book has been devoted in one way or another to describing, assessing, and analyzing the relative merits of such proposals. Ultimately, however, municipal governments must be judged by the extent to which they do what the majority of their residents want done. By this simple measure, Canadian local government probably succeeds.

RESOURCES

This book did not outline various theoretical approaches to urban politics at the beginning because there is no such approach or combination of approaches that is especially helpful in understanding all of Canadian local government as it has been discussed here. Some theoretical approaches, such as 'public choice' and regime theory, were introduced when and where they were relevant. For many theorists of urban politics broadly defined, some of the institutional issues discussed here would be considered quite unimportant, and some important theoretical issues (such as rescaling) have scarcely been touched. For alternative approaches to those used in this book, see the writings by Boudreau, Keil, Bradford, and Phillips listed in the Bibliography, as well as the writings that these authors cite.

STUDY QUESTIONS

1. What are the connections among globalization, neo-liberalism, and rescaling? How do these concepts help you understand what has happened in Canadian cities and local governments over the last 30 years?

2. What, in your view, have been the most important changes in Canadian local government over the past 20 years?

3. Would you ever stand as a candidate for election to a municipal council? Why or why not?

NOTES

Introduction

1. For Canadian urban geography, see Trudi Bunting and Pierre Filion, eds, *Canadian Cities in Transition: Local Through Global Perspectives*, 3rd edn (Toronto: Oxford University Press, 2006), as well as Bunting, Filion, and Ryan Walker, eds, *Canadian Cities in Transition: New Directions in the Twenty-First Century*, 4th edn (Toronto: Oxford University Press, 2010); for urban sociology, see Harry H. Hiller, ed., *Urban Canada*, 2nd edn (Toronto: Oxford University Press, 2010).

Chapter 1

1. For a brief account of the historical evolution of the Corporation of the City of London, see the following entry on its website: <www.cityoflondon.gov.uk/Corporation/LGNL_Services/Leisure_and_culture/Local_history_and_heritage/development.htm>.
2. For a review of the historical origins of municipal government in Canada, see Kenneth Grant Crawford, *Canadian Municipal Government* (Toronto: University of Toronto Press, 1954), ch. 2.
3. Hendrik Hartog, *Public Property and Private Power: The Corporation of the City of New York in American Law, 1730–1870* (Chapel Hill: University of North Carolina Press, 1983).
4. Section 15(b) of the Ontario Freedom of Information and Protection of Privacy Act, as quoted in Ontario, Ministry of the Attorney General, Information and Privacy Commissioner, *Final Order PO-1915-F*, 22 June 2001.
5. Ibid.
6. *Godbout v. Longueuil (City)*, [1997] 3 S.C.R. 844.
7. Commonwealth Local Government Forum, *Canada Profile*, at: <www.clgf.org.uk/user files/1/File/2008_Country_Files/CANADA.pdf> (23 June 2010).
8. Statistics Canada, *Financial Information System (FMS) 2004*, Catalogue no. 68F0023XIB, p. 131.
9. Warren Magnusson, 'The Local State in Canada: Theoretical Perspectives', *Canadian Public Administration* 28, 4 (1985): 575–99.
10. Crawford, *Canadian Municipal Government*, 59.

Chapter 2

1. David Bulger and James Sentance, 'Prince Edward Island', in Andrew Sancton and Robert Young, eds., *Foundations of Governance: Municipal Government in Canada's Provinces* (Toronto: University of Toronto Press, 2009), 314–44.
2. For a full discussion criticizing assumptions about the inherent virtues of political decentralization, see Daniel Treisman, *The Architecture of Government: Rethinking Political Decentralization* (Cambridge: Cambridge University Press, 2007). See also Gerry Stoker, 'Introduction: Normative Theories of Local Government and Democracy', in Desmond King and Gerry Stoker, eds, *Rethinking Local Democracy* (Houndsmills, Basingstoke, Hampshire: Macmillan), 1–25.
3. For a discussion of this and related issues, see Ronald J. Oakerson, *Governing Local Public Economies: Creating the Civic Metropolis* (Oakland, Calif.: ICS Press, 1999), esp. 16.
4. For a discussion of allocative efficiency in the Canadian context, see Harry Kitchen, *Municipal Revenue and Expenditure Issues in Canada*, Canadian Tax Paper 107 (Toronto: Canadian Tax Foundation, 2002), ch. 3.
5. Charles Tiebout, 'A Pure Theory of Local Expenditure', *Journal of Political Economy* 64 (1956): 416–24. For background on how Tiebout developed his approach, see William A. Fischel, *The Homevoter Hypothesis: How Home Values Influence Local Government Taxation, School Finance, and Land-use Policies* (Cambridge, Mass.: Harvard University Press, 2001), 76–80. For a relatively recent survey of the public choice approach to American

local government, see Oakerson, *Governing Local Public Economies*. Those at the lower end of the socio-economic scale—poor people—often are not in position to 'vote with their feet', and since they usually are not property-owners in any case, their concerns and needs can get pushed aside in the public choice model.

6. John Stuart Mill, *Considerations on Representative Government* (London: Parker, Son, and Bourn, 1861), 275.
7. Paul E. Peterson, *City Limits* (Chicago: University of Chicago Press, 1981), ch. 6.
8. Alan Norton, *International Handbook of Local and Regional Government* (Brookfield, Vt: Edward Elgar, 1994).
9. David Siegel, 'Ontario', in Sancton and Young, eds, *Foundations of Governance*, 20–69.
10. The following discussion of municipal functions in Canada is an updated version of the account found in Andrew Sancton, 'Introduction', in Sancton and Young, eds, *Foundations of Governance*, 6–8. Research on this subject was part of the project on Public Policy in Municipalities, based at the University of Western Ontario, funded by the Social Sciences and Humanities Research Council of Canada (SSHRC), and headed by Robert Young.

Chapter 3

1. These documents can be found at: <laws.justice.gc.ca/en/const/index.html>.
2. Canada, National Capital Commission, *The Capital of Canada: How Should It Be Governed* (Ottawa, 1974), I, 14.
3. School boards will be explored more fully in Chapter 4.
4. David M. Cameron, 'Provincial Responsibilities for Municipal Government', *Canadian Public Administration* 23, 2 (1980): 222–35. See also the articles by Warren Magnusson cited in the 'Resources' section of this chapter.
5. C. Richard Tindal and S. Nobes Tindal, *Local Government in Canada*, 7th edn (Toronto: Nelson, 2009), 177.
6. Ibid, 180.
7. For details, see: <www.scics.gc.ca/menu_e.html>.
8. For BC's Agricultural Land Commission, see: <www.alc.gov.bc.ca/>.
9. John G. Chipman, *A Law unto Itself: How the Ontario Municipal Board Has Developed and Applied Land-Use Planning Policy* (Toronto: University of Toronto Press, 2002), 10–11.
10. Ibid., 12.
11. For a detailed analysis of the effect of the OMB on municipal decision-making in the city of Toronto, see Aaron Alexander Moore, 'Planning Institutions and the Politics of Urban Development: The Ontario Municipal Board and the City of Toronto, 2000–2006', Ph.D. thesis, University of Western Ontario, 2009.
12. Serge Belley et al., 'Quebec', in Andrew Sancton and Robert Young, eds, *Foundations of Governance: Municipal Government in Canada's Provinces* (Toronto: University of Toronto Press, 2009), 122.
13. Neil Bradford, 'Rescaling for Regeneration? Canada's Urban Development Agreements', paper presented at the 2008 annual meeting of the Canadian Political Science Association, at: <www.cpsa-acsp.ca/papers-2008/Bradford.pdf>.
14. Harry Kitchen, *Municipal Revenue and Expenditure Issues in Canada*, Canadian Tax Paper No. 107 (Toronto: Canadian Tax Foundation, 2002), 226.
15. For links to each of the agreements, see: <www.infc.gc.ca/ip-pi/gtf-fte/agree-entente/agree-entente-eng.html>. For more information, see Fabio Bojorquez, Eric Champagne, and François Vaillancourt, 'Federal Grants to Municipalities in Canada: Nature, Importance and Impact on Municipal Investments from 1990 to 2005', *Canadian Public Administration* 52, 3 (2009): 439–55.
16. John A. Chenier, 'The Evolving Role of the Federation of Canadian Municipalities', *Canadian Public Administration* 52, 3 (2009): 395–416.
17. For sustainable initiatives by the FCM, see: <www.sustainablecommunities.fcm.ca/GMF/>.
18. Andrew Sancton, 'The Urban Agenda', in Herman Bakvis and Grace Skogstad, eds, *Canadian Federalism: Performance, Effectiveness, and Legitimacy*, 2nd edn (Toronto: Oxford University Press, 2008), 314–33. See also Robert Young and Kelly McCarthy, 'Why Do Municipal Issues Rise and Fall on the Federal Policy Agenda in Canada?', *Canadian Pub-*

lic Administration 52, 3 (2009): 347–70; Christopher Stoney and Katherine A.H. Graham, 'Federal–Municipal Relations in Canada: The Changing Organizational Landscape', *Canadian Public Administration* 52, 3 (2009): 371–94.

19. For the Association of Municipalities of Ontario, see: <www.amo.on.ca/AM/Template.cfm?Section=AMO_By_law_No_1&Template=/CM/ContentDisplay.cfm&ContentID=149942>.

Chapter 4

1. Ronald A. Manzer, *Public Schools and Political Ideas: Educational Policy in Historical Perspective* (Toronto: University of Toronto Press, 1994), 52; David M. Cameron, *Schools for Ontario: Policy-making, Administration, and Finance in the 1960s* (Toronto: University of Toronto Press, 1972), 34–5.
2. Cameron, *Schools for Ontario*, 36.
3. Joseph P. Viteritti, ed., *When Mayors Take Charge: School Governance in the City* (Washington: Brookings Institution Press, 2009).
4. H.C. Barnard, *A History of English Education from 1760*, 2nd edn (London: University of London Press, 1964), 210.
5. Manzer, *Public Schools*, 60.
6. Ibid, 54.
7. <www.mels.gouv.qc.ca/sections/electionsscolaires/pdf/resultats2003-2007.pdf>.
8. P.C. Stenning, 'The Role of Police Boards and Commissions as Institutions of Municipal Police Governance', in C.D. Shearing, ed., *Organizational Police Deviance* (Toronto: Butterworths, 1981), 165.
9. Ibid, 168; N. Rogers, 'Serving Toronto the Good: The Development of the City Police Force, 1834–84', in Victor L. Russell, ed., *Forging a Consensus: Historical Essays on Toronto* (Toronto: University of Toronto Press, 1984, 122–3; John C. Weaver, *Crimes, Constables, and Courts: Order and Transgression in a Canadian City, 1816–1970* (Montreal and Kingston: McGill-Queen's University Press, 1995), 87.
10. Robert L. Bish and Eric G. Clemens, *Local Government in British Columbia*, 4th edn (Vancouver: Union of British Columbia Municipalities, 2008), 99–102.
11. Ontario, Ministry of the Attorney General, The Ipperwash Inquiry, Vol. 2, *Policy Analysis* (2007), ch. 12, at: <www.attorneygeneral.jus.gov.on.ca/inquiries/ipperwash/report/vol_2/index.html>.
12. M.E. Beare and T. Murray, eds, *Police and Government Relations: Who's Calling the Shots?* (Toronto: University of Toronto Press, 2007).
13. Quoted in Ontario, *Policy Analysis*, 311.
14. Quoted ibid, 312.
15. Ibid, 313.
16. Ontario, *Report of the Royal Commission on Metropolitan Toronto*, vol. 2: *Detailed Findings and Recommendations* (1977), 279.
17. Susan Eng, 'Commentary', in Beare and Murray, eds, *Police and Government Relations*, 290–4. For more on this point, see John Sewell, *Police in Canada: The Real Story* (Toronto: James Lorimer, 2010), especially ch. 8.
18. Ontario, *Policy Analysis*, 328.
19. Section 485 of the Vancouver Charter, which can be found at: <www.bclaws.ca/EPLibraries/bclaws_new/document/ID/freeside/vanch_00>.
20. <vancouver.ca/parks/info/publications/AnnualReport2007English.pdf>.
21. Section 492.3 of the Vancouver Charter.
22. Christopher Armstrong and H.V. Nelles, *Monopoly's Moment: The Organization and Regulation of Canadian Utilities, 1830–1930* (Philadelphia: Temple University Press, 1986), 12.
23. Ibid, 37.
24. Ibid, 75–6.
25. <www3.ttc.ca/PDF/Transit_Planning/Annual_Report_2007U.pdf>.
26. <www.toronto.ca/divisions/pdf/org_chart.pdf>.
27. In 2009, six were members of the Montreal city council. The seventh was the mayor of Westmount, a municipality totally surrounded by the City of Montreal. For more details about municipal organization in the Montreal area, see Chapter 8.

28. Frances Frisken, 'A Triumph for Public Ownership; The Toronto Transportation Commission, 1921–53', in Russell, ed., *Forging a Consensus*, 249.

29. Ibid, 262–4.

30. Frances Frisken, *The Public Metropolis: The Political Dynamics of Urban Expansion in the Toronto Region, 1994–2003* (Toronto: Canadian Scholars' Press, 2007), 84.

31. For details, see: <www.conservation-ontario.on.ca/>.

32. Bish and Clemens, *Local Government in British Columbia*, 127–34.

33. The information on this special-purpose body is updated from Andrew Sancton, Rebecca James, and Rick Ramsay, *Amalgamation vs. Inter-municipal Cooperation: Financing Local and Infrastructure Services* (Toronto: ICURR Press, 2000).

34. Roger Tassé, *Review of Toronto Port Authority Report* (Toronto: Royal Commission on the Future of the Toronto Waterfront, 2006), at: <www.tc.gc.ca/eng/policy/report-acf-torontoportauthority-e-955.htm#table_of_contents_>.

35. Tom Urbaniak, *Her Worship: Hazel McCallion and the Development of Mississauga* (Toronto: University of Toronto Press, 2009), 186–9.

36. Ibid, 186.

37. The municipal appointments are formally made by the Communauté métropolitaine de Montréal, an upper-tier level of metropolitan government (to be discussed in Chapter 7), which also assigns municipal costs of the commuter rail system to its member municipalities on the basis of each municipality's share of total assessed property.

38. For a discussion of Nova Scotia that contains helpful general analysis and references, see Martha Black and Katherine Fierlbeck, 'Whatever Happened to Regionalization: The Curious Case of Nova Scotia', *Canadian Public Administration* 49, 4 (2006): 506–27. For Ontario, see Ontario, Ombudsman, *The LHIN Spin: Investigation into the Hamilton Niagara Haldimand Brant Local Health Integration Network's Use of Community Engagement in its Decision-making Process*, Aug. 2010. For the abolition of regional health authorities in Alberta in 2008, see Susan Ruttan, 'Supersized: Forged in Secrecy, Alberta's New Health Superboard Continues the Dismantling of Public Healthcare', *Alberta Views* (Nov. 2009): 32–7.

39. Québec, *Pacte 2000, Rapport de la Commission nationale sur les finances et la fiscalité locales* (1999), 290–2.

40. Dale Richmond and David Siegel, eds, *Agencies, Boards, and Commissions in Canadian Local Government* (Toronto: Institute of Public Administration of Canada, 1994).

Chapter 5

1. Louis Wirth, 'Urbanism as a Way of Life', *American Journal of Sociology* 44 (1938): 3–24.

2. Harry H. Hiller, 'Introduction: Urbanization and the City', in Harry H. Hiller, ed., *Urban Canada*, 2nd edn (Toronto: Oxford University Press, 2010), xii.

3. <www12.statcan.ca/census-recensement/2006/ref/dict/geo049a-eng.cfm>.

4. Ibid.

5. Calculated from data found at: <www12.statcan.gc.ca/census-recensement/2006/dp-pd/hlt/97-550/Index.cfm?TPL=P1C&Page=RETR&LANG=Eng&T=801&PR=0&SR=1&S=3&O=D>. The Toronto urban area was the most populous (4,753,120); Thunder Bay was in twenty-ninth place (103,247); Moncton was next (97,065).

6. For details of how the calculations are made, and additional rules, see <www12.statcan.ca/census-recensement/2006/ref/dict/geo009a-eng.cfm>.

7. Ray D. Bollman and Heather A. Clemenson, 'Structure and Change in Canada's Rural Demography: An Update to2006 with Provincial Detail', Statistics Canada Research Paper, Agriculture and Working Paper Series, Dec. 2008, Catalogue no. 21–601–M, No. 90, 16–17.

8. <geodepot.statcan.ca/Diss/Highlights/Page9/Page9_e.cfm>.

9. <www.placestogrow.ca/index.php?option=com_content&task=view&id=9&Itemid=14>.

10. Robert Lewis, *Manufacturing Montreal: The Making of an Industrial Landscape, 1850 to 1930* (Baltimore: Johns Hopkins University Press, 2000).

11. For a summary of the 'world cities' literature from a Canadian perspective, see Trudi Bunting and Tod Rutherford, 'Transitions in an Era of Globalization and World City Growth', in Trudi Bunting and Pierre Filion, eds, *Canadian Cities in Transition: Local Through Global Perspectives*, 3rd edn (Toronto: Oxford University Press, 2006), 65–85.

12. On this subject, see the work of Richard Florida, now a prominent faculty member at the University of Toronto. For more information on all his work, see his website at: <www.creativeclass.com/richard_florida/>. An important recent and related book containing considerable Canadian content is Mario Polèse, *The Wealth and Poverty of Regions: Why Cities Matter* (Chicago: University of Chicago Press, 2009).
13. Eric Fong, 'Immigration and Race in the City', in Harry Hiller, ed., *Urban Canada*, 2nd edn (Toronto: Oxford University Press, 2010), 132–54.
14. For a careful and nuanced interpretation of the relevant demographic data, see, Evelyn J. Peters, 'Aboriginal Peoples in Urban Areas', in Hiller, ed., *Urban Canada*, 2nd edn., 156–74.
15. David Ley and Heather Frost, 'The Inner City', in Bunting and Filion, eds, *Canadian Cities in Transition*, 192–210.

Chapter 6

1. For a more detailed discussion of this hypothetical example, see Andrew Sancton, *The Limits of Boundaries: Why City-Regions Cannot Be Self-governing* (Montreal and Kingston: McGill-Queen's University Press, 2008), 59–64.
2. For information on the property tax, see Chapter 14.
3. Andrew Sancton, *Governing the Island of Montreal: Language Differences and Metropolitan Politics* (Berkeley: University of California Press, 1985), 23.
4. Paul-André Linteau, *Histoire de Montréal depuis la Confédération* (Montreal: Boréal, 1992), 75.
5. Sancton, *Governing the Island of Montreal*, 26–7.
6. Paul-André Linteau, *The Promoters' City: Building the Industrial Town of Maisonneuve, 1883–1918* (Toronto: James Lorimer, 1985).
7. E.W. Villeneuve, quoted in Andrew Sancton, 'Montreal', in Warren Magnusson and Andrew Sancton, eds, *City Politics in Canada* (Toronto: University of Toronto Press, 1983), 64.
8. Ibid.
9. Calculated from data in Table 1 of the Appendix in Magnusson and Sancton, eds, *City Politics in Canada*, 321.
10. This account is based on Sancton, *Governing the Island of Montreal*, 93–101.
11. James Lightbody, 'Edmonton', in Magnusson and Sancton, eds, *City Politics in Canada*, 283.
12. Ibid., 259.
13. Ibid., 276.
14. T.J. Plunkett and James Lightbody, 'Tribunals, Politics, and the Public Interest: The Edmonton Annexation Case', *Canadian Public Policy* 8, 2 (1982): 207.
15. Lionel D. Feldman, 'Editor's Note', in Lionel D. Feldman, ed., *Politics and Government of Urban Canada*, 4th edn (Toronto: Methuen, 1981), 431.
16. Calculated from data in Table 1 of the Appendix in Magnusson and Sancton, eds, *City Politics in Canada*, 321.
17. Plunkett and Lightbody, 'Tribunals, Politics, and the Public Interest', 216.
18. Edmonton, City of, 'Submission to the Local Authorities Board of Alberta: Written Argument', Sept. 1980. For details of the area in question, see P.J. Smith and H.L. Diemer, 'Equity and the Annexation Process', in P.J. Smith, ed., *Edmonton: The Emerging Metropolitan Pattern* (Victoria, BC: University of Victoria Department of Geography, 1978), 263–89.
19. Alberta LAB as quoted in Plunkett and Lightbody, 'Tribunals, Politics, and the Public Interest', 217.
20. Ibid., 218.
21. Ibid.
22. Lightbody, 'Edmonton', 278.
23. Statistics Canada, *2006 Census of Canada*.
24. Timothy Cobban, 'The Role of Municipalities in Stimulating Economic Growth: Evidence from the Petroleum Manufacturing Industry in Southern Ontario, 1860–1960', Ph.D. thesis, University of Western Ontario, 2008, 18.
25. Ibid., 30.
26. Ibid., 32.

27. Ibid., 60–1.
28. Ibid., 61.
29. Ibid., 113–15.
30. For more details, see John F. Meligrana, 'The Politics of Municipal Annexation: The Case of London's Territorial Ambitions in during the 1950s and 1960s', *Urban History Review* 29, 1 (2000): 91–103.
31. Ontario Municipal Board, FFM 7054, 9 May 1960, 37.
32. Ibid., 11.
33. Ibid., 25–6.
34. Ibid., 31–2.
35. Ibid., 32.
36. Ibid., 35–6.
37. Ibid., 7.
38. City of London, 'Proposal for Boundary Adjustments', 18 Nov. 1988, transmittal letter. For more details of this case, see Andrew Sancton, 'Negotiating, Arbitrating, Legislating: Where Was the Public in London's Boundary Adjustment?', in Katharine A. Graham and Susan D. Phillips, eds, *Citizen Engagement: Lessons in Participation from Local Government* (Toronto: Institute of Public Administration of Canada, 1998), 163–87.
39. Letter from John Sweeney, Ontario Minister of Municipal Affairs, to M.C. Engels, London city administrator, 25 Apr. 1990.
40. Ontario, Ministry of Municipal Affairs, Office of the Greater London Area Arbitrator, 'Co-opportunity: Success through Co-operative Independence', Apr. 1992, Appendix 1.
41. Ibid., 1.
42. As quoted in the *London Free Press*, 27 Apr. 1992.
43. Ibid.
44. Geoff Ghitter and Alan Smart, 'Mad Cows, Regional Governance, and Urban Sprawl: Path Dependence and Unintended Consequences in the Calgary Region', *Urban Affairs Review* 44, 5 (2009): 628.
45. Richard Parker, 'Calgary: A Uni-City at 50 Years', *Plan Canada* 45, 3 (2005): 29–31.
46. Max Foran, *Expansive Discourses: Urban Sprawl in Calgary, 1945–1978* (Edmonton: University of Alberta Press, 2009), ch. 5.
47. Ibid., 44.
48. Ibid., 52.
49. Ibid., 53.
50. Ghitter and Smart, 'Mad Cows', 622.
51. Ibid., 637.
52. Sancton, *The Limits of Boundaries*, 76.

Chapter 7

1. A huge academic literature exists on the government of the London metropolitan area. For a relatively recent example, see Ben Pimlott and Nirmala Rao, *Governing London* (Oxford: Oxford University Press, 2002).
2. David C. Hammack, *Power and Society: Greater New York at the Turn of the Century* (New York: Russell Sage Foundation, 1982).
3. For elaboration, see G. Ross Stephens and Nelson Wikstrom, *Metropolitan Government and Governance: Theoretical Perspectives, Empirical Analysis, and the Future* (New York: Oxford University Press, 2000), ch. 2.
4. The urban application of the public-choice approach is especially associated with the work of Vincent Ostrom and Elinor Ostrom and their students at the Workshop in Political Theory and Policy Analysis at Indiana University. A much broader public-choice perspective is concerned with applying market principles to all forms of political analysis. In this perspective, the work of such authors as James Buchanan, Gordon Tullock, Mancur Olson, Kenneth Arrow, and William Niskanen is especially important.
5. For a summary, see Stephens and Wikstrom, *Metropolitan Government and Governance*, ch. 6.
6. For a Canadian example of this kind of analysis, complete with references to all the relevant American academic literature, see Robert L. Bish, *Organization and Opportunities:*

Local Government Services Production in Greater Saint John, The AIMS Urban Futures Series, Paper #4 (Halifax: Atlantic Institute for Market Studies, 2004).

7. For elaboration on these points, see Ronald J. Oakerson, *Governing Local Public Economies: The Civic Metropolis* (Oakland, Calif.: ICS Press, 1999).

8. Frances Frisken, *The Public Metropolis: The Political Dynamics of Urban Expansion in the Toronto Region, 1924–2003* (Toronto: Canadian Scholars' Press, 2007), 55.

9. Ibid.

10. Andrew Sancton, *Governing the Island of Montreal: Language Differences and Metropolitan Politics* (Berkeley: University of California Press, 1985), 28.

11. Frisken, *The Public Metropolis*, 68.

12. Unless otherwise noted, this discussion of Metro Toronto is based on material in Andrew Sancton, *Governing Canada's City-Regions* (Montreal: Institute for Research on Public Policy, 1994), 77–8.

13. Frisken, *The Public Metropolis*, 81.

14. As quoted ibid., 124.

15. Meyer Brownstone and T.J. Plunkett, *Metropolitan Winnipeg: Politics and Reform of Local Government* (Berkeley: University of California Press, 1983), 18–32.

16. S. George Rich, 'Winnipeg: Innovations in Governing a Metropolis', in R. Charles Bryfogle and Ralph R. Krueger, eds, *Urban Problems*, rev. edn. (Toronto: Holt, Rinehart, and Winston, 1975), 344.

17. Ibid., 344–6.

18. Stewart Fyfe, 'Local Government Reform in Toronto: 1853–1973', in Bryfogle and Krueger, eds., *Urban Problems*, rev. edn., 362.

19. Tom Urbaniak, *Her Worship: Hazel McCallion and the Development of Mississauga* (Toronto: University of Toronto Press, 2009), 36.

20. For a discussion of Mayor McCallion's role as mayor, see Chapter 11. The discussion both here and in Chapter 11 relies heavily on Tom Urbaniak's superb biography, *Her Worship*, which is must reading for any student of Canadian urban politics.

21. Ibid., 208.

22. Ibid., 210–11.

23. Ibid., 214.

24. Ibid., 216.

25. Two 'restructured counties' subsequently were created in Oxford and Lambton. The main feature of the restructuring was that the cities of Woodstock and Sarnia were no longer 'separated' and became part of the county system.

26. Sancton, *Governing the Island of Montreal*, 28–30, 38–9.

27. Ibid., 108–9.

28. Quoted ibid., 110.

29. Ibid., 132–5.

30. Ibid., 132–43.

31. Ibid., 147.

32. For information about the three different categories of MRCs after 2002, see Serge Belley et al., 'Quebec', in Andrew Sancton and Robert Young, eds, *Foundations of Governance: Municipal Government in Canada's Provinces* (Toronto: University of Toronto Press, 2009), 76–7.

33. Ibid., 78.

34. Patrick J. Smith and Kennedy Stewart, 'British Columbia', in Sancton and Young, eds, *Foundations of Governance*, 282–313. See especially the references in footnotes 4–7 on pages 306–7.

35. Patrick J. Smith, 'Even Greater Vancouver: Metropolitan Morphing in Canada's Third-Largest City Region', in Don Phares, ed., *Governing Metropolitan Regions in the 21st Century* (Armonk, NY: M.E. Sharpe, 2009), 142.

36. Mike Harcourt and Ken Cameron, with Sean Rossiter, *City Making in Paradise: Nine Decisions that Saved Vancouver* (Vancouver: Douglas & McIntyre, 2007), ch. 4.

37. Smith, 'Even Metro Vancouver', 248.

38. Edward C. LeSage Jr, 'Municipal Reform in Alberta: Breaking Ground at the New Millenium', in Joseph Garcea and Edward C. LeSage Jr, eds. *Municipal Reform in Canada: Reconfiguration, Re-empowerment, and Rebalancing* (Toronto: Oxford University Press, 2005), 69–70.

39. Alberta, Municipal Affairs, Alberta Capital Region Governance Review, *Final Report: An Agenda for Action* (2000), 11–12.
40. Ibid., 19.
41. Lesage, 'Municipal Reform in Alberta', 74.
42. <www.capitalregionboard.ab.ca/>.
43. Calgary Regional Partnership, *Calgary Metropolitan Plan* (2009), 17.
44. Ibid., 18.
45. Ibid., 8.
46. <www.calgaryregion.ca/crp/aboutus/faqs.aspx>.
47. <www.rockyview.ca/Top_Menu/Media_Center/EntryId/114/Rocky-View-withdraws-from-Regional-Partnership.aspx>.

Chapter 8

1. For brief descriptions of events in Britain, Australia, and New Zealand, see Andrew Sancton, *Merger Mania: The Assault on Local Government* (Montreal and Kingston: Mc-Gill-Queen's University Press, 2000), 84–8.
2. Andrew Sancton, Rebecca James, and Rick Ramsay, *Amalgamation vs. Inter-municipal Cooperation: Financing Local Infrastructure Services* (Toronto: ICURR Press, 2000), ch. 6.
3. Larry Kusilek and Trevor Price, 'Ontario Municipal Policy Affecting Local Autonomy: A Case Study Involving Windsor and Toronto', *Urban History Review* 16, 3 (1988): 257.
4. Ibid., 257–8.
5. Ibid., 258.
6. Ibid., 260.
7. Ibid., 261, 268–9.
8. Ibid., 261.
9. As quoted ibid., 262.
10. Ibid.
11. Kenneth Grant Crawford, *Canadian Municipal Government* (Toronto: University of Toronto Press, 1954), 70.
12. Sancton, Merger Mania, 51–7.
13. Meyer Brownstone and T.J. Plunkett, *Metropolitan Winnipeg: Politics and Reform of Local Government* (Berkeley: University of California Press, 1983).
14. Ibid., 41.
15. Quoted ibid., 42.
16. Quoted ibid.
17. Tom Carter, 'Manitoba', in Andrew Sancton and Robert Young, eds, *Foundations of Governance: Municipal Government in Canada's Provinces* (Toronto: University of Toronto Press, 2009), 250–2.
18. For details, see Andrew Sancton, *Governing Canada's City-Regions* (Montreal: Institute for Research on Public Policy, 1994), 26.
19. Calculated from Statistics Canada, *2006 Census of Canada*.
20. For the law establishing the partnership, see: <www.canlii.org/en/mb/laws/stat/ccsm-c-c23/latest/ccsm-c-c23.html>.
21. Allan O'Brien, *Municipal Consolidation in Canada and Its Alternatives* (Toronto: ICURR Press, 1993), 24.
22. Quoted in Sancton et al., *Amalgamation vs. Inter-municipal Cooperation*.
23. For an evaluation and further discussion, see ibid., ch. 5.
24. John Crossley, 'Municipal Reform in Prince Edward Island: Uneven Capacity and Reforms', in Joseph Garcea and Edward C. Lesage Jr, eds, *Municipal Reform in Canada: Reconfiguration, Re-empowerment, and Rebalancing* (Toronto: Oxford University Press, 2005), 228.
25. John C. Robison, 'Public Participation in Restructuring Local Governments to Create the City of Miramichi', in Katherine A. Graham and Susan D. Phillips, eds, *Citizen Engagement: Lessons in Participation from Local Government* (Toronto: Institute of Public Administration of Canada, 1998), ch. 9; Igor Vojnovic, 'Municipal Consolidation, Regional Planning, and Fiscal Accountability', *Canadian Journal of Regional Science* 23, 1 (2000): 49–72.

26. Daniel Bourgeois, 'Municipal Reform in New Brunswick: To Decentralize or Not To Decentralize,' in Garcea and Lesage, eds, *Municipal Reform*, 247.

27. Ibid.

28. George Betts, 'Municipal Restructuring, New Brunswick Style: The Saint John Experience', *Municipal World* 51, 9 (1997): 3–8.

29. *Globe and Mail*, 28 Oct. 1994.

30. Sancton et al., *Amalgamation vs. Inter-municipal Cooperation*, ch. 5.

31. This account of the Halifax amalgamation follows Andrew Sancton, 'Reducing Costs by Consolidating Municipalities: New Brunswick, Nova Scotia, Ontario', *Canadian Public Administration* 39, 3 (1996): 275–8. Full references for this material can be found there. See also Vojnovic, 'Municipal Consolidation'.

32. Igor Vojnovic, 'The Fiscal Distribution of the Provincial–Municipal Service Exchange in Nova Scotia', *Canadian Public Administration* 42, 2 (1999): 512–41.

33. For details, see Sancton, *Merger Mania*, 93–101. See also Ian Stewart, 'The Dangers of Municipal Reform in Nova Scotia', in Peter Clancy et al., *The Savage Years: The Perils of Reinventing Government in Nova Scotia* (Halifax: Formac, 2000), 199–227.

34. James C. McDavid, 'The Impacts of Amalgamation on Police Services in the Halifax Regional Municipality', *Canadian Public Administration* 45, 4 (2002): 538–65.

35. Andrew Sancton, 'Amalgamations, Service Realignment, and Property Taxes: Did the Harris Government Have a Plan for Ontario's Municipalities', *Canadian Journal of Regional Science* 33, 1 (2000): 135–56.

36. John Ibbitson, *Promised Land: Inside the Mike Harris Revolution* (Toronto: Prentice-Hall, 1997).

37. The material that follows, until the discussion of Kawartha Lakes, is based on Sancton, 'Amalgamations, Service Realignment, and Property Taxes', 137–42.

38. Material on Kawartha Lakes was originally published in French. See Andrew Sancton, 'Fusions et défusions municipales au Québec et en Ontario', in François Pétry, Éric Bélanger, et Louis M. Imbeau, eds, *Le parti Libéral: Enquête sur les réalisations du gouvernement Charest* (Québec: Les Presses de l'Université Laval, 2006), 321–38.

39. For a more detailed comparison of the de-amalgamation movements in Quebec and Ontario, see ibid.

40. The former chief of staff to the Minister of Municipal Affairs at the time has dismissed this possible reason for the amalgamation as 'nonsense'. Frances Frisken, *The Public Metropolis: The Political Dynamics of Urban Expansion in Toronto, 1924–2003* (Toronto: Canadian Scholars' Press, 2007), 241.

41. Material on 'saving money' follows Sancton, *Merger Mania*, 125–7. Full references can be found there.

42. Although there might not have been chaos in the delivery of services, there was much confusion (and worse) behind the scenes. For details, see Toronto Computer Leasing Inquiry/Toronto External Contracts Inquiry (the Bellamy Inquiry) *Report* (2005). The report is discussed in ch. 12 of this book.

43. Toronto City Summit Alliance, 2003: 4, at: <www.torontoalliance.ca/docs/TCSA_report.pdf>.

44. Ibbitson, *Promised Land*, 248, 250.

45. Martin Horak, 'The Power of Local Identity: C4LD and the Anti-amalgamation Mobilization in Toronto', Research Paper 195, Centre for Urban and Community Studies at the University of Toronto, 1998; Julie-Anne Boudreau, *The Megacity Saga* (Montreal: Black Rose, 2000).

46. *East York (Borough) v. Ontario* (1997), [1998] 36 O.R. (3d) 733 [1998]. For more details, see Beth Moore Milroy, 'Toronto's Legal Challenge to Amalgamation', in Caroline Andrew, Katherine A. Graham, and Susan Phillips, eds, *Urban Affairs: Back on the Policy Agenda* (Montreal and Kingston: McGill-Queen's University Press, 2002), 157–78.

47. For more details on all these changes, see Sancton, *Merger Mania*, ch. 6.

48. David Siegel, 'Ontario', in Sancton and Young, eds, *Foundations of Governance*, 28.

49. Ibid., 30.

50. Serge Belley et al., 'Quebec', in Sancton and Young, eds, *Foundations of Governance*, 72, 75.

51. Material in this subsection is an English-language version of part of Sancton, 'Fusions et défusions'. For more references, see the French-language publication.

52. Quebec, *Pacte 2000: Rapport de la Commission nationale sur les finances et la fiscalité* (Québec: Gouvernernent du Québec, 1999).

53. As quoted in Kathleen Lévesque, '25 élus dirigeront la suprarégion de Montréal', *Le Devoir*, 15 June 1999, A1. Author's translation.

54. Québec, Municipal Affairs and Greater Montreal, *Municipal Reorganisation: Changing the Ways to Better Serve the Public* (Québec: Gouvernment du Québec, 2000).

55. Québec, Ministère des Affaires municipales, *Regroupements municipaux dans la région métropolitaine de Montréal: Recommendations du mandataire* (2000), at: <www.mamm.gouv. qc.ca/accueil/livre_blanc_2000/documents/montreal/rap_mand_ber.pdf>, 6–7. Author's translation.

56. I was a consultant for the city of Westmount in 1999–2000. My work for Westmount resulted in the publication of *Merger Mania: The Assault on Local Government* (Montreal and Kingston: McGill-Queen's University Press, 2000). At the time that Mayor Trent responded to the Bernard report, I had no contractual relationship with Westmount.

57. Henry Milner and Pierre Joncas, 'Montreal: Getting through the Megamerger', *Inroads* 11 (2002): 49–63.

58. For an extended analysis along these lines, see Andrew Sancton, 'Why Municipal Amalgamations? Halifax, Toronto, Montreal', in Robert Young and Christian Leuprecht, eds, *Municipal–Federal–Provincial Relations in Canada* (Montreal and Kingston: McGill-Queen's University Press, 2004), 119–38.

59. Material in this subsection is an English-language version of part of Sancton, 'Fusions et défusions'. For detailed references, see the French-language publication.

60. 'Editorial: Demergers Still an Issue', *The Gazette* (Montreal), 18 Mar. 2003.

61. Jean-Pierre Collin and Mélanie Robertson, 'The Borough System of Consolidated Montréal: Revisiting Urban Governance in a Composite Metropolis', *Journal of Urban Affairs* 27, 3 (2005): 307–30.

62. Henry Aubin, 'Those Pesky Mergers', *The Gazette* (Montreal), 15 Mar. 2003.

63. Lawrence Poitras, 'La défusion municipale au Québec', Report from the Montreal law office of Borden, Ladner, Gervais, 17 Mar. 2003, 35.

64. Ibid., 72.

65. <www.electionsquebec.qc.ca/english/municipal/election-results/2004-referendums.php>.

66. <election-montreal.qc.ca/userfiles/file/fr/Actualites-documentation/20091103-Resultats-Sommaires.pdf>.

67. Belley et al., 'Quebec', 76.

68. Joseph Garcea, 'Saskatchewan's Municipal Reform Agenda: Plethora of Processes and Proposals but Paucity of Products', in Garcea and Lesage, eds, *Municipal Reform in Canada*, 83–105.

Chapter 9

1. Floyd Hunter, *Community Power Structure* (Chapel Hill: University of North Carolina Press, 1953).

2. Nelson W. Polsby, *Community Power and Political Theory*, 2nd edn (New Haven: Yale University Press, 1980); Alan Harding, 'The History of Community Power', in Jonathan S. Davies and David L. Imbroscio, eds, *Theories of Urban Politics*, 2nd edn (Los Angeles: Sage, 2009), 27–39.

3. David M. Rayside, *A Small Town in Modern Times: Alexandria, Ontario* (Montreal and Kingston: McGill-Queen's University Press, 1991).

4. Ira Katznelson, *City Trenches: Urban Politics and the Patterning of Class in the United States* (New York: Pantheon, 1981).

5. For a fuller discussion, with extensive references, see Warren Magnusson, 'Introduction', in Warren Magnusson and Andrew Sancton, eds, *City Politics in Canada* (Toronto: University of Toronto Press, 1983): 13–20.

6. Paul E. Peterson, *City Limits* (Chicago: University of Chicago Press, 1981), ch. 6.

7. Donald Gutstein, 'Vancouver', in Magnusson and Sancton, eds, *City Politics in Canada*, 196.

8. Timothy Lloyd Thomas, *A City with a Difference: The Rise and Fall of the Montreal Citizens' Movement* (Montreal: Véhicule Press, 1997).

9. James Lightbody, 'Finding the Trolls under Your Bridge: The New Case for Party Politics in Canadian Cities', *Journal of Canadian Studies* 34, 1 (1999): 172–83.

10. For the argument that immigrants who are non-citizens should have the right to vote in municipal elections, see Myer Siemiatycki, 'The Municipal Franchise and Social Inclusion in Toronto: Policy and Practice', *Inclusive Cities Canada* (Oct. 2006): 9–13.

11. Ontario Municipal Board, Decision No. 0605, 8 Mar. 2003.

12. Calculated from information on the city of Ottawa website at: <www.ottawa.ca/city_hall/ward/index_en.html>.

13. <www.electionsquebec.qc.ca/english/municipal/electoral-map/criteria-for-delimitation.php>.

14. Ontario Municipal Board, Decision #3072, 22 Nov. 2005.

15. Paul J. Bedford, 'Reconsidering the Ward System of Governance', *Ontario Planning Journal* 20, 6 (2005): 25–7.

16. Patrick J. Smith and Kennedy Stewart, 'British Columbia', in Andrew Sancton and Robert Young, eds, *Foundations of Governance: Municipal Government in Canada's Provinces* (Toronto: University of Toronto Press, 2009), 299.

17. Vancouver, 'A City of Neighbourhoods: Report of the 2004 Electoral Reform Commission'.

18. Ibid., 16–17.

19. Irene Bloemraad, 'Diversity and Elected Officials in the City of Vancouver', in Caroline Andrew et al., eds, *Electing a Diverse Canada: The Representation of Immigrants, Minorities, and Women* (Vancouver: University of British Columbia Press, 2008), 61.

20. M. Rick O'Connor, *Open Local Government: How Crucial Legislative Changes Impact the Way Municipalities Do Business in Canada*, 2nd edn (St Thomas, Ont.: Municipal World, 2004), 23–5.

21. Ibid., 28–9.

22. For a more detailed discussion of some of the issues involved, see Andrew Sancton and Paul Woolner, 'Full-time Municipal Councillors: A Strategic Challenge for Canadian Urban Government', *Canadian Public Administration* 33, 4 (1990): 482–505.

23. <www.mississaugainquiry.ca/li/pdf/Ruling_Conflict_of_Interest.pdf>.

24. Determined from the various provincial essays in Sancton and Young, eds, *Foundations of Governance*.

25. Joseph Kushner, David Siegel, and Hannah Stanwick, 'Ontario Municipal Elections: Voting Trends and Determinants of Electoral Success in a Canadian Province', *Canadian Journal of Political Science* 30, 3 (1997): 539–53.

26. Joseph Kushner and David Siegel, 'Why Do Municipal Electors Not Vote?', *Canadian Journal of Urban Research* 15, 2 (2006): 264–77.

27. Kushner et al., 'Ontario Municipal Elections'.

28. Andrew et al., eds, *Electing a Diverse Canada*.

29. Ibid, 262–3.

30. Ibid, 263.

31. <www.localelectionstaskforce.gov.bc.ca/library/Campaign_Finance_Overview.pdf>, 9.

32. <www.mah.gov.on.ca/Page7045.aspx>.

33. <www.localelectionstaskforce.gov.bc.ca/library/Campaign_Finance_Overview.pdf>, 14.

34. <www.calgary.ca/docgallery/bu/cityclerks/election/2007/candidate_contributions/bronconnier.pdf>.

35. Robert MacDermid, 'Funding City Politics: Municipal Campaign Funding and Property Development in the Greater Toronto Area', CSJ Foundation for Research and Education and Vote Toronto, Jan. 2009, 39.

Chapter 10

1. Material on London was originally collected as part of a research project from 1990 to 1995, called 'Does Local Government Matter? Community Policy-Making in London, Ontario', funded by the Social Sciences and Humanities Research Council of Canada. Most of the findings remain unpublished, except for: Andrew Sancton and Byron Montgomery, 'Municipal Government and Residential Land Development: A Comparative

Study of London, Ontario in the 1920s and 1980s', in Frances Frisken, ed., *The Changing Canadian Metropolis* (Berkeley: Institute of Governmental Studies, University of California, 1994), vol. 2, 777–98. Some of the material in the early sections of this chapter derives from this publication.

2. Ian M. Rogers, *Canadian Law of Planning and Zoning* (Toronto: Carswell, 1973), 75.

3. Ibid., 76.

4. Ontario, Committee on Taxation, *Report* (Toronto: Queen's Printer, 1967), vol. 2, 310.

5. For a full list of all the relevant land-use planning terminology in the various provinces, see Gerald Hodge and David L.A. Gordon, *Planning Canadian Communities: An Introduction to the Principles, Practice, and Participants*, 5th edn (Toronto: Nelson, 2008), 218–19.

6. Michael R. Pearce, Carman Cullen, Donna Green, and Chow-Hou Wee, *The London Retailing Study* (London, Ont.: City of London, 1984), 332–3.

7. Ibid., 335.

8. Jane Jacobs, *The Death and Life of Great American Cities* (New York: Random House, 1961).

9. Christopher Leo, *The Politics of Urban Development: Canadian Urban Expressway Disputes*, Monographs on Canadian Urban Government, No.3 (Toronto: Institute of Public Administration of Canada, 1977).

10. Pierre Gauthier, Jochen Jaeger, and Jason Prince, *Montréal at the Crossroads: Superhighways, the Turcot and the Environment* (Montreal: Black Rose, 2009).

11. Aaron Alexander Moore, 'Planning Institutions and the Politics of Urban Development: The Ontario Municipal Board and the City of Toronto, 2000–2006', Ph.D. thesis, University of Western Ontario, 2009.

12. Warren Magnusson, 'Toronto', in Andrew Sancton and Warren Magnusson, eds, *City Politics in Canada* (Toronto: University of Toronto Press, 1983), 118–26.

13. Hodge and Gordon, *Planning Canadian Communities*, 5th edn, ch. 12.

14. William A. Fischel, *The Homevoter Hypothesis: How Home Values Influence Local Government Taxation, School Finance, and Land-Use Policies* (Cambridge, Mass.: Harvard University Press, 2001).

15. John R. Logan and Harvey L. Molotch, *Urban Fortunes: The Political Economy of Place* (Berkeley: University of California Press, 1987).

16. Paul Peterson, *City Limits* (Chicago: University of Chicago Press, 1981).

Chapter 11

1. James P. Feenan et al., 'Newfoundland and Labrador', in Andrew Sancton and Robert Young, eds, *Foundations of Governance: Municipal Government in Canada's Provinces* (Toronto: University of Toronto Press, 2009), 478.

2. Allan Levine, 'Stephen Juba; The Great City Salesman', in Allan Levine, ed., *Your Worship: The Lives of Eight of Canada's Most Unforgettable Mayors* (Toronto: James Lorimer, 1989), 68.

3. Ibid.

4. Ibid., 76.

5. Ibid., 78.

6. Ibid., 95.

7. Statistics Canada, *2006 Census of Canada*.

8. Tom Urbaniak, *Her Worship: Hazel McCallion and the Development of Mississauga* (Toronto: University of Toronto Press, 2009).

9. Ibid., 9.

10. Ibid., 235.

11. Ibid., 9.

12. Ibid., 107.

13. Ibid., 226.

14. Ibid., 237.

15. Ibid., 238.

16. Robert E. Lang and Jennifer B. Lefurgy, *Boomburbs: The Rise of America's Accidental Cities* (Washington: Brookings Institution Press, 2006).

17. Urbaniak, Her Worship, 238.
18. Ibid., 237–8.
19. Robert A. Dahl, *Who Governs? Democracy and Power in an American City* (New Haven: Yale University Press, 1961).
20. Clarence Stone, *Regime Politics: Governing Atlanta, 1946–1988* (Lawrence: University Press of Kansas, 1989), 3.
21. Ibid., 4.
22. Karen Mossberger, 'Urban Regime Analysis', in Jonathan S. Davies and David L Imbroscio, eds, *Theories of Urban Politics*, 2nd edn (Los Angeles: Sage, 2009), 40–54.
23. Christopher Leo, 'Global Change and Local Politics: Economic Decline and the Local Regime in Edmonton', *Journal of Urban Affairs* 17, 3 (1995): 280.
24. Ibid., 295.
25. Ibid., 280.
26. Ibid., 295.
27. Timothy Cobban, 'The Political Economy of Urban Development: Downtown Revitalization in London, Ontario, 1993–2002', *Canadian Journal of Urban Research* 12, 2 (2003): 231–48.
28. Ibid., 243.
29. Christopher Leo, 'Are There Urban Regimes in Canada? Comment on: Timothy Cobban's "The Political Economy of Urban Development: Downtown Revitalization in London, Ontario, 1993–2002"', *Canadian Journal of Urban Research* 12, 2 (2003): 346.
30. Ibid., 348.
31. Timothy Cobban, 'Timothy Cobban's Reply to Christopher Leo's Comment "Are There Urban Regimes in Canada?"', *Canadian Journal of Urban Research* 12, 2 (2003): 352.
32. Clarence Stone, 'Rethinking the Policy–Politics Connection', *Policy Studies* 26, 3 (2005): 250.
33. Kristin R. Good, *Municipalities and Multiculturalism: The Politics of Immigration in Toronto and Vancouver* (Toronto: University of Toronto Press, 2009), 132.
34. Ibid., 133.
35. Ibid., 189.
36. Ahmed Allahwala, Julie-Anne Boudreau, and Roger Keil, 'Neo-Liberal Governance: Entrepreneurial Municipal Regimes in Canada', in Trudi Bunting, Pierre Filion, and Ryan Walker, eds., *Canadian Cities in Transition: New Directions in the Twenty-First Century* (Toronto: Oxford University Press, 2010), 218.
37. Ibid., 221.
38. Douglas Yates, *The Ungovernable City: The Politics of Urban Problems and Policy Making* (Cambridge Mass.: MIT Press, 1977), 165.
39. Martin Horak, *Governance Reform from Below: Multilevel Politics and the 'New Deal' in Toronto, Canada*, Human Settlements and Dialogue Series 4 (Nairobi: UN-HABITAT, 2008).
40. Nick Ternette, 'Glen Murray's Failed New Deal', *Canadian Dimension* 38, 5 (Sept.–Oct. 2004), at: <canadiandimension.com/articles/1961>.
41. Emmanuel Brunet-Jailly, 'Vancouver: The Sustainable City', *Journal of Urban Affairs* 30, 4 (2008): 375–88.
42. Robert Young, 'Multilevel Governance: Benefits, Costs, Possibilities', presentation to the Workshop on Cities and Multilevel Governance—American and Canadian Perspectives, annual meeting of the Canadian Political Science Association, Ottawa, 27 May 2009.
43. Roger Tassé, *Review of Toronto Port Authority Report* (Toronto: Royal Commission on the Future of the Toronto Waterfront, Oct. 2006), at: <www.tc.gc.ca/eng/policy/report-acf-torontoportauthority-e-955.htm#table_of_contents_>.

Chapter 12

1. <www40.statcan.gc.ca/l01/cst01/govt54a-eng.htm>.
2. For a valuable recent commentary on this subject, see David Siegel, 'The Leadership Role of the Municipal Chief Administrative Officer', *Canadian Public Administration* 50, 2 (2010): 139–61.

3. Thomas J. Plunkett, *City Management in Canada: The Role of the Chief Administrative Officer* (Toronto: Institute of Public Administration of Canada, 1992), 13.
4. Ibid., 16.
5. <icma.org/main/bc.asp?bcid=104&hsid=1&ssid1=17&ssid2=22&ssid3=276>.
6. Toronto Computer Leasing Inquiry/Toronto External Contracts Inquiry, *Report* (2005).
7. City of Waterloo Judicial Inquiry, *Final Report of the Commissioner* (2003).
8. Ibid., 1–2.
9. Ibid., 64, 141.
10. Ibid., 26.
11. Ibid., 28.
12. Ibid., 30.
13. Ibid., 30–1.
14. Ibid., 25.
15. Ibid., 228.
16. Ibid., 125.
17. Ibid., 36.
18. Ibid., 68.
19. Ibid., 166.
20. Ibid.
21. Ibid., 182–3.
22. Ibid., 7.
23. Mr Justice John Gomery was charged with investigating how federal public servants distributed public funds in Quebec in the aftermath of the 1995 referendum on Quebec sovereignty. The judge determined, in his 2006 report, that large amounts of money were not used in accordance with the purposes for which they were officially intended.
24. James C. McDavid, 'Solid Waste Contracting-out, Bidding Practices, and Competition, among Canadian Local Governments', *Canadian Public Administration* 44, 1 (2001): 1–25. See also Benjamin Dachis, *Picking Up Savings: The Benefits of Competition in Municipal Waste Services*, C.D. Howe Institute Commentary No. 308, Sept. 2010.
25. James C. McDavid and Annette E. Mueller, 'A Cross-Canada Analysis of the Efficiency of Residential Recycling Services', *Canadian Public Administration* 51, 4 (2008): 569–88.
26. Frank K. Oheming and John J. Grant, 'When Markets Fail to Deliver: An Examination of the Privatization and Deprivatization of Water and Wastewater Services Delivery in Hamilton, Canada', *Canadian Public Administration* 51, 3 (2008): 475–99.
27. <www.pppcouncil.ca/pdf/brockton.pdf>.
28. Ontario, *Report of the Walkerton Inquiry* (Toronto: Queen's Printer for Ontario, 2002).
29. David Cameron, 'The Relationship between Different Ownership and Management Regimes and Drinking Water Safety', Discussion Paper for the Walkerton Inquiry, June 2001, 127–8.
30. Timothy Cobban, 'The Political Economy of Urban Redevelopment: Downtown Revitalization in London, Ontario, 1993–2002', *Canadian Journal of Urban Research* 12, 1 (2003): 240.
31. An exception is James R. McVittie, 'Local Government Unionism in Ontario 1935–1963: Study of the Determinants of Union Growth', Ph.D. thesis, University of Western Ontario, 1991.
32. T.J. Plunkett and G.M. Betts, *The Management of Canadian Urban Government: A Basic Text for a Course in Urban Management* (Kingston, Ont.: Institute of Local Government, Queen's University, 1978), 283–4.
33. Katherine Graham, 'Collective Bargaining in the Municipal Sector', in Gene Swimmer and Mark Thompson, eds, *Public Sector Collective Bargaining in Canada: Beginning of the End or End of the Beginning?* (Kingston, Ont.: Industrial Relations Centre, Queen's University, 1995), 182–3.
34. <www.metrovancouver.org/services/labour/Pages/default.aspx>.
35. Graham, 'Collective Bargaining in the Municipal Sector', 191.
36. Richard L. Jackson, 'Police and Firefighter Labour Relations', in Swimmer and Thompson, eds, *Public Sector Collective Bargaining*.
37. Larry Savage, 'Organized Labour and Local Politics: Ontario's 2006 Municipal Elections', *Labour/Le Travail* 62 (Fall 2008), 174.

38. Ibid.
39. Ibid., 175.
40. The Ontario Region of the Canadian Labour Congress did engage in similar activities during the 2010 Ontario municipal elections. See: <www.canadianlabour.ca/ontario-region/ontario-municipal-election-2010>.
41. John D. Donahue, *The Warping of Government Work* (Cambridge, Mass.: Harvard University Press, 2008).
42. Ibid., 79.
43. Leo Troy, *The Twilight of the Old Unionism* (Armonk, NY: M.E. Sharpe, 2004), 111–38.

Chapter 13

1. An excellent example of such writing relating to the federal government is David A. Good, *The Politics of Public Money: Spenders, Guardians, Priority Setters, and Financial Watchdogs inside the Canadian Government* (Toronto: University of Toronto Press, 2008).
2. Calculated from Statistics Canada, CANSIM Table 3850024.
3. Ibid.
4. Ibid.
5. Ibid.
6. Harry M. Kitchen, *Municipal Revenue and Expenditure Issues in Canada*, Canadian Tax Paper No.107 (Toronto: Canadian Tax Foundation, 2002), 187.
7. Ibid., 127.
8. Ibid., 147–52.
9. Ibid., 152.
10. Many of the issues covered in this section are dealt with in more detail in Steven Renzetti, *Wave of the Future: The Case for Smarter Water Policy*, Commentary No, 281 (Toronto: C.D. Howe Institute, Feb. 2009).
11. Christopher Armstrong and H.V. Nelles, *Monopoly's Moment: The Organization and Regulation of Canadian Utilities, 1830–1930* (Philadelphia, Temple University Press, 1986), 18.
12. Ibid., 32.
13. E.V. Buchanan, *London's Water Supply: A History* (London, Ont.: London Public Utilities Commission, 1968), 9.
14. Ibid., 86.
15. <www.ec.gc.ca/Water-apps/MWWS/pdf/MWWS_2006_WaterUse_May2010.pdf>.
16. Quebec, Bureau d'audiences publiques sur l'environnement, Rapport de la Commission sur la gestion de l'eau au Québec, Tome 2, *L'eau, ressource à protéger, à partager et à metre en valeur* (Québec, 2000), 105.
17. Ibid., 105–6. Author's translation.
18. Ontario, Ministry of Public Infrastructure Renewal, Water Strategy Expert Panel, *Watertight: The Case for Change in Ontario's Water and Wastewater System* (Toronto: Queen's Printer for Ontario, 2005), 55.
19. For details, see Kitchen, *Municipal Revenue and Expenditure Issues*, 141.
20. Ibid., 132.
21. Ibid., 133.
22. Ibid., 134–5.
23. For example, see Saeed Mirza, *Danger Ahead: The Coming Collapse of Canada's Municipal Infrastructure*, Report for the Federation of Canadian Municipalities, Nov. 2007.
24. Steven Renzetti and Colin Busby, 'Water Pricing: Infrastructure Grants Hinder Necessary Reform', *Policy Options* (July–Aug. 2009): 32–5.
25. <www.buildingcanada-chantierscanada.gc.ca/plandocs/booklet-livret/booklet-livret08-eng.html#drinkingwater>.
26. Ontario, *Watertight*, 50.
27. Ibid., 58.
28. Ibid., 50.
29. Pierre J. Hamel, 'Les compteurs d'eau résidentiels: une mauvaise idée', *Bulletin de la ligue des droits et libertés* (Spring 2006): 22–3.
30. Ontario, *Watertight*, 59.

Chapter 14

1. Andrew Sancton, 'Introduction', in Andrew Sancton and Robert Young, eds, *Foundations of Governance: Municipal Government in Canada's Provinces* (Toronto: University of Toronto Press, 2009), 7.
2. Harry Kitchen, *Municipal Revenue and Expenditure Issues in Canada*, Canadian Tax Paper 107 (Toronto: Canadian Tax Foundation, 2002), 67–72.
3. Ibid., 64.
4. Ibid., 79.
5. <www.ourcommonwealth.org>. See also Francis K. Peddle, *Cities and Greed: Taxes, Inflation and Land Speculation* (Ottawa: Canadian Research Committee on Taxation, 1994).
6. Constitution Act, 1867, s. 125.
7. Kitchen, *Municipal Revenue and Expenditure Issues*, 64.
8. Calculated from Statistics Canada CANSIM Table 385-0024; see also Kitchen, *Municipal Revenue and Expenditure Issues*, 181.
9. Ibid., 64.
10. For Ontario, see Elizabeth Bloomfield, 'Municipal Bonusing of Industry to 1930', *Urban History Review* 9, 3 (1981): 59–76; Timothy William Cobban, 'The Role of Municipalities in Stimulating Economic Growth: Evidence from the Petroleum Manufacturing Industry in Southern Ontario, 1860–1960', Ph.D. thesis (University of Western Ontario, 2008), 115–47.
11. John D. Donahue, *Disunited States* (New York: Basic Books, 1997).
12. Kitchen, *Municipal Revenue and Expenditure Issues*, 109–12.
13. Ibid., 85–90.
14. Ibid., 76–7.
15. Ibid., 94.
16. Wade Locke and Almos Tassonyi, 'Shared Tax Bases and Local Public Expenditure Decisions', *Canadian Tax Journal* 41, 5 (1993): 941–57.
17. Enid Slack, 'Revenue Sharing Options for Canada's Hub Cities', a report prepared for the Meeting of Canada's Hub City Mayors, 17–18 Sept. 2004.
18. Kitchen, *Municipal Revenue and Expenditure Issues*, 229.
19. Ibid.

Chapter 15

1. Julie-Anne Boudreau, Roger Keil, and Douglas Young, *Changing Toronto: Governing Urban Neoliberalism* (Toronto: University of Toronto Press, 2009), 27.
2. Ibid., 25.
3. Julie-Anne Boudreau, 'Intergovernmental Relations and Polyscalar Social Mobilization', in Robert Young and Christian Leuprecht, eds, *Municipal–Federal–Provincial Relations in Canada* (Montreal and Kingston: McGill-Queen's University Press, 2006), 162.
4. Boudreau et al., *Changing Toronto*, ch. 4. Although the book as a whole is about 'governing urban neo-liberalism', and Chapter 4 is about the amalgamation, the word 'neo-liberalism' is not used in the chapter, except in the very last sentence where it is not applied to the amalgamation.
5. Andrew Sancton, 'Why Municipal Amalgamations? Halifax, Toronto, Montreal', in Young and Leuprecht, eds, *Municipal–Federal–Provincial Relations*, 119–37.
6. Susan D. Phillips, '"You Say You Want an Evolution?" From Citizen to Community Engagement in Canadian Cities', in Emmanuel Brunet-Jailly and John F. Martin, eds, *Local Government in a Global World: Australia and Canada in Comparative Perspective* (Toronto: University of Toronto Press, 2010), 56.
7. Ibid., 57.
8. Ibid., 69. For Broadbent's latest work on this subject, see Alan Broadbent, *Urban Nation: Why We Need to Give Power Back to the Cities to Make Canada Strong* (Toronto: Harper-Collins, 2008).
9. Andrew Sancton, *The Limits of Boundaries: Why City-Regions Cannot be Self-governing* (Montreal and Kingston: McGill-Queen's University Press, 2008).

10. Joseph Garcea and Edward C. LeSage Jr, eds, *Municipal Reform in Canada: Reconfiguration, Re-empowerment, and Rebalancing* (Toronto: Oxford University Press, 2005).

11. Phillips, "'You Say you Want an Evolution'", 71.

12. Andrew Sancton, *Merger Mania: The Assault on Local Government* (Montreal and Kingston: McGill-Queen's University Press, 2000).

13. Phillips, "'You say You Want an Evolution'", 73.

14. Neil Bradford, *Place-Based Public Policy: Towards a New Urban and Community Agenda for Canada*, Research Paper F/51 (Ottawa: Canadian Policy Research Networks, 2005).

15. For elaboration on this point and for brief discussions of the exceptions to this general statement, see Sancton, *The Limits of Boundaries*, ch. 2.

BIBLIOGRAPHY

Alberta, Municipal Affairs, Alberta Capital Region Governance Review. *Final Report: An Agenda for Action*. Edmonton, 2000.

Allahwala, Ahmed, Julie-Anne Boudreau, and Roger Keil. 'Neo-Liberal Governance: Entrepreneurial Municipal Regimes in Canada', in Bunting, Filion, and Walker (2010: 210–24).

Andrew, Caroline, et al., eds. *Electing a Diverse Canada: The Representation of Immigrants, Minorities, and Women*. Vancouver: University of British Columbia Press, 2008.

Armstrong, Christopher, and H.V. Nelles. *Monopoly's Moment: The Organization and Regulation of Canadian Utilities, 1830–1930*. Philadelphia: Temple University Press, 1986.

Barnard, H.C. *A History of English Education, from 1760*, 2nd edn. London: University of London Press, 1964.

Beare, M.E., and T. Murray, eds. *Police and Government Relations: Who's Calling the Shots?* Toronto: University of Toronto Press, 2007.

Bedford, Paul J. 'Reconsidering the Ward System of Governance', *Ontario Planning Journal* 20, 6 (2005): 25–7.

Belley, Serge, et al. 'Quebec', in Sancton and Young (2009: 70–137).

Betts, George. 'Municipal Restructuring, New Brunswick Style: The Saint John Experience', *Municipal World* 51, 9 (1997): 3–8.

Bish Robert L. *Organization and Opportunities: Local Government Services Production in Greater Saint John*. The AIMS Urban Futures Series, Paper #4. Halifax: Atlantic Institute for Market Studies, 2004.

—— and Eric G. Clemens. *Local Government in British Columbia*, 4th edn. Vancouver: Union of British Columbia Municipalities, 2008.

Black, Martha, and Katherine Fierlbeck. 'Whatever Happened to Regionalization: The Curious Case of Nova Scotia', *Canadian Public Administration* 49, 4 (2006): 506–27.

Bloemraad, Irene. 'Diversity and Elected Officials in the City of Vancouver', in Andrew et al. (2008: 46–69).

Bloomfield, Elizabeth. 'Municipal Bonusing of Industry to 1930', *Urban History Review* 9, 3 (1981): 59–76.

Bojorquez, Fabio, Eric Champagne, and François Vaillancourt. 'Federal Grants to Municipalities in Canada: Nature, Importance and Impact on Municipal Investments from 1990 to 2005', *Canadian Public Administration* 52, 3 (2009): 439–55.

Bollman, Ray D., and Heather A. Clemenson. 'Structure and Change in Canada's Rural Demography: An Update to 2006 with Provincial Detail'. Statistics Canada Research Paper, Agriculture and Working Paper Series, Dec. 2008, Catalogue no. 21–601–M, No. 90.

Boudreau, Julie-Anne. *The Megacity Saga*. Montreal: Black Rose, 2000.

——. 'Intergovernmental Relations and Polyscalar Social Mobilization', in Young and Leuprecht (2006: 161–80).

——, Roger Keil, and Douglas Young. *Changing Toronto: Governing Urban Neoliberalism*. Toronto: University of Toronto Press, 2009.

Bourgeois, Daniel. 'Municipal Reform in New Brunswick: To Decentralize or Not To Decentralize', in Garcea and Lesage (2005: 242–68).

Bradford, Neil. *Place-Based Public Policy: Towards a New Urban and Community Agenda for Canada*. Research Paper F/51. Ottawa: Canadian Policy Research Networks, 2005.

——. 'Rescaling for Regeneration? Canada's Urban Development Agreements', paper presented at the 2008 annual meeting of the Canadian Political Science Association. At: <http://www.cpsa-acsp.ca/papers-2008/Bradford.pdf>.

Broadbent, Alan. *Urban Nation: Why We Need to Give Power Back to the Cities to Make Canada Strong*. Toronto: Harper-Collins, 2008.

Brownstone, Meyer, and T.J. Plunkett. *Metropolitan Winnipeg: Politics and Reform of Local Government*. Berkeley: University of California Press, 1983.

Brunet-Jailly, Emmanuel. 'Vancouver: The Sustainable City', *Journal of Urban Affairs* 30, 4 (2008): 375–88.

Buchanan, E.V. *London's Water Supply: A History*. London, Ont.: London Public Utilities Commission, 1968.

Bulger, David, and James Sentance. 'Prince Edward Island', in Sancton and Young (2009: 314–44).

Bunting, Trudi, and Pierre Filion, eds. *Canadian Cities in Transition: Local Through Global Perspectives*, 3rd edn. Toronto: Oxford University Press, 2006.

——, ——, and Ryan Walker, eds. *Canadian Cities in Transition: New Directions in the Twenty-First Century*. Toronto: Oxford University Press, 2010.

—— and Tod Rutherford. 'Transitions in an Era of Globalization and World City Growth', in Bunting and Filion (2006: 65–85).

Calgary Regional Partnership. *Calgary Metropolitan Plan*. 2009.

Cameron, David. 'The Relationship between Different Ownership and Management Regimes and Drinking Water Safety'. Discussion Paper for the Walkerton Inquiry, June 2001.

Cameron, David M. *Schools for Ontario: Policy-making, Administration, and Finance in the 1960s*. Toronto: University of Toronto Press, 1972.

——. 'Provincial Responsibilities for Municipal Government', *Canadian Public Administration* 23, 2 (1980): 222–35.

Canada, National Capital Commission. *The Capital of Canada: How Should It Be Governed?* Ottawa, 1974.

Carter, Tom. 'Manitoba', in Sancton and Young (2009: 223–81).

Chenier, John A. 'The Evolving Role of the Federation of Canadian Municipalities', *Canadian Public Administration* 52, 3 (2009): 395–416.

Chipman John G. *A Law unto Itself: How the Ontario Municipal Board Has Developed and Applied Land-Use Planning Policy*. Toronto: University of Toronto Press, 2002.

Cobban, Timothy. 'The Political Economy of Urban Development: Downtown Revitalization in London, Ontario, 1993–2002', *Canadian Journal of Urban Research* 12, 2 (2003): 231–48.

——. 'Timothy Cobban's Reply to Christopher Leo's Comment "Are There Urban Regimes in Canada?"', *Canadian Journal of Urban Research* 12, 2 (2003): 349–52.

——. 'The Role of Municipalities in Stimulating Economic Growth: Evidence from the Petroleum Manufacturing Industry in Southern Ontario, 1860–1960', Ph.D. thesis, University of Western Ontario, 2008.

Collin, Jean-Pierre, and Mélanie Robertson. 'The Borough System of Consolidated Montréal: Revisiting Urban Governance in a Composite Metropolis', *Journal of Urban Affairs* 27, 3 (2005): 307–30.

Commonwealth Local Government Forum. *The Local Government System in Canada*. At: <www.clgf.org.uk/userfiles/1/File/2008_Country_Files/CANADA.pdf>.

Crawford, Kenneth Grant. *Canadian Municipal Government*. Toronto: University of Toronto Press, 1954.

Crossley, John. 'Municipal Reform in Prince Edward Island: Uneven Capacity and Reforms', in Garcea and Lesage (2005: 218–41).

Dachis, Benjamin. *Picking Up Savings: The Benefits of Competition in Municipal Waste Services*. Toronto: C.D. Howe Institute Commentary No. 308, Sept. 2010.

Dahl, Robert A. *Who Governs? Democracy and Power in an American City*. New Haven: Yale University Press, 1961.

Donahue, John D. *Disunited States*. New York: Basic Books, 1997.

——. *The Warping of Government Work*. Cambridge, Mass.: Harvard University Press, 2008.

Eng, Susan. 'Commentary', in Beare and Murray (2007: 290–4).

Feenan, James P., et al. 'Newfoundland and Labrador', in Sancton and Young (2009: 453–86).

Feldman, Lionel, ed. *Politics and Government of Urban Canada: Selected Readings*, 4th edn. Toronto: Methuen, 1981.

Fischel, William A. *The Homevoter Hypothesis: How Home Values Influence Local Government Taxation, School Finance, and Land-use Policies*. Cambridge, Mass.: Harvard University Press, 2001.

Fong, Eric. 'Immigration and Race in the City', in Hiller (2010: 131–54).

Foran, Max. *Expansive Discourses: Urban Sprawl in Calgary, 1945–1978*. Edmonton: University of Alberta Press, 2009.

Frisken, Frances. 'A Triumph for Public Ownership: The Toronto Transportation Commission', in Victor L. Russell, ed., *Forging a Consensus: Historical Essays on Toronto*. Toronto: University of Toronto Press, 1984.

——. *The Public Metropolis: The Political Dynamics of Urban Expansion in the Toronto Region, 1924–2003*. Toronto: Canadian Scholars' Press, 2007.

Fyfe, Stewart. 'Local Government Reform in Ontario: 1853–1973', in R. Charles Bryfogle and Ralph R Krueger, eds, *Urban Problems*, rev. edn. Toronto: Holt, Rinehart, and Winston, 1975, 352–66.

Garcea, Joseph, and Edward C. LeSage Jr, eds. *Municipal Reform in Canada: Reconfiguration, Re-empowerment, and Rebalancing*. Toronto: Oxford University Press, 2005.

Gauthier, Pierre, Jochen Jaeger, and Jason Prince. *Montréal at the Crossroads: Superhighways, the Turcot and the Environment*. Montreal: Black Rose, 2009.

Ghitter, Geoff, and Alan Smart. 'Mad Cows, Regional Governance, and Urban Sprawl: Path Dependence and Unintended Consequences in the Calgary Region', *Urban Affairs Review* 44, 5 (2009): 617–45.

Good, David A. *The Politics of Public Money: Spenders, Guardians, Priority Setters, and Financial Watchdogs inside the Canadian Government*. Toronto: University of Toronto Press, 2008.

Good, Kristin R. *Municipalities and Multiculturalism: The Politics of Immigration in Toronto and Vancouver*. Toronto: University of Toronto Press, 2009.

Graham, Katherine A. 'Collective Bargaining in the Municipal Sector', in Gene Swimmer and Mark Thompson, eds, *Public Sector Collective Bargaining in Canada: Beginning of the End or End of the Beginning?* Kingston, Ont.: Industrial Relations Centre, Queen's University, 1995.

——— and Susan D. Phillips, eds. *Citizen Engagement: Lessons in Participation from Local Government*. Toronto: Institute of Public Administration of Canada, 1998.

Gutstein, Donald.'Vancouver', in Magnusson and Sancton (1983: 189–221).

Hamel, Pierre J. 'Les compteurs d'eau résidentiels: une mauvaise idée', *Bulletin de la ligue des droits et libertés* (Spring 2006): 22–3.

Hammack, David C. *Power and Society: Greater New York at the Turn of the Century*. New York: Russell Sage Foundation, 1982.

Harcourt, Mike, and Ken Cameron, with Sean Rossiter. *City Making in Paradise: Nine Decisions That Saved Vancouver*. Vancouver: Douglas & McIntyre, 2007.

Harding, Alan. 'The History of Community Power', in Jonathan S. Davies and David L. Imbroscio, eds, *Theories of Urban Politics*, 2nd edn. Los Angeles: Sage, 2009, 27–39.

Hartog, Hendrik. *Public Property and Private Power: The Corporation of the City of New York in American Law, 1730–1870*. Chapel Hill: University of North Carolina Press, 1983.

Hiller, Harry H. 'Introduction'. in Hiller (2010: xii–xxi).

———, ed. Urban Canada, 2nd edn. Toronto: Oxford University Press, 2010.

Hodge, Gerald, and David L.A. Gordon. *Planning Canadian Communities: An Introduction to the Principles, Practice, and Participants*, 5th edn. Toronto: Nelson, 2008.

Horak, Martin. 'The Power of Local Identity: C4LD and the Anti-amalgamation Mobilization in Toronto'. Research Paper 195, Centre for Urban and Community Studies, University of Toronto, 1998.

———. *Governance Reform from Below: Multilevel Politics and the 'New Deal' in Toronto, Canada*. Human Settlements and Dialogue Series 4. Nairobi: UN-HABITAT, 2008.

Hunter, Floyd. *Community Power Structure*. Chapel Hill: University of North Carolina Press, 1953.

Ibbitson, John. *Promised Land: Inside the Mike Harris Revolution*. Toronto: Prentice-Hall, 1997.

Jackson, Richard L. 'Police and Firefighter Labour Relations', in Gene Swimmer and Mark Thompson, eds., *Public Sector Collective Bargaining in Canada: Beginning of the End or End of the Beginning?* Kingston, Ont.: Industrial Relations Centre, Queen's University, 1995.

Jacobs, Jane. *The Death and Life of Great American Cities*. New York: Random House, 1961.

Katznelson, Ira. *City Trenches: Urban Politics and the Patterning of Class in the United States*. New York: Pantheon, 1981.

Kitchen, Harry. *Municipal Revenue and Expenditure Issues in Canada*. Canadian Tax Paper 107. Toronto: Canadian Tax Foundation, 2002.

Kushner, Joseph, and David Siegel. 'Why Do Municipal Electors Not Vote?', *Canadian Journal of Urban Research* 15, 2 (2006): 264–77.

———, ———, and Hannah Stanwick. 'Ontario Municipal Elections: Voting Trends and Determinants of Electoral Success in a Canadian Province', *Canadian Journal of Political Science* 30, 3 (1997): 539–53.

Kusilek, Larry, and Trevor Price. 'Ontario Municipal Policy Affecting Local Autonomy: A Case Study Involving Windsor and Toronto', *Urban History Review* 16, 3 (1988): 255–70.

Lang, Robert E., and Jennifer B. Lefurgy. *Boomburbs: The Rise of America's Accidental Cities*. Washington: Brookings Institution Press, 2006.

Leo, Christopher. *The Politics of Urban Development: Canadian Urban Expressway Disputes*. Monographs on Canadian Urban Government, No.3. Toronto: Institute of Public Administration of Canada, 1977.

———. 'Global Change and Local Politics: Economic Decline and the Local Regime in Edmonton', *Journal of Urban Affairs* 17, 3 (1995): 277–99.

———. 'Are There Urban Regimes in Canada? Comment on: Timothy Cobban's

"The Political Economy of Urban Development: Downtown Revitalization in London, Ontario, 1993–2002'", *Canadian Journal of Urban Research* 12, 2 (2003): 344–8.

LeSage, Edward C., Jr. 'Municipal Reform in Alberta: Breaking Ground at the New Millennium', in Garcea and LeSage (2005: 57–82).

Levine, Allan. 'Stephen Juba, the Great City Salesman', in Allan Levine, ed., *Your Worship: The Lives of Eight of Canada's Most Unforgettable Mayors*. Toronto: James Lorimer, 1989, 67–96.

Lewis, Robert. *Manufacturing Montreal: The Making of an Industrial Landscape, 1850 to 1930*. Baltimore: Johns Hopkins University Press, 2000.

Ley, David, and Heather Frost. 'The Inner City', in Bunting and Filion (2006: 192–210).

Lightbody, James. 'Edmonton', in Magnusson and Sancton (1983: 255–90).

———. 'Finding the Trolls under Your Bridge: The New Case for Party Politics in Canadian Cities', *Journal of Canadian Studies* 34, 1 (1999): 172–83.

Linteau, Paul-André. *The Promoters' City: Building the Industrial Town of Maisonneuve, 1883–1918*. Toronto: James Lorimer, 1985.

———. *Histoire de Montréal depuis la Confédération*. Montreal: Boréal, 1992.

Locke, Wade, and Almos Tassonyi. 'Shared Tax Bases and Local Public Expenditure Decisions', *Canadian Tax Journal* 41, 5 (1993): 941–57.

Logan, John R., and Harvey L. Molotch. *Urban Fortunes: The Political Economy of Place*. Berkeley: University of California Press, 1987.

MacDermid, Robert. 'Funding City Politics: Municipal Campaign Funding and Property Development in the Greater Toronto Area'. The CSJ Foundation for Research and Education and Vote Toronto, Jan. 2009.

McDavid, James C. 'Solid Waste Contracting-out, Bidding Practices, and Competition among Canadian Local Governments', *Canadian Public Administration* 44, 1 (2001): 1–25.

———. 'The Impacts of Amalgamation on Police Services in the Halifax Regional Municipality', *Canadian Public Administration* 45, 4 (2002): 538–65.

——— and Annette E. Mueller. 'A Cross-Canada Analysis of the Efficiency of Residential Recycling Services', *Canadian Public Administration* 51, 4 (2008): 569–88.

McVittie, James R. 'Local Government Unionism in Ontario 1935–1963: Study of the Determinants of Union Growth', Ph.D. thesis, University of Western Ontario, 1991.

Magnusson, Warren. 'Introduction', in Magnusson and Sancton (1983: 3–57).

———. 'Toronto', in Magnusson and Sancton (1983: 94–139).

———. 'The Local State in Canada: Theoretical Perspectives', *Canadian Public Administration* 28, 4 (1985): 575–99.

———. 'Protecting the Right of Local Self-Government', *Canadian Journal of Political Science* 38, 4 (2005): 897–922.

———. 'Urbanism, Cities, and Local Self-Government', *Canadian Public Administration* 48, 1 (2005): 96–123.

——— and Andrew Sancton, eds. *City Politics in Canada*. Toronto: University of Toronto Press, 1983.

Manzer, Ronald A. *Public Schools and Political Ideas: Educational Policy in Historical Perspective*. Toronto: University of Toronto Press, 1994.

Meligrana, John F. 'The Politics of Municipal Annexation: The Case of London's Territorial Ambitions during the 1950s and 1960s', *Urban History Review* 29, 1 (2000): 91–103.

Mill, John Stuart. *Considerations on Representative Government*. London: Parker, Son, and Bourn, 1861.

Milner, Henry, and Pierre Joncas. 'Montreal: Getting through the Megamerger', *Inroads* 11 (2002): 49–63.

Milroy, Beth Moore. 'Toronto's Legal Challenge to Amalgamation', in Caroline Andrew, Katherine A. Graham, and Susan Phillips, eds, *Urban Affairs: Back on the Policy Agenda*. Montreal and Kingston: McGill-Queen's University Press, 2002, 157–78.

Mirza, Saeed. *Danger Ahead: The Coming Collapse of Canada's Municipal Infrastructure*. A Report for the Federation of Canadian Municipalities, Nov. 2007.

Moore, Aaron Alexander. 'Planning Institutions and the Politics of Urban Development: The Ontario Municipal Board and the City of Toronto, 2000–2006', Ph.D. thesis, University of Western Ontario, 2009.

Mossberger, Karen. 'Urban Regime Analysis', in Jonathan S. Davies and David L. Imbroscio, eds, *Theories of Urban Politics*, 2nd edn. Los Angeles: Sage, 2009, 40–54.

Norton, Alan. *International Handbook of Local and Regional Government*. Brookfield, Vt: Edward Elgar, 1994.

Oakerson, Ronald J. *Governing Local Public Economies: Creating the Civic Metropolis.* Oakland, Calif.: ICS Press, 1999.

O'Brien, Allan. *Municipal Consolidation in Canada and Its Alternatives.* Toronto: ICURR Press, 1993.

O'Connor, M. Rick. *Open Local Government: How Crucial Legislative Changes Impact the Way Municipalities Do Business in Canada,* 2nd edn. St Thomas, Ont.: Municipal World, 2004.

Oheming, Frank J., and John J. Grant, 'When Markets Fail to Deliver: An Examination of the Privatization and Deprivatization of Water and Wastewater Services Delivery in Hamilton, Canada', *Canadian Public Administration* 51, 3 (2008): 475–99.

Ontario. *Report of the Royal Commission on Metropolitan Toronto,* vol. 2: *Detailed Findings and Recommendations.* Toronto, 1977.

———. *Report of the Walkerton Inquiry.* Toronto: Queen's Printer for Ontario, 2002.

———, Committee on Taxation. *Report.* Toronto: Queen's Printer, 1967.

———, Ministry of Public Infrastructure Renewal, Water Strategy Expert Panel. *Watertight: The Case for Change in Ontario's Water and Wastewater System.* Toronto: Queen's Printer for Ontario, 2005.

———, Ministry of the Attorney General. *The Ipperwash Inquiry,* vol. 2: *Policy Analysis.* Toronto, 2007.

———, Ombudsman. *The LHIN Spin: Investigation into the Hamilton Niagara Haldimand Brant Local Health Integration Network's Use of Community Engagement in Its Decision-making Process.* Toronto, Aug. 2010.

Parker, Richard. 'Calgary: A Uni-City at 50 Years', *Plan Canada* 45, 3 (2005): 29–31.

Peddle, Francis K. *Cities and Greed: Taxes, Inflation and Land Speculation.* Ottawa: Canadian Research Committee on Taxation, 1994.

Peters, Evelyn J. 'Aboriginal Peoples in Urban Areas', in Hiller (2010: 156–74).

Peterson, Paul E. *City Limits.* Chicago: University of Chicago Press, 1981.

Phillips, Susan D. '"You Say You Want an Evolution?" From Citizen to Community Engagement in Canadian Cities', in Emmanuel Brunet-Jailly and John F. Martin, eds, *Local Government in a Global World: Australia and Canada in Comparative Perspective.* Toronto: University of Toronto Press, 2010, 55–80.

Pimlott, Ben, and Nirmala Rao. *Governing London.* Oxford: Oxford University Press, 2002.

Plunkett, Thomas J. *City Management in Canada: The Role of the Chief Administrative Officer.* Toronto: Institute of Public Administration of Canada, 1992.

——— and G.M. Betts. *The Management of Canadian Urban Government: A Basic Text for a Course in Urban Management.* Kingston, Ont.: Institute of Local Government, Queen's University, 1978.

——— and James Lightbody. 'Tribunals, Politics, and the Public Interest: The Edmonton Annexation Case', *Canadian Public Policy* 8, 2 (1982): 207–21.

Poitras, Lawrence. 'La défusion municipale au Québec', Report from the Montreal law office of Borden, Ladner, Gervais, 17 Mar. 2003. At: <www.cric.ca/pdf/guide/defusions/defusion_rapport_poitras.pdf>.

Polèse, Mario. *The Wealth and Poverty of Regions: Why Cities Matter.* Chicago: University of Chicago Press, 2009.

Polsby, Nelson W. *Community Power and Political Theory,* 2nd edn. New Haven: Yale University Press, 1980.

Québec. *Pacte 2000: Rapport de la Commission nationale sur les finances wt la fiscalité locales.* Quebec, 1999.

———, Bureau d'audiences publiques sur 'l'environnement, Rapport de la Commission sur la gestion de l'eau au Québec, Tome 2. *L'eau, ressource à protéger, à partager et à metre en valeur.* Quebec, 2000.

———, Municipal Affairs and Greater Montreal. *Municipal Reorganisation: Changing the Ways to Better Serve the Public.* Quebec: Gouvernment du Québec, 2000.

———, Ministère des Affaires municipals. *Regroupements municipaux dans la région métropolitaine de Montréal: Recommendations du mandataire.* Quebec, 2000.

Rayside, David A. *A Small Town in Modern Times: Alexandria, Ontario.* Montreal and Kingston: McGill-Queen's University Press, 1991.

Renzetti, Steven. *Wave of the Future: The Case for Smarter Water Policy.* Commentary No. 281. Toronto: C.D. Howe Institute, Feb. 2009.

——— and Colin Busby. 'Water Pricing: Infrastructure Grants Hinder Necessary Reform', *Policy Options* (July–Aug, 2009): 32–5.

Rich, S. George. 'Winnipeg: Innovations in Governing a Metropolis', in R. Charles Bryfogle and Ralph R. Krueger, eds, *Urban Problems,* rev. edn. Toronto: Holt, Rinehart, and Winston, 1975, 341–51.

Richmond, Dale, and David Siegel, eds. *Agencies, Boards, and Commissions in Cana-*

dian Local Government. Toronto: Institute of Public Administration of Canada, 1994.

Robison, John C. 'Public Participation in Restructuring Local Governments to Create the City of Miramichi', in Graham and Phillips (1998: 188–99).

Rogers, Ian M. *Canadian Law of Planning and Zoning*. Toronto: Carswell, 1973.

Rogers, N. 'Serving Toronto the Good: The Development of the City Police Force, 1834–84', in Victor L. Russell, ed., *Forging a Consensus: Historical Essays on Toronto*. Toronto: University of Toronto Press, 1984.

Ruttan, Susan. 'Supersized: Forged in Secrecy, Alberta's New Health Superboard Continues the Dismantling of Public Healthcare', *Alberta Views* (Nov. 2009): 32–7.

Sancton, Andrew, 'Montreal', in Magnusson and Sancton (1983: 58–93).

———. *Governing the Island of Montreal: Language Differences and Metropolitan Politics*. Berkeley: University of California Press, 1985.

———. *Governing Canada's City Regions*. Montreal: Institute for Research on Public Policy, 1994.

———. 'Reducing Costs by Consolidating Municipalities: New Brunswick, Nova Scotia, Ontario', *Canadian Public Administration* 39, 3 (1996): 267–89.

———. 'Negotiating, Arbitrating, Legislating: Where Was the Public in London's Boundary Adjustment?', in Graham and Phillips (1998: 163–87).

———. 'Amalgamations, Service Realignment, and Property Taxes: Did the Harris Government Have a Plan for Ontario's Municipalities?', *Canadian Journal of Regional Science* 33, 1 (2000): 135–56.

———. *Merger Mania: The Assault on Local Government*. Montreal and Kingston: McGill-Queen's University Press, 2000.

———. 'Why Municipal Amalgamations? Halifax, Toronto, Montreal', in Young and Leuprecht (2006: 119–37).

———. 'Fusions et défusions municipales au Québec et en Ontario', in François Pétry, Éric Bélanger, and Louis M. Imbeau, eds, *Le parti Libéral: Enquête sur les réalisations du gouvernement Charest*. Québec: Les Presses de l'Université Laval, 2006, 321–38.

———. *The Limits of Boundaries: Why City-Regions Cannot Be Self-governing*. Montreal and Kingston: McGill-Queen's University Press, 2008.

———. 'The Urban Agenda', in Herman

Bakvis and Grace Skogstad, eds, *Canadian Federalism: Performance, Effectiveness, and Legitimacy*, 2nd edn. Toronto: Oxford University Press, 2008, 314–33.

———. 'Introduction', in Sancton and Young (2009: 3–19).

———, Rebecca James, and Rick Ramsay. *Amalgamation vs. Inter-municipal Cooperation: Financing Local and Infrastructure Services*. Toronto: ICURR Press, 2000.

——— and Byron Montgomery. 'Municipal Government and Residential Land Development: A Comparative Study of London, Ontario in the 1920s and 1980s', in Frances Frisken, ed., *The Changing Canadian Metropolis*, vol. 2. Berkeley: Institute of Governmental Studies, University of California, 1994, 777–98.

——— and Paul Woolner. 'Full-time Municipal Councillors: A Strategic Challenge for Canadian Urban Government', *Canadian Public Administration* 33, 4 (1990): 482–505.

——— and Robert Young, eds. *Foundations of Governance: Municipal Governance in Canada's Provinces*. Toronto: University of Toronto Press, 2009.

Savage, Larry. 'Organized Labour and Local Politics: Ontario's 2006 Municipal Elections', *Labour/Le Travail* 62 (Fall 2008): 171–85.

Sewell, John. *Police in Canada: The Real Story*. Toronto: James Lorimer, 2010.

Siegel, David. 'Ontario', in Sancton and Young (2009: 20–69).

———. 'The Leadership Role of the Municipal Chief Administrative Officer', *Canadian Public Administration* 50, 2 (2010): 139–61.

Siemiatycki, Myer. 'The Municipal Franchise and Social Inclusion in Toronto: Policy and Practice', *Inclusive Cities Canada* (Oct. 2006).

Slack, Enid. 'Revenue Sharing Options for Canada's Hub Cities', a report prepared for the Meeting of Canada's Hub City Mayors. 17–18 Sept. 2004.

Smith, P.J., and H.L. Diemer. 'Equity and the Annexation Process', in P.J. Smith, ed., *Edmonton: The Emerging Metropolitan Pattern*. Victoria, BC: University of Victoria Department of Geography, 1978, 263–89.

Smith, Patrick J. 'Even Greater Vancouver: Metropolitan Morphing in Canada's Third-Largest City Region', in Don Phares, ed., *Governing Metropolitan Regions in the 21st Century*. Armonk, NY: M.E. Sharpe, 2009, 237–63.

———— and Kennedy Stewart. 'British Columbia', in Sancton and Young (2009: 282–313).

Statistics Canada. *Financial Information System (FMS)*. Catalogue no. 68F0023XIB, 2004, 131.

————. *2006 Census of Canada*.

Stenning, P.C. 'The Role of Police Boards and Commissions as Institutions of Municipal Police Governance', in C.D. Shearing, ed., *Organizational Police Deviance*. Toronto: Butterworths, 1981.

Stephens, G. Ross, and Nelson Wikstrom. *Metropolitan Government and Governance: Theoretical Perspectives, Empirical Analysis, and the Future*. New York: Oxford University Press, 2000.

Stewart, Ian. 'The Dangers of Municipal Reform in Nova Scotia', in Peter Clancy et al., *The Savage Years: The Perils of Reinventing Government in Nova Scotia*. Halifax: Formac, 2000, 199–227.

Stoker, Gerry. 'Introduction: Normative Theories of Local Government and Democracy', in Desmond King and Gerry Stoker, eds, *Rethinking Local Democracy*. Houndsmills, Basingstoke, Hampshire: Macmillan, 1996, 1–25.

Stone, Clarence. *Regime Politics: Governing Atlanta, 1946–1988*. Lawrence: University Press of Kansas, 1989.

————. 'Rethinking the Policy-Politics Connection', *Policy Studies* 26, 3 and 4 (2005): 241–60.

Stoney, Christopher, and Katherine A.H. Graham. 'Federal–Municipal Relations in Canada: The Changing Organizational Landscape', *Canadian Public Administration* 52, 3 (2009): 371–94.

Tassé, Roger. *Review of the Toronto Port Authority Report*. Toronto: Royal Commission on the Future of the Toronto Waterfront, Oct. 2006. At: <www.tc.gc.ca/eng/policy/report-acf-torontoportauthority-e-955.htm#table_of_contents_>.

Ternette, Nick. 'Glen Murray's Failed New Deal', *Canadian Dimension* 38, 5 (Sept.–Oct. 2004). At: <canadiandimension.com/articles/1961>.

Thomas, Timothy Lloyd. *A City with a Difference: The Rise and Fall of the Montreal Citizens' Movement*. Montreal: Véhicule Press, 1997.

Tiebout, Charles. 'A Pure Theory of Local Expenditure', *Journal of Political Economy* 64 (1956): 416–24.

Tindal, C. Richard, and S. Nobes Tindal. *Local Government in Canada*, 7th edn. Toronto: Nelson, 2009.

Toronto Computer Leasing Inquiry/Toronto External Contracts Inquiry. *Report*. 2005.

Treisman, Daniel. *The Architecture of Government: Rethinking Political Decentralization*. Cambridge: Cambridge University Press, 2007.

Troy, Leo. *The Twilight of the Old Unionism*. Armonk, NY: M.E. Sharpe, 2004.

Urbaniak, Tom. *Her Worship: Hazel McCallion and the Development of Mississauga*. Toronto: University of Toronto Press, 2009.

Vancouver. 'A City of Neighbouhoods: Report of the 2004 Electoral Reform Commission'. 2004.

Viteritti, Joseph P., ed. *When Mayors Take Charge: School Governance in the City*. Washington: Brookings Institution Press, 2009.

Vojnovic, Igor. 'The Fiscal Distribution of the Provincial-Municipal Service Exchange in Nova Scotia', *Canadian Public Administration* 42 (1999): 512–41.

————. 'Municipal Consolidation, Regional Planning, and Fiscal Accountability', *Canadian Journal of Regional Science* 23, 1 (2000): 49–72.

Waterloo, City of, Judicial Inquiry. *Final Report of the Commissioner*. 2003.

Weaver, John C. *Crimes, Constables, and Courts: Order and Transgression in a Canadian City, 1816–1970*. Montreal and Kingston: McGill-Queen's University Press, 1995.

Wirth, Louis. 'Urbanism as a Way of Life', *American Journal of Sociology* 44 (1938): 3–24.

Yates, Douglas. *The Ungovernable City: The Politics of Urban Problems and Policy Making*. Cambridge, Mass.: MIT Press, 1978.

Young Robert, and Christian Leuprecht, eds. *Municipal–Federal–Provincial Relations in Canada*. Montreal and Kingston: McGill-Queen's University Press, 2006.

———— and Kelly McCarthy. 'Why Do Municipal Issues Rise and Fall on the Federal Policy Agenda in Canada?', *Canadian Public Administration* 52, 3 (2009): 347–70.

CREDITS

Grateful acknowledgement is made for permission to reprint the following:

Page 97–8, block quote: Timothy Cobban, 'The Role of Municipalities in Stimulating Economic Growth: Evidence from the Petroleum Manufacturing Industry in Southern Ontario, 1860-1960', unpublished PhD thesis in Political Science at The University of Western Ontario, 2008, pp 60–1.

Page 118, numbered list: Stewart Fyfe, 'Local Government Reform in Toronto: 1853–1973', in Bryfogle and Krueger, eds., *Urban Problems*, rev.edn., p. 362.

Page 130, block quote: Alberta, Municipal Affairs, Alberta Capital Region Governance Review, Final report: An Agenda for Action (2000), pp. 11–12.

Page 136, block quote: Larry Kusilek and Trevor Price, 'Ontario Municipal Policy Affecting Local autonomy: A Case Study Involving Windsor and Toronto,' *Urban History Review* 16, 3 (February 1988): 257.

Page 277, block quote: Allan Levine, 'Stephen Juba; The Great City Salesman', in Allan Levine, ed., *Your Worship: The Lives of eight of Canada's Most Unforgettable Mayors* (Toronto: James Lorimer, 1989), p. 68.

Page 229, block quote: Tom Urbaniak, *Her Worship: Hazel McCallion and the Development of Mississauga* (Toronto: University of Toronto Press, 2009), p. 238.

Page 245, block quote: 'History of ICMA and the Local Government Management Profession.' *http://icma.org/main/bc.asp?bcid=104&hsid=1&ssid1=17&ssid2=22&ssid3=276*. Web.

Page 282, block quote: Quebec, Bureau d'audiences publiques sur l'environnement, Rapport de la Commission sur la gestion de l'eau au Québec, Tome 2, L'eau, resssource à protéger, à partager et à metre en valeur (Québec 2000), p. 105.

INDEX